Accession no.
36112309

KV-191-229

Sustainability in Practice
From Local to Global: Making a Difference

WITHDRAWN

LIS - LIBRARY	
Date 8/1/14	Fund G
Order No. DONATION	
University of Chester	

Sustainability in Practice
From Local to Global: Making a Difference

Editors: Nicola Corrigan, Sarah Sayce, Ros Taylor

Copyright © 2009 by the Authors

Cover image by July3rd Designs
Cover design by Robert Mann

All rights reserved.

No part of this book may be reproduced in any form or by any electronic or mechanical means including information storage and retrieval systems, without permission in writing from the Authors. The only exception is by a reviewer, who may quote short excerpts in a review.

The editors of this volume have made every effort to contact and to acknowledge any other publisher of and/or copyright holder of all text and diagrams herein. We do ask that any possible omissions be brought to our attention and we will endeavour to correct them in any subsequent edition.

Published by Kingston University Press Ltd.
Kingston University, Penrhyn Road, Kingston upon Thames, KT1 2EE
http://fass.kingston.ac.uk/KUP/index.shtml

Printed in the United Kingdom by Beamreach Printing

Printed on paper taken from sustainably managed forests

ISBN 978-1-899999-44-6

KUP is grateful to the Editors for providing permission for the publication of these essays as part of their conference material.

Contents

Page

Greening People and Places

Sustainable Solutions: An Everyday Experience

Empowerment and Change

Case Studies in Sustainable Development

Policy to Practice

Educational Change

Sustainability and the Professions

Transformation and Change

List of Figures

Page

List of Tables

Page

List of Appendices
Reclaiming the Future - From Re-using Construction Materials to One Planet Living®

Preface

This book engages with and amplifies debates which were aired at the Sustainability in Practice Conference 2007 held at Kingston University, London. These essays bring together academia, business, local government and other practitioners to evaluate and discuss the extent to which real progress in sustainability has been achieved, and to explore together ways of moving towards a more sustainable future. As Professor Susan Buckingham has stated, 'this book gives higher education institutions, and people working and studying in them, useful strategies for becoming more environmentally sustainable'.

Contributions are arranged according to themes: Greening People and Places; Sustainable Solutions - An Everyday Experience; Empowerment and Change; Case Studies in Sustainable Development; Policy to Practice; Educational Change; Sustainability and the Professions and Transformation and Change. Lively exchanges here emphasize the importance of education as a transformational tool. Furthermore, the essays demonstrate that education needs to be developed within an institution or organisation that is striving to achieve sustainability in day-to-day practice, in strategic management and in governance. Several writers stress the importance of leadership; leadership that is guided by knowledge and wisdom in the context of sustainable development; leadership that generates positive action rather than yet more rhetoric and discussion. Indeed, the need to operationalise theory to achieve change emerges as a dominant theme: a case of 'real world' sustainability.

Key note speakers set the scene for the perspectives developed by the authors in this essay collection. Sara Parkin (Founder Director, Forum for the Future) highlighted the significant role of universities as educators not only of our political leaders, but also in giving the skills and confidence for entrepreneurship in a field not obviously associated with corporate business and international trade. She argues that an appropriately-educated public could make more sustainably informed consumer choices.

Edward Douglas Miller (Remarkable) regaled us with his (by now multi-million pound) sustainable business development; he highlighted the value of confidence to make the leap from theory into practice, thinking through opportunities and marketing appropriately. 'Green' or sustainable products, he argues, should be market leaders in their own right; attractively designed, minimally but appropriately-packaged, and with wide market appeal. They should be designed with a view to re-use.

Another speaker from industry, Clare Lissaman (Adili) toured us through ethical supply chains and the big questions we must ask when evaluating products such as the dilemmas of 'locally -sourced' versus 'fairly-traded' goods. She showed us that 'ethically-sourced' does not have to mean expensive; it also depends on leadership, the business philosophy of corporations, and on the behaviour of consumers. The question of 'expensive to whom' was highlighted in this context.

With Professor Tim O'Riordan (Sustainable Development Commission, UK) we explored the complexities these considerations reveal and the cultural changes needed for sustainable futures, while Clare Shuttleworth posed the challenge, 'what has happened to sustainable development?' She touched on the concerns of many contributors; the superficiality of much that claims to be sustainable development; and the piecemeal approach and the seemingly inevitable dilution of sustainability issues associated with short timeframes and cost cutting requirements for live projects. Saskia Merriman (Accenture) reviewed the challenges to creating institutional and business change – how to engage tired and weary people and promote a new culture of sustainability activity.

So what to do? In practice these challenging contributions inspired us here at Kingston to take things forward. Clare Shuttleworth, in her conference address, likened the complexities of sustainability to a spider's web - how things seemingly at the periphery may yet prove integral to fundamental solutions. We explored some of these ideas with Professor Tim O'Riordan, and conceived the potential for a *Sustainability in Practice Regional Hub* based at Kingston University London. Metaphorically, in both a far-reaching and a practical sense, we hope this will move the 'wheel' of sustainability forward.

The inauguration of the *Kingston University Sustainability Hub* took place in June 2009. For this we add our thanks to Deputy Vice Chancellor of Kingston University, Professor Mary Stuart, who gave the welcoming address to delegates at the Sustainability in Practice Conference 2007 and who subsequently has engaged with and promoted our work. The new *Sustainability Hub* consolidates the work of the three prime movers for the

Conference - Kingston University's Steering Group for Sustainability, C-SCAIPE*, (Kingston's HEFCE funded CETL) and the Kingston University Sustainability Team - and extends and develops the sustainability agenda across the University.

This enabling mechanism encourages new participants, spawns new programmes, reveals new relationships and introduces new ideas. The *Hub* reaches out to other HEIs and educational establishments in the UK and beyond; it engenders cross-disciplinary research to solve practical problems and explore the polemics of sustainable development; it also fosters deep engagement with sustainability across the curriculum and promotes cross curricula collaboration and cooperation at Kingston University and with external agents promoting technological and cultural change.

Significantly, we hope that the *Sustainability Hub* engages and revitalises people's interest in sustainability issues across the 'Triple Bottom Line'. Amidst these complexities we aim to identify for our wider audience achievable progress and measurable outcomes to stimulate interest and retain commitment.

We invite you to reflect on the issues and discussion in this book. We look forward to engaging you in our new developmental work. We wish you all a more sustainable future.

Nicola Corrigan	Sarah Sayce	Ros Taylor
Sustainability Team	C-SCAIPE	Steering Group for Sustainability
		Director, *Kingston University*
		Sustainability Hub

*Centre for Sustainable Communities Achieved through Integrated Professional Education

Nicola Corrigan

Nicola Corrigan has over ten years experience in environmental management and corporate social responsibility, having worked as a consultant and in private and public sector organisations. In her current role as Sustainability Facilitator at Kingston University, she leads the University's multi-award winning Sustainability Team which focuses on issues such as carbon management, sustainable buildings and community involvement. Nicola has a BSc (Hons) in Environmental Science, an MSc in Environmental Management for Business and is an Associate of IEMA. For a number of years she was a Charitable Trustee and Director of the Environmental Association for Universities and Colleges.

Sarah Sayce

Sarah Sayce is a Chartered Surveyor by profession. Following some years in practice as a valuer and commercial property manager, she became an academic and is now Professor and Head of the School of Surveying and Planning at Kingston University. Her extensive research portfolio includes a body of work on sustainable property and professional education. She is Chair of the University's Centre for Sustainable Communities Achieved through Integrated Professional Education (C-SCAIPE) which aims to promote in graduates the skills and value sets to assist in the move towards a more sustainable society. Outside the University she maintains an active involvement with the RICS (Royal Institution of Chartered Surveyors).

Ros Taylor

Ros Taylor is an ecologist by background. She has many years experience teaching environmental issues and polices at undergraduate and postgraduate levels. At Kingston she has developed and run the environmental sciences undergraduate programmes and has instigated undergraduate and postgraduate courses on sustainable development and led sustainability initiatives with local businesses. Ros has written widely around these themes and she is a regular contributor to BBC Radio 4's topical environmental discussion programme, *Home Planet*. She is now director of Kingston University's Sustainability Hub.

Acknowledgements

Without singling out individuals, we would like to thank all those at Kingston University who helped us to run a successful conference. We are especially indebted to the participants who devoted extra time and effort to prepare their contributions for this book.

We are equally grateful to the keynote speakers who triggered our debates and discussions; Sara Parkin, Founder Director, Forum for the Future; Edward Douglas Miller, Managing Director, Remarkable; Clare Lissaman, Ethical Trading Consultant, Adili; Tim O'Riordan, Sustainable Development Commission; Clare Shuttleworth, Sustainability Bureau Manager, White Young Green; and Saskia Merriman, Environmental Lead, Accenture.

We also wish to thank Will Anderson, Eco-builder and author, who enlivened the Conference 'after dinner' discussions at Denbies Vineyard.

We express our gratitude to the conference sponsors, media partners, exhibitors and other supporters who helped us to promote this event.

Sponsors
Canon, the Carbon Trust, Veolia Environnement

Media Partners
The Ecologist, Forum for the Future, Institute of Environmental Management and Assessment, White Young Green

Exhibitors
The Environmental Association of Universities and Colleges, London 21, Office Depot, Royal Borough of Kingston, Thames Landscape Strategy, Surrey Chambers of Commerce

Supporters
DTZ, i-think.com, Market Ecology, Flipside Vision, Schumacher College, Sustainable Building

Our especial gratitude goes to:
Robert Gant and Nor Aziz at Kingston University who worked meticulously, with enthusiasm and good humour, in the preparation of this manuscript; and Kingston University Press and Siobhan Campbell for their expert guidance at all stages in the publication.

Sustainability and Changing University Culture and Curriculum: Grand Valley State University Case Study

Steve Glass, Norman Christopher and Wendy Wenner
College of Interdisciplinary Studies, Grand Valley State University
Elena Lioubimtseva
Geography and Planning Department, Grand Valley State University

Abstract

In the past two decades the higher education cultures in many countries have embedded significant changes in understanding the role of sustainability. While many universities and colleges in the United States have embraced this concept as the major driver of environmental, social, economic and technological progress, only a few programmes offer undergraduate or graduate degrees in sustainability studies or sustainable development. Recently, however, interdisciplinary scholarship on the role of sustainability in higher education has been boosted by research and public debate on global climate change, globalisation and free trade. Nevertheless, some US universities still do not consider sustainability as a serious priority in scholarship and curriculum, focusing primarily on campus operations and facilities. This paper contests this simplistic approach and argues that it represents only the first step in building a truly sustainable community on campus.

Grand Valley State University (GVSU) believes that sustainable campus facilities and routine campus operations can be effectively used as powerful resources for interdisciplinary research and hands-on problem solving education. In 2004 GVSU created a Sustainability Initiative which aimed to bring together student, faculty, facility and community groups to create awareness and gain momentum in campus and community sustainability. This paper outlines the engagement of groups and their activities. Student activities include: the production of a student sustainability guide for all first years, living centre energy conservation competitions, student internships with businesses interested in sustainability, campus sustainability week and a host of other student activities. Facility activities embrace a wind energy study, energy efficiencies, recycling practices, food service sustainability and LEED buildings. Faculty and curriculum goals cover research, outreach service, teaching sustainability in the classroom and academic programmes such as environmental studies, the sustainability certificate and establishment of a faculty sustainability consortium. Furthermore, community partnerships have been nurtured where the university serves as a catalyst. In all cases, GVSU seeks to demonstrate enhancement in value arising from engagement with the framework of sustainability.

Keywords United States, sustainability, curriculum, campus culture, higher education

Introduction

The Talloires Declaration (signed in France in 1990) agreed to increase awareness of environmentally sustainable development, create an institutional culture of sustainability, educate for environmentally responsible citizens, and foster environmental literacy for all. Over 315 universities world-wide, including more than one hundred in the United States, have subscribed to The Declaration that claims that 'universities educate most of the people who develop and manage society's institutions. For this reason, universities bear profound responsibilities to increase the awareness, knowledge, technologies, and tools to create an environmentally sustainable future'.

Grand Valley State University (GVSU) mission is educating students to shape their lives, their professions and societies. As a leader of higher education in West Michigan, the university bears profound responsibilities to increase the awareness, knowledge, technologies and tools to create an environmentally sustainable future. However, like many other US campuses, the conscious awareness of sustainability is a relatively recent phenomenon at Grand Valley. Since 2004 GVSU has been actively engaged in building its new Sustainability Initiative and published the first Sustainability Report in October 2005. That report addresses all three areas of the triple bottom line (TBL), including social, environmental and economic indicators of sustainable development and utilises 64 sustainability indicators or metrics:

> The university is a microcosm of the larger community, and the manner in which it carries out its daily activities is an important demonstration of ways to achieve environmentally responsible living. By practising what it preaches, the university can both engage the students in understanding the institutional metabolism of materials and activities, and have them actively participate to minimize pollution and waste. (Talloires Declaration, 1990)

Driven both by student and faculty demands, the past three years have been a time of dramatic changes in understanding of the role of sustainability in GVSU curriculum, campus culture, research policies, operations, student life, and community outreach. This paper summarises some major steps in this direction, success stories, lessons as well as some major challenges presented to the creation of a truly sustainable campus model at GVSU.

Importance of Sustainability for Grand Valley

Grand Valley State University is situated in Allendale, Michigan, home to Grand Valley's main campus, established in 1960, and situated on 1,237 acres, 12 miles west of Grand Rapids. Classes are also offered at the University's Pew Campus in Grand Rapids (15 miles away), Meijer Campus in Holland (20 miles), and through centres at Muskegon (40 miles) and Traverse City (150 miles) established in cooperation with local community colleges. Enrolling 23,500 students, it has been the fastest growing comprehensive university in the state for over ten years. Located in west Michigan, near Lake Michigan, it enjoys access to water resources, agriculture, and recreation and is situated within a regional population in excess of one million.

As the university grows, its social, economic and environmental impact on the region is substantial. Six hundred million dollars (US) of economic value is attributed to the university, and over 80% of the graduates remain in the region. Like any community, Grand Valley seeks to create lasting value to the region, students and environment. Sustainability becomes an essential part of the mission of: 'Educating students to shape their lives, their professions, and their societies. The university contributes to the enrichment of society through excellent teaching, active scholarship, and public service'. Grand Valley, therefore, seeks to become a model community of sustainability through its actions and role in education.

Development of Sustainability at Grand Valley State University

In July of 2004 Grand Valley began to engage in the development of sustainability across a wide range of campus activities. The Sustainability Initiative was launched; a programme headed by Mr. Norman Christopher, and was given the directive to produce Grand Valley's first Sustainability Indicator report. This report outlined the key markers for sustainability performance on the campus. Compilation of the report provided the impetus to bring together Deans, facility managers, food services and other key players in campus activities. Following the completion of the report in 2005, several teams were created. First, an advisory group of Deans, managers and key faculty began to meet quarterly to discuss strategic planning. A smaller tactical team comprising the Sustainability Director, Facilities Director, Student Senate President and the Associate Dean of Interdisciplinary Studies met to plan key strategies. Lastly, a group of faculty form an 'education for sustainability' team charged with piloting curricular changes through the faculty review process. Future plans include curriculum development, campus events, online and real time indicator reports, and a published strategic plan covering the next two years.

Sustainability in the design of all new campus buildings has become a leading topic. GVSU has made a commitment to energy efficiencies in newly-constructed buildings. Adhering to LEED (Leadership in Energy and Environmental Design) standards, and within the constraints of space (university founded in 1960), construction this year will exceed US$100 million. New construction using green building materials and striving for LEED certification includes:

(i)   The Michigan Alternative and Renewable Energy Center - a LEED certified building, self- powered through the use of biofuels and solar energy. It is an incubator for alternative energy research

(ii)   Lake Ontario Hall - a LEED silver building for classes and offices uses the most up to date energy and water efficient designs

(iii) Kennedy Engineering - a LEED building that incorporates rooftop gardens to reduce water run-off and help insulate the building

(iv)   New Construction - Indoor practice facility for sports; New Honors living centre (classes and living spaces for 1,000 students); building additions which use LEED design methods

Partnerships

Grand Valley has worked closely with the city of Grand Rapids (population 300,000) drawing organisations, businesses and other educational institutions into a partnership dedicated to promoting sustainable practice. The Community Sustainability Partnership (*www.grpartners.org*) which holds quarterly summits to discuss sustainable practices related to the Triple Bottom Line is making progress towards purposeful change in the region. Partnerships are now forming in other communities and the intention is to develop a west Michigan regional partnership serving the million-plus population. The university has committed both to Education for Sustainability, by the President's signing of the Talloires Declaration, and carbon neutrality, as evidenced by the signing of the ACU President's Climate Commitment in 2007.

Operations

Energy savings

As the fastest growing university within the state of Michigan, GVSU casts a large footprint and expends vast resources. Recent campus efforts are focusing on improving energy efficiencies to hold down cost increases. Purchasing bulk fuel and electricity has enabled Grand Valley to reduce natural gas costs per square foot whilst water consumption has remained stable. Bulk purchasing efforts are being expanded to include office materials, paper and other expendables.

To improve efficiency Grand Valley has installed, recently, a new boiler which re-uses heated air within the system. Cost savings will pay for the improvement within three years. GVSU has also recently completed a wind analysis project where wind velocity readings are obtained across the campus. The goal is to determine whether GVSU can augment its electricity use, specifically for edge-of-campus facilities that pay a higher rate for electricity. In 2007, Grand Valley is investing US$1.0 million on various energy efficiency projects. Facilities is investing US$25,000 to initiate a CFL bulb replacement programme where incandescent bulbs are exchanged for compact fluorescent bulbs. Energy savings should pay for the cost of the replacement within a few years.

With almost 90 campus buildings, a switch to 'green' cleaning products will further reduce environmental impact. Currently Facilities is testing floor polishes and cleaning solutions that are environmentally sound. Floor polishes have been adopted that are more durable and require less frequent stripping than conventional polishes. Grand Valley has formed a partnership with Nichols (http://www.enichols.com/), a supplier of cleaning products and member of the Community Sustainability Partnership (*http://www.grpartners.org/*) which has funded two scholarships in Sustainability for Grand Valley undergraduate students.

Transportation

A bus ridership programme has been initiated as a joint venture between GVSU and the city of Grand Rapids. Grand Valley has two campuses, the Allendale main campus and a downtown Grand Rapids campus, 15 miles away. Buses run every six minutes, and use has grown exponentially since the programme began in 2000. Estimated gasoline savings in 2005 alone were 550,000 gallons costed at US$2 million. Recently, the city and Grand Valley have purchased two hybrid buses which help to greatly improve energy efficiency and help meet the daily demand of over 7,000 riders. Additional savings both by students and GVSU reduced the demand for downtown parking passes (at a cost of US$120) as well as negating the need to build additional downtown parking. Campus facilities have also purchased plug-in electric maintenance vehicles and more energy efficient lawn mowers in an effort to further reduce the carbon footprint. A preliminary study has been completed to examine Grand Valley's carbon footprint, with additional work scheduled in estimating transportation impact (air travel, commuting) and carbon offset by the natural surroundings (tree survey).

Water

Water saving is very important to Grand Valley. Situated 20 minutes from the Great Lakes, water conservation and water quality is essential for maintaining a sustainable environment. New LEED buildings, with waterless urinals and low volume toilets reduce water use by over 70%. Grand Valley has a retention pond in the centre of campus to help capture storm water run off; however, water run off is a serious problem for Grand Valley, as it is situated along high ravines that line the adjacent Grand River. Increased run off has already contributed to local ravine erosion. Future plans to combat the storm water problem include additional holding ponds, rain gardens, porous pavement for parking lots, increased native plantings, rain meters on irrigation systems and a change in mowing practices along the ravine edges to reduce water run off.

Recycling

Michigan lags behind the nation in its recycling efforts. Grand Valley also struggles with recycling participation, with only 24% of materials recycled. Efforts are underway to improve recycling on campus. Recycling locations are expanding and being made more visible. An area where Grand Valley is taking the lead is on the use of recycled materials. The bookstore has switched its paper purchase to recycled paper. While the initial cost is slightly higher, the environmental impact (water use) is reduced. Food service has now switched almost entirely to recycled products, including cups, napkins, utensils and other packaging. The shirts worn by employees are made from hemp, purchased from a local sustainable clothing vendor. Food services also purchase farm produce from local vendors. Future plans include composting and growing food on campus gardens.

Facilities is trying to encourage students on-campus to think more responsibly about discarded possessions at the end of the year. Project Donate is designed to allow students who would normally discard beds, appliances and other living items to donate via specially designated dumpsters for sorting and distribution to agencies and those in need. In 2007, over 25 metric tons of items were so donated.

Community garden

Project planning has started for nearby farm land recently purchased by Grand Valley to provide for future overflow construction projects and joint community and campus use as a community garden. Facilities plans to use some of the land as a campus tree nursery while food services propose to grow food and develop a site for composting food waste.

Students

Students at Grand Valley have become significant drivers of the sustainability agenda on-campus. They have a strong history of volunteerism and community activity. Sustainability is proving to be a cause uniting student groups around a common theme. This year the Student Senate will be hosting a series of meetings and dinners for over 20 student groups having a tie to sustainability. The Senate President's goal is to create a student coalition that pools resources to impact sustainability on-campus. In addition, the Student Senate crafted a resolution in 2007 supporting the creation of a Sustainability Certificate programme which faculty will develop in the Fall.

Sustainability guidebook

In 2006, students and the Director of Facilities at Grand Valley teamed up to create the first Sustainability Guidebook. The small booklet described what sustainability is and how students might become involved. In 2007, students revised the booklet, added information on what can be done to reduce, re-use, and recycle. The attractive booklet was distributed at first year student orientation to 3,500 incoming freshmen. Orientation leaders were also provided with information on sustainability. The Guidebook continues to be successful and over 10,000 have been printed for 2007 (see *http://www.gvsu.edu/cms3/assets/1ACDDEF0-A15A-67B1-F268BE06B2416593/sustainabilty_guide/Stu SustainFinal.pdf*).

Web page

In 2005, students working with the Director of the Sustainability Initiative (Mr. Norman Christopher) created a sustainability web page (*http://main.gvsu.edu/sustainability/*). The page, updated by student interns, contains information about sustainability-related courses, campus events, news articles, and opportunities for student participation. A faculty page has recently been added (see *www.gvsu.edu/cois*).

Student projects

Since sustainability is a new topic for local communities and businesses, Grand Valley students have been given rare opportunities to become involved in high level planning for some businesses. Recently, for example, when a local hospital wanted to produce a report on its sustainable practices and track key indicators it turned for assistance to Grand Valley. A senior business student, completing a two semester independent study, researched, interviewed key staff, and created an indicator report for the hospital. The hospital recently hired a sustainability coordinator to maintain the hospital's sustainability momentum. Other projects include assistance given to an area High School for underprivileged students in mathematics tutoring, mentorship and curricular help with art and design. Meanwhile, the university's Service Learning Centre has partnered local communities in need to help and linked students to sustainability-related projects. In addition, students are: assisting Campus Operations to establish the extent of the university footprint; conducting audits on transportation costs for the hybrid buses; and calculating estimates for campus-wide green-house gas emissions. Facilities will continue collaboration with students in the collection of data related to energy conservation. In addition, students from the School of Nursing work with low income and disadvantaged school children whilst nursing students visit schools and provide, on-site and free of charge, basic health care services.

Students are widely involved in promoting sustainability across the campus. Working with Campus Operations, Food Services, and the Sustainability Initiative students are helping to host Campus Sustainability Week. Held during October and immediately prior to Make a Difference Day, the three day event hosts speakers, music, fair trade food and demonstrations such as a 'green' living space. Each day focuses on one of the three aspects of the 'Triple Bottom Line' (environmental stewardship, economic prosperity, social justice). The event is designed to involve faculty and their classes.

In addition student living centres are becoming more involved with sustainability. Energy competitions were held across campus during 2006 and 2007. Buildings were told to reduce electricity use as the competition goal. Living centres reduced usage in one month by 120,000 Kwh, enough energy to power 234 homes for one month. Cost savings exceeded US$15,000. Future activities will be extended to faculty and staff buildings.

Faculty and Staff

Getting Faculty together

In the spring of 2007, the Associate Dean launched a faculty listserv for sustainability and invited the campus community, faculty and community members to join. Faculty identified on campus as participants in any event or activity relating to sustainability were targeted. To date, 30 members comprise the listserv, with 20 more faculty identified as having an interest in sustainability. In the spring information was sought from faculty about personal research related to sustainability. As is often the case, many faculty are unaware of the activities of colleagues in other departments. The intention is to encourage sustainability research across disciplines that provides greater value to the university community.

Starting in the Fall 2007, an internal grant has funded a 'teaching circle' to promote discussion on teaching sustainability in various classroom settings (disciplines). The goals of the teaching circle are to:
  (i)   increase familiarity with sustainability
  (ii)   generate case examples of sustainability issues that cross disciplines
  (iii)   identify and gather interested faculty to underpin the development of a Sustainability Certificate programme
  (iv)   compile material for an introductory text on sustainability

As part of an internal grant to promote the teaching of sustainability, Faculty are expected to read *147 Tips on Teaching Sustainability*, and a website has been launched (see *www.gvsu.edu/cois*).

Faculty research

Sustainable development has become an important focus of faculty research at Grand Valley. Efforts have been made to facilitate communication among faculty and students and promote multidisciplinary collaboration. Faculty have been surveyed to devise a database of current research activities as the basis for stimulating collaborative work (see *http://www.gvsu.edu/cois/index.cfm?id=41B D8AA3-9683-8B58-805E66FBB2188DF6*).

7

Curriculum

The 2005 Indicator Report listed courses that covered aspects of sustainability. That list was expanded in 2007 to over 200 courses, including a hard core of 60 that were heavily focused on sustainability. These courses span a variety of disciplines. Many are part of the General Education curriculum while others are concentrated in specific majors. For guidance, students have been given access to a dedicated web site (*http://www.gvsu.edu/cms3/assets/1ACDDEF0-A15A-67B1-F268BE06B2416593/NEW%20revised%20sustainability_Courses2007-08.xls*).

In the summer of 2006, a group of GVSU faculty conducted a pilot study on the role of sustainability in the higher education curriculum in the US and Europe to identify best practices and criteria-based, bench-mark institutions. Faculty surveyed sustainability initiatives in the UK, Belgium and Spain and established a preliminary network for collaborative research on sustainability indicators.

Across campus, faculty are coming together to form interdisciplinary programmes that involve sustainability. An Environmental Studies Minor is being approved by the university curricular committees. In the Fall 2007, faculty will begin to work on a Sustainability Certificate programme and the possible inclusion of sustainability as a part of general education.

The Business College has seen the need for sustainability within its curriculum. Working with the Director of Sustainability, the College Dean co-taught a topics course 'Sustainable Business and Organizations' for MBA students. The class was very well-received and the business student advisory group has requested the College to develop coursework for undergraduate students. Discussions are underway between the Business College and the College of Interdisciplinary Studies to coordinate development efforts.

Engineering has identified a substantial need for training in sustainability. Engineering faculty now teach sustainable design practices in many classes. Students have helped design and build a 'green' home for a low income resident as a class project and have participated in design competitions related to energy efficiency and sustainable design. Student research projects in alternative energy (solar, wind), energy use tracking (i.e. bus system) and efficiency design now revolve around sustainability. A recent extension to the engineering building recently received LEED Silver rating for environmental design.

Initiatives for sustainability now arise spontaneously from faculty and staff. For example, information staff are pursuing best practices in sustainable printing and use paper and printing supply chains certified by the Forestry Stewardship Council (FSC). Another example is the campus bookstore selling re-usable shopping bags with half of the profit directed to the Sustainability Initiative. The international programme is initiating a tree planting programme to offset carbon use from air travel by the study-abroad programme. These examples demonstrate clearly the on-campus expansion of a stakeholder ownership of sustainability and growth of a positive culture.

Clearly, the momentum for education in sustainability is taking shape and accelerating in growth. The Sustainability Initiative, housed in the College of Interdisciplinary Studies, is uniquely positioned as the 'dot connector'. It provides the link between different disciplines making possible an integration of sustainability education across the university.

Outreach

Connecting Grand Valley to the local community is an important role of a regional university. In addition to its economic impact, Grand Valley offers an intellectual capital and service resource that can greatly benefit west Michigan. One key resource for the region is the Annis Water Resources Institute (AWRI) (*http://www.gvsu.edu/wri/*). AWRI is a research and education arm of Grand Valley, located on the shores of Lake Michigan. Conducting water quality studies for local communities as well as larger, grant-funded initiatives, AWRI is a vital resource for the Great Lakes region. In addition to research activities, AWRI maintains a fleet of two vessels and a laboratory for educational purposes. The boats take school children onto Lake Michigan to collect water samples for analysis in the laboratory. AWRI also provides training for educators on water quality experiments for the classroom. The Institute provides services to government and often testifies on water quality issues. It has received grant funding to host 'Café Scientific' sessions for the local community to discuss sustainability among interested community members and business owners.

The Lake Michigan shoreline is an unique resource for GVSU. The Michigan Alternative and Renewable Energy Center (MAREC) is the first fully-integrated demonstration facility for distributed generation of electricity using alternative and renewable energy technologies in the United States. As a LEED building, it is fully self-sufficient in energy generation. This energy Centre will create and attract new business to the region. MAREC is positioned to establish west Michigan as a leader in the application of alternative energy technologies - technologies that can be widely employed globally. In addition, MAREC ensures that Grand Valley State University will be a leader in developing interdisciplinary alternative energy education and product development programmes.

A 30 kW Capstone micro turbine has been installed and integrated with MAREC's advanced electric generating technologies that have operated continuously in the past 14 months: a 250 kW molten carbonate fuel cell (Fuel Cell Energy), a 30 kW photovoltaic solar roof tiles (Unisolar) and a nickel metal hydride battery (COBASYS). A Kane heat exchanger was integrated for exhaust gas heat recovery. In addition, in November 2007, MAREC will be hosting an Energy conference for local business to create strategies for business becoming involved in wind energy production.

From the perspective of social justice and education, Grand Valley has been active in establishing relationships with schools and non-profit organisations. The Sustainability Initiative, for example, was contacted by a local Alternative School, a school for students who are well below the margin in reading and mathematics. Moving these children towards graduation is a difficult task, and often the schools are under-funded. This school needed assistance in mathematics tutoring, visual and graphics arts instruction and creating a model for sustainability in practices. A partnership was created and key resources to assist the school were identified at Grand Valley. This partnership model can be extended to other schools and local colleges. Another example involves partnership with a school where 95% of the students come from families living in poverty and without access to health care and personal transportation. In partnership, students from the nursing programme at Grand Valley benefit from visiting the school where they provide free basic health care and treatment. In addition, the College of Interdisciplinary Studies which houses the sustainability initiative has chosen poverty and economic justice as its theme for 2007-08, linking this initiative to broader programmes offered across campus.

Summary and Conclusion

Sustainability efforts at Grand Valley are becoming more visible with each passing year. Efforts are widespread and involve multiple entities. Rather than a top down management, the GVSU Initiative seeks to draw together stakeholders who will work in partnership to achieve its goals. Future plans include an analysis of the feasibility of achieving carbon neutrality, receiving a LEED Campus designation and enhancing green energy use. Grand Valley aims to be a model that communities and other Universities can look to for sustainable practice. With sustained links to the community and region, Grand Valley intends to become a centre of excellence in sustainability, one to which communities can look for guidance and achievement.

References

Annis water resources Institute. [Internet]. <http://www.gvsu.edu/wri/>.[Accessed 7th June 2007].

Community Sustainability Partnership. [Internet].<www.grpartners.org>. [Accessed 7th June 2007].

Grand Valley Accountability Report 2008 [Internet]. <http://www.gvsu.edu/forms/accountabilityreport.pdf>. [Accessed 21st August 2007].

Grand Valley Sustainability Web Page. [Internet]. <http://www.gvsu.edu/sustainability/>. [Accessed 7th June 2007].

Grand Valley Faculty Research in Sustainability. [Internet].
<http://www.gvsu.edu/cois/index.cfm?id=41BD8AA3-9683-8B58-805E66FBB2188DF6>. [Accessed 7th June 2007].

Grand Valley Sustainability Curriculum. [Internet]. <http://www.gvsu.edu/cms3/assets/1ACDDEF0-A15A-67B1-F268BE06B2416593/NEW%20revised%20sustainability_Courses2007-08.xls>. [Accessed 7th June 2007].

GVSU Community Garden. [Internet]. <http://www.gvsu.edu/sustainability/index.cfm?id=01B8BB60-ED9F-2ED7-8EF5DFA03EE1829E>. [Accessed 17 November 2008].

Nichols Cleaning Products. [Internet]. <http://www.enichols.com/sustainability.php>. [Accessed 7th June 2007].

Report and Declaration of the Presidents Conference (1990) - Talloires Declaration. [Internet]. <http://www.ulsf.org/programs_talloires_report.html>. [Accessed 7th June 2007].

Student Sustainability Guidebook. [Internet]. <http://www.gvsu.edu/cms3/assets/1ACDDEF0-A15A-67B1-F268BE06B2416593/sustainabilty_guide/StuSustainFinal.pdf>. [Accessed 7th June 2007].

Campus Greening at the University of Plymouth: Some Highs and Lows in a Two Year Collaborative Experience

Mhairi Mackie, James Gray-Donald, Sue Turpin Brooks, Alan Dyer, Robert Score and Paul Lumley
University of Plymouth

Abstract

The greening of university campuses is becoming more common, yet there is a paucity of research about this process, institutional learning and the connection of campus greening to staff and student experience. This paper explores a capital spend project with a £2 million budget which aimed 'to establish an infrastructure which directly impinges on the students' life on campus and overtly models a 'green' outlook and sound sustainability policies' (Dyer and Selby, 2004). The paper looks at the dynamics of collaborative working within the project activities, the benefits and difficulties of drawing together a very disparate team, the opportunities afforded by such cross-boundary work and the lessons learned. The main lessons learned were that a growing understanding and development of shared objectives amongst a diverse group (with different backgrounds and specialist knowledge) has proved successful in the stimulation of a more holistic, inclusive approach while completing projects to time and budget. Local circumstances, and the pressures of pre-existing policy on the physical development of the Plymouth Campus over the same time period, have led to both synergies and frustration. There is evidence of institutional learning at several levels with links to core policy issues already agreed and other significant changes in process. The paper concludes with some recommendations for others developing university campuses which aim to be a valuable resource for learning and teaching (about, in and through) sustainability.

Keywords Education for Sustainable Development (ESD), sustainability, campus greening, collaboration

Introduction

Campus greening is becoming more common but there are few, if any, examples of a comprehensive commitment by a university that has been carried forward into action (Walder and Clugston, 2002). The Centre for Sustainable Futures (CSF) has a mandate to transform the University of Plymouth to be a model of education for sustainable development, and for its campus to 'overtly model a "green" outlook and sound sustainability policies' (Dyer and Selby, 2004). Two years into a five year project the university has spent over £2 million on campus greening projects that have reduced the university's ecological footprint, engaged a range of stakeholders and connected with curriculum development in innovative ways (Gray-Donald and Selby, 2006). Building on the success of the capital spend and relationships built with chancellery, CSF has put in place what is likely the most holistic sustainability policy and action plan yet seen for a university.

This paper investigates some of the reasons for the success of the capital spend project, as well as frustrations, lessons learned and recommendations. It is based on interviews with eight key people in the university, including academics, estates managers, students and a procurement officer. Following an explanation of why the research is needed, the background to the project and the research methodology, six main themes from the research are presented:

(i)   'We were doing this all before the CETL ESD arrived'
(ii)   'We didn't achieve as much as we might have done'
(iii)   Continuing confusion over the university decision making processes and plans
(iv)   Problems with capital expenditure timescales
(v)   Setting clearer agendas for consultants
(vi)   Academics talking to administration and support staff

The paper concludes with recommendations for each of the themes identified.

Need for Research

In *Greening the University Curriculum: Appraising an International Movement*, Martin Haigh states that 'There now seems to be growing agreement that HEIs should equip all their students with "environmental literacy" and that sustainability should be central to concerns both in HEI curricula and operational practice'. This is echoed by a wide array of academics and policy makers including the more than 100 university presidents and vice-chancellors who have signed up to sustainability declarations (Tilbury, 2004).

This is especially true in England. In 2005, the Higher Education Funding Council of England (HEFCE) published a statement of policy *Sustainable development in higher education* which sets out their approach to promoting the sustainable development agenda (HEFCE, 2005). Sustainable development is now being promoted from the highest places. In addition, the Environmental Association for Universities and Colleges (EAUC) now has a membership of over 200 universities and colleges and is very active across the nation as an environmental and sustainability champion (EAUC, 2007). To complement these endeavours, HEEPI (Higher Education Environmental Performance Improvement) supports the work of energy managers, develops the capacity of environmental-related staff and runs yearly Green Gown Awards (HEEPI, 2007). It is therefore clear that there is a great deal of interest and action around environmental and sustainability issues at universities in the UK.

A study conducted by one of the most recognised and respected organisations in the field, University Leaders for a Sustainable Future (ULSF), concluded that 'While many campuses have begun to redesign their operations based on eco-efficiency, waste reduction and recycling, few schools have made a comprehensive commitment to such practices' (Calder and Clugston, 2002). This is in spite of the fact that such practices can lead to significant cost savings[1] (Calder and Clugston, 2002). However, while there has been a lot of campus greening, 'there is little guidance available for campus sustainability advocates and scholars' (Calder and Clugston, 2002, p.3). In light of this, Shriberg conducted a detailed study of US colleges and universities that have signed the Talloires Declaration

---

[1] See also (Sharp, 2002), his conclusions and description of the Harvard revolving eco-loan fund.

in order to identify 'organisational factors which determine why and how some campuses are emerging as sustainability leaders while most campuses lag behind' (Shriberg, 2002, p.3).

He continues, stating that:

> The results indicate that collaborative decision making structures, progressive/liberal political orientation, a collegial atmosphere, and image-seeking behaviour represent strong positive conditions for success in campus sustainability. Initiatives are most successful when driven by diverse stakeholders - with the support of top leaders - acting in a coordinated manner and capitalizing on or creating a 'spark'.

That same year, Leith Sharp published an excellent paper entitled *Green campuses: the road from little victories to systemic transformation* based upon seven years of experience at Harvard University and a study of thirty other universities. He provides very good advice on general principles of organisational management that help institutionalise a commitment to campus environmental sustainability. However, to the knowledge of the authors, neither Sharp, Shriberg nor anyone else have published papers about a particular university's comprehensive effort to redesign its operations (green their campus) looking, in particular, at decision-making and institutional learning. This paper aims to start filling that niche.

Project Background[2]

The Centre for Sustainable Futures (CSF) at the University of Plymouth opened on 1 June 2005, following a successful bid by a group of academics representing several disciplines to HEFCE (Higher Education Funding Council of England) for initial capital and five-year recurrent funding for a Centre in Excellence in Teaching and Learning: Education for Sustainable Development (CETL ESD). In the bidding process with HEFCE, the Plymouth team had to demonstrate already-existing excellence in ESD curriculum and pedagogical development. Those 'excellent' Faculties and Schools from which the team was drawn were: Education, Law, Geography, Architecture and Design, Environmental Building Group (Engineering), Agriculture and Rural Management, and Earth, Ocean and Environmental Sciences.

The goal of CSF, as laid out in the bid document, is 'to transform the University of Plymouth from an institution characterised by significant areas of excellence in Education for Sustainable Development (ESD) to an institution modelling university-wide excellence and, hence, able to make a major contribution to ESD regionally, nationally and internationally' (Dyer and Selby, 2004, p.1). To that end, a core staff of seven was appointed and arrangements were made for the partial buy-out on an annual basis of academics as affiliated Centre Fellows. There were 24 Fellows in 2006/07 and a new cohort of 12-plus academics from other disciplines starting in the academic year 2007/08.

A programme of capital work totalling £2 million was developed with the CETL ESD bid authors and representatives of the Environmental Building Group and School of Architecture and Design. A condition of funding was that all the money had to be spent and projects completed within two years.

---

[2] The next three paragraphs are an excerpt from Gray-Donald and Selby (2006) quoted with the authors' permission.

It was recognized that the expenditure of such a sum of money on capital works within the first two years of the CETL was a challenge in terms of typical project development, design, contract agreement and building programmes. For this reason, and a desire to model the sustainability principles of transparency and participation, a diverse team was brought together to move forward the CSF capital spend. The inclusion of academics within a capital spend project at the university was unusual. Indeed the inclusion of architecture and engineering faculty is unusual at an international level:

> Sustainable design on campuses is perhaps the most exciting recent trend in the HESD movement. It is particularly critical since estimates indicate that our built environment will double size over the next 20 to 40 years. Ironically, the impetus for green buildings appears to be coming more from the liberal arts side of the academy (rather than the graduate schools of design)(Calder and Clugston, 2002).

The budget laid out in the CETL ESD bid document is presented as Table 1.

Table 1   CETL ESD Sustainability budget

KIRKY LODGE	
£250k	Conversion/upgrade to CSF

GATEWAY : Rowe Street Project	
£1,000k	BREEAM assessment

ECO CAMPUS	
£500k	(£460k) total
£200k	Energy efficiency measures
£40k	Eco-landscaping measures
£60k	External socialising areas
£30k	Waste reduction measures
£50k	Cycle storage/changing
£80k	Disab. and gender landscape

VIDEO-CONFERENCING	
£250k	Schumacher
	partner coll.
£45k	Thermal imaging camera

Source: Dyer and Selby, 2004, Appendix 4b

Students and staff representatives were included in the early discussions of each of the projects. Meetings typically included: The Project Manager, Estates liaison person, ESD CETL Deputy Director, academics from School of Architecture, Manager of the Student's Union, President of the Student's Union, Student's Union Environmental Officer, Quantity Surveyor, Project Architect and Master-plan Consultant.

By early October 2005, it became apparent that despite the urgency for day-to-day decision making to take place, there was a real need for a more integrated overview and discussion of the university campus as a whole. A campus forum began with its aim 'To contribute to the development of the university campus in Plymouth as a rich resource for teaching and learning for Sustainability, and as a high quality environment in terms of the social, technical, cultural, biodiversity, and aesthetic aspects of the site and its buildings'. The campus forum met roughly once per month and had an attendance fluctuating from 15-30 drawn from across the university.

The campus greening initiative was noteworthy for its high level of consultation with students and stakeholders on the following projects:

- ensuring the high BREEAM rating of the new iconic seven-story Levinsky Arts Building
- refurbishing Kirky Lodge (which had been condemned) with minor structural work, eco-paints, eco-carpet, replacing the panes of old windows with double-glazing
- creating a Student Union garden with native vegetation offering one of the few useful outdoor social spaces on campus
- increased cycle storage
- infrastructure for the first ever University of Plymouth recycling scheme
- lastly, conducting a detailed analysis of opportunities and feasibility of alternative energy creation on two University of Plymouth campuses and surrounding areas

Each of these projects is making a significant contribution to reducing the carbon footprint of the university. Because CSF is mandated to promote education for sustainable development, we have worked hard to link each of the projects with the curriculum and with informal student learning on campus. Examples include:

- making the educational value of a building a criterion in design
- exhibiting leading edge digital artistic displays of resource use and sustainability issues on the outside and inside of various buildings
- consulting architectural and construction students on the design of new buildings and entrusting them with such changes
- involving other students in landscaping changes
- having an open and accessible archive of the campus greening project notes and designs
- establishing institutional spaces for participatory processes

Methodology

This paper is overtly insider research. Almost all of the research at CSF is action based. This is no exception. The research is meant to provide insight into the operation of CSF and its efforts to promote ESD in all aspects of the university. Campus greening is not conceived of separately from curriculum development, community engagement or cultural change. They are all embedded within each other. As such there are nine overlapping strands of research and over 20 individual research projects at CSF related to sustainability at the university. In 2006, *Through the (not so) Green Door* investigated how CSF is connecting campus greening and curriculum change (Gray-Donald and Selby, 2006). The Environmental Building Group has published a series of articles looking at curriculum change and the student experience (Murray *et al.*, 2006). There is a forthcoming chapter in a book about campus greening based on a three week think tank at Schumacher College with international experts, university staff and regional representatives.

All this research complements, and is evidence of, the insider knowledge of the authors about the campus greening process at the University of Plymouth. There is an extensive documentary trail that has been reviewed which includes minutes of campus forum meetings, minutes of project meetings, project reports, emails and interviews for other lines of research. Semi-structured interviews were also conducted with eight key people within the university who were involved in the CSF capital spend. These interviews lasted 15 - 45 minutes. They were then transcribed and circulated to the authors. The authors read the transcripts independently and identified key passages and themes. Very close agreement was found between the themes identified. These themes were then written up by different authors and edited by the remainder. Further information about CSF and the capital spend projects is presented at http://csf.plymouth.ac.uk, clicking on campus.

Key Themes

'We were doing this all before the CETL ESD arrived'

The original bid document confirmed that the university had already implemented sustainability in several academic fields and, after CSF began operating, it became clear that individuals in the Learning Resources Department/ Estates had defined environmental responsibilities and high levels of awareness. For example, Paul Lumley was highly commended in 2005 by HEEPI Green Gown awards for £1.6million in savings from water conservation. Several other respondents, including the Head of Procurement and the Head of Estates Planning, indicated that at the time of CSF's initiation their existing practices had involved the consideration of sustainability. This included corporate social responsibility concerns and BREEAM assessment of building projects.

Others involved were less confident. A number of personnel having lower levels of responsibility indicated that they were able to use the CSF project to build on their existing knowledge and values by expanding their understanding of sustainability and education for sustainability.

Several areas of capital expenditure, such as the recycling systems, had been seen as important in advance of CSF's involvement, and the university had already established a 'Smarter Campus' initiative which combined discussions on transport (particularly bicycle use and provisions), litter and bins, landscape and street furniture and lighting provision. Indeed discussions about recycling had been on-going for over a decade. Many of these initiatives benefited greatly from the Capital funding (and indeed provided a basis for the bid) which made possible, for the first time, the university-wide implementation of bicycle storage and high quality refuse sorting facilities. It is generally thought that the use of external funding was the key to moving forward agendas that did not fit into annual budget lines.

The two-year timescale of capital expenditure made it difficult to initiate building projects which could be wholly completed by the closing date. However, there was an opportunity to raise awareness and standards of buildings to which the budget could make a contribution. Even at a late stage in the project's development, in the summer of 2005 whilst the site clearance work for the Roland Levinsky building was underway and the contract had been let, CETL requested that project managers undertake a BREEAM assessment of the design to explore opportunities for improvement of the specification and design decisions. The discussion (Mackie, 2005) raised several issues, principally why such an appraisal had not been undertaken earlier in the building design process.

So while many of the processes and procedures associated with different aspects of running the estates service and the commissioning and procurement of buildings and landscape designs and products were well established, it is clear that the additional funding encouraged key discussions to take place. Given that CSF management had to sign off on various budget items, they were able to raise the importance of sustainability in the decision making hierarchy. This meant that CSF had a significant impact on the way that such issues were considered.

What is clear is that the initial response of the Estates team, in particular, was enthusiastic and the subsequent assistance that was given in the development of capital projects was good tempered, thoughtful and extremely valuable. Estates staff were amazed at the spaces for discussion that CSF created, the way out-of-the-box thinking was encouraged and the public valorisation of sustainability principles that, previously, had been held in private.

'We didn't achieve as much as we might have done'

There is undoubtedly a sense of frustration in many of the responses, from fellows, managers and estates representatives. Initially, the clear ambition was to make a significant difference to the quality of the campus landscape, including projects which increased biodiversity, raised the profile of local plant species, used natural materials, and which created rich cultural and social environments full of opportunities for interaction, learning and teaching.

A real inhibition on such projects in practice was the university's existing re-organisation agenda, initiated by the Vice Chancellor in 2001, to bring the staff and students from the three outlying campuses from Exmouth, Exeter and Newton Abbot, onto the Plymouth site. This wider project required the building of new Arts Faculty (Roland Levinsky), Education building (James Street) a Sports Hall, major extensions to four existing buildings (Scott, Davey, the Students Union and Portland Square) and total disruption during the 2005-2007 sessions to the pedestrian and built environments of the Plymouth campus.

The impact of these university-initiated projects on the developing CETL capital projects (for CSF and the Experiential learning CETL), including the provision of office space for all four CETLs awarded to Plymouth in 2005, was enormous. The impact on Estates staff was very heavy. They had to oversee a raft of developments which meant: co-ordinating building sites and access; scaffolding areas; protection for pedestrian routes; site access; and contractors' site huts and stores. This work was in addition to their normal site maintenance, health and safety and utilities responsibilities. No extra staff were hired by Estates during this time.

However, several key projects were initiated. The following three illustrate gains and losses:

- *Roland Levinsky*: the contribution to this building, although it came too late to revise major design decisions, ensured significant community use, and that the Gateway building also had high class building monitoring systems and data output opportunities. The Theatre, cinema, major exhibition and lecture rooms will provide a highly valuable on-campus resource for local, national and international sustainability events

17

- *The Vision Theatre*: a joint project with the experiential learning CETL which had reconditioned an existing small planetarium building on-campus to provide 360 degree, state of the art projection and acoustic environmental simulation. Our contribution was to design and fund the external building fabric and associated external social and display spaces. This proved extremely valuable in engaging designers and architects, but was severely curtailed by the unpredicted encroachment of neighbouring building works, and the late change in location of the Portland Square memorial sculpture site. The university asked us to allocate part of the budget to the project for upgrading the existing Drakes Park which was transferred to the university in December 2006

- *The Students Union Garden*: the subject of an additional funding bid in the Autumn of 2005, was perhaps the most successful so far. Owing to the timing of the Students Union rebuild contract, we were able to use the same contractor and take advantage of an existing programme of works and reduced overhead costs. The final design, selected from four sketch options by students and the Students Union Manager, was developed in terms of the materials specification (oak seating and planters), detailed design - to increase seating areas and opportunities for supporting day and evening events, and to improve access for disabled students, recycling storage capacity, and planting specification - through discussions with students and staff at the Campus Forum. The intention to engage students from Bicton College (a University of Plymouth partner College) in planting the area with local, native species has yet to be implemented

This unprecedented period of rebuilding with several contractors, architects and other building design consultants already working at full stretch was not perhaps the best time to initiate a sustainability debate about the university environment, very little of which was even visible. The impact on the visual and social landscape of the campus to date has been slight, and the interpretation initiatives are only now beginning to come together. However, the developing contacts within the Capital Spend Team encouraged the inclusion of several CETL ESD fellows as members of the University Strategic Plan: Urban Design Group chaired by Rob Score. This group created the landscape strategy for the university as part of the Strategic Plan draft, published in July 2006, which made significant proposals for the future of the campus as a whole, including many of the original CETL ESD objectives, and focused on the role of the buildings and landscapes as teaching and learning resources for sustainability in their own right. The recent Sustainability Policy Action Plan includes the setting up of a 'Campus as a Learning Resource Group', bringing together learning resource managers and academics and estates representatives in a body which can take forward many of the CETL's objectives in the coming years.

Continuing confusion over the university decision making processes and plans

The University of Plymouth is a hierarchical organisation. This is the norm for universities. There was some tension with the CSF capital-spend because CSF was trying to be open and transparent in its decisions while also encouraging participation of groups normally left out of decision-making processes. While CSF staff were praised for their ability to make compromises and adapt to university structures, restrictions and realities there was a further difficulty. Even senior members of estates and chancellery were not aware of how the university made decisions about capital projects and policies in general. Indeed, chancellery were unable to state when and how policies were being revised, updated or monitored.

Incomplete information was given to the Capital Spend Team. This was not malicious, but just the reality of a very busy university in the midst of closing down three campuses and undergoing significant structural changes. While the confusion over decision making processes can be explained locally, Leith Sharp points out that there is a prevalent myth of the rational university:

> As a result of this cultural assumption [of a rational university], universities in general, persist in designing processes and structures that are based on assumptions of rationality, despite the inevitable dysfunction of such approaches, because it supports the greater goal of appearing rational. From personal experience, it appears that one of the most significant and prevalent forms of stress experienced by staff within universities is the stress of having to sustain the myth of organisational rationality while facing the reality of organisational irrationality....The myth prevents institutional analysis and reform as a response to dysfunction since the political payoff for accepting dysfunction is much greater than the payoff for dealing with root causes (Sharp, 2002, p.136).

The University of Florida provides a very good model of how to reach some clarity and transparency of reporting structures within a university. They have adapted the Global Reporting Initiative (GRI), a tool used by sustainably progressive cities around the world and many major corporations, for use by a university. A GRI report is created each year by a city/company/university. Each report clearly presents the operating budget, assets, decision-making structure, mission and vision statements and goes through a triple bottom-line accounting. The University of Florida:

> ...united the interests of the administration with those of campus greening and social progressive constituents and, in the process, established a baseline with which to compare future metrics...The University of Florida's publication of a GRI-consistent sustainability report is a first step in recognizing its role both within and outside the academic community. The university recognizes that using this system for sustainability measurement provides a baseline on which improvements can be made, identifying specific activities in need of immediate attention (Newport et al. 2003, p.357; pp.361-2).

Struggling through the decision making structures at the University of Plymouth has had some positive outcomes. It led to strong connections formed across disciplines, with support staff and senior management. Building on this network of relations the CSF Director drove forward a holistic sustainability policy and action plan that has been approved by chancellery and the Board of Governors (University of Plymouth, 2007).

Problems with capital expenditure timescales

Simply put, it is extremely difficult to design and execute a successful building project within two years of acceptance of a funding bid. The timescales which might be desirable for a fully sustainable project - by implication highly consultative, collaboratively designed (to consider all aspects of material, environmental, social and cultural requirements and impacts) and fully audited - were not available for the capital spend, within two years, of the £2+ million CETL budget. This challenge was both helped and hindered by the extensive on-going and forthcoming construction and refurbishment projects on the Plymouth main campus. It was helped because there were a number of projects that the estates team wanted to do but did not have the money. This included the Student Union Gardens and the Drakes Place Gardens. It proved very challenging because there were literally very few places on campus where work was physically possible due to the impact of the many projects associated with the university reorganisation. An already dense urban campus saw existing landscapes, sites and pedestrian alleys closed off to provide working and storage areas for other projects.

A requirement of the HEFCE funding was to spend the whole budget in two years. Although this creates limitations, the pressures of the timescale meant that everyone involved had to learn more rapidly through having to implement the projects. Had we had additional time at the start of the projects we might have had less of a sense of urgency, and not travelled so far. Particularly useful for us was the concurrent activity of both other Plymouth CETLs, and the wide range of scales and types of projects supported (transport, refuse, building, landscape, interpretation, etc.) which meant that a large number of individuals were involved in at least part of the process. This involvement significantly improved communication and built a shared understanding in the team. CSF accomplished the originally budgeted projects as well as applying for roughly £300,000 of additional funds. This is credit to the amount of work put in by the Capital Spend Team on top of their teaching or management duties.

Setting clearer agendas for consultants

For many of those involved, one of the real successes of the project has been the greatly increased interaction between academic and support staff. The need for exploration of the agendas and brief requirements of the capital projects increased discussion with building and landscape design consultants, heating and ventilating engineers, sculptors, structural engineers and many specialist Energy and Communication contractors. The high level of discussions with people from different disciplines provided a rapid learning environment for those involved.

The university's building contracting process which appoints framework consultants (and contractors) for all key roles for a period of five years, made it possible to work with consultants who were familiar with the university's requirements, and the physical campus and buildings. This proved to be a double edged sword:

- saving time and costs which would have made normal bidding and tendering processes impossible within the two year window
- but meaning that in some cases it was difficult for the consultants to respond to the very different expectations of a sustainability driven briefing and design process

All consultants were very familiar with the university priorities for buildings to 'come in on time and on cost'. The idea that the CETL should invest additional fee costs in exploring options, widening the debate to include students (Students' Union Garden) and community members (Drakes Park) was initially very difficult for quantity surveyor and project management teams. However several of the consultants tried hard to rise to the challenge. The discussion did lead to some very innovative and experimental thinking, even though in several cases (e.g. geological sample cladding and geo-thermal energy supplies to the Vision Theatre) these did not go ahead for good technical or organisational reasons. What became apparent however was that although in some cases individual consultants were either enthusiastic or knowledgeable about environmental issues, their inputs were inconsistent and, to a certain extent, unpredictable.

As the two year project evolved, a more detailed discussion with Estates and Procurement staff emerged about the university processes of appointing and evaluating design consultants, and about the quality of the design briefing provided. The CETL has now been able to provide the Procurement Division with new sustainability criteria for use in the promotion and assessment of the Framework contracts for December 2006 - April 2007. The university can now reliably expect consultants to have good skills in a wide range of technical and process related areas of design development.

A sustainability brief had already been devised, prior to the CETL project, by the firm of Battle McCarthy, with funding secured from EAUC through the work of the energy and procurement managers. However the sustainability brief was only one of 20 sections in a University Design Brief which included everything from general instructions for design consultants to the specification of light bulbs in lecture theatres. The brief was therefore not given central importance. The design brief is currently in the process of reorganisation, in response to the university's new 'Sustainability Policy' (University of Plymouth, 2007) which was written with wide and deep consultation across the university and, in particular, with the help of Estates and CSF staff.

Academics talking to administration and support staff

A member of the estates team mentioned in an interview that 'I had never gone into an academic's office by choice before the CSF capital spend. I mean, of course I went in plenty of offices, but it was always for meetings. Now that I have met some lecturers I will actually stop in and say hi. That is a change'. Indeed estates staff started questioning their label as 'support' staff which had a pejorative tone within the university.

Academic staff, too, found that their view of the learning resources team changed with the much closer contact and improved understanding of the range of their colleagues' responsibilities which the capital spend process required. Initial suspicion on both sides was gradually modified by the trust which the collaboration built, allowing everyone to appreciate better the others', often complementary, strengths in what became a very integrated project.

Recommendations

The following recommendations, drawing on the themes outlined above, may be useful for those setting out, like us, on the process of greening their own universities:

1. *Find out what everyone is already doing!*

This seems obvious but it was surprising how long it has taken to establish both the key roles and responsibilities for environmental, cultural and social aspects of sustainability within the university support and academic staff. Useful documents and policies continued to surface which we wished we'd known about earlier. Many incredibly valuable people are already well on the way in their own fields of expertise, and will be very useful and positive allies and collaborators in the project. Our Campus Forum which included students, academics, estate support, librarians, public relations staff and others provided a good point of contact for this discussion to emerge, and also helped link through informal networks those individuals who might otherwise have slipped through the net. We recommend working within existing structures, meeting people through informal networks and creating a new space for green campus advocates to meet, discuss, strategise and support each other.

2. Be realistic about what it is possible to achieve!

Find out what the university is already planning, who is planning it and when they think it is going to happen. Then tailor your projects to take advantage of synergies, and to avoid major conflicts of space, time and energy. This sounds straightforward, but has proved to be one of the most intractable difficulties in the whole capital expenditure process. Universities are complex and many faceted organisms and even without the added burden of the upheavals that were going on around us in Plymouth they are often difficult to tie down. The university itself has many agendas that are not necessarily intended for public consumption, and commercially sensitive data may make it hard to understand the full picture. Even full support from the top (which we enjoyed) does not ensure that everyone in the organisation will wish to be completely open about their own agendas. Time, working together, making mistakes and learning from them are perhaps the only effective ways to build understanding and trust.

3. Clarify the organisation's decision making processes and plans

A great deal of time can be spent in discussions which will in the end have no influence on those taking decisions. The real, as opposed to theoretical, decision making responsibilities of individuals and groups will have a profound effect on how projects can be initiated, developed and completed. Identifying key people, committees and groups, and understanding their timescale and remits early in the process is essential. Finding appropriate levels of approach to such systems can be a subtle and challenging task, and will require a range of different points of intervention, to ensure that the best possible overview of the systems is available. The use of the Global Reporting Initiative shows great potential for helping a university become more transparent.

4. Problems with capital expenditure timescales

The difficulty of achieving anything truly sustainable within a two year capital funding timescale is debateable. However the pressure of the timescale does mean that everyone involved can learn more rapidly through having to implement the projects. Had we had additional time at the start of the projects we might have had less of a sense of urgency, and not travelled so far. However there is a real need for HEFCE timescales and briefing budgets which encourage whole life costing, proper environmental and social auditing, and ensure that post occupancy analysis are a fundamental requirement for every project.

5. Setting clearer agendas for consultants

Look carefully at the technical competencies of both in-house and external technical staff and consultants. It is difficult to achieve sustainability in either landscape or building projects working with designers who do not have congruent experience and abilities. Sustainability in the procurement process is becoming an increasingly significant focus for government attention (OGC, 2005; DEFRA,

2006; Addis and Talbot, 2001). Identifying key dates and opportunities for raising standards in Framework Contracts will be crucial.

6. Academics talking to administration and support staff

Universities have a lot of formal and informal structures and boundaries. Education for sustainable development questions the value of these boundaries and the way the world is carved up into disciplines and support services. By challenging these assumptions and creating comfortable places for a diversity of people to come together, academics, administration and support staff began talking to each other in new and more trusting ways. People were able to understand the reasons for previous decisions and policies while also making recommendations for future changes. An atmosphere of conviviality and commitment to a common (but often quite general) purpose is key.

References

Calder, W. and Clugston, R. 2002 'U.S. Progress Toward Sustainability in Higher Education', in Dernbach, J.C. (ed) *The Environmental Law Institute.* Also available from: [Internet]. <http://www.ulsf.org/dernbach/assess.htm>.

Dahle, M. and Neumayer, E. 2001 Overcoming barriers to campus greening: A survey among higher educational institutions in London, UK. *International Journal of Sustainability in Higher Education*, **2**, 139-160

Dyer, A. and Selby, D. 2004 *Centre for Excellence in Teaching and Learning: Education for Sustainable Development: Stage Two.* Plymouth: University of Plymouth

Department for Environment, Food and Rural Affairs 2006 *Procuring the Future: Sustainable Procurement National Action Plan: recommendations from the Sustainable Procurement Task Force.* London: DEFRA

Addis, B. and Talbot, R. 2001 *Sustainable Construction Procurement: A guide to delivering environmentally responsible projects.* London: Department of Trade and Industry and CIRIA

EAUC 2007 Home Page [Internet].<http://www.eauc.org.uk/home>. [Accessed 30th August 2007].

Gray-Donald, J. and Selby, D. 2004 Through the (not so) green door: Connecting campus greening and curriculum change. *Ekistics*, **71**, 203-212

Haigh, M. 2005 Greening the University Curriculum: Appraising an International Movement. *Journal of Geography in Higher Education*, **29**, 31-48

HEFCE 2007 *Sustainable Development in Higher Education: Statement of Policy.* [Internet]. <http://www.hefce.ac.uk/pubs/hefce/2005/05_28/05_28.pdf>. [Accessed 30th August 2007].

HEEPI 2007 *About HEEPI* [Internet]. <http://www.heepi.org.uk/>. [Accessed 30th August 2007].

Mackie, M. 2005 *Report on the BREEAM Assessment meeting on the Rowe Street Building, 15th August 2005.* Internal CETL ESD report

M'Gonigle, M. and Starke, J. 2006 *Planet U: Sustaining the World, Reinventing the University.* Gabriola Island: New Society Publishers

Murray, P., Goodhew, S. and Turpin-Brooks, S. 2006 Environmental sustainability: Sustainable construction a UK case study. *International Journal of Environmental, Cultural, Economic and Social Sustainability*, **2**, 2

Newport, D., Chesnes, T. and Lindner, A. 2003 The 'environmental sustainability' problem: ensuring that sustainability stands on three legs. *International Journal of Sustainability in Higher Education*, **4**, 357-363

Office of Government Commerce 2005 *Sustainability: Achieving Excellence in Construction Procurement Guide.* OGC

Parkin, S., Johnstone, A., Buckland, H., and White, E. 2004 *Learning and Skills for Sustainable Development: Developing a Sustainability Literate Society.* London: Forum for the Future/Higher Education Partnership for Sustainability

Pike, l., Shannon, T., Lawrimore, K., McGee, A., Taylor, M. and Lamoreux, G. 2003 Science education and sustainability initiatives: a campus recycling case study shows the importance of opportunity. *International Journal of Sustainability in Higher Education,* **4**, 218-229

Sharp, L. 2002 Green campuses: the road from little victories to systemic transformation. *International Journal of Sustainability in Higher Education,* **44**, 128-145

Shriberg, M. 2002 Sustainability in U.S. Higher Education: organizational factors influencing campus environmental performance and leadership. Doctoral dissertation University of Michigan. [Internet]. <http://sitemaker.umich.edu/snre-student-mshriber/files/shriberg.pdf>. [Accessed 3rd September 2007].

Simpson, W. 2003 Energy Sustainability and the Green Campus. *Planning for Higher Education,* **March-May**, 150-158

Tilbury, D. 2004 'Environmental education for sustainability: a force for change in higher education', in Corcoran, P.B. and Wals, A. E. J. *Higher Education and the Challenge of Sustainability.* Dordrecht: Kluwer Academic Publishers

University of Plymouth April 2007 Sustainability Policy. [Internet]. <http://csf.plymouth.ac.uk/node/428>. [Accessed 3rd September 2007].

Changing Behaviours for a More Sustainable London

Shalini Jayasinghe, Afsheen Rashid and Gayle Burgess
London Sustainability Exchange

Abstract

If everyone in the world lived as Londoners do we would need three planets to sustain us (London Remade/London First, 2003). Furthermore, there is a lot of evidence to suggest that although citizens want to live more sustainably and feel fairly well informed about what they could do, the majority are not acting on these desires. London Sustainability Exchange (LSx)'s experience (Motivation Kit CD-Rom, LSx, 2006) demonstrates that a one-size-fits-all approach will not work in helping people from all communities achieve 'One Planet' lifestyles. With almost 30% of 7.2 million residents representing a BAME (Black, Asian and Minority Ethnic) group, London presents an ideal test-bed for a variety of behaviour change campaigns that aim to close the so-called 'value-action' gap.

LSx's Behaviour Change Programme[1] delivers initiatives to help shift Londoners' behaviour and cascade a lasting, rather than transient, legacy of change. Pilot projects identify key motivators, and barriers and effective ways to address these, and test the effectiveness of a range of creative and culturally-appropriate outreach activities and communication channels. Comedy plays, environmentally-themed sermons and street dance workshops are all examples of approaches that have successfully inspired Londoners to adopt more sustainable 'One Planet' lifestyles.

Keywords   London, behaviour, BAME, champion, sustainable

Introduction

The challenge of getting Londoners to lead 'greener' lives - to reduce their waste, conserve energy and water, recycle more, and so on - is a mighty one. Much evidence exists to show that although citizens want to live more sustainably, and often feel well informed about the kinds of things they could do, the majority are just not acting on these desires.

According to results from the 'City Limits' ecological footprint analysis of London, in the year 2000 the city's ecological footprint was 42 times its bio-capacity and 293 times its geographical area (roughly twice the size of the UK) (IWM(EB), 2002). Further calculations published by London Remade and London First (2003) demonstrate that while the average person on earth requires 2.3 global average hectares (gha) to provide for his or her consumption, the average person living in the UK requires over 5.3 gha. The footprint of London's residents and organisations is 10% above this national average at 5.8 gha per person (London Remade and London First, 2003); 35.7% is attributed to goods, services and waste management, 23.6% to food, 19.5% to direct energy consumption (except transport), 13.9% to personal mobility, 5.7% to the provision of housing and 1.5% to pollution abatement. This provides a useful proxy for the amount of behaviour change required to secure quality of life for all Londoners and the capital's future as the most sustainable world city.

---

[1] Behaviour Change: http://www.lsx.org.uk/whatwedo/behaviourchange_page2554.aspx

Meeting the Challenges of a Transient London

London is a unique city with dynamic demographics. It is the largest city in Europe with a population of 7.2 million, and this is estimated to expand to over 8 million by 2020 (ONS, 2007). London is also a culturally diverse city. Nearly 30% of Londoners represent a minority ethnic group (ONS, 2007). Over 300 languages are spoken by school children in London (Baker and Eversley, 2000) and there are more than 50 non-indigenous communities that have a population of more than 10,000 (ONS, 2007). In addition, the psychosocial, socio-cultural and political environments are highly complex and dynamic, providing constantly changing opportunities and challenges for businesses, organisations and communities, and a challenging context for behaviour change campaigns.

A Strategic Approach to Changing Behaviour: The Use of Networks, Champions and Hooks

LSx aims to accelerate the transition to a sustainable London. This requires not only an increased awareness and change in attitudes amongst Londoners but also, crucially, a change in behaviours. Through research mapping, LSx has identified a variety of barriers that prevent Londoners from adopting more sustainable 'One Planet' lifestyles, and classified these into four broad groups: apathy, attitudes, awareness and accessibility. Whilst these barriers influence against behaviour change, motivators exist to effectively influence for it. LSx has classified these into five broad groups: empathy, encouragement, awareness, accessibility and empowerment.

London's large population and complex demographics pose multi-faceted challenges to behaviour change campaigns, with particular issues associated with access to, and engagement of, communities, as well as the practical ability to deliver appropriate change programmes. In addition, campaign activities need to cascade a lasting or transformative, rather than transient, legacy of change.

Evidence presented in LSx's Motivation Kit CD-Rom (LSx, 2006), demonstrates that a 'one size fits all' approach will not work in helping people from all communities break the cycle of unsustainable consumption. As the list below indicates, behaviour change campaigns need to develop approaches that are aspirational and relevant to people's everyday lives, to successfully inspire them to adopt more sustainable lifestyles.

1. Be inspired – check out other campaigns, copy what works. Be inspired by behaviour change theories and models.
2. Everyone's different – one size does not fit all. Understand your audience – their needs and wants, likes and dislikes. Design messages to fit and engage with what's important to them.
3. Create the 'AIDA' factor – design messages which grab attention, spark interest, generate desire that leads to action.
4. Keep it simple – use language that people understand – avoid jargon
5. Use multi media – people absorb information in different ways. Use varied methods – graphics, text, sound, visuals.
6. People influence people – work with 'influencers' who are trusted and listened to by your audience.
7. Create the right conditions – ensure that they have enough support and infrastructure to make the change.
8. Put your heart into it – find out what makes people happy, sad, excited, bored. Then use it: appeal to values and beliefs. Use stories and role models.

9. Say goodbye to guilt – don't make people switch off by attacking them. Make them feel good and give them incentives to change their behaviour.
10. Review, revise and renew – build in monitoring and evaluation throughout, that way you'll be able to respond quickly to what's not working so well.

Social networks

LSx's experience suggests that it is only through the co-operation of partners and individuals that we can achieve a fundamental shift in the take up of sustainable lifestyles. Communities tend to be built on social networks (Krebs and Holley, 2002-2006). Networks provide a wealth of social capital and are a useful tool for strategic access to communities, whilst providing influential connections. Social network theory views social relationships as nodes and ties, nodes being the individuals (or communities or organisations) and ties being the relationships/connections between them. Thus each individual and each community form nodes within one or more networks including family networks, local community groups, residents associations, school groups, offices and faith groups. These networks not only provide access into the community, but also provide an infrastructure of familiarity and identity to that particular community.

LSx utilises social networks extensively as a key strategic tool to achieve a breadth and depth of outreach and community engagement. Key nodes and ties relevant to the community/communities are mapped out at the start of each project, and relationships, stakeholders and knowledge flows are identified (Fig. 1). LSx is in itself a networking organisation, providing organisations and networks of individuals with the motivation, knowledge, and connections they need to put sustainability into practice. The organisational strategy is thus incorporated into project delivery.

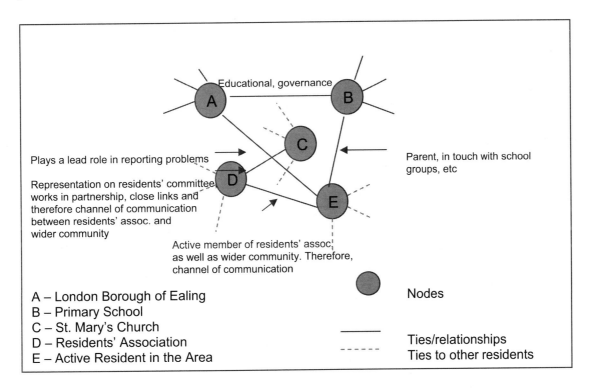

Figure 1 Network map of West-Twyford, LB Ealing: site for the 'Rewarding Green Householders' pilot study

Champions of change

Although leaflets and brochures have a place in behaviour change campaigns, peer influence, advocacy and/or subtle pressure from key community leaders and opinion formers are frequently much more crucial. As communications agency Futerra explain:

> Social learning theory states that people learn from each other all the time, by modelling the behaviour around them and by using individual human contact and communication to set their behaviour and attitudes. This is why it is so difficult to change an individual's attitude without taking into account the attitudes of his or her family, friends, colleagues and community. (Futerra, 2005)

Gladwell (2000) further examines the power of 'social epidemics' or sudden and often chaotic changes from one state to another. He explains that epidemics have clear examples of contagious behaviour, similar to viral marketing, in which little changes can have big effects, while the smallest change can shatter the epidemic's equilibrium.

The complex demographics of London, coupled with the patterns of behaviour change explained in Futerra (2005) and Gladwell (2000), mean that typically, having a key point of contact, or *champion*, within the community not only helps to secure a breadth and depth to outreach and community engagement, but also a highly efficient and effective way of 'getting people on board'. Such people - those who are locally active, sensitive to cultural nuances and aware of local issues, priorities and barriers to action - often prove pivotal to the success of any behaviour change campaign.

When selecting/appointing Champions, it is important to select those with the most suitable personality type. LSx adopts the model by Gladwell (2002), who identifies good Champions as protagonists, skilled friendship makers who maintain their friendships, are persuasive, gather information and are well-respected. Within the group of protagonists, Gladwell (2002) further identifies three types of people who have the power to produce the phenomenon of a social epidemic and thereby the biggest impact. These are, Connectors - people specialists: those who know lots of people; Mavens - information specialists: those who accumulate knowledge, but are socially motivated, so that they want to spread this knowledge; and Salesmen - persuaders: noted for their charm, enthusiasm and likeability. Each type of person plays a unique and crucial role in delivering a behaviour change campaign successfully. Ideally, therefore, for each given project, it is important to choose *champions* that represent each of these personality types.

In order to ensure representation across the personality types, LSx asks each potential *champion* to self-assess themselves and assess their peers (Table 1). This also helps tailor activities to each *champion* and, accordingly, allocate appropriate behaviour change campaign tasks.

Table 1 Assessment of personality types of community champions working in West-Twyford on the 'Rewarding Green Householders' pilot project

	Champion 1	Champion 2	Champion 3
Champion 1	Maven	Salesman	Maven
Champion 2	Maven	Connector	Maven/Connector
Champion 3	Salesman/Connector	Salesman/Connector	Maven
Concluded Personality Type	**Maven/Salesman/ Connector**	**Salesman/Connector**	**Maven/Connector**

'Hooks' and incentives

Whilst networks and *champions* provide useful tools for motivating behaviour change, the complex demographics of London make a 'one-size fits all' approach unsuitable for the delivery of effective programmes that have a lasting legacy of change. Specifically-tailored activities that empathise with the different communities of London are consequently essential. Behaviour change campaigns therefore require 'hooks' which networks and *champions* can use to deliver activities effectively. 'Hooks' are a mechanism through which campaign messages can be made relevant to, and resonate with, target community aspirations and values: faith is, therefore, one example of this.

As part of its strategic approach, LSx has developed and delivered a number of pilot projects with culturally diverse communities across the capital, identifying key motivators, barriers and 'hooks' to overcome these, and effective ways to integrate these into successful behaviour change campaigns. Our pilot studies test the effectiveness, on the ground, of a variety of 'hooks' and the delivery of campaign messaging through creative and culturally appropriate outreach activities and channels. For example: using fun as a 'hook', we have commissioned comedy plays with an environmental theme tailored to the Turkish speaking community, using faith as a 'hook', we have worked with partners to deliver environmentally themed sermons, highlighting Quranic scripture promoting resource efficient behaviours, amongst Muslim communities. 'Hooks' for SMEs tend to orient around the 3 C's of competitive advantage, cost efficiency and compliance, while 'hooks' for young people include a 'cool' element. As such we coordinated the delivery of street dance workshops choreographed around environment-friendly behaviours such as riding a bicycle, turning off the lights for our *Children as Change Agents Initiative* which was instrumental in helping young people to act as *champions* of behavioural change in their households and contribute to improved cohesion in their Camden communities.

Learning from these pilots is shared amongst LSx's 'Motivate London Learning Network', a 350 strong pan-London network of individuals and public, private and third sector organisations working to motivate various behaviour changes across the capital. Learning from LSx's pilot projects has shown that incentives are a useful tool to motivate people to change their behaviour and often provide the 'stepping stone' from awareness raising to behaviour change and the take up of more sustainable actions.

Using incentives to change people's attitudes, beliefs and behaviour is an interesting study in itself. Theory suggests that when a situation involves incentives, incentives of different sizes yield different results that may not be in direct correlation with what may be expected (Lidwell *et al.*, 2003). When incentives for an unpleasant task are small, it is suggested that people tend to do the task by reassuring themselves that it is in keeping with their beliefs. When incentives for an unpleasant task are large, people do it because they feel that they are compensated for doing the task that may otherwise not be in keeping with their beliefs. This phenomenon is attributed to a reduction in dissonance (Lidwell *et al.*, 2003). This can manifest as an inconsistency between the beliefs one holds or between one's actions and one's beliefs.[1] In accordance with our aim to produce a lasting legacy of change, we are thus required to carefully choose incentives that would motivate a lasting behaviour change, rather than one that stops once the incentive is removed. Our experience suggests that a 'Goody Bag' or 'Sustainability Starter Kit' containing items such as an energy saving light bulb, save-a-flush, information on local, organic and fair-trade produce, green tariffs, cycle maps, eco-friendly products provide a useful initial incentive to make the first change to lifestyles. Other incentives to secure longer term change include: communication materials such as mugs advocating 'Boil a cupful not a kettleful'; calendars displaying culturally appropriate and seasonal messages; and competitions giving prizes for the best performing household, street and most innovative approaches.

Motivating Londoners to Adopt Sustainable Lifestyles

In order to accelerate the shift to a sustainable London and encourage Londoners to move towards 'One Planet' lifestyles, LSx has adopted the above strategy. This section includes details of how a selection of LSx projects have incorporated social marketing techniques with the use of *champions of change*, hooks and incentives, and how the resultant behaviour change campaigns have been communicated through culturally-appropriate channels and materials. Qualitative and quantitative evidence is also presented to demonstrate the strategy's effectiveness.

Rewarding green householders

The *Rewarding Green Householders Pilot Project* explores how effective a range of incentives are in encouraging householders to adopt 'greener' lifestyles driven forward using *Community Champions*. Instead of using an individual reward or incentive the range of mechanisms include mobilising *Community Champions*, 'A Give or Take day', distribution of starter kits and a competition to reward the 'best household', 'most innovative practice' and 'best street'. During the early part of the year 2007, three *Community Champions* actively worked within the West Twyford community to promote residents to take up more sustainable lifestyles. *Champions* distributed leaflets to the 750 households, community centres, the Church and other common spaces in the area. From these 100 householders received sustainability starter kits to enable them to take on greener practices. Activities such as 'A Give or Take day' held in March for the locals saw the participation of several residents - both 'giving' and 'taking'.

---

[2] American Psychological Association (APA): dissonance. (n.d.). Merriam-Webster's Medical Dictionary. Retrieved January 15, 2007, from Dictionary.com website: http://dictionary.reference.com/browse/dissonance

As Figure 2 demonstrates, the project had an impact on the householders as a majority of the respondents admitted that changes in behaviour had occurred. None of the respondents were disinterested in environmental issues although the sample might be biased with those responding tending to be those more interested in the issue.

It was interesting to note which of the mechanisms brought about behaviour change. Participant responses, illustrated in Figure 3, show that the starter kits were largely instrumental in changing behaviour as the kits encouraged and enabled participants to take immediate action:

The bags of samples distributed free introduced many (including myself) to cycle routes, pink garden waste bags and more awareness of the water/electricity saving issue. (Participant)

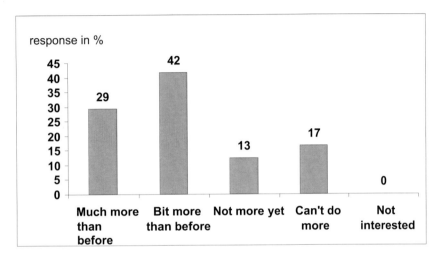

Figure 2   Participants' level of change after the project

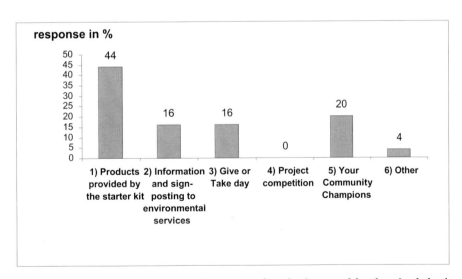

Figure 3   Participants' views on the effectiveness of mechanisms used for changing behavior

The second most influential factor was the *Community Champions*, which reinforced the effectiveness of other incentives. The starter kits were distributed through direct interaction with the *champion* at appropriate community gatherings.

Significantly, the competition was not seen, at all, as an incentive. This is reassuring as it implies that people change due to better awareness and for long-term benefits ensuring a lasting legacy of change.

Children as change agents

This Motivate London pilot project explored how effective children can be as agents of behaviour change within their households and communities. Children constitute a large, unique and wide reaching network within a predominantly young and culturally diverse London, linking streets, cultures and religions. They often have far-reaching ties to various groups of society. LSx's previous experience suggested that developing the capacity of London's children to act as agents of change would be a key aspect of securing London's future as a more sustainable world city.

The *Children as Change Agents Pilot Study* aimed to encourage and empower young people in the Camden Goods Yard estate to act as agents of behavioural change to promote and cascade sustainable lifestyles amongst their households and local communities, and increase social cohesion. The estate is owned and managed by Community Housing Group and the demographics include approximately 220 children of whom about 100 are younger than five years, and 176 adults almost all of whom are aged under 50 years. All residents have been classed as either vulnerable or identified as some other priority group for housing. There is a 69% unemployment rate amongst the residents and 47% are single parent families. Approximately half of the residents are British White, while half belong to a Black Asian or Minority Ethnic (BAME) group.

Children were approached through the Housing Associations' youth engagement team and encouraged to explore their perceptions of the environment and adopt more sustainable behaviour through artistic expression and other activities. The activities were selected according to feedback from initial feasibility assessment which suggested they would be welcome and warmly received. Activities included:

- visiting Camley Street nature reserve
- building floating wildlife gardens on Regents Canal
- environmentally-themed street dance workshops
- bag painting with a quiz on sustainability
- Halloween-themed bat walk
- football match with half-time quiz

The project worked directly with 55 young people to develop their capacity and support them as agents of behavioural change to motivate residents in taking up sustainable lifestyles. Through articles in Community Housing Group newsletters, personalised correspondence and local publicity, the project reached out to over 600 Camden residents.

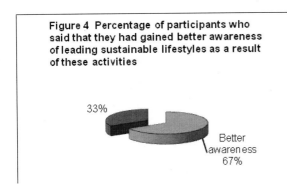

Figure 4 Percentage of participants who said that they had gained better awareness of leading sustainable lifestyles as a result of these activities

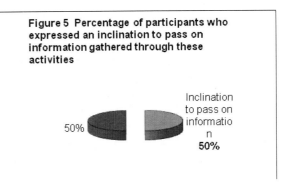

Figure 5 Percentage of participants who expressed an inclination to pass on information gathered through these activities

Following the activities, participants showed a greater commitment to environmentally sustainable behaviour through improved knowledge and skills, as well as a desire to spread the knowledge and skills gained to other people. Figures 4, 5 and 6 show participant expression of interest following activities: 67% of participants said that their awareness on how to lead a sustainable lifestyle had improved as a result of these activities; 50% of participants expressed an interest to get further involved in activities 'to make a difference'; and 50% expressed an inclination to pass on information gained through these activities to others.

Many parents were surprised at how engaged their children became with environmental issues. The mother of one child commented 'I was taken aback by how much they felt about the planet and their home-town'. The parents also agreed that they themselves were often set in their ways but that encouragement from their children can help to motivate them to change their behaviour. However, parents also recognised that their own behaviour can also influence their children.

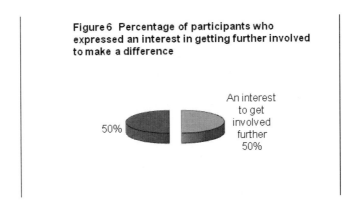

Figure 6 Percentage of participants who expressed an interest in getting further involved to make a difference

The project activities also helped in developing further links and ties in the community. The floating wildlife gardens succeeded in bringing together children and even some of the parents from the estates to engage in joint activities. Feedback indicated that participants recognised and appreciated this opportunity, one commenting that 'It was good that we all got to interact with each other'.

Evaluating the impact of the project on the participants' households, it was found that the projects had certainly stirred some will in both children and their parents to take up more sustainable behaviour.

Hinduism and H2O

Working in partnership with Thames Water, LSx developed and implemented an initiative employing innovative social marketing techniques to promote water conservation as part of a wider move towards 'One Planet' lifestyles amongst culturally diverse communities, notably representatives of the Hindu community, in East London. LSx identified *champions* within the community to help understand religious customs and cultural sensitivities. Community leaders, Temple Committee members and teachers who fell under the categories of 'mavens', 'connectors' and 'salesman' personality types were trusted faces in the community and able to reassure others of the legitimacy of the project and effectively cascade core campaign messages:

> I'm very keen to support the environment and save resources that are no longer regarded as free and endless. Returning home yesterday I instantly placed the water saving devices in the toilet flush. I run my business from home and meet many customers everyday. If you give me more of these devices I'll try to encourage others to save water during flushes. (Champion)

This initiative reinforced LSx's experience that faith is an effective 'hook' with which to motivate sustainable behaviour as culturally-appropriate messages drawing the links between theological beliefs and the environment were well received:

> It is a very good idea to have these talks on Hinduism and nature because it is fundamental to what we believe. Conservation and preservation is the core of our lives and every Hindu has this duty to respect nature. (Participant)

Outreach activities included Temple talks, workshops, children's activities and participation at festivals delivered during the summer of 2006. These reached over 2800 members of the East London Hindu community. Incentives, water saving tools such as save-a-flush and visually engaging communication materials, including themed mugs, t-towels, leaflets and calendars, were distributed to enable water saving action and provide regular prompts. Three volunteers agreed to complete water diaries over a two-week period when offered a relevant incentive such as a water butt. As LSx staff were unable to source volunteers whose water use was metered, volunteers estimated and recorded daily water use associated with a range of everyday activities in quantities of five litre buckets (volunteers were shown what a five litre bucket looked like in order to reduce error).

As Figure 7 shows, on average, the three participants reported managing to reduce their water consumption after they received campaign messages through at least one of the project activities and the communication materials, resources and devices in the goody bags.

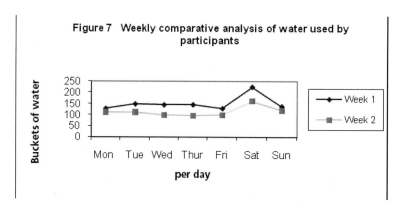

34

A sample survey of 208 participants conducted at the end of the project showed that: 35% expressed an interest in getting further involved and making a difference; 40% were keen to make a difference by taking up sustainable lifestyles; and 25% felt that the activities had helped them to gain a better understanding of environmental issues.

Champions proved pivotal to the success of the initiative. In order to secure a lasting legacy of change from this project, LSx is now working with Thames Water to implement Phase 2 which will include building the capacity of these *champions* to organise practical 'in house' demonstrations such as plumbing workshops for key household decision makers.

Other projects

LSx continues to employ innovative social marketing techniques to put sustainability into practice:

- The Diverse London Community Ambassador Scheme supports 10 ambassadors to engage with 1000 representatives of culturally diverse communities across London
- As a part of the Greener Food Project, LSx has recruited *sustainability champions* to encourage London's food and drink sector SME's to reduce their eco-footprint
- We are currently building the capacity and skills of 6 ambassadors in the Marks Gate and Pepys Estate to map out hot spots of environmental inequalities and develop tools and networks to address these effectively

Conclusions

Behaviour change campaigns have a pivotal role to play in securing London's future as a sustainable world city and a decent quality of life for all citizens. London's size and complexity offer a number of opportunities and challenges for behaviour change campaigns in the capital. With nearly 30% of Londoners representing a minority ethnic group (ONS, 2007), over 300 languages spoken by school children in the capital (Baker and Eversley, 2000) and more than 50 non-indigenous communities with a population of more than 10,000 (ONS, 2007), a one-size-fits-all approach in promoting 'One Planet' and healthier, wealthier lifestyles, communities and businesses will not work. LSx consequently employs the following strategic approach to changing behaviours in London:

1. *Social networks*

LSx utilises social networks extensively as a key strategic tool to achieve a breadth and depth of outreach and community engagement. As illustrated above, LSx's experience suggests that social networks are one of the most effective ways to cascade campaign messages and achieve a fundamental shift in behaviour. Existing networks such as family, schools, offices, faith groups provide access into the community and an infrastructure of familiarity and identity which in turn facilitates behaviour change in addition to increased awareness.

2. *Champions of change*

Champions have proven to be pivotal to the success of LSx's behaviour change campaigns. As demonstrated, *champions* are respected faces and trusted sources within target communities, familiar with local nuances and able to exert subtle influence and 'peer pressure' to successfully transform community behaviours towards 'One Planet' lifestyles. *Champions* were instrumental in stimulating behaviour change in several of our projects. LSx's experience shows that the personality of the *champions* is a key factor in effectively motivating individuals to change behaviour. This is highlighted specifically in the findings of the *Rewarding Green Householders Pilot Project.*

3. *'Hooks' and incentives*

'Hooks' are a crucial mechanism through which behaviour change messaging is made relevant to, and resonates with, campaign target audiences. Hooks can often be a value system such as faith, and LSx has delivered several projects promoting the links between theological messaging around stewardship of creation and living more sustainable 'One Planet' lifestyles. This is demonstrated through our 'Hinduism and H2O' initiative, which helped to secure more water and other resource-efficient behaviour amongst almost 3,000 members of the Hindu community in East London.

Evaluation processes support the premise that these elements, when used in combination with incentives such as the sustainability starter kits, can be highly effective in securing a long-term, rather than transient, behaviour change.

References

Baker, P. and Eversley, J. (eds) 2000 *Multilingual Capital, The Languages of London's Schoolchildren and Their Relevance to Economic, Social, and Educational Policies.* Battlebridge. [Internet].< http://www.battlebridge.com/mc.htm>. [Accessed 5th August 2007].

Futerra 2005 *The Rules of the Game: Principles of Climate Change Communication.* [Internet]. <http://www.defra.gov.uk/ENVIRONMENT/climatechange/pubs/pdf/ccc-rulesofthegame.pdf>. [Accessed 9th August 2007].

Gladwell, M. 2002 *The Tipping Point: How Little Things Can Make a Big Difference.* Boston: Back Bay

IWM(EB) 2002 *City Limits: A resource flow and ecological footprint analysis of Greater London.* [Internet].<http://www.citylimitslondon.com/downloads/Complete%20report.pdf>.[Accessed 9th August 2007].

Krebs, V. and Holley, J. 2002-2006 *Building Smart Communities Through Network Weaving.* [Internet]. <http://www.orgnet.com/BuildingNetworks.pdf>. [Accessed 9th August 2007].

Lidwell, W., Holden, K. and Butler, J. 2003 *Universal Principles of Design: 100 Ways to Enhance Usability, Influence Perception, Increase Appeal, Make Better Design Decisions, and Teach Through Design.* Rockport Publishers

London Remade and London First 2003 *Towards a sustainable London: reducing the capital's footprint. Phase 1 report: Determining London's ecological footprint and priority impact areas for action.* [Internet]. <http://www.londonremade. com/download _files/ Phase%201%20Final.pdf>. [Accessed 9th August 2007].

LSx 2006 *The Motivation Kit: Means of motivation and powers of persuasion.* London: London Sustainability Exchange

ONS 2007 *The office of national statistics.* [Internet]. <http://www.statistics.gov.uk/>. [Accessed 9th August 2007].

Acknowledgements

- Penny Noy
- Jerome Veriter
- London Councils
- DEFRA
- City Parochial Foundation
- Thames Water

'LIKE THE FLOORS': VISIONING A NEW ART OF LIVING[1]

John Blewitt
University of Exeter

Abstract

To live with the earth's ecological limits requires, among other things, new approaches to learning and new approaches to living, seeing the experience of everyday life as part of a wider social ecology encompassing the interrelationship of 'three ecologies' - social relations, human subjectivity and the natural world. The everyday is where our direct relationship with the social and natural worlds, our desires, capabilities, identities and potential are formulated, developed and experienced. Everyday life is the site where we can fashion a critique of dominant, alienating and exploitive ideas and practices and nurture new or alternative ways of doing, thinking, producing and being.

To this end, the presentation will explore the experience of wood in the built, and particularly the domestic, environment. One of the most important aspects of wood is that it affords a wonderful sensory and aesthetic experience. Think of a handcrafted oak table, an applewood breadboard, timber frame house … You don't have to be a craftsperson to know this; you just have to touch, see, smell or stand on it to understand. And, when combined with sustainable production and design, wood offers a significant moral significance, too.

Keywords   Sustainability, everyday life, wood, learning, experience

Felix Guattari argues that the wider social ecology of everyday life encompasses the interrelationship existing between 'three ecologies' - (capitalist) social relations, human subjectivity and the natural world or environment. Guattari (2000, pp.41-2) writes:

> The increasing deterioration of human relations with the socius, the psyche and 'nature', is due not only to environmental and objective pollution but is also the result of a certain incomprehension and fatalistic passivity towards these issues as a whole, among both individuals and governments. Catastrophic or not, negative developments are simply accepted without question. Structuralism and, subsequently, postmodernism has accustomed us to a vision of the world drained of the significance of human interventions, embodied as they are in concrete politics and micropolitics. The explanations offered for this decline of social praxes - the death of ideologies and the return to universal values - seem to me unsatisfactory. Rather, it appears to be the result of the failure of social and psychological praxes to adapt, as well as a certain blindness to the erroneousness of dividing the Real into a number of discrete domains. It is quite wrong to make a distinction between action on the psyche, the socius and the environment. Refusal to face up to the erosion of these three areas, as the media would have us do, verges on a strategic infantalisation of opinion and a destructive neutralisation of democracy. We need to 'kick the habit' of seductive discourse, particularly the 'fix' of television, in order to be able to apprehend the world through the interchangeable lenses or points of view of the three ecologies.

Our environment is what surrounds us. It is our environs, our homes, communities, streets, artefacts and relationships. Not every aspect of our environs is attractive, pleasurable, life enhancing, valuable or interesting. Neither are they necessarily sustainable in any direct or indirect sense. As the architect

---

[1] A full development of these ideas can be found in Blewitt (2006) from which some material for this article has been drawn.

and thinker Christopher Day (2004) writes 'we become attuned to noise, ugliness, polluted air and hard shapes and when this happens they, and we, do their, and our, most damage'. Our senses and sensitivities become dulled which is reflected and reproduced in the way we live and see our lives unfolding and the environment shapes us and we, it.

Designers, architects, manufacturers, domestic workers, business and crafts people, in fact everyone, should be concerned to nourish what makes us us, feeding and animating the soul, rather than to diminish, degrade or denude it and us. Here, it is important to recognise that all the senses are engaged in our day-to-day encounters with our life world, that designed and natural objects speak to them all together and rarely in isolation. Things, places, object, artefacts may therefore offer life, health, warmth, meaning and pleasure. An example: I have a breadboard made of wood from an apple tree. It is smooth to touch, sensual and sensuous; when touched it seems as if it touching me, it has a wondrous rich dark colour and is perfectly round with no hard edges. The sensing and the sensible interact sympathetically, reciprocally. As Abram (1996) writes 'neither the perceiver nor the perceived is totally passive in this relationship. They become attuned to one another', the breadboard and me - the breadboard and owner, user, eater ... However, when we objectify or conceptualise our experience we tend to repress and block our sensuous involvement, our participation. We see it differently, perhaps. It becomes simply a utilitarian commodity, a possession, an object without soul. Materials therefore affect, strike a chord, with us through our perception of them and the way we relate to them. As the French phenomenologist Maurice Merleau-Ponty (1962, p.317) has written:

> ...in so far as my hand knows hardness and softness, and my gaze knows the moon's light, it is as a certain way of linking up with the phenomenon and communicating with it. Hardness and softness, roughness and smoothness, moonlight and sunlight, present themselves in our recollection, not pre-eminently as sensory contents, but as kinds of symbiosis, certain ways the outside has of invading us and certain ways we have of meeting this invasion, and memory here frees the framework of the perception from the place where it originates.

Our senses do not operate singularly but in combination. I can see, touch, smell, hear and even taste that breadboard. We speak of cool or warm colours, sweet smells, hard sounds, and from 2000 - 2006 the Countryside Agency even ran a programme called 'eat the view' which attempted to link in the perceptions of consumers sustainable local products with the countryside. Taste what you can see, taste what you see. This is more than mere gastronomic, slow food sustainable tourism but an invitation to experience and perceive differently.

These linguistic labels for our five senses put into words the means and basis for our pre-theoretical environmental awareness and it is this process, this capability, that any new art of sustainable living needs to retrieve and communicate. So, like any other breadboard worth its salt you can cut bread on it but the experience of the applewood breadboard makes the task a little bit special. Something to relish, enjoy and to repeat because of the joy involved in handling the material, sensing the craft and skill that went into its making. What's more the pleasure it affords invites a caring relationship to emerge and a disposition to search for other useful objects that are more than simply functional but have an intrinsic beauty in their meaning, matter and form. As any person who works with wood will tell you, different materials offer different possibilities, suggest different shapes, ideas and pleasures. Wood is not naturally 'dead straight' though can be made so. Edges need not be hard or harsh and in time rarely remain so. Wood lives, has its own qualities and character and as you get to know different timbers their characters emerge too. Wood can even have an afterlife through its reuse, reworking and reapplication. For Day (2004, p.168) 'wood is warm, redolent of life even after the tree is long felled'. We respond to the 'being' of materials by the effects they have on our selves, bodies and emotions. Natural materials bring our human-made environment closer to what it depends on. Natural materials, like natural rather than processed foodstuffs, give us roots, and a way, in to the ecological realities of our existence because they hardly ever, even in their finished state, completely lose their connection to the natural world. This is probably why there is a growing interest in the restoration of old and the construction of new timber framed dwellings and why writers such as Roger Deakin can produce such a beautiful and eloquent rhapsody as *Wildwood* (2007).

Wood is also one of the healthiest building materials - a natural regulator of indoor climate. It 'breathes' and assists ventilation stabilising humidity, purifying the air and absorbing sound (Pearson, 1989). Neither does wood disturb natural electrical and magnetic fields. But it is important to remember that the widespread tree felling that has characterised so much of human history, has literally fuelled civilisations over the millennia, has been environmentally damaging and for some cultures and ecosystems ultimately disastrous. Wood then needs now to be sourced from reliable and sustainable places. It needs to be conserved. Where possible it needs to be reused, recycled, reshaped and reworked to be given new life and new purpose... and can be, quite easily. As Williams (2006) concludes in his massive study of deforestation from ancient times to the present, deforestation is no longer a purely economic matter. It is wrought with long term ethical, humanitarian and ecological concerns. Unless forests are in some way perceived as 'sacred', as something that although outside of us defines and constitutes our inner natures, the land and places in which we dwell, then wooded lands will continue to be destroyed without thought or care. For the German philosopher Heidegger (1993), to dwell is to remain at peace, to be at one with the primal verities of existence, to be free from harm and danger, to stay with things and locales over time. Only when we are capable of dwelling are we capable of building homes and communities, of using wood sustainably, caringly and meaningfully. It is an ethical imperative.

I remember speaking to Laura after a community development meeting I had attended about her community involvement, her ideas, hopes and consumer purchases. She told me of her desire to buy a wooden coffee table but could not easily find one that was fairly-traded or locally-sourced. She first went to a local store in a nearby town and found something she liked and quite reasonably priced but the wood was not from a sustainable source. Although beautifully crafted and 'exactly what I wanted' it was suspiciously half the price of a similar product imported from France. The oak table in question was from China and the shop couldn't say whether it was a fairly-traded product or not. The trader was slightly surprised, and perhaps affronted, that this ethical issue was preventing Laura from completing a purchase. She then went home to search the Internet looking at the online catalogue of *John Lewis* - a major store with both a reputation for quality and ethical trading. The problems continued. She found an attractive table made of wood from a rubber tree at a fifth of the price of the Chinese oak table and wanted to learn a little more. It isn't always simple being green or ethical. Like many other things you either have to work at it, compromise and/or face disappointment:

> I was looking on the website for a coffee table and I thought that store would do good quality, that they'd be ethical and they'd know who their sources are which they did, I suppose, but as it turned

out they couldn't guarantee that it was from a fairly-traded organisation. The timber - I suppose they replace rubber plantations, but I don't know how quickly rubber trees grow and it was so cheap, I couldn't imagine anyone making it would have been paid anything more than a pittance. I think everything should be fairly-traded. No one should be classed as a slave anymore, which is in effect what it is. No one should be working ridiculous hours and be paid nothing to do it. People should expect a fair wage for what they do, and we should expect to pay a suitable amount that enables people to have that. We wouldn't do it ourselves or expect our families to do it. Why should we expect other people in Third World countries to have a lesser standard of life, so we can have luxury items at their expense. Fairly-traded goods promote the right work ethic and right work relations. I don't know how the company reacted to me cancelling the order. You don't know whether you are a lone voice in the wind but if more people took notice, I guess, and cared about where their products came from, then they would cease to trade with that particular organisation or make certain they could reassure their customers like me that where they were from and the people making the goods, were treated with respect, had a fair wage and had a reasonable standard of life, which we all expect. (Laura, interview)

No sale. She eventually found what she wanted with the help of an ethical consumer guide in *The Ecologist* and a number of additional Google searches on the computer which identified a number of small local businesses specialising to the crafting of furniture from reclaimed wood. Laura visited one workshop, spoke to the craftsman about her needs, questioned him about where he sourced his materials, examined examples of the work he had produced for others - tables, bookcases, benches - and, together, the two sketched out what would be the right shape and size, be fit for purpose, and be aesthetically and sensuously pleasing into the bargain. The wood would be reclaimed from renovated or demolished buildings and the table could be fashioned in either pine or oak. And the cost, certainly a little more than John Lewis, IKEA or MFI and the Chinese oak table but having opted for pine was by no means in a league that would place it out of bounds for the majority of households.

Laura's was an ethical choice with the pleasure derived from the ability to actualise values, participate in the design and fashioning, of a household good. Relationships of care were established and pleasure derived from that and from the artistry and ethic that went into its making. As Walter Crane (1893, p.18), President of the Arts and Crafts Exhibition Society from 1880 to 1912 and follower of William Morris, noted 'cheapness as a rule, in the sense of low priced production, can only be obtained at the cost of cheapness - that is, cheapening of human life and labour; sure, in reality a most wasteful and extravagant cheapness!'. When I asked why she went to so much trouble Laura had problems answering, articulating her reasoning and her actions. It was simply the right thing to do. She could not really recall when she had started to think and consume 'ethically'. It just seemed to have developed as she learnt more about the world from her engagement with it, from what she read, what she surfed and who she observed. Her understandings and perceptions had gradually altered as the profligate and ephemeral aspects of our consumer culture seemed increasingly unjustified, unrewarding and unnecessary.

Some additional insights may be learnt from the sociology of Henri Lefebvre (1991; 2002) and the social anthropology of Tim Ingold (2000). Lefebvre argues that the everyday is where we are in terms of our direct relationship with the social and natural worlds and where our desires, capabilities, identities and potential are, in the first instance, formulated, developed and made real. Everyday life is also the site from where we can fashion a critique of dominant, alienating and exploitive ideas and practices and where we can start to create new or alternative ways of doing things, of thinking and acting, of producing, perceiving and consuming - of developing a new art of living:

> Everyday life is profoundly related to all activities, and encompasses them with all their differences and their conflicts; it is in their meeting place, their bond, their common ground. And it is in everyday life that the sum total of relations which make the human - and every human being - a whole takes shape and its form. In it are expressed and fulfilled those relations which bring into play the totality of the real, albeit in a certain manner which is always partial and incomplete: friendship, comradeship, love, the need to communicate, play, etc. (Lefebvre, 1991, p.97)

For Lefebvre, the modern world has led us to take a privatised (deprived) and instrumental approach to life and living, the natural and social worlds, work and leisure, the ideal and the mundane. Dominant modes of communication, of information gathering and storage, often seem separated from everyday social relationships and social experience. Everything seems to have been commodified, packaged in images or oven-ready experiences that have their own peculiar meaning and purpose and which function to keep the economic wheels turning. We buy, we consume processed foods, processed holidays and processed entertainments divorced from what we are actually capable of creating by and for ourselves. Goods are good, and more goods are better. Our being is increasingly divorced and distanced from what ultimately our existence depends upon - the 'natural world'. Lefebvre, therefore, is no fan of 'the consumer society'; but nonetheless recognises a certain degree of ambiguity:

> .....'consumer society' manipulates needs; the masters of production are also the masters of consumption, and they also produce the demands for which and according to which they are supposed to be producing. Deliberately or not, they leave other equally valid needs and other equally objective demands to one side. It is not very often that a voice makes itself heard to criticize this illusion which is not entirely an illusion, this appearance which is not entirely an appearance, since needs - even if they are provoked and prefabricated - can not all be equally phoney and artificial. Ambiguity between individual and social needs and desires papers over unperceived contradictions, blunting them and coinciding with the three dimensional 'realness' of the everyday. Only when there is this ambiguity can the illusion and appearance be sustained. (Lefebvre, 2002, p.223)

I certainly need to get about, to be mobile, to have access to places of work and leisure, get to the shops and occasional holiday destinations. I certainly need to eat, preferably fresh food, and I certainly like to fit in and be part of things. But do I really need to replace my car every couple of years, eat strawberries all year round, wear clothes which display a tick or a whoosh? If I do, and act accordingly, then I am my own worst enemy, contributing personally and directly to a system that offers me less by promising and delivering more. Everyday life is therefore a mix of what is seemingly repressive and functional (in terms of reproducing capitalist social relations) and what is potentially emancipatory, better and different. Consumerism and advertising also nurtures authentic needs and desires that may remain unfulfilled - food that looks good but is nutritious and not packed with salt, sugar, saturated fats and 'E's. Mobility and access should not be subject to traffic gridlock, pollution, poor public transportation or degradation of the countryside. Urban environments can and should provide cultural and economic opportunities and pleasant social, green, spaces. Community gardens, allotments, urban farms, places and spaces where people can connect or just be. Lefebvre argues for an urban revolution - a transformation of urban spaces manifesting 'a creative capacity in its effects on daily life' (Lefebvre, 1991b, p.54), the starting point for a metamorphosis of the everyday and which in many cases is closely associated with the city as poly- or trans-functional, as play as well as work.

In social life, play has a role. What is it? Relaxation and entertainment, yes; but more than that, it is rediscovered spontaneity, and even more, it is activity which is not subjected to the division of labour and the social hierarchies. At first sight, humanly and socially speaking, play seems to be a minor, marginal activity, sidelined and tolerated by the important functions of industrial society. Compared with the reality of practical life and the truth of representations, it seems to be an illusion, a lie, something phoney. On closer scrutiny, the reverse is true. Play recalls forgotten depths and summons them up to the light of day. By making them stay within the everyday, it encompasses art and many other things as well. It uses appearances and illusions which - for one marvellous moment - become more real than real. And with play another reality is born, not a separate one, but one which is 'lived' in the everyday, alongside the functional. Play will enliven experience, render people more active and less passive, substitute quality for quantity, intensify material and non-material exchange ensuring that human creativity is nurtured and expressed. It is this creative quality that ensures productive human learning; and agency can push us beyond the quotidian, beyond business as usual. A new play ethic could well be a theme of a more sustainable and liveable world (Kane, 2004) and this resonates well with those theorists of the everyday that see beyond the routine and the mundane to the vital, 'puissance' (the will to live) and the creative (Maffesoli, 1996; Crook, 1998). And when are we at play? When we are becoming ourselves by stepping out of our selves. When we interact with others and with things. When we create, when we touch, when we smell, see and hear and when we go down to the woods ... today.

Following Borgmann (1984), Higgs (2003, p.185) suggests that it is the 'communion between self, thing and environment (and perhaps also spirit) that generates profound meaning in our lives'. A 'thing' is inseparable from its context involving both bodily and social engagement whereas a 'device' is simply itself - a commodity to be consumed. There are particular practices, focal practices, that generate this meaning - going slow perhaps, enjoying celebratory meals, reading a bedtime story to one's children, or being in tune with an experience of the natural world that hasn't been served up as a Disneyfied, commodified, package. You don't have to go to Disneyland to experience the commodification of nature, leisure or fulfilment. You can buy it in the mall or maybe just go to a leisure resort or nature theme park. New technologies which Higgs and Borgmann refer to as *devices* ultimately do not deliver happiness or satisfaction but rather distract us from what really matters, things that have focussing qualities, that enable us to realise ourselves as human persons rather than adjuncts of consumerism.

For Borgmann, our fascination with mass produced artefacts (devices again) - new cars, games consoles, DVDs, digital cameras - prevent, even destroy our capacity, for focal practice because increasingly we experience the world through our engagement with these objects, commodities or services, which are disconnected and disposable. Places become sites and homes machines for living in. The means become not simply constitutive of the ends, but rather the ends themselves. The response then is to promote a practice that restores natural and human ecologies, social and bodily engagement with place, and in doing so generate and regenerate meaning. This focal restoration is not a return to a myth of a golden past but the reality is that little things may actually count for quite a lot.

To illustrate his position, Borgmann offers a seemingly antiquated illustration but one which today is perhaps not so quaint. I first came across Borgmann and Higgs when my wife and I were looking to replace the oil fired central heating in our house with a couple of wood burning stoves. The increasing price of oil, its impact on the environment, the possibility of purchasing the wood from local sustainable sources and the desire to have a more 'natural' domestic environment figured in our discussions. Borgmann (1984, pp.41-42) writes:

> The experience of a thing is always and also a bodily and social engagement with the thing's world. In calling forth a manifold engagement, a thing necessarily provides more than one commodity. Thus a stove used to furnish more than mere warmth. It was a focus, a hearth, a place that gathered the work and leisure of a family and gave the house a centre. Its coldness marked the morning, and the spreading of its warmth the beginning of the day. It assigned to the different family members tasks that defined their place in the household. (…) It provided for the entire family a regular and bodily engagement with the rhythm of the seasons that was woven together of the threat of cold and the solace of warmth, the smell of wood smoke, the exertion of sawing and of carrying, the teaching of skills, and the fidelity to daily tasks. (…) Skill is intensive and refined world engagement. Skill, in turn, is bound up with social engagement. It moulds the person and gives the person character. Limitations of skill confine any one person's primary engagement with the world to a small area.

I have learnt about different type of wood. What burns well and what doesn't. What grows well, can be coppiced and when harvested. I have learnt the time it takes for wood to be seasoned and I have learnt that wood, a renewable resource if renewed, is only part of the answer to the meeting of our energy requirements. Focal things and focal practices require skill, patience and continual engagement. They are 'centering' things. Lighting a fire is a pleasure. They need to be nurtured … and practised. In restoring degraded land or building a new community people necessarily collaborate, cooperate, share and learn socially and individually. They learn facts and skills. They learn to listen to others, to understand their own and others' emotions. They learn to be. So for Higgs adding the social to the ecological, adds value to restoration practices because such activities promote value in nature and community.

Ingold notes that although the universal reason of western science tends to be placed above and beyond the world of everyday material reality and our own vernacular, or indigenous, knowledge and understanding of it, science is still rooted in our lived experience of it. Following Bateson (1972), Ingold attempts to outline not so much an ecology of learning or an ecology of mind but something more fundamental - a (sentient) ecology of life. There is no hard and fast boundary between mind and the world. As Bateson (1972, p.460) stated in his lecture *Form, Substance and Difference*, 'the mental world - the mind - the world of information processing - is not limited by the skin'. Rather, as Ingold explains (2000, p.18), the mind should be envisaged as extending outwards towards the environment along multiple sensory pathways leading to the unfolding of the whole system of relations constituted by a multifarious involvement of the perceiver in his/her environment. Information only exists by our moving in and through the world. Ingold (2000, p.19) writes:

> Organic life, as I envisage it, is active rather than reactive, the creative unfolding of an entire field of relations within which beings emerge and take on the particular forms they do, each in relation to the others. Life in this view, is not the realisation of pre-specified forms but the very process wherein forms are generated and held in place. Every being, as it is caught up in the process and

carries it forward, arises as a singular centre of awareness and agency; an enfoldment, at some particular nexus within it, of the generative potential that is life itself (....)

'Organism plus environment' should denote not a compound of two things, but one indivisible totality. The totality is, in effect, a developmental system, and an ecology of life - in my terms - is one that would deal with the dynamics of such systems. Now if this view is accepted - if, that is we are prepared to treat form as emergent within the life-process - then, I contend, we have no need to appeal to a distinct domain of mind, to creatura rather than pleroma, to account for pattern and meaning in the world. We do not, in other words, have to think of mind or consciousness as a layer of being over and above that of the life of organisms, in order to account for their creative involvement in the world.

Ingold (1992) also discusses how information does not turn into knowledge simply by one piece of data being added to another. Data only becomes information when it is put into some context and information only becomes knowledge once we have begun to understand its meaning within a context of direct perceptual engagement with our various environments - the three ecologies. We develop this capacity to understand and to know by being shown things, which act as clues to the world as it is and as it could be. We are shown things by family, parents, friends, elders, teachers, television programmes, internet sites, travel agencies, books, movies, adverts, material artefacts, consumer goods, animals, images in magazines, on billboards, in newspapers, and so on. These elements inform our view of the world, help constitute the way in which we fashion our meaning schemes and perspectives. Formal and informal learning can be understood to be an *education of attention* involving science, logic, rationality, skills and capacities of various descriptions but also intuition derived from and underpinning the constant unfolding of our creative relationships with the wider environmental contexts of meaning-making. Laura learnt from the internet, from the craftsman from the wood. I learnt from my engagement with apple wood breadboard. Plastic would not have afforded the same experience or offer the same rich learning opportunities.

Gibson (1979) suggested an alternative to the western notion that there is the mind and there is the world and we can only act on the world through our cultural representations or constructions of it. Gibson discussed the *affordances* of the environment which exist as inherent potentials of the objects within the world, independent of any use made of them by individuals or other sentient creatures. Different people may share different perceptions of a shared environment, of what it affords, and people themselves are capable of designing and constructing their environment, putting to use what is there, in various ways and in various combinations. Termites construct their world in one way because they are termites. Humans can chose one of many possible options if they have the brain and will to, and create a few more through learning leading to the development of knowledge, reflexive capabilities and greater understanding. Importantly, Ingold distinguishes *nature* from *environment* with the former consisting of essentially neutral objects apparent only to detached or 'indifferent' observers and the latter constituted in *relation* to the person whose environment it is. He (1992, p.44) recognises that humans may have the capacity to engage or disengage with the world, to effect outer-directed actions and inner-directed thoughts but life he emphasises 'is given in engagement, not in disengagement'. More importantly to the themes found in this paper, Ingold (1992, p.44) writes:

Although humans undoubtedly have the capacity to adopt such a 'designer orientation' towards the environment, I do not think this is the way it is normally perceived in everyday life. No more than other animals can human beings live in a permanently suspended condition of contemplative detachment. If the animal is always and immediately 'one with its life activity', so is the human for much (if not all) of the time. Thus with Gibson, I believe that our immediate perception of the environment is in terms of what it affords for the pursuit of the action in which we are currently engaged. The man throwing the stone did not, we suppose, first 'construct' the stone as a missile by attaching a meaning or 'throw-quality' to impressions of it received through the senses. Nor was the act of throwing merely the bodily execution of a command subsequently issued by the mind of the basis of this construct. Rather, it was the very involvement of the man in his environment, in the practical context of throwing, that led him to attend to the 'throwability' of the object, by virtue of which it was perceived as a missile. Such direct perception of the environment is a mode of engagement with the world, not a mode of construction of it.

Gibson's concept of *affordances* can be productively used to outline a theory of how technology, including the materiality of artefacts, shape everyday social life enabling as well as constraining action (Hutchby, 2001). Although Gibson himself says little beyond the notion that 'behaviour affords behaviour', this rather undeveloped notion is picked up by Reed (1988) who suggests that social agents directly perceive their mutual affordances and share with others their direct perceptions of the environment. Being socialised into the same culture, having had similar experiences through living in the world individuals will become familiar with the same information. Everyday social life is therefore a consequence of our direct perceptual involvement in the world. Objects take on their meaning and significance by being part of the routine pattern and social relationships of day-to-day activities - doing the washing, driving to work, eating a burger, painting the cupboard, cutting the grass, shopping to fill the freezer, looking good, having fun, watching a DVD.

You can buy a guide to green living but first you have to want to make that investment, see the need and believe that something can be done and then do it. One important way of influencing people's attitudes, values and behaviour is art and design which, combined with public discussion and community involvement, may realise the positive benefit of ecologically sound concepts. Eco-design is relevant to those living on ordinary housing estates or in upper middle class gated communities. It may help fashion an alternative, more sustainable, view of the world. Experience of space and place of which sustainable design form a part, as the indigenous peoples know so well, therefore become key elements within an overall ecology of learning about our selves, our understandings of how we connect with the wider social and natural worlds. This ecology of learning is experiential in the broadest sense incorporating emotional, intuitive, rational, scientific and possibly mystical elements. We may attempt to consciously make sense of this experience by putting it all into words, concepts and theories - environmental justice, civic participation, social capital, sustainability, design, makeover - but often we simply feel things. We feel that composting or standing up to a developer or replacing dusty carpets with wooden flooring is the right thing to do. It is possible to feel safe and secure in a virtual community or feel injustice or environmental shame in the country or the city. It is possible to feel that we are living healthy and contented lives, that the open or closed spaces, the coriander or concrete, are not alternate realities but integrated realities created by ourselves.

Some residents of the eco-friendly Housing Association development of Oak Meadow in North Devon have been persuaded by their new eco-house to think and act differently. Dorothy and Ken live in a home with three children and feel that everyone in the neighbourhood 'gel up together'. There is a generalised trust symbolised by the comment of one resident that she would trust her house key to any one of her immediate neighbours. Living at Oak Meadow is both special and normal. The materials from which the house is constructed are natural. High energy efficiency, optimum solar gain, rain water harvesting, triple glazed windows, grey water recycling, blown newspaper insulation, photo voltaic power, cool larders and plenty of wood. The external oak cladding gives the housing an aesthetic warmth even though for some residents wooden walls reminded them of Trago Mills - 'the West Country's unique family shopping and leisure parks'. No wall to wall carpets either, but crisp and warm wooden floors that make the home 'natural' and sensuous to the touch - both living and lived. Dorothy told me:

> I think a lot of people thought that just because you had one of these houses you had to change everything about you. No. This is my home. I have to have it for me. I'm not going to do it just because someone says you have to. No carpets - that's fine. I love the floor, no problem. Love the floors.

However, living at Oak Meadow has, for some, subtly but positively affected everyday routines without any sense of intrusive or disturbing change, so that after a short while it is other, (less green), people who seem different, lazy or uncaring. Cultural norms and values have shifted and meanings have altered. A green community isn't a green or alternative community but a decent one, a responsible, a pleasant and a desirable one. Other areas seem different, too, and these feelings are shared and create a sense of pride and satisfaction, of belonging and togetherness, of being different but necessarily so.

The experience of green space, of 'nearby nature', is pleasing to the eye and other senses, has a restorative function often helping to clear the head after a busy day or relieve feelings of stress and anxiety. The psychologists Kaplan and Kaplan (1995, p.196) identify the benefits aesthetic natural environments offer. Aesthetic natural environments give pleasure; they are satisfying to experience. Second, such settings support human functioning. They provide a context in which people can manage information effectively; they permit people to move about and to explore with comfort and confidence. And, finally, such environments foster the recovery from mental fatigue. They permit tired individuals to regain effective functioning.

Roof gardens are also becoming increasingly popular with planners, architects and urban inhabitants in North America, Japan and parts of Europe. Apart from the aesthetic pleasures they provide, roof gardens also absorb urban pollution, increase the energy efficiency of buildings by providing insulation, produce cooling in summer, absorb noise, create wildlife habitats, offer additional space for vegetable growing which could in turn reduce environmental damage by cutting down on the need for imported food and reduce rainwater run-off. Green roofs can absorb up to 80% of the moisture and retain it. There are some interesting examples on both public and private buildings. The Ford Motor Company's Rouge Factory in Michigan boasts the largest roof garden at 454,000 square feet and the CUE building (Centre for Understanding and the Environment) at the Horniman Museum in London has as its roof a living and evolving wildflower meadow. Also in London companies that design and create roof gardens for private houses and flats are doing good business.

For Worpole (2000) green space, particularly parks, offer privacy and escape from domestic demands and responsibilities and although other, harder, (semi) public spaces can also generate feelings of belonging and even intimacy, there is no associated sense of guilt, as there may be on a therapeutic trip to a shopping mall that one is not spending money on consumer goods when one should be. However, the meanings people attach to various places differ - a park or a public square may be a place for solitary reflection or for meeting people. An urban woodland may be desirable because it offers a connection to nature. Wilder urban places, for example, former derelict sites or railway sidings, may encourage birds and animals to return enhancing biodiversity and are no longer being crudely perceived as 'waste ground'. The protection of open spaces, the nurturing of a vibrant and convivial street culture, farmers' markets, safe places for walking and cycling and more environmentally friendly dwellings and refurbishments are public supports and places facilitating a more sustainable and healthier everyday life.

The urbanist Kevin Lynch (1981, p.115) saw cities and urban areas not so much as an ecosystem but as an evolving 'learning ecology'. For Lynch, an ecological ecosystem is essentially made up of 'unthinking organisms' not conscious 'of their fatal involvement in the system and its consequences'. Ecosystems change and develop, reach maturity or a state of dynamic equilibrium but they cannot be said to learn or initiate progressive developments: 'The inner experiences of the organisms - their purposes and images - are irrelevant; only their outward behaviour matters' (Lynch 1981, p.115). Within a human settlement people are conscious, capable of modifying their attitudes and behaviour, of envisioning a different future, altering their way of doing things, and of learning to see wasteland as a reserve for wildlife. Human imagination, values, intentions, knowledge creation, information flows, the connection of inner experience with outer action all contribute to altering the conditions of possibility, of being flexible and adaptable, of organising ideas and of successfully dealing with tensions, difficulties and conflict.

For Lynch, a good settlement is one that is characterised by a dynamic openness, accessibility, diversity, tolerance, adaptability and decentralised decision-making. Stability or recurrence is not something to be valued for itself or as a primary defining feature. If settlements are to become adaptable, tolerant and flexible then the only way this can happen is if its inhabitants become adaptable, tolerant and flexible, too. What people do in their neighbourhoods and communities, what constraints or freedoms they work with or within, will shape the nature of this learning ecology and their learning within them. Although writing before the term sustainability or sustainable development came into general use, Lynch's understanding of 'development' is worth reflecting on. He writes (1981, pp.116-7):

> If development is a process of becoming more competent and more richly connected, then an increasing sense of connection to one's environment in space and time is one aspect of growth. So that settlement is good which enhances the continuity of culture and the survival of its people, increases a sense of connection in time and space, and permits or spurs individual growth: development, within continuity, via openness and connection.

As Lefebrve (1991, p.289) argues, every social organisation or society has a characteristic spatial practice, i.e. the close association between daily reality and urban reality, that offers an understanding of its values and domain assumptions – 'the space of a (social) order is hidden in the order of space'. When the rational and the abstract become real the possibility of violence becomes real, too, for space is instrumental, 'the most general of tools'. It does violence to the everyday as seen in Thamesmead, the Aylesbury and Heygate estates and possibly in Seaside. This is because, for Lefebrve (1991, pp.38-

39), societies produce space in two ways. Firstly, conceptual *'representations of space'* designed or produced by scientists, planners, architects, urbanists, academics, etc. Secondly, experiential space, *representational spaces*, the space of users, people, inhabitants - 'space as directly lived through its associated images and symbols - the dominated space - and hence passively experienced space which the imagination seeks to change and appropriate'. Representational spaces, therefore, overlay physical spaces and both together shape and are shaped by economic and social forces, tensions and conflicts; or, for Lefebrve, capitalism and neo-capitalism. Nonetheless, there are implications attached to the dominance of *representations of space* over lived experiences of space and this boils down to the marginalisation of ordinary people, ordinary dwellers in the land, producing a subjectivity, a way of living and being, subject to a world conceived, designed, constructed and policed by others.

The user's space is lived and created, but without art and poetry it will not be humanised, customised, personalised, created, decorated and painted. Without nature it will remain barren. As Bachelard (1969) said, 'we grow more attached to the tree in our garden when it is populated by birds'. When we share our life world with other life worlds. Why? We live the spaces and places as well as what's in them. We live in and through them. We sense them and they us, we communicate, commingle and participate in them perceiving their softness, hardness, light, darkness, pleasure or pain. If we do not, or cannot, approach our spaces, places, artefacts and objects of desire artistically, then we can live our lives in a full and flourishing manner. For art is what we produce, it is something other than the raw material of wood, stone, paint, sight or sound. It is a symbol of what we are, our lived experience, our connection and connectedness with the earth which nurtures and sustains us. We need a new art of living and working that symbolises in its matter and form sustainable development in all its manifestations and senses. We need to feel sustainability. What does sustainability smell like? We need to love the floors. Until we are able to gain genuine pleasure from the common surroundings of life and work, all the accessories of life will, as William Morris argued in *Commonweal* as long ago as 1885, our life worlds will remain 'mean, trivial, ugly - in a word, *vulgar'*.

References

Abram, D. 1996 *The Spell of the Sensuous.* New York: Vintage Books

Bachelard, G. 1969 *The Poetics of Space.* Boston: Beacon Press

Bateson, G. 1972 *Steps to an Ecology of Mind.* Chicago: University of Chicago Press

Blewitt, J. 2006 *The Ecology of Learning: sustainability, lifelong learning and everyday life.* London: Earthscan

Borgmann, A. 1984 *Technology and the Character of Contemporary Life.* Chicago: University of Chicago Press

Crane, W. 1893 'Of the Revival of Design and Handicraft: with notes on the work of the Arts and Crafts Exhibition Society', in Members of the Arts and Crafts Exhibition Society (eds) *Arts and Crafts Essays.* London: Rivington, Percival and Co

Crook, S. 1998 Minotaurs and Other Monsters: 'Everyday Life' in Recent Social Theory. *Sociology,* **32,** 523-540

Day, C. 2004 *Places of the Soul: architecture and environmental design as a healing art.* Oxford: Architectural Press

Deakin, R. 2007 *Wildwood: a journey through trees.* London: Hamish Hamilton

Gibson, J.J. 1979 *The Ecological Approach to Visual Perception.* Boston: Houghton Mifflin

Guattari, F. 2000 *The Three Ecologies.* London: Athlone Press

Heidegger, M. 1993 'Building Dwelling Thinking', in Krell, D.F. (ed) *Basic Writings: Martin Heidegger.* Routledge: London

Higgs, E. 2003 *Nature by Design.* Cambridge Massachusetts: MIT Press

Ingold, T. 1992 'Culture and the Perception of the Environment', in Croll, E. and Parkin, D. (eds) *Bush Base: Forest Farm: Culture, Environment and Development.* London: Routledge

Ingold, T. 2000 *The Perception of the Environment.* London: Routledge

Lefebvre, H. 1991 *Critique of Everyday Life, Volume One.* London: Verso

Kane, P. 2004 *The Play Ethic.* London: Pan Books

Lefebvre, H. 2002 *Critique of Everyday Life, Volume Two.* London: Verso

Lynch, K. 1981 *Good City Form.* Cambridge Massachusetts: MIT Press

Maffesoli, M. 1996 *The Time of the Tribes: the Decline of Individualism in Mass Society.* London: Sage

Merleau-Ponty, M. 1962 *Phenomenology of Perception* (trans. S. Colin). London: Routledge

Morris, W. 1994 'The Worker's Share of Art', in Salmon, W. (ed) *Political Writings: contributions to* Justice *and* Commonweal *1883-1890 by William Morris.* Bristol: Thoemmes Press

Pearson, D. 1989 *The Natural House Book: creating a healthy, harmonious and ecologically sound home.* London: Gaia Books

Williams, M. 2006 *Deforesting the Earth: from prehistory to Global Crisis.* Chicago: Chicago University Press

Intelligent Sustainable Solutions for the Fashion Industry

Ewa Szczotka
Associate Lecturer, Kingston University

Abstract

In his paper *Enabling solutions, social innovation and design for sustainability*, Professor Ezio Manzini, a leading thinker in sustainable design, suggests looking to creative communities who have moved away from dominant trends and found solutions in new and innovative ways. He sees designers as 'facilitators' rather than just part of the design process. With the clothing and footwear industry in the UK being responsible for 59 MtCO2, the designer has to become more than just a facilitator; he has to become an educator, innovator and create a movement of awareness and responsibility within the industry encouraging methods of design as if our very lives depended on it.

The *Stern Report*, Al Gore's *An Inconvenient Truth* and Eugenie Harvey and her hugely successful campaign *'We are what we do'* which started off a whole new way of thinking about how we lead our lives and how we affect others will act as catalysts in the quest for workable, intelligent sustainable solutions within the fashion industry. A change of mindset is required in an industry which has been about fast profits and a disregard for ethics. Sustainability awareness does not have to be boring - it just needs to be accepted and this will stimulate a new thinking process and the necessary debate.

Keywords Sustainability, solutions, change, mindset, fashion

Introduction

Curator (n.) - keeper/ custodian
Origin Latin 'curare' to take care of or to care for

In this fragile world it has become apparent that fashion needs its own 'curator', someone who wants to protect and uphold something which is seen as valuable and endangered. 'Curator' has evolved through research and the understanding of the fashion industry; it is an umbrella name for a set of ideas which have acted as a catalyst for this paper. It is hoped that at the end of the research 'Curator' will offer an educational programme on sustainability for the fashion industry starting at graduate level through to designers and buyers. Its aim would be to bring in an awareness of the impact which design has on our day-to-day lives and to show that designers through their design actions, re-evaluations and choices are in fact the driving force of change:

> Education is the most powerful weapon you can use to change the world. (Nelson Mandela)

The Catalyst

The fashion industry sector has until now been all about fast profits and disregard for the environment and ethical trading, and has been profiting from a live-for-today attitude. McKenzie (1994) observed that 'fashion by its very nature exhibits an indulgence for conspicuous waste'. As the green fashion and textiles editor of *Eco Design Journal* she worked with some of the early innovators for eco fashion design such as Kate Fletcher and Helen Storey raising very important questions and showing that the fashion industry had to become more responsible and re-evaluate its whole design process from 'cradle to grave'. Many cynics did not want to believe that the fashion industry could ever become sustainable; but this is as much about being 'sustainably aware' and designing with these new principles in mind. Companies are using the new mindset to solve the old problems, but often the solutions are not what the fashion industry wants to hear.

To understand sustainability is to understand all that it incorporates and through this knowledge we can then move on and reform the deeply-rooted problems found within the fashion industry. Sustainability is defined as the development that meets the needs of the present without compromising the ability of future generations to meet their own. This definition was created in 1987 at the World Commission on Environment and Development. It was in 1992 at The Earth Summit in Rio that more than 100 heads of state agreed on five separate agreements concerning sustainable development. Agenda 21, one of the agreements, calls governments and local governments to focus on economic, social and environmental agenda and develop solutions to problems through encouraging better and more efficient practices.

Quite simply, as industries and consumer demands have grown so have their demands on earth's natural resources and the equation has stopped balancing as the earth is not being given enough time to renew and replenish. Let's be honest: we don't have a couple of spare millennia to stock up on oil, coal and water nor do we have time to allow the centuries-old rainforests to grow back. Therefore, we have to get involved in balancing the equation by finding ways of not taking out more than we put back in. This careful balancing applies also to human issues as well as the environment. The Native American Iroquois Confederacy have the 'seventh generation' philosophy which relates to sustainability, mandating that chiefs always consider the effects of their actions on their descendants seven generations in the future. The fashion industry, historically, has never thought in this way and it will be a long education process, at every level, to make the industry move towards sustainability.

When looking at sustainability it is easy to be confused trying to understand how ethical trading, fair trading, organic, recycling, off-setting of carbon emissions, durability and scientific textile innovation of clothing can contribute to sustainability. However, each is valid in the context of 'sustainability awareness' and it is a step closer to achieving sustainability - one does not work without the other and together they give the change of mindset which will encourage innovative design thinking.

Victor Papanek, in his book *The Green Imperative* (1995), suggests we must examine what each of us can contribute from our own specific role in society. He goes on to say that ecology and environmental equilibrium are the underpinnings of all human life on earth; there can neither be human life nor human culture without them. Design must be the bridge between human needs, culture and ecology. He underlines the collaborative efforts of all disciplines which are necessary to ensure change, and highlights the fine balance between improving life style and well-being yet still preserving natural resources and eco-systems.

Of all the industrial sectors, the clothing industry has been very slow in its uptake of responsibilities to the environment. The Carbon Trust issued statistics that attributed to the clothing and footwear industry 59 million tonnes of CO_2 emissions annually in the UK. The fashion industry has educated its consumers to expect up-to-the-minute fashion from the catwalks, almost as quickly as it comes off it, and all at affordable prices. Kelsey (2007) notes in her article *Embrace the death of cheap chic* that 'for more than a decade while the cost of practically everything else has been going up the price of clothing has been coming down, thanks mostly to cheap labour and production', but as Jane Shepherdson, ex-Top Shop brand director, said consumers cannot keep buying cheap clothes and 'not ask where they come from'.

Fashion has deadlines. It is these deadlines and the constant fight to keep clothing at certain price points for the consumer which has caused the current set of problems. Fashion businesses are no longer content with just two seasonal collections. There are four seasonal buys with tasters constantly appearing just to keep the consumer interested and to encourage repeat visits to the stores and boutiques. E-newsletters from fashion retailers are used to tempt the consumer to spend more as they inform their customers of new weekly arrivals of stock.

Retailers are obsessed with keeping their shops always full of stock at the beginning, middle and end-of-season. In addition, buyers make special purchases made just for sale periods to ensure the shops look well-stocked, encouraging customers to spend as much time there to bag that all important sale. Whether the reason for this is consumer-led because of increased spending power or industry-led through educating the consumer to expect more and spend more, statistics from the Cambridge University Institute of Manufacturing (2008) give food for thought:

- consumers in the UK purchase around 2.15 million tonnes of clothing and textiles each year
- this equates with about 3 billion garments per year - approximately 50 items per person
- it amounts to 35kg per person
- £780 per head per year is spent on clothes
- one eighth is sent for re-use through charities and rest is discarded
- 1 million tonnes of textile waste is tipped into Britain's landfill sites every year

Such statistics are becoming more readily available: consumers are starting to take notice and are gradually re-evaluating their spending habits; and are more willing to incorporate changes into their lives by spending less and certainly choosing retailers who reflect their own beliefs. Some of the major high street retailers have already started to reform their business practices and are re-evaluating their supply chains due to pressure from campaigners such as 'Labour behind the label' and 'Ethiscore' who name and shame companies using factories in their supply chain where workers are not paid a living wage. Companies such as 'Historic Futures' may help to address this problem. They are able to offer supply chain traceability and transparency; this allows the clothing to be traced through all of its processes and the necessary information to be attached electronically.

Ethical trading should not be seen as a separate issue but as a step towards sustainability. The fashion industry has never had an ethical reputation. Historically, workers within the textile industry have always been paid badly and worked in poor conditions. Constant pressure on the manufacturers to keep their prices down has meant that they squeeze where they can, especially the wages of their workers. For many factory owners, paying higher wages means demanding higher prices for their product but they in turn are being squeezed by buyers. If this is not achieved it means either closure or re-location to countries where the conditions are more favourable and their shareholders remain satisfied with the company's profit margins. At the moment, many factory owners in China are considering Africa as a destination for the re-location of their business and where labour laws are far more favourable due to a variety of concessions for textile and garment manufacturing.

These facets of sustainability, such as fair and ethical trade, seem to have grabbed the consumers' imagination. Whether this has occurred due to celebrity-led pressure groups or to empowerment of doing good by choice, there is no doubt that the hard work of campaigners has paid dividends. There are so many components to consider when looking at the fashion supply chain - the ethics can be readily addressed, the wrong is so apparent and the remedy so obvious. However, sustainability demands a completely different mindset which requires all those involved to look to the future and run their businesses so as to ensure that there is a future.

Inspiration for change can be found in the Craft Council's *Well Fashioned - Eco Style in the UK* Exhibition (2006) where individual designers showed their own take on eco-fashion. Rebecca Earley, the Curator of the exhibition, brought the designers together for a one-day workshop to share the inspirations which had acted as catalysts in eco design. From this emerged a Collaborative Sketchbook which gave visitors an insight into the minds of the designers; and, in turn, visitors were asked to respond to the eco-fashion which they saw by leaving comments for live re-evaluation during the exhibition. There were no right or wrong design processes: each had a valid take on finding their own solutions to the environmental problems to which the fashion industry is contributing.

Despite there being no definitive solution, the Stern Report, Al Gore's *An Inconvenient Truth* and regular media reports have served as constant reminders of what the future holds for us if nothing is done and that 'doing nothing is not an option' (Stuart Rose, CEO Marks and Spencers). Governments, ecologists, environmentalists, scientists but most importantly the consumer are now asking for 'sustainability awareness' to be at the head of all companies' agendas. Currently, in the fashion industry there are two mindsets - there are those that are taking their responsibilities seriously and are looking to reform and re-evaluate business practices, and there are those who are hoping that this is just another political fad which will just disappear.

Newer companies are finding it far easier to address this problem. They are setting their own standards as to how they want to run their businesses, and how the company's practices will reflect their own beliefs. *Howies* clothing company, recently bought out by *Timberland, Terraplana* and *Innocent* fruit drinks are examples of companies which have taken their own beliefs and incorporated them into company' long-term strategies as well as daily business practice.

Terraplana has set its sustainability standards very high and 'aims to be the most innovative and sustainable designer shoe brand in the world'. They do this through careful eco-friendly design, choice of materials (coffee bags, jackets, shirts, jeans are re-used) and they plan to create products of 'total beauty'. *Terraplana* has worked hard to get its message over clearly to the consumer by devising simple, informative, icons which tell the consumer what they are buying into. Once the product has been designed they go ahead with a detailed life-cycle analysis to see if anything can be done in a better and more sustainable way.

Innocent fruit drinks tell us that they aren't perfect, but 'we're trying to do the right thing'. Their approach is simple: use 100% natural, ethically-sourced, products. Their packaging is ecologically sound and, each year, they offset their carbon emissions as well as giving 10% of their profits to charity. *Howies* uses a different approach: their aim is to make clothes which are of a higher quality and therefore more durable, thereby lengthening the time between replacement. They also use re-cycled cotton and polyester and use innovative more ecological ways to achieve the different denim finishes.

These companies are constantly re-evaluating and re-visiting their business and design practices. Although they may not be sustainable, they are 'sustainably aware' and are looking constantly becoming more so in the future. They are looking for total transparency in company core beliefs and what they represent, and this has been rewarded with growth and consumer brand loyalty.

The Consumer

Just-style (2007) quotes in *UK: Ethical trading key to consumers' choices* survey findings by Deloitte that 59% of consumers think about ethics and green issues while shopping and buying products. This consumer is difficult to identify but it is their philosophies and ideologies which unite them. They cross generations and professions. Viewpoint calls them the 'Nu-austeres - consumers who are forsaking consumption and pleasure for self-denial, austerity and simplicity' an antidote for the decadent 1970's and 1980's. Other forecasters and analysts of trends call them 'consumers with a conscience'. Whatever their label, motivation or political leanings they are growing in force and they are demanding products which conform to their beliefs. This is a very exciting time for product designers as this is a captive audience wanting to buy products which will fit in with their beliefs on environmental and spiritual matters.

There is the added bonus for those businesses that are willing to make changes to accommodate the needs of this consumer. This business in the UK has been calculated to be worth in the region of £25 billion whereas ten years ago it was only £1 million. This is just estimation: but with the marketplace so receptive to eco products there has never been a better time to turn a company into the company it should have been and still can be, namely one which puts sustainability at the centre of each design and production decision.

Product Red has already caught the imagination of these 'cause related consumers' - why not have a luxury item and part of your spend goes to a worthy cause. And what could more worthy than to alleviate HIV and Aids in Africa? Product Red has caught the imagination of its target audience and is giving them the ultimate partnership - that of helping their fellow man, a most meaningful of all retailing experience. Products which have joined this partnership have spent small fortunes finding out whether it would be worth their while joining the partnership. They have been buying reports predicting consumer spending trends and carrying out their own research. Moreover, they have come to the same conclusion: 'brands that are in tune with the values of their customers are more successful' (Ben Stimson, Sky's Director of Corporate Social Responsibility).

Economists Carol Graham and Richard Lanyard authors of *Happiness: Lessons from a New Science* say that we no longer ask ourselves 'Do I look good in this?' it is all about how we feel. Happiness is moving up in importance so much that the *Economist* magazine runs a quality of life index. These consumers really do not want use, eat or wear products formed through other people's misery or that damage the environment. However, in this tightly timetabled world they live in they do not want to spend time reading labels on food or clothing or read lengthy reports. They want to believe in the ideology of the company and want to trust the company to buy in products which will not compromise their beliefs. Getting it wrong for the company will mean the consumer will go elsewhere to places where their own standards can be met.

The Confusion

> Whatever you can do or dream you can, begin it. Boldness has genius, power and magic in it. (Goethe)

The confusion for the fashion industry lies in knowing what to do and where to begin, especially in established large companies. Globally there are around 26.5 million people working in textiles and clothing and 182,000 in the UK. The good part is that despite the scale of the task companies have started to change their business practices. To help bring about the changes large companies are hiring dedicated CSR Managers who help them focus on social, environmental and ethical issues. Burberry's good management in areas such as the environment has had direct financial benefits. They are following their recent CSR appointment in the UK with hiring a CSR Manager in the Far East dedicated to working with suppliers on ethical supply chain issues.

GAP and Marks and Spencer's have all felt the wrath of their customer when stories have appeared in the press about these major brands using sweatshops to produce their garments and their products were boycotted for a period. Since the sweatshop exposé, Marks and Spencer have taken mammoth leaps forward and are now looking to take the lead on environmental issues concerning the retail industry. January 2007 saw them announce plans to spend £200 million over the next five years putting in place their 100-point plan covering climate change, waste, raw materials, fair trade and healthy living.

The Calculations

In their 2006 publication *Well dressed?* The Institute for Manufacturing at Cambridge University showed the best illustration of what needs to be done. There are many parts to this report which should make the consumer and the fashion industry sit up and take action. Some of the key points are those which focus on energy consumption and toxicity when producing and using a cotton T-shirt and a viscose blouse, but the conclusion applies to most natural or man made garments. In the example of a T-shirt (of which 8 are bought by each person in the UK each year), they determine the primary energy profile as 16 Mega Joules and show that this quadruples during its use phase (65

Mega Joules). This latter statistic is calculated by taking the energy needed in washing at 60°c and drying 25 times.

It then represents the strikingly-different primary energy analysis for a viscose blouse. In this case, the production of the material uses up most energy (33 Mega Joules) whereas the use phase accounts for only seven Mega Joules. It only uses a sixth of the energy that cotton needs in the use phase as it is washed at much lower temperatures and there is no need for tumble drying or ironing. Dr Kate Fletcher (2006) has already recognised the impact that washing and drying has had on the environment. She argues that improved labelling by manufacturers could lead to better washing and drying practices which would reduce energy consumption. Perhaps this would act as a catalyst to spur the industry to think about better performing fabrics and investment in research.

There are other issues when considering which textiles are more or less sustainable. There are the obvious advantages of growing cotton organically but still with huge amounts of water needed to get a healthy crop. This has already had disastrous consequences for the Aral Sea where natural resources have been mismanaged the consequences have been disastrous. The Aral Sea has almost divided into two and there are more sandstorms causing salt contamination of agricultural land. Since the cotton was not organic, pesticide and fertiliser residue flowed into the sea as pollutants. Recent reports, however, have shown that vegetation and fishing are returning to the area due to careful water management.

Man-made fibres and synthetic fibres also pose problems; they use large amounts of energy in initial production. However, research progresses on the reduction of environmental impact. These man-made and synthetic textiles are now exhibiting more of the attributes of natural fibres favoured by consumers for so many years. There have been considerable advances in man-made (cellulosic) textiles which give designers real sustainable options for the garment industry. Furthermore, synthetic textiles are proving to be sustainable, despite being oil-based, as they are totally recyclable and quality does not degenerate.

Tencel is a good example of a sustainable textile made from cellulosic wood pulp fibres which, unlike cotton, does not place a heavy demand on water. The manufacturers of Tencel claim that the manufacturing process was designed with the environment in mind; most importantly, it is biodegradable and does not pose a landfill problem. More and more textile innovators are looking to the 'cradle and grave' design concept mimicking nature's processes. Tencel and Ingeo are examples of non-traditional fibre sources; there are many others, such as peat, alginate, metal fibres, mineral fibres, paper, rubber, bio fibres and nano fibres, all of which have a future in the garment industry. Textiles with new properties and finishes which might reduce the need for washing the garment such as self cleaning, scent emitting and wicking properties are essential to reduce the need for garment washing and drying. Ros Hibbert, a textile consultant specialising in sustainability and author of the excellent *Textile Innovation* confirms the importance of non-traditional fibres and examines smart and interactive textiles. She also provides in depth information on developments in commercial and non-traditional fibre sources and has researched information on fibre engineering and the finishing of textiles to give new attributes.

Suzanne Lee, Senior Fellow at Central Saint Martins College of Art and Design (2005) in her book *Fashioning the future* explores the future of fashion. She suggests: '...guests could leave a fashion show wearing entirely different outfits to those in which they arrived; mimicking molecules could allow editors to re-organise their own clothes, copying the new look they have viewed just seconds earlier'.

If we are to believe what Mark Tungate (2005) tells us that 'clothes and accessories are expressions of how we feel, how we see ourselves and how we wish to be treated by others', then choosing what we wear will become more of a political and environmental statement.

Many designers claim that the lack of readily available information on textiles from suppliers is the reason for the restricted collections. Information in the fashion industry gives companies the competitive edge and, for many, keeping suppliers for themselves has meant they have kept their market advantage. Anna Cohen, an American designer from Portland, says that her designs demand certain types of fabrics and the sustainable options are just not out there. Her designs show innovation and her mission statement states that she wants to make lines that can maintain a competitive edge but also be 100% sustainable. However, she finds sourcing new fabrics so difficult as she is a small company and the textile suppliers inevitably prefer to work with companies which will place large orders.

Another problem that eco-fashion faces is that it has a reputation for being very earthy, scratchy and unexciting - in essence boring. So much so, that fashion designers such as Peter Ingwersen, one half of Noir, who use organic and fair trade cotton explains '...I totally respect what everyone is doing for ethical clothing, but at the same time, I don't want to be lumped as that ethical clothes label; our garments look like normal stylish clothes, made form luxurious fabrics'. Linda Loudemilk, an American designer, talks about 'Luxury eco' and is proud of her green credentials. She uses innovative new textiles made from sasawashi, bamboo, sea cell, soya and other self-sustaining plants. She even set up The Loudermilk Institute for Sustainability, a non-profit organisation which faciliates and manages research projects specifically aimed at sustainable product design.

The success of the campaign organisation 'We are what we do' and their book *Change the World for a Fiver* can serve only as an inspiration for planting seeds of change in society. 630,890 have been inspired to make promises for change on a variety issues not so much to do with fashion, but society as a whole. The success of the movement towards sustainability within the fashion industry will rely on re-evaluating how design schools teach design principles and how highly they regard sustainability in the design process.

The solutions are there and have been for many years. These include: efficient re-cycling; choice of textile; scientific innovation; new fibre sources; simply cutting down on the number of garments we possess or washing at lower temperatures; and not using a tumble dryer. Perhaps simple measures such as fashion companies being made to be responsible for the disposal of the garment after it has stopped being useful would speed up the process of finding efficient recycling methods or biodegradable alternatives. Takashimaya, Japan's largest department store, has already set up collection points outside stores for unwanted clothes and are taking responsibility for used-garment disposal. The important part of the education process is to start to question, re-evaluate and then bring in the changes. The objective is to create a movement of awareness and responsibility within the fashion industry that encourages methods of design, as if our very lives depended on it.

Ezio Manzini (2005), a leading thinker in sustainable design, opens his thought provoking paper *Enabling solutions, social innovation and design for sustainability* with an ancient wisdom - 'if someone is hungry do not give them fish. Give them a fishing rod and teach them how to fish' - it is now imperative to teach the next generation to fish.

References

Books

Braddock, S.E. and O'Mahoney, M. 1998 *Techno Textiles: Revolutionary fabrics for fashion and design.* London: Thames and Hudson Ltd

Cumming, V. 2004 *Understanding Fashion History.* London: BT Batsford

Ewing, E. 2005 History *of 20th Century Fashion.* London: BT Batsford

Harvey, E. 2004 *Change the World for a Fiver.* London: Short books Ltd

Institute for Manufacturing 2006 *Well Dressed?* Cambridge: University of Cambridge Institute for Manufacturing

Hibbert, R. 2004 *Textile Innovation.* Line Publishing

Jones, J.S. 2005 *Fashion Design.* London: Lawrence King Publishing

Lee, S. 2005 *Fashioning the Future – Tomorrow's Wardrobe.* London: Thames and Hudson

Lindstrom, M. 2005 *Brand Sense.* New York: Free Press Simon and Schuster

McQuaid, M. 1998 *Extreme Textiles Designing for the High Perfomance.* London: Thames and Hudson

Quinn, B. 2002 *Techno Fashion.* Oxford: Berg Publishers

Papanek, V. 1995 *The Green Imperative.* London: Thames and Hudson

Tungate, M. 2005 *Branding Style from Armani to Zara.* London: Kogan Page

Journals and Newspapers

Austerity and the city (Editorial) 2006 Viewpoint 18

Eco-textile News 2007 Issue 1

Eco-textile News 2007 Issue 2

Eco-textile News 2007 Issue 3

Eco-textile News 2007 Issue 4

Fletcher, K. 1997 Alternative Fibres. *Eco-design,* **5,** 30

Kelsey, L. 2007 Embrace the death of cheap chic. *The Times,* 8 August

Sunday Times 2006 Mrs Bono Saves the Day (Editorial). February 2006

Vogue 2006 Moral Fibre (Editorial). December 2006

McKenzie J. 1994   Green Fashion. *Eco-design*, **3**, 40

Shah, D. 2006   The Fashion with a conscience. *View*, 76

Papers

Earley, R. 2006   Well-fashioned: Towards our eco future, essay for Well fashioned. *Eco Style in the UK exhibition*

Fletcher, K. 2006   Well-laundered, short text for well fashioned. *Eco-style in the UK exhibition*

Fletcher, K. 2006   Fashion, where people and the environment matter, *Well fashioned: Eco style in the UK exhibition*

Manzini, E. 2005   Enabling solutions, social innovation and design for sustainability, Politecnico di Milano

Websites

www.brandchannel.com/features
www.carbontrust.co.uk
www.cleanclothes.org
www.craftscouncil.org/Well fashioned Eco-Style in the UK
www.c2ccertified.com
www.edun.ie
www.forumforthefuture.org.uk
www.greenfibres.com
www.howies.co.uk
www.innocentdrinks.co.uk/us/
UK: ethical trading key to consumer's choices. [Internet]. <www.just-style>. [Accessed 3rd January 2007].
US: global market booming for organic cotton apparel. [Internet]. <www.just-style>. [Accessed 28th June 2006].
www.kingston.ac.uk/sustainability
www.katefletcher.com/lifetimes
www.marksandspencers.com
www.noir-illuminati2.com
www.labourbehindthelabel.org
www.peopletree.co.uk
www.soilassociation.com

Film

An Inconvenient Truth 2006 Paramount

Empowering Student Sustainability Practitioners: The Kaliro Link Project

Jane Roberts
Centre for Active Learning, University of Gloucestershire

Abstract

The University of Gloucestershire (UoG) and the National Teachers' College, Kaliro (NTCK), Uganda, have been in partnership since 1999 and there are regular visits of Gloucestershire students to the College. The programme mixes academic and voluntary work to support the Link Project. This includes fundraising to improve learning resources at NTCK, and mentoring Ugandan staff and students in ICT skills development during the field class. Other voluntary projects have developed from this partnership, for example fund-raising to support an orphanage. A small number of students have returned to Uganda post-graduation to work in sustainability-related projects, both commercial and voluntary.

This paper reports on research undertaken on the development of students' skills as sustainability practitioners through the active experiential learning opportunities of the Link Project and module. Data are drawn from post-fieldtrip interviews, video diaries, and student self-evaluations. This narrow approach to evaluation finds very positive outcomes. There is evidence that the trip and associated activities have improved students' sustainability skills, changed attitudes towards sustainability and empowered students to make changes to their own lifestyles and career plans. However, a broader evaluative approach to the project, taking into account the risks to participants, environmental impacts, and issues of equity between the link project stakeholders raises interesting questions about its overall sustainability.

It is concluded that it is very likely that the benefits of the project outweigh the costs, but that the project leaders need to remain vigilant in reviewing and take, where possible, credible actions to mitigate potential and actual negative impacts.

Keywords   Uganda, digital divide, field work, skills for sustainability

Introduction

In 1999 the University of Gloucestershire established a link partnership with the National Teachers' College, Kaliro (NTCK), Uganda. The link has two aims:

(i)   to provide opportunities for staff and student development at the two institutions
(ii)   to enhance the provision of learning resources at NTCK where this was possible in a cost effective way

At Level II, students from the Community Development, Geography, Environmental Management and Environmental Science degree and HND programmes have the opportunity to undertake a field visit to Uganda to fulfil the compulsory module *EL201 Fieldweek,* rated at 15 CATS points. Students are invited to choose from a list of possible destinations. The Uganda option is usually oversubscribed and students are selected on a first come, first served basis. The group size is about 18 each year.

Normally, *EL201* involves a European destination, five or six preparatory sessions, 7-10 days residential fieldwork, plus up to three classroom-based sessions on return. Students opting for the Uganda option, however, are asked to commit their support to the Link Project, as well as fulfilling the academic outcomes of the module. This they do in various ways:

(i)   Fundraising: about £2000 is raised by students each year. These monies are not used to subsidise the trip; instead they pay for the export of second-hand books and computer equipment and for the purchase of computer consumables and peripherals for NTCK

(ii)   In 2002 there was enough money available to pay for two senior NTCK staff to visit the university for three weeks for staff development in information and communication technology (ICT) skills and quality management

(iii)   Mentoring: prior to the visit students are encouraged to undertake the European Computer Driving Licence (ECDL) course in order to develop their confidence in using ICT. During the visit, they offer mentoring to their Ugandan peers in the use of these technologies

(iv)   Other practical assistance: for example, collecting and packing learning resources such as second-hand books and computers for the partner institution

In order to include mentoring work as well as academic projects, the trip is of 17 days duration. For students choosing projects with a Community Development or Human Geography focus there may be some synergies between Link Project activities and their academic work. For example, past projects have examined the potential gender bias in access to ICT resources at NTCK. Students whose discipline is more scientific are more likely to undertake projects which have no direct relevance to the Link Project, for example on water quality in townships close to Kaliro or on fisheries management. In all cases, however, the quality of learning is greatly enhanced by the advice and local expertise of NTCK academics and the willingness of NTCK students to act as guides and translators. It is important to both partners that this is the case, as it means that both are contributing substantially, albeit in different ways, to the quality of learning in each other's institution.

Academically, Uganda offers a wealth of active learning opportunities allowing students to undertake field-based project work in line with the learning outcomes set for the *EL201* module. The opportunity for ICT training and mentoring is also of benefit, as are the enhanced project management skills associated with organising fundraising events. The opportunity to engage in an extended project brings its own benefits - most students' involvement with the Link Project extends over a 12 month period or longer, in contrast to the usual 15 week span of the module. This engenders commitment to the project and enthusiasm for learning.

This paper evaluates the sustainability of the field class using two approaches. Firstly, the potential and actual development of students' sustainability skills and their empowerment as sustainability practitioners is examined using three different data sets. Secondly, a more holistic evaluation is attempted, taking into account broader costs and benefits, including those related to the health of participants, the environmental impact of the field class and some social and cultural aspects.

Student Skills: Methodology

Efforts have been made to gather a range of detailed evaluative data focusing on the student experience of the Uganda trip and associated activities over a number of years. This is because the trip is costly to students and in terms of staff time. From the earliest days of the Link Project there has also been a recognition of the need to evaluate, carefully, the benefits to check that they justified, in particular, the health and safety-related risks, but also negative factors such as flight-related carbon emissions. In this paper three main sources of data are used for analysing the development of sustainability skills through participation in the Link Project and module:

(i)   Interviews with participants from the 2001 group which were undertaken as part of a more general investigation of skills development

(ii)   'Reflective-self evaluations' required as a component of assessment 2003-2007

(iii)   Video diaries kept by some of the 2006 and 2007 group

1. Interviews (2001 group)

In 2001, the first year of the Uganda field class, a small research project was conducted with the primary aim of investigating students' skills development through participation in the Link Project activities, in particular the ICT mentoring component of the programme. Six students from the cohort of 13 were interviewed prior to the trip and again during the following term. The remaining seven did not take the opportunity to participate in the study. The interviews were recorded and transcribed. It was made clear to students that participation in the study was voluntary and that the interviews were confidential and not related to module assessment.

Although the project was focused mainly on the development of ICT skills through the preparation for, and participation in, ICT training at Kaliro, interviews also included questions that explored broader aspects of skill development, using the framework developed by Murphy *et al.* (1997, Section 4.2):

a)   personal skills (such as improving their own learning, action planning)
b)   interpersonal skills (working with others, group work, teamwork)
c)   communication, numeracy, skills in using information technology
d)   problem solving, critical thinking, objective reasoning, reflection, lateral thinking

[....] also associated attitudes and understandings such as:

e)   a positive attitude to change
f)   values and personal integrity
g)   understanding the worlds of work, politics and society

This list was developed 10 years ago and published to coincide with the Dearing Report's call for Higher Education curricula to pay more attention to employability skills (National Committee of Inquiry into Higher Education, 1997). It may seem surprising, from a 2007 standpoint, that no link between key skills and environmental education, nor education for sustainable development, was made in Murphy's report, despite the earlier and influential Toyne Report on the importance of cross-curricular environmental education (Department for Education, 1992). However, it can be noted that there is considerable overlap between the 'key skills' of the 1990s and the 'skills for sustainability' that are currently recognised; the former are largely a generic version of the latter. In their review of current initiatives on education for sustainability in UK Higher Education, Dawe *et al.* (2005, para. 91) note:

> The following knowledge, skills and attitudes were identified as factors developed by students through ESD courses:
>
> - Interdisciplinary skill
> - Ethical skills and the understanding necessary to put sustainability into practice
> - Critical and reflective thinking
> - Knowledge of the practical impacts that their decisions will have
> - Awareness of the facts surrounding sustainability challenges, and the skills necessary to play a part in their solution

For the purposes of this evaluation, it was decided to review and re-analyse data collected originally for the 2001 study, although this had not been specifically designed to investigate sustainability skills. The five point framework presented by Dawe *et al.* was used, initially, for the re-analysis and evaluation of the development of students' sustainability skills gained from participation in the project. However, a sixth category was added to capture themes emerging from the data relevant to leadership, for example teamwork and self-confidence.

2. Reflective self-evaluations

Annually, each annual field class has been evaluated as part of mainstream quality assurance processes within the university. Results from evaluations in the early years of the trip surprised the organisers. Although in informal and semi-formal, social and teaching, group and one-to-one situations during the field class, students made deeply personal verbal comments on their learning, the development of their skills, attitudes and values and how they felt themselves to have been transformed by their experiences, they seemed reluctant or unable to articulate these in writing when asked for a formal evaluation. Various evaluation formats were used but all gave similar results. The timing of the process seemed to make no difference: responses gathered towards the end of the trip in Uganda were similar to those taken on campus a week or two after the return. Students tended to give very mundane comments about, for example, the organisation, transport arrangements and food but, even when asked directly, would not focus to any great extent on their learning or skill development.

By 2003, in an attempt to capture better evidence of reflection on skills development, the assessment brief included as an assignment a 200 word 'reflective self-evaluation of how your personal skills and confidence in self-management have developed through participation in the entire module. The subject matter in this section should not be restricted to the research topic chosen for this assessment'. The responses are analysed below using the six point framework introduced above.

3. Video diaries

Students registered for the Uganda trip from the 2006 and 2007 cohorts were invited to make video diaries during the field class. They were given a short explanation in class of what was involved and then issued with consent forms. It was stressed that participation was voluntary and that they could withdraw at any time; that participating students had complete control over the content of the tape, including the opportunity to edit it on return to the UK; and that only the module tutor and one or two technical staff would be able to view the material once it was submitted. By way of an incentive, students were offered a DVD copy of their footage as a souvenir.

Take-up at the initial stage was high from both groups. From the 38 (19 + 19) students in both cohorts 28 returned consent forms and were issued with a digital video tape. The case and tape were labelled with the student's name. The case also bore the questions in Table 1 as an *aide memoire*. Students were told that they could talk about anything at all, but that the researcher was most interested in their learning about Uganda, the UK, their subject, the field class group and themselves. During the trip, periodical reminders were issued to encourage students to record their diaries by borrowing one of the two video cameras available. A small number of students had their own cameras and did not need the university equipment.

Table 1 Text attached to video tape cases

What have I learned:
About Uganda?
About the UK?
About my subject?
About the group?
About me?

On return to the UK the tapes were transferred to DVD, transcribed and analysed using the six point framework.

Student Skills: Findings

As expected, the three methods used generated a range of data, some more successfully than others. In this section the quality of the data from each source will first be discussed, followed by an holistic analysis based on the six sustainability skill headings.

1. Interviews (2001 group)

The main focus of the original investigation had been skill development through ICT mentoring. This meant that responses were most relevant to the skill headings: interdisciplinary skills (focusing primarily on the relationship between ICT skills and development); knowledge of the practical impacts that their decisions will have; awareness of the facts surrounding sustainability challenges, and the skills necessary to play a part in their solution; and leadership, teamwork and self-confidence.

2. Reflective self-evaluations

Despite tutorial support for this task during the field class, the success of this approach to data collection was limited. As in the module evaluation responses, the majority of students wrote fairly stilted, pedestrian and non-evaluative accounts, although there were a few excellent submissions.

Although students were very positive about the value of the field trip, overall there was not the anticipated level of reflection. This may be due to student perceptions of what is appropriate in an exercise labelled 'evaluation' or 'assessment', combined with a lack of experience in reflective writing. The assessment criteria had been drafted to reward honest reflection rather than bland assurances that skills had been developed but this subtlety may have escaped the students.

The accounts are, with a few exceptions, markedly less candid than the interview data and video diaries. Observations are almost universally positive, in contrast to the overall positive but more rounded comments obtained in the other formats. Again, this is probably related to the student's perceptions of what is required in an assessment and the fear of being marked down.

The evaluations are useful, however, as a way of identifying which skills students perceived as actually or potentially relevant to their participation in the Link Project. These mainly fell into three categories, in descending order of significance: leadership, teamwork and self-confidence; ethical skills and the understanding necessary to put sustainability into practice; and awareness of the facts surrounding sustainability challenges, and the skills necessary to play a part in their solution.

3. Video diaries

Due to logistical difficulties, only 11 of the 28 tapes issued were returned with usable data, although several tapes contained contributions from more than one student. A comprehensive analysis of the content of the diaries is presented in Roberts (2007). As would be expected from the 'What have I learnt?' brief the content is rich and covers a broad range of topics. The analysis in this section is concerned solely with the six categories of skill development. Of these, four featured most prominently in this data set: knowledge of the practical impacts that their decisions will have; ethical skills and the understanding necessary to put sustainability into practice; awareness of the facts surrounding sustainability challenges, and the skills necessary to play a part in their solution; and leadership, teamwork and self-confidence.

Interdisciplinary skills

EL201 Fieldweek is an interdisciplinary module and part of an integrated curriculum of environmental disciplines. Components in assessment are 50% individual project and 50% group project. It is usual for the groups to contain students from different disciplines. For example, a group comprising a Human Geographer, Environmental Scientist and Biologist might undertake a study on aspects of the actual and perceived quality of borehole water. Although interdisciplinary skills are not part of the assessed learning outcomes of the module, it is likely that such skills are enhanced for the majority of students, albeit within the environmental disciplines.

There is evidence from the datasets that students are exercising interdisciplinary skills. Students on joint programmes without the environmental courses mentioned linkages with their other subjects. A Geography and Psychology student spoke in a video diary of the different attitudes to mental illness in Europe and Africa; a Geography and Sports Science student spoke of the importance of football in Ugandan culture and the challenges for coaches and clubs with little access to resources. This suggests the field class is encouraging students to come out of disciplinary silos and make connections between different fields of knowledge.

This came through most clearly in the interviews with the 2001 class who were the first cohort to visit Uganda and whose arrival coincided with the first batch of computers sent from Cheltenham. Although they had been trained in ICT and mentoring skills beforehand, they were unprepared for the intense and often chaotic conditions under which they were attempting, in a limited time span, to train key staff and students in the basic use of the machines. Frequent power cuts disrupted the programme. All those interviewed were enthusiastic about the Link Project and mentoring and some were passionate. This experience brought out for them clearly the relationships between ICT and development (Computing and Geography *via* Education), and the implications of being rich and being poor (Economics):

> I could never forget this one guy's smile after I taught him to type. It was so … forget all the Oxfam and the Christian Aid videos you see on the TV about poverty and disaster in the world, these are poor people learning something, people who haven't had the chance to learn before and okay I say poor, in Uganda they're relatively well advanced, but obviously to us they would still be counted as poor people. But the benefits they've gained from computers they show, they show to you and it's just like they express it in this way and you just, you feel really…. We paid to do this, we paid money and we haven't actually been given anything from it, so it's not selfish, to take away satisfaction from it, I really feel like I've done something. (Student A, 2001)

Ethical skills and the understanding necessary to put sustainability into practice

Ethical issues are frequently mentioned in the *reflective self-evaluations*, although little detail is given. For example, a student might say 'I have completely changed my attitude towards poverty' without saying in what ways the attitude had changed. The video diaries give a much richer picture of the ethical challenges which students perceive during the trip. Some of these are religious in origin (one student was troubled by a challenge from Christian Ugandans and their accusation that UK had converted Uganda to Christianity but was now itself apostate); more frequently they are related to past colonialism and present economic and social inequalities. Many students received begging letters or were disconcerted by direct requests for gifts by their Ugandan peers. Many were uncomfortable with the assumption that they were rich. One was embarrassed at the prospect of buying a large sum of phone credit and considered going into several shops to split the purchase. Some students reflected without reaching a conclusion on what could be done: others recognised the need for ethical lifestyle changes:

> There was this little girl in Iganga, I was sat in the bus and I put my hand out and shook her hand and she bowed down or curtsied me which was quite shocking. (Student B, 2006/07)

> The kids are amazing, like I said before, they touch you and they really touch you inside your heart but something that does annoy me is the fact that if I was in the same situation I'd do the same thing as what they do, they all ask for money all the time. They see a white man and they think money, loaded, you know. They're just all the time msungo, msungo, money, money and that's what's annoyed me today. (Student C, 2006/07)

I've learnt that you don't need to have as much stuff as you've got in England. It's just unnecessary the way that we live. …. We just use up too many resources, just selfish. When you actually think about it you only need a third of what you actually own. That's the best thing I've learnt. (Student D, 2006/07)

A minority, particularly those who had travelled in the developing world before, recognised the potential for disparity between intentions and actions on return to the UK:

As soon as I got back I gave away most of my clothes last time. Now when you get back to uni you kind of get absorbed into a culture. …. At university it is so different and there are so many pressures to do different things like drinking and having proper clothes and everything. And so it's been weird in that way that I've really been disappointed with myself and how I am living my life. ………. [on return to the UK] It's hard being back in the UK ……. I am lazy here. (Student E, 2006/07)

Critical and reflective thinking

Each of the methods gave participating students the opportunity to reflect critically on different aspects of the field class, the Link Project, and their own responses to the various challenges that they had met. Although there was evidence in the interviews of critical and reflective thinking, it was not clear from the data if this faculty had been developed as a result of participation in the Link Project i.e. that students emerged from the experience with an enhanced capacity for reflection rather than just practising their existing reflective skills.

As previously noted, data from the *reflective self-evaluations* was, paradoxically, the most discouraging of the three data sets. Only a minority of students responded to the brief with deep reflection. This was despite evidence from verbal communications during and after the field class that such reflection was taking place and at quite a profound level - the main reason for initiating the video diary project (Roberts, 2007).

Compared to the interview data, there was much richer evidence in the video diaries of critical and reflective thinking, some of this at a profound level. Although there is again no direct evidence that students' capabilities had been enhanced, it is clear that some students were consciously reflecting very hard:

A thinking day for me. I just quite wanted to be on my own just sat there and thought about, thought about life, had a bit of a cry. Not a sad cry, because it's not sad, it's not sad here. People are so happy but… I don't know, maybe it was a guilty cry about how much I've got …. But it's good to have a think and quite a nice place to do it as well. (Student F, 2006/07) I think that's all linked into the fact that there's just so much to do here because you are always, always thinking and you're always thinking about everything. You have to. (Student G, 2006/07)

Knowledge of the practical impacts of decisions

The reality of living without piped water, dependent on pit latrines, a sporadic electricity supply and food prepared from fresh ingredients on open fires raised many questions for students about their lifestyles and consumption in the UK. A typical observation must be read in the context of concerns about the disparity between intentions and actions noted above:

> Water usage as well, that's a massive thing over here and when I get back I'm gonna try and change my water usage ways. Try not to leave taps on or anything and electricity as well. These guys over here, they get it seems like four hours of power a day, if that and at home we're all going round leaving lights on, leaving TVs on and daft things like that. Play stations, stupid stuff like that.... (Student H, 2006/07)

Mentoring in the computer room gave most mentors a solid feeling of achievement. Besides the direct satisfaction of face-to-face tuition, the first 2001 cohort showed that the early development work and fundraising they had invested in the project had resulted in the establishment of a resource which was greatly valued by the recipient institution.

Awareness of the facts surrounding sustainability challenges, and the skills necessary to play a part in their solution

Living close to the environmental sources and sinks, without the apparatus of commerce and industry to process resources and wastes, revealed to students the rewards and challenges available to those who live in this way, full-time. Academic projects enabled deeper understanding, but all students were exposed to a range of social and environmental problems in Uganda: the demographic challenge for a nation 50% of whose population is under 15 years of age; over-crowded and under-resourced schools; AIDS and its effects on orphans and widows; the failure of the economy to meet the basic needs of many; deforestation and fishery depletion; and the challenges of biodiversity conservation in a land-hungry subsistence economy.

During each annual field class, without exception, students have reflected verbally as to why it is that, with such serious problems to contend with, people in Uganda are seemingly so much happier than in the UK. These reflections are an important theme in the video diaries:

> They've got such stronger communities than we have at home at all and with their family as well. We had a bit of a debate about whether who's happiest the English people or the Ugandan people. Ugandan. I think Ugandan, but I'm kind of undecided. Definitely Ugandan. It's just we're so materialistic and get happy about things. (Student I, 2006/07)

> I have learnt about the UK that it is not a happy place. ... Walking down the street everyone has their head down and those that don't have their head down are giving you evils. It's quite a negative place to be. (Student J, 2006/07)

Despite this profound diagnosis of the roots of unsustainability at a global level, what is absent from all three data sets is any sense that community or political action could be a vehicle for change. Most students raise the question of consumer-related and lifestyle changes they could make. A minority discuss making their career in development. But none seems to have a sense of empowerment as citizens.

Leadership, teamwork and self-confidence

This is probably the most significant category of the six in terms of the empowerment of students as sustainability practitioners. There was clear evidence from all three data sets that the module and Link Project had given students the opportunity to grow in confidence within a safe framework. Students mentioned enhancements in self-confidence; short- and long-term planning; self-management; communication within the group and with Ugandans; and social and teamwork skills. The more reflective went on to recognise which of these skills still needed further development. Students associated these improvements in skills to the range of academic and voluntary activities associated with the field class.

Evaluation

The Link Project has been an undoubted success in terms of its aims, with both institutions reporting benefits which are out of proportion to the inputs each has contributed. As well as the educational benefits, there is evidence of increased cultural understanding within both institutions; strong friendships; and some spin off projects (Sullivan, 2007).

The data analysed here show that, together, the module and Link Project offer challenging opportunities to develop, through active and experiential learning, skills which are directly relevant to sustainability. The ICT mentoring project, in particular, gives students direct practitioner experience and seems to be a powerful learning experience. Two firm conclusions can be drawn. Firstly, the field class offers all participants the opportunity to develop sustainability skills and, through active and experiential learning, to become empowered as novice sustainability practitioners. Secondly, as with all learning opportunities, some participants gain more from the experience than others. All those who contributed to the data sets seem to have recognised at least some of the sustainability challenges raised by the trip and started to reflect upon them. A minority of students have fully embraced these opportunities and have significantly enhanced their skills and attitudes. Several have returned to Uganda, either for dissertation research or to become involved in commercial or voluntary development projects (Sullivan, 2007). Others have worked to raise money to support an orphanage which was founded by a former student at NTCK. Overall, it is clear that the impact of the field class upon sustainability skill development for student participants is large and positive. As an active learning experience participation in the module and Link Project has empowered students as sustainability practitioners.

Against this needs to be set the disbenefits of the activities. This case study has focussed so far on the development of students' skills as sustainability practitioners through active learning by participation in the Link Project, although other substantial benefits have been achieved. These include successful staff development experiences for both partner institutions and the transfer of more than 40 computers, over 3,500 books and other learning resources to National Teachers' College, Kaliro and its partner schools. There are, however, negative aspects to the trip: environmental, health-related and social, which raise questions about its sustainability.

Each passenger's return journey from Heathrow to Entebbe generates ~1.47 tonnes of carbon dioxide emissions (Climate Care, 2007) which is probably more than three times the annual per capita average for Uganda (UNEP/GRID-Arendal, 2007). This is ironic as one important focus of the academic programme is the potential impacts of climate change on vulnerable local ecosystems, such as Lake Victoria, and those whose livelihoods depend on these (Adger *et al.*, 2003). During the trip a further significant environmental impact is generated through the necessity, for reasons of health and safety, for students and staff to drink up to four litres of water a day, purchased in 500 ml plastic bottles.

Piped and borehole water is not safe to drink untreated and it is important that fluid levels are kept high to avoid dehydration and heat stroke. Of the estimated 2,300 waste bottles generated each year during the 17 day visit a very small number are reused as containers or toys by villagers and their children. The rest are disposed of into inadequate waste management systems. Not only are there no plastic recycling facilities available in Uganda, for most of the locations on the itinerary there are no available municipal systems. In Uganda's rural areas domestic waste (including plastics) is either burned or buried in small pits. This is an appropriate solution in areas of low population density when the waste stream consists almost entirely of biodegradable domestic food waste but highly unsatisfactory for non-biodegradable wastes.

Ugandan and European students mix well during the visit and there is a programme of social, cultural and sporting activities to encourage this. However, there are difficulties within the overall positive experience and these arise in part from the perceived and actual disparities in wealth between the two cohorts, as noted above. Other identified cultural problems include the impact of European visitors, not only on the remote rural settlements visited during the trip, but also on some of the more urban localities on the programme. Some students in their video diaries express unease about project work which involves them in asking questions of local people as they feel they do not give anything back; but if gifts are given they then feel uncomfortable in the persona of a 'rich westerner'.

There are a range of medical and other risks to students and staff associated with the trip and these are assessed and mitigated as far as is possible in advance of the visit. The most significant and difficult to control risk is that of a road traffic accident, as driving standards and road conditions in Uganda are poor. Members of the group have become ill on occasion due to minor cases of diarrhoea or dehydration, and sometimes with more serious ailments such as malaria and dysentery, despite the sometimes forceful advice of staff on prophylactic measures.

Lastly, there is also the question of the social, cultural and environmental appropriateness of the mostly-second-hand ICT resources that have been exported as part of the project (James, 2003). As previously noted, the waste management infrastructure is very poor and it is unclear how the computers will be disposed of once the ingenuity of the technician at NTCK is exhausted and they can no longer be kept in service.

Conclusion

These multifarious impacts, positive, negative, multi-dimensional and mixed, are of course incommensurable. The profound learning experience, enhancement of sustainability related skills and the empowerment of students to envisage the need for changes in their own lifestyles and careers is extremely valuable, but it comes with costs. Some of these, for example the health risks, are borne by the participants themselves. More troubling are the externalities, especially if these fall on those already in poverty. Overall, the benefits can be judged to outweigh the costs but organisers must take two actions. The first is to minimise and mitigate the costs wherever practicable. The second is ensure students have the opportunity to reflect on these conundrums and thus enrich still further the learning experience.

Acknowledgements

The success of the Uganda Field class has depended on the support, goodwill and expertise of many colleagues at the National Teachers' College, Kaliro, Uganda, especially Robert Bagalama and Sam Waiswa. This project was undertaken as part of a Fellowship granted by the Centre for Active Learning, University of Gloucestershire. My colleagues Martin Jenkins, Alex Steele, Kenny Lynch and Chris Hall are thanked for their input, especially their assistance with data collection, as are the student participants. Sonia Chilton efficiently and accurately transcribed the audio and video tapes. The 2001 study was supported financially from the University of Gloucestershire's Small Teaching Grants Fund (2000-2001). Financial support for the field class over several years by the Janet Trotter Trust and the St Paul and St Mary Fund is gratefully acknowledged.

References

Adger, W. N., Huq, S., Brown, K., Conway D. and Hulme, M. 2003   Adaptation to climate change in the developing world. *Progress in Development Studies*, **3**, 179-195. [Internet]. <http://pdj.sagepub.com/cgi/content/abstract/3/3/179>. [Accessed 24th August 2007].

Climate Care 2007 *Flights calculator.* [Internet]. <http://www.climatecare.org/britishairways/calculators/flight/>. [Accessed 24th August 2007].

Dawe, G., Jucker, R. and Martin, S. 2005 *Sustainable development in Higher Education: Current practice and future developments, A report for The Higher Education Academy.* York: HEA. [Internet]. <http://www.heacademy.ac.uk/misc/sustdevinHEfinalreport.pdf>. [Accessed 30th December 2006].

Department for Education 1992 *Environmental responsibility: An agenda for further and higher education.* London: HMSO

James, J. 2003 *Bridging the Global Digital Divide.* Cheltenham: Edward Elgar

Murphy, R. *et al.* 1997 Supporting Key Skills in Higher Education: A Staff Development Pack. Nottingham: University of Nottingham

National Committee of Inquiry into Higher Education 1997 *Higher Education in the Learning Society* [Internet]. <http://www.leeds.ac.uk/educol/ncihe/>. [Accessed 24th August 2007].

Roberts, J. 2007 'Capturing values: a triangulation of academic frameworks, concepts of education and the student experience', in *ESD: Graduates as Global Citizens Conference,* 10-11 September, Bournemouth University

Sullivan, K. 2007 'Footballs to Africa: Or, from theory to action', in Roberts, C. and Roberts, J. (eds) *Greener by Degrees: Exploring Sustainability through Higher Education Curricula.* Cheltenham: Geography Discipline Network

United Nations Environment Programme/GRID-Arendal 2007 *Emissions of carbon dioxide, in Africa and selected OECD countries.* [Internet]. <http://maps.grida.no/go/graphic/emissions_of_carbon_dioxide_in_africa_and_selected_oecd_countries>. [Accessed 24th August 2007].

Science, Society, Politics, and the Media – Joining Efforts to Manage the Risk of Termite Infestation in the Azores

Ana Moura Arroz, Ana Cristina Palos, Isabel Estrela Rego and Paulo Borges
Universidade dos Açores, Portugal

Abstract

Termites are well-established pests which infest structural timber in many parts of the world. In the Azores archipelago (Portugal), the drywood termite *Cryptotermes brevis* (Insecta, Isoptera) has been found in four of the nine islands, and has caused serious damage to buildings and other artefacts, especially in the main towns. In the last five years, control measures have included investment in scientific research involving surveys to classify infestations and the development of mitigation strategies. Nevertheless, the infestation is far from being controlled and Azorean citizens are still largely unaware of the dangers and risks associated with this urban pest. However, the losses from *C. brevis* can be greatly reduced through the introduction of effective educational programmes and management practices.

This research project has four aims: firstly, to understand people's perspectives on the consequences of termite infestation and their perceptions regarding the effectiveness of existing and proposed management strategies; secondly, to comprehend the role of the media in the formation of public opinion; thirdly, to develop means of communicating complex technical information so as to avoid misunderstandings between the public and the scientific community, politicians and urban managers; and, finally, to develop and introduce channels of communication between the main stakeholders, securing the engagement of citizens in termite control.

The presentation integrates evidence from stakeholders and identifies communication problems as the basis for resolving conflicts, facilitating dialogue and partnerships, and promoting an awareness of the risk of termites. Data were collected from interviews, the descriptive-interpretative analysis of media reports, scientific discourses and existing operational programmes. Lack of integration among stakeholders was identified as a significant challenge to effective communication.

Keywords   Azores, termite infestation, citizen participation, risk management and communication

The Problem

Six years ago, some homeowners in Angra do Heroísmo, the major town of Terceira Island in the Azores (Portugal), began to observe pellets, elates, and wings of drywood termites in their furniture and historic buildings. However, not until 2002 was *Cryptotermes brevis* identified in Terceira and São Miguel islands (Borges *et al.*, 2004; Myles 2004) where, at present, it is considered a well-established and serious pest for structural timbers. It now exists in four of the nine islands in the archipelago (Santa Maria, São Miguel, Terceira and Faial) and has caused severe damage to the buildings and other artefacts in major towns. The capacity of this termite to attack different types of dry wood enables it to invade all fixed parts of the house structure, including the roof, ceiling, wooden pavement, windows and doors. Given that it can eat both soft and hard woods, and its strong preference for sapwood over heartwood (Myles *et al.*, 2007), it is the only termite commonly found in furniture. These characteristics explain its introduction and dispersion in the Azores and heighten the probability of its further spread to the remaining islands (Borges *et al.*, 2007).

Even though other termite species such as the *Kalotermes flavicollis* (an European dampwood termite) and the *Reticulitermes grassei* (a Mediterranean subterranean termite), have been recently identified in the Azores (Borges and Myles 2007), the scale of infestation by the West Indian dry wood termite *C. brevis*, is a major cause of concern. At present, hundreds of residential, governmental and commercial buildings in the islands of São Miguel, Terceira, and Faial are infested with *C. brevis* (Borges *et al.*, 2004, Borges and Myles, 2007). Each year, additional structures will be colonized through seasonal dispersal flights from untreated buildings (Guerreiro *et al.*, 2007).

Since the identification of this pest, the University of the Azores, in partnership with other national and international institutions, has hosted research devoted to:

(i)   identification of termite species in the Azores and characterisation of their biology
(ii)   determination of patterns of termite distribution and abundance in Terceira, particularly in the Angra do Heroísmo district
(iii)   analysing the environmental factors involved in the propagation of termites in Terceira island
(iv)   development of testing techniques, in the laboratory and *in situ*, for the mitigation of infection and propagation control
(v)   making comparative studies of assorted chemical and physical methods for treating infested furniture (see Borges, *et al.*, 2004; Myles, 2004; Borges and Myles, 2007)

To evaluate the incidence of the pest in the district of Angra do Heroísmo, the research team conducted an exploratory study of 10 randomly selected houses in each rural village, and in ten randomly selected houses in each street suspected of infestation in the only town (Borges *et al.*, 2004). Later, following a campaign to inform local residents, this sample was extended to include all houses reporting infestation to the local authorities until the end of May of 2004.

Figure 1 shows that the pest is much more harmful in less humid regions. In the historical centre of Angra do Heroísmo infestation was confirmed in 43% of the inspected houses; half of these exhibited signs of severe infestation or a sufficiently high level of damage to foundation structures so as to endanger their occupants (Borges *et al.*, 2004; Myles, 2004). This level of infestation was not consistent across the island; drywood termites were absent from rural areas of the interior.

**Figure 1 Distribution pattern of the drywood *Cryptotermes brevis* termite in Angra do
Heroísmo district and in Biscoitos, December 2004 (based on Borges *et al.*, 2004)**

In 2006, inspections revealed that infestation was more severe in S. Miguel Island, and particularly in the historical centre of its major town, Ponta Delgada (Myles *et al.*, 2007). Results from other studies (Ferreira *et al.*, 2007) confirm that the two most common types of wood typically used in building construction (*Cryptomeria japonica* and *Eucalyptus* spp.) are among the species favoured by the *Cryptotermes brevis*. In addition, these are the two species that support higher levels of egg production and termite survival (Guerreiro *et al.*, 2007).

Given that termite infestation has reached such a level that it cannot be completely eradicated, these statistics emphasise the vulnerability of the local socioeconomic system and the seriousness of the potential threat. Costs of restoration, repairs to damaged property and measures for the prevention of attack and propagation demand rapid intervention by local authorities. These concerns extend to the restoration, conservation and protection of innumerable monuments of historical and cultural value (Borges *et al.*, 2007).

The Termipar Project – Citizen Participation in the Control of Termite Infestation in the Azores

To date, public perception of the risks associated with urban termites has not been systematically surveyed. In addition, there has been little publicity and few requests to civic authorities for property inspection. This indicates a general lack of awareness of both the gravity of the problem and the responsibility for action. Risk management experts, however, feel that the impact of their recommendations on the target population has been weak (Borges *et al.*, 2007). Moreover, previous research (Borges *et al.*, 2004) has demonstrated the existence of a wide gap between what people actually know and what they need to know about termites. This reflects a disjunction in communication between experts and the public.

In reaction to the threats presented by nuclear power, since the 1960s practitioners in disaster management have identified a convergence in thinking between the social, natural and technological sciences. A paradigm shift has occurred which replaces distance between lay and expert positions with a nexus of interacting variables related to the cultural (Lupton, 1999; Lima and Castro, 2005), social (Lima 1998; Sjöberg, 2000), cognitive (Kraus and Slovic, 1988) and emotional (Lowenstein, *et al*, 2001; Slovic *et al.*, 2004) dimensions of risk perception. In parallel, forms of communication that were mainly informative, unidirectional and geared to persuading people to follow experts' prescriptions have been replaced by approaches that are dialogical and bi-directional (Fischhoff, 1995). These bring together the public and risk management experts in a social learning process that fosters mutual trust through recognition of legitimate interests and concerns (Renn, 2005).

The organization and mediation of a risk communication process should embrace the risk perceptions of the public, experts and decision-makers, their beliefs regarding respective roles and actual responses to situations. This research project - Citizen Participation in the Control of Termite Infestation in the Azores (TERMIPAR) - focuses on the involvement and commitment in partnership of interested groups in termite control and the communication network. The aim is to investigate risk communication as a two-way process of social influence and conflict mediation in an efficient management of the pest infestation. The objectives are now outlined and phases of the study presented with key research questions and methodologies.

Objectives

The objectives set for the project are to:

(i)   understand the assumptions and perspectives of citizens, experts, decision-makers and the mass media regarding the consequences of termite infestation, the effectiveness of existing and proposed management strategies, and the potential conflicts between perceptions, concerns, attribution of causes and estimates of risk

(ii)   examine the cultural frames of reference in media discourse and the formation of public opinion in communicating the termite pest problem

(iii)   identify factors underlying public trust and social participation in local communities and the communication of risk management strategies

(iv)   develop, implement and evaluate communication strategies for participation in decision making between the main stakeholders and the public regarding termite control

(v)   devise simple methods for communicating complex technical information, in recognition of perceptions of accountability and trust, so as to avoid misunderstandings between scientists, political representatives, managers and society

(vi)   contribute to the development of a plan for the efficient management of environmental risks by facilitating access by decision-makers and the public to scientific and technical knowledge

Phases of the project

Five key tasks were addressed in the two phases of the TERMIPAR project.

Phase 1 – Characterization of termite risk

(i) *Social response to risk.* In the past six months the project has focused on: the characteristics of state management practices and procedures implemented, and an analysis of the social dynamics stakeholder groups (Figure 2). A number of key issues were addressed: firstly, how do experts interpret risk; secondly, what is the position of environmental problems on the political agenda; thirdly, what policies are officially undertaken; fourthly, what institutional means exist for monitoring environmental risk prevention and mitigation; and, finally, what sort of mechanisms do responsible institutions use to reach different groups in society? For an evaluation of the social response to termite risk, the research team sought to integrate two approaches: firstly, an external focus on the phenomenon as it appeared to the team; secondly, an appreciation based on the public, scientific and institutional modes of interpretation.

(ii) *Risk profiles.* An understanding of the beliefs and values shared by individuals in a given society is essential in determining the level of threat and risk estimation (Bernardo, 1998, p.3). Judgements on risk and coping strategies have to be evaluated for the design of communication devices. Answers were sought to the following questions: firstly, how is a given risk understood by the different groups involved in the situation; secondly, what kinds of information do these groups have about the situation and ways of dealing with it; thirdly, how do different groups estimate the probability of risk exposure, the severity of consequences, and the possibility of eradicating and controlling termite spread to other islands; and, fourthly, the extent to which people are aware that small-scale financial investment can alter agricultural practices and modify the wood processing industry, thereby reducing risk.

These questions have a direct bearing on the role of government in alleviating outcomes and providing information as to levels of public vulnerability to hazards. They also highlight the socio-cultural dimensions of human existence, whereby certain groups may take fewer precautions, trusting in providence and believing that 'everything will be settled with the help of God'. However, the fundamental question remains: who is responsible for what aspects of risk prevention and mitigation? Answers to these core questions inform an understanding of the relationship between risk perception and the attribution of responsibility, and the definition of risk management strategies. This study, therefore, aims to establish how different groups perceive and react to the risk of termite infestation. Interviews and questionnaire surveys were used to establish that relationship.

The significance of the media in shaping Portuguese public opinion regarding environmental issues and the political agenda remains central to this investigation. This has been highlighted in several studies (Almeida *et al.*,1997; Almeida, 2004; Gonçalves *et al.*, 2004) which suggest that although the public attached a decreasing measure of reliability to information from the media, it was still regarded as the primary source and transmitter of information on environmental risks. Nevertheless, and in spite of media intervention, the important question remains as to why the public is less than fully engaged in the control of termites. In this context, key questions posed for investigation focus on: the strategies opinion makers can use to persuade citizens to react to the dual problems of control and management; selecting pressure groups for mobilisation; and developing culturally-specific instruments to enhance public communication in dealing with the termite problem. To answer these questions the research team applied content analysis to newspaper reports, radio programmes, and TV productions.

(iii) *Risk communication factors.* The willingness of citizens and stakeholders to participate in the process of behavioural change, a pre-condition for public responsibility, and development of confidence in the institutions responsible for risk governance is essential. An understanding of the processes involved in the communication of risk to the public is vital for decision-making and conflict mediation, and has a bearing on levels of uncertainty and trust (Eiser and White, 2006; Renn, 2005; Taylor-Gooby, 2004). Hence, it is important to identify spokespeople who are trusted by different sections of the public, and effective communication practices and factors that build trust and confidence. Answers to these questions can inform the style and design of communication instruments and channels as related to specific needs, participation and socio-cultural characteristics in building relationships of trust and sound risk governance.

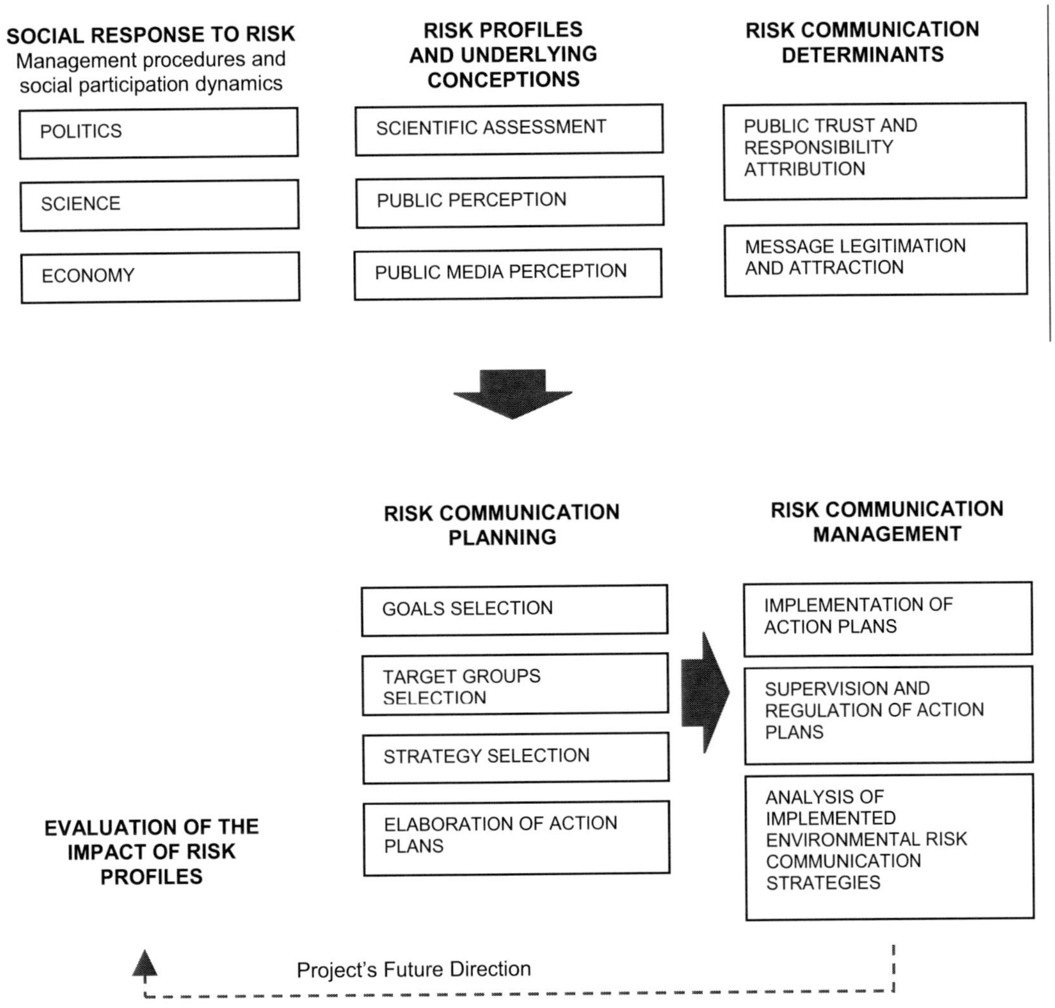

SOCIAL RESPONSE TO RISK Management procedures and social participation dynamics	RISK PROFILES AND UNDERLYING CONCEPTIONS	RISK COMMUNICATION DETERMINANTS
POLITICS	SCIENTIFIC ASSESSMENT	PUBLIC TRUST AND RESPONSIBILITY ATTRIBUTION
SCIENCE	PUBLIC PERCEPTION	MESSAGE LEGITIMATION AND ATTRACTION
ECONOMY	PUBLIC MEDIA PERCEPTION	

EVALUATION OF THE IMPACT OF RISK PROFILES	RISK COMMUNICATION PLANNING	RISK COMMUNICATION MANAGEMENT
	GOALS SELECTION	IMPLEMENTATION OF ACTION PLANS
	TARGET GROUPS SELECTION	SUPERVISION AND REGULATION OF ACTION PLANS
	STRATEGY SELECTION	ANALYSIS OF IMPLEMENTED ENVIRONMENTAL RISK COMMUNICATION STRATEGIES
	ELABORATION OF ACTION PLANS	

Project's Future Direction

Figure 2 Phases of the TERMIPAR Project

These issues were addressed through an analysis and interpretation of the background legislation and political public debate, the measures implemented by government and local authorities, reports from site inspection visits requested by citizens, and the media (local newspapers, radio and TV news) output produced since the pest infestation was first identified in 2002. This task was achieved by an interpretative content analysis of oral and written discourse, using methodologies and instruments appropriate to the task. In addition, to identify the interplay between various factors at the personal level, the perspectives, vulnerabilities and experiences of termite research specialists, decision-makers, pest management specialists from private companies, municipal authorities and target groups from the population were captured using a structured questionnaire.

Phase 2 – Intervention strategies and practices

The second phase of the project relates to the implementation of communication strategies pertaining to the management of risk perception and communication. It aims: firstly, to provide information about termite risk and ways of handling it; secondly, to assist people in learning forms of action for coping with termite infestation; thirdly, to contribute towards public recognition of competence and fairness in institutions; and, finally, to promote participation in conflict resolution and decision making processes related to risk.

Obstacles and resistances to the flow of communication have been identified in an earlier phase of the project. The stated objectives of the case-specific and targeted communication processes are to: provide information; promote behavioural change; offer experts, decision-makers and stakeholders the possibility of sharing perspectives; and implement and regulate risk management processes in accordance with agreed institutional compromises. Important questions are raised for resolution: firstly, how to negotiate so as to ensure that all participants are involved in the decision-making process; secondly, how to get participants to sign-up to the aims of intervention; thirdly, how to mobilize the NGO's experience and knowledge of environmental issues in the mediation between individuals and groups in decision-making processes; and, finally, to identify and agree regulation mechanisms for monitoring processes and their social impact on groups and risk mitigation. Although the time required for evaluation extends beyond the scope of the project, the eradication of termites in the Azores demands the development of regulation mechanisms to secure the continuity of communication processes identified in this project.

Where Do We Stand Now?

Phase 1 of the project continues and has already uncovered issues associated with the low impact of scientific knowledge and legislation on personal behaviour in dealing with termite infestation. This section explores more fully the social aspects and dimensions of 'pest governance'.

Institutional measures and control

In the past six years, the effects of pest infestation on economy and heritage have triggered scientific research. However, knowledge gained on the risk source and efficacy of mitigation strategies have not resulted in the intended social outcomes due to the absence, at a regional level, of effective measures for mitigation, control, prevention, and dissemination of good practice. To deal with that situation, a mission team comprising representatives from different government departments was created and charged with developing a programme of pest management. The programme devised a set of integrated recommendations for stakeholders. These encompassed:

(i)   information about the sources of risk and the strategies for management
(ii)   support and technical advice to the populations at risk
(iii)   strategies to mitigate and control the source of risk
(iv)   legal measures for prevention, disinfection and removal of previously-infected waste (Borges, 2007)

Despite the diversity of these recommendations, political engagement was restricted to the financial support of scientific studies (Borges and Myles, 2007), provision of a short technical course to train inspection workers, and drafting legislation for the attribution of financial support connected with the rehabilitation of buildings. It also facilitated building inspection when required by citizens. However, financial support from government is restricted to families with a gross salary of 413 euros per person (minimum national salary) and is removed when at least two individual members of the family have a gross salary in excess of that threshold. However, the difficulty experienced in designing a management structure for coordinating operations suggests an absence of the political will to control this environmental threat, notwithstanding its social priority. Consequently, in the absence of clear guidelines, it becomes difficult for experts to assume responsibility and for citizens to understand what action they should take and from whom they should seek support.

Contrary to the intentions of the Mission Group which identified the responsibilities of the state and municipal authorities, the current situation is limited to a somewhat piecemeal case-by-case response and depends heavily on the awareness and engagement of individuals, including their financial ability to support remedial work. Government measures are targeted mainly at underprivileged people; many buildings of considerable importance from the viewpoint of heritage are vulnerable. Furthermore, the main political thrust is directed at citizens' and private companies' responsibilities for detection, treatment, recovery and waste management, rather than the coordination of measures for prevention. In this respect a situation of risk privatisation emerges which increases the state of vulnerability within the social system. In particular, the absence of control in the transport of wood between islands can lead to the dispersal of termites elsewhere in the archipelago. Although the complete eradication of termites from the Azores is impracticable, evidence concludes that losses from *C. brevis* can be reduced if effective mitigation practices and more stringent inspection of imported goods are initiated.

Public information

Although incomplete, the content analysis of media reports indicates that, in contrast to radio coverage, local periodicals and television broadcasts have presented extensive coverage on termite infestation. Characteristically, they have introduced stakeholders to readers and viewers and represented the diverse viewpoints of home-owners, scientists, pest managers, private companies, and politicians. In contrast, radio programmes have featured reports from scientists. As yet, however, audience research statistics for each of these media are not available, thus hindering a comprehensive interpretation of their particular roles in the formation of public opinion.

Research has investigated and identified the main source of information for homeowners (Borges *et al*. 2007; Borges and Myles, 2007). This comprises a user-friendly book that specifies practical methods for managing termite infestation in Azorean buildings in the three main affected islands (Borges and Myles, 2007). In addition, workshops - a communication strategy based on a bottom up curricula construction with great flexibility in content and which facilitates interaction between the public and the scientist - have been organised for the public. Such workshops need to be sensitive to place-specific and deep cultural differences in economic relations and group dynamics. These events have provided an opportunity for representatives from government departments to meet stakeholders and debate issues in a local setting.

Economic sectors and private initiative

As yet, the full economic impact of termite infestation and its social consequences have not been determined. It seems likely, however, that agriculture and the wood processing industries will experience change with the substitution of termite-resistant tree species in home construction (e.g.

Cryptomeria japonica and *Eucalyptus* spp.). Even though these changes were recommended in the *Programa de Combate às Térmitas nos Açores* (Anonymous, 2004), the lack of financial incentives and training programmes has retarded progress. Evidence from the workshop programme, however, indicates that leading wood processors have expressed an interest in such measures, but in only one of the three most heavily infested islands. Likewise, as yet, only two local pest control companies are conducting termite control operations using non-specialised termiticides available on the international market (Borges and Myles, 2007). In this context, further training is needed and the use of environmentally-sensitive pesticides merits investigation. Finally, in the absence of specific regulations governing the movement of timber, including import and export, local transport companies need to be made aware of their role in termite infestation and its spatial diffusion.

Final Considerations

This research programme is on-going. So far, evidence confirms that lack of effective interaction between the main stakeholders - government, civic, commercial and individual - presents a significant barrier to the control and eradication of termite infestations in the Azores. It points to the need for more stringent regulation, the development of place-specific and culturally-sensitive solutions, and strategic partnerships between stakeholders in combating the challenges presented by termite infestation.

References

Almeida, J.F. (ed) 2004. Os Portugueses e o Ambiente - Resultados do II Inquérito Nacional. Oeiras: Celta Editora

Almeida, J.F., Lima, A..V., Nave, J.G., Casanova, J.L. and Schmidt, L. (eds) 1997 *Inquérito nacional - Os portugueses e o ambiente*. Resumo 2001. Lisboa: Observa

Anonymous 2004 Grupo de Missão para Estabelecer um Programa de Combate às Térmitas nos Açores - *Programa de Combate às Térmitas nos Açores*. Unpublished Report

Bernardo, F. 1998 'Percepção pública de riscos e planos de intervenção', in Santos, M. A. and Silva, D.S. (eds) *Risco e gestão de crises em vales a juzante de barragens*. Lisboa: Nato and LNEC

Borges, P.A.V. 2007 ' Introdução', in Borges P.A.V. and Myles, T. (eds) *Térmitas dos Açores*. Lisboa: Princípia

Borges, P.A.V., Lopes, D.H., Simões, A.M.A., Rodrigues, A.C., Bettencourt, S.C.X. and Myles, T. 2004 *Relatório do Projecto – Determinação da Distribuição e Abundância de Térmitas (Isoptera) nas Habitações do Concelho de Angra do Heroísmo*. Universidade dos Açores: Ciências Agrárias

Borges, P.A.V. and Myles, T.G. 2007 *Térmitas dos Açores*. Lisboa: Princípia

Borges, P.A.V., Myles, T.G., Lopes, D.H., Ferreira, M., Borges, A., Guerreiro, O. and Simões, A. 2007 'Estratégias para combate e gestão das térmitas nos Açores', in Borges P.A.V. and Myles, T. (eds) *Térmitas dos Açores*. Lisboa: Principia

Eiser, J. R. and White, M. P. 2006. 'A Psychological approach to understanding how trust is built and lost in the context of risk', in *Social Contexts and Responses to Risk Network (SCARR), Working Paper, No. 12*. [Internet]. < http://www.kent.ac.uk/scarr/>. [Accessed 22nd May 2007].

Ferreira, M., Myles, T.G., Borges, A. Guerreiro, O. and Borges, P.A.V. 2007 'Consumo de madeiras e produção de partículas fecais pelas espécies de térmitas açorianas da família *Kalotermitidae: Kalotermes flavicollis* e *Cryptotermes brevis'*, in Borges, P.A.V. and Myles, T. (eds) *Térmitas dos Açores*. Lisboa: Principia

Fischhoff, B. 1995 Risk perception and communication unplugged: Twenty years of process. *Risk Analysis*, **15**, 137-145

Gonçalves, M. E., Delicado, A., Domingues, M. and Raposo, H. 2004 *Novos riscos, tecnologia e ambiente.* Relatório Final, OBSERVA, ISCTE

Guerreiro, O., Myles, T.G., Ferreira, M., Borges, A. and Borges, P.A.V. 2007 'Voo e fundação de colónias nas térmites dos Açores, com ênfase na *Cryptotermes brevis',* in Borges, P.A.V. and Myles, T. (eds) *Térmitas dos Açores.* Lisboa: Princípia

Kraus, N. N. and Slovic, P. 1988 Taxonomic analysis of perceived risk: modelling individual and group perceptions within homogeneous hazard domains. *Risk Analysis,* **8**, 435-455

Lima, M. L. and Castro, P. 2005 Cultural theory meets the community: worldviews and local issues. *Journal of Environmental Psychology,* **25**, 23-35

Lima, M. L. 1998 Factores sociais na percepção de riscos. *Psicologia,* **12**, 11-28

Lowenstein, G. F., Weber, E. U., Hsee, C. K. and Welch, E. 2001 Risk as feelings. *Psychological Bulletin,* **127,** 267-286

Lupton, D. 1999 *Risk.* New York: Routledge

Myles, T.G. 2004. *Report on termites in the Azores with emphasis on Cryptotermes brevis and its control.* Unpublished

Myles, T.G., Borges, P.A.V., Ferreira, M., Guerreiro, O., Borges, A. and Rodrigues, C. 2007 'Filogenia, Biogeografia e Ecologia das Térmitas dos Açores', in Borges, P.A.V. and Myles, T. (eds) *Térmitas dos Açores.* Lisboa: Principia

Renn, O. 2005 *Risk Governance. Towards an integrative approach,* White Paper No 1. Geneve: International Risk Governance Council.

Sjöberg, L. 2000 Factors in risk perception. *Risk Analysis,* **20**, 1-11

Slovic, P., Finucane, M., Peters, E. and MacGregor, G. 2004 Risk as analysis and risk as feelings: some thoughts about affect, reason, risk, and rationality. *Risk Analysis,* **24,** 1-12

Taylor-Gooby, P. 2004. 'Psychology, Social Psychology and Risk', in *Social Contexts and Responses to Risk Network (SCARR),* Working Paper, No. 3 [Internet].<http://www.kent.ac.uk/scarr/>.[Accessed 22nd February 2007].

LIBRARY, UNIVERSITY OF CHESTER

Undergraduates Push for a Carbon-Neutral Field Course!

Duncan Reavey, Joan Whibley and Hannah Connon
University of Chichester

Abstract

University undergraduate students have taken the initiative to offset carbon dioxide emissions from their travel to overseas field courses. Results are a new 70-tree organic apple orchard and a new 300-tree native hedgerow planted at a nearby country centre. However, the processes that led to this outcome were seeded by the carefully considered actions of university tutors in providing a thought-provoking task on the outward flight, a casual statement in a campfire conversation, prior sourcing of trees and a pre-arranged site for planting. Even so, as far as the students are concerned, everything was a result of their initiative. Subsequent coursework planned by tutors for these same students to deliver environmental education to primary school children at 'their' orchard is likely to reinforce the affective benefits of the original plantings. Here we explore the learning approach used, the benefits of this approach to the students and the wider community, and lessons learned about the practicalities of the initiative. The initiative sits somewhere between the formal curriculum and voluntary activities. We begin to consider some of the tensions and the opportunities this raises.

Keywords   Carbon neutral, tree planting, student-led, environmental education, ownership of end product

The Official Line

It started around a campfire on a Lanzarote beach. A few days before, Adventure Education undergraduates had the chance to do a short task on the aeroplane - calculating the levels of carbon dioxide emitted as a result of the field course, mostly from the air travel. But on the beach someone began to talk about whether we should offset this by some positive action that uses up the carbon dioxide we had produced.

Heated debate and careful thinking followed, but a month after the group returned to UK, we saw a result. A new organic apple orchard of 70 fruit trees, some of them rare Sussex varieties, was planted at the Aldingbourne Country Centre (www.aldingbournetrust.co.uk) by University of Chichester students (Fig. 1).

Figure 1
Once a field, now an orchard (and the barrows of manure helped)

As well as benefiting Aldingbourne's clients (adults with learning disabilities undertaking horticultural training), we then invited local school children to visit the Country Centre in the autumn to find out more about the rare varieties of apple. Half day sessions for Year 2, 5 and 6 classes from local schools were led by University of Chichester undergraduates from the same degree course, keen to develop their own skills in environmental education as they led storytelling, apple tasting, apple bobbing, biodiversity sampling, mapping and a lot more.

What Worked, What Didn't (But Don't Tell the Students)

That's the official storyline, but what really happened? For some time tutors have grappled with the dilemma of whether or not to run field courses abroad. So far we have argued that useful learning coming from students working in unfamiliar and challenging environments (lava fields, craters and lava tubes, surf and reefs, and so on) was more beneficial than anything we would achieve by restricting activities to our own backyard. Environmental costs are, we'd argue, offset by the benefits of us producing effective outdoor educators who would have a powerful impact far and wide for decades to come.

But the task on the aeroplane was no accident. The hint that got the conversations going on the beach was slipped in by a tutor, and again it was no accident that it happened in an informal, out-of-hours setting. Tutors did nothing to fuel discussions, though provided facts in response to questions from students (Note that the tutors appeared to be more focussed on the *cerveza* than the conversation about climate change). We were not surprised when students decided to plant trees to offset emissions - after all it's been touted as a way forward for years (e.g. Carbon Neutral Company, 2007) - and were happy to provide support when asked. Throughout, the students did not realise that tutors had already pencilled in a time for possible plantings (to keep it free from coursework), found a location, booked minibuses to get students there, and arranged for the purchase of young trees. As far as the students were concerned, everything was a result of their initiative, and tutors were simply helpful facilitators as students moved their ideas forward. After a long discussion, they decided among themselves that it should be optional to get involved.

Table 1   The cost of 'our' orchard. (We assumed two trees per student offset the CO_2 emissions from their travel to the Lanzarote field course)

	£
60 organic apple trees @ £6.80 each	408.00
70 buckle ties @ £1 each	70.00
delivery	58.75
10 rare variety trees@ £15 each	150.00
delivery	23.00
70 tree stakes @ 95 p each	66.50
Total	**£776.85**

They realised there would be a cost beyond giving their time. Some asked for the actual costing of the planting so they could decide how much cash they should contribute personally. Planting an organic orchard isn't cheap, especially when using rare and organic apples which fit in with the priorities of

Aldingbourne Country Centre. Our 70 trees cost £776.85 (Table 1). Of course, students could have offset their CO_2 emissions by getting cheaper trees that grow bigger (not expensive rare or organic apples!). In the circumstances tutors decided it was not essential that student contributions covered the full cost price and we sourced alternative funds to make up a shortfall. It was agreed that students should contribute whatever they wished as individuals and that the size and number of contributions would not be broadcast. All would have the chance to take part in the plantings whether or not they paid anything. Not surprisingly, but disappointing all the same, only a minority of the students contributed financially though passing the money to a student representative would have been easy to do.

Double Take?

We dared to do exactly the same thing the next year. If anything, the tutors looked even more closely into their beer in an attempt to give greater ownership to the students, but the conversations and outcomes (and the tutors' background preparations) were very much the same. This time we planted a 300-tree native hedgerow alongside the apple orchard. Surprisingly, this second cohort of students had not picked up from the previous cohort any knowledge of the orchard planting the year before. The cover was almost blown by a member of the Aldingbourne staff, but a tutor changed the subject just in time. The hedgerow cost around £360. More students contributed to the financial cost, but still not more than half.

Changes for Next Time

We are returning to Lanzarote, but we have listened to student feedback. Once again we will work hard to ensure that our students have ownership of the initial idea for the project. Once again we will work behind the scenes to set up a project that is worthwhile and sustainable. We will certainly be open to alternative solutions they suggest (e.g. purchase of two energy efficient light bulbs by each student for use in student houses?) though the affective nature of the experience would be far less than the digging holes, shifting manure, and planting trees in sticky mud and soaking drizzle. We are considering adding £10 per head to the cost of the field course to ensure that any proposal is financially viable if we are not able to source alternative funds. At the moment we would not propose to tell the students about this 'climate change levy' of our own - we would prefer students to opt in to paying a personal contribution once they have considered the issues, and would accept any additional voluntary contribution.

Benefits of the Learning Approach to the Students and the Wider Community

Recent research has questioned the benefits of tree planting *per se* as an approach to offsetting carbon dioxide emissions over the long term. However, we believe that sensitive tree planting can have a range of additional benefits. While these vary according to location and context, they include:

- change in presence and abundances of wildlife species (important for effective functioning of an aspiring organic setting like Aldingbourne)
- a contribution in a small way to the conservation of rare crop varieties (another important principle for Aldingbourne, where practicable)

In our case, planting at a centre for adults with learning difficulties had a variety of unusual additional benefits including:

- creation of new teaching resource for use by clients in their horticultural studies
- providing a source of organic fruit for sale in the centre's shop (thus providing income for this educational charity)
- developing the students' teamwork and communication skills as well as raising practical awareness of disability issues

Further benefits come from having trees planted personally by those directly responsible for the CO_2 emissions. These include:

- better awareness among students of the science of climate change issues and ways our personal actions contribute to the problem
- development of vocational and generic skills that can be applied in a range of contexts and career development
- affective learning, which leads to increased interest, attention, concern and responsibility. We believe this is greatly enhanced by the students' view that planting the trees was their own initiative. In due course, having the students lead environmental education activities for children in 'their' orchard and 'their' hedgerow is likely to enhance these affective benefits

Which of these benefits matters most? It is difficult to say, though perhaps our mission in the university focuses our attention on the developing attitudes of the students. So how did they respond? We asked open questions about students' views on the orchard project three months after the planting Answers were diverse and emphasised both the functional and the emotional. Typical responses were:

I think it's morally a really good thing to do, which makes some absent minded people think. And makes the interested people think a bit more.

Got us thinking in an interesting and easy way to understand … very hands-on and enjoyable.

A brilliant idea …… fantastic and made even more worthwhile seeing the heartfelt appreciation of those we helped.

Figure 2 Satisfied undergraduates and clients of the Centre after the planting

However, others added:

> Don't rely on us to do it … force us all to pay … add the cost to the cost of the trip.

> I feel I must mention that if this solution were left entirely up to us students to organise,
> I fear it might not have had such wide participation.

Subsequently, we asked students involved in planting 'their' orchard and 'their' hedgerow whether the tree-planting experience had affected, firstly, their perception of sustainability issues; and secondly, their personal action to live more sustainably in the subsequent 18/6 months. Though there has been only a small response rate so far, students have highlighted and/or demonstrated:

- increased personal reflection on their personal environmental impacts
- greater awareness that individual lifestyle choices can contribute to making a difference and greater willingness to change
- some genuine behavioural change in some areas (though none has planted any more trees)

Diverse undergraduate reflections 6 months or 18 months after tree planting include:

> Everyone seemed to understand why they had spent the morning digging holes in a cold field. After this, everyone has thought a lot more about their carbon debt even if they haven't acted on it after arriving at a destination after a flight. The concept is definitely well embedded in all our minds. I personally have informed many people how we repaid our carbon debt … many people have seemed interested in the concept.

> Although I still want to travel I'm going to make sure I do something to repay the environment.

> It has definitely changed my perceptions and opinions on the use of non-sustainable fuels. Every time I fill up my car, I'm not really thinking about the cost but rather how much has been thrown out the back of my exhaust pipe. However I accept that there are some things in this life I can deal with and sort out and there are some things I can't.

> The experience has also changed my behaviour to an extent. I recycle a lot more (although how much that helps environmental conservation is up for debate, it appears). The camp I work at insists on using paper plates and cups. I have my own cup with me, so I use that to save on the waste.

> Planting the trees in itself has not made me more aware of the issues. Rather, the media bandwagon and plethora of airtime that this issue has received since then has increased my perception of whether we can cope with a sustainable lifestyle in western society… Through my awareness I have started to make small changes, but not anything near a sustainable lifestyle.

> Personally I'm not entirely convinced that one group of people planting trees can make much difference, but it definitely can't hurt.

> I think for me, the tree planting was more of a 'quick fix' for the trip to Lanzarote. I haven't changed my lifestyle because or since then. I do, however, have to say that I have always led (or tried to) an environmentally positive lifestyle.

> Personally I think this issue can only be fixed by individuals and individuals only … Since we have planted the trees, I have sadly not been as great as I could have been. I have sadly flown to Australia and back to work there. Although I have planted trees in Australia and worked in nature reserves preserving their endangered wildlife, the point is I flew and contributed towards global warming. Given my first comment, I could sound like a hypocrite, but now that I am back I am most certainly

going to be 'greener' and I am now currently looking at personal ways to reduce my carbon footprint. I feel as though I have helped the environment in both countries, but I have also created lots of damage. It is so easy to fly, drive and not even think about the damage or effect we cause and create, but my mission is to now change my personal contribution and also to commit myself to introducing my friends and family into sustainability and their carbon footprint and how they can change this.

Is the Learning Approach Appropriate?

Typically, university colleagues from Chichester and elsewhere have commended the tutors for the careful behind-the-scenes facilitation of this project. It is clear that allowing the students to feel this was their own initiative increased their motivation and encouraged engagement. However, we remain a little uncomfortable about being not entirely open with the students. This is an interesting tension which we have not yet resolved. Is it really 'skilful teaching' as some of our colleagues describe it? In due course we will ask a small number of students, rather than risk losing the apparent continuing benefits of students regarding the project as their own.

Volunteering – A More Rapid Route to Sustainability Education in the Universities?

Typically, changes in university curricula are slow to happen. However, we demonstrate here how a good idea has been put into action almost immediately. One reason is that it was not a formal part of the curriculum written into course documentation. Instead, it was a voluntary initiative of students to which they could opt in or out. As such, we were helped by the support of the university's volunteer office which was able to contribute discretely to the administration and to the funding of the project using money dedicated to helping students carry out volunteer activities in/for the community. By using volunteers who owned their own project, we have shown a way of achieving a rapid change in understanding. We believe this is a more rapid response to a sustainability challenge than achieved by many conventional tutor-led changes to courses or to university policies. Extra-curricular activities and external influences are increasingly recognised as one of the most effective ways of students learning for sustainable development (Elliott, 2007; Sjerps-Jones, 2007). While linked more closely to a particular university course than some volunteer activities, our case study carries many of the features that make extra-curricular volunteering so effective for learning and for personal growth.

Extending the Approach to Trainee Teachers

Affective experiences in the outdoors are an important prerequisite for many before they are ready and/or willing to engage fully in learning about environmental and sustainability issues (Boyle *et al.*, 2007; Reavey, 2007). In this, Adventure Education undergraduates are not typical university students. Most already have a love of the outdoors from years of climbing, kayaking, sailing, surfing, caving and more. A greater challenge comes from engaging students of other disciplines. We have found that trainee primary school teachers, for example, have a surprisingly poor knowledge and understanding of environmental issues, and a disappointingly low motivation to make change happen.

We surveyed a typical cohort of 2nd year undergraduate trainee primary teachers at the University of Chichester in 2006 (n=93; 93% female; 66% aged under 25). We repeated questions from opinion poll surveys of the UK general public conducted at about the same time so that we could compare our data. While 57% felt climate change will affect their lives (public: 48%) and 85% thought human-made causes contribute most (public: 71%), only 44% felt climate change is one of Britain's most important issues (public: 53%). Only 7% felt they knew a lot about climate change (public: 23%). Only 18% named the gas that most contributes to global warming (public: 30%). 71% thought changing personal behaviour would make a difference (public: 54%) and 95% claimed to be prepared to change (public: 85%). However, compared to the public, fewer would spend money insulating homes or installing more efficient heating (56% versus 92%), use less energy at home (83% versus 92%), buy more expensive but more energy-efficient products (28% versus 82%), buy local food and pay more for it (34% versus 77%), fly less (12% versus 62%), pay more for flying (9% versus 51%), and pay more for petrol (9% versus 37%).

In a classroom-based lecture for trainee primary teachers, each of 100 students estimates their CO_2 emissions from their daily commute from home to the university and back [crudely, 1kg for every five miles driven per car, divided among passengers]. Each adds their own estimate to the running total of the class, typically giving a total of around 0.7 tonnes CO_2 for around 100 students to attend campus each day. This is an eye-opener for tutors as well as students. For example, if we're serious about cutting carbon emissions, shouldn't we reduce the number of days each week when students are required on campus? However, only one or two students ask after the lecture what they can do to offset the emissions. Expecting whole cohorts of 100+ busy trainee teachers to volunteer time and money to offset carbon emissions is not likely to be successful. Instead, we plan to use the tree-planting approach to provide an affective experience to start them thinking, giving us a foundation on which to build later in their training. We believe this is important for the students who have not had these kinds of experiences so far in their lives. We want them to experience the sticky mud, the soaking drizzle and the barrow loads of manure.

Choosing dates in late October is no accident. But we also want them to have the satisfaction of planting trees that we believe many will return to visit in times to come. The camaraderie, and a campfire and barbecue afterwards, will help. The activity will be voluntary, but in a timetable slot usually taken up by a conventional lecture and workshop that will no longer happen. We anticipate a full attendance because of the positive pre-publicity we will provide. Around 250 student teachers will together plant a Battle of Britain Memorial Woodland at Tangmere, with trees and tree-guards funded by a Lottery grant, and each student will be on-site for three hours. Those who can't make that event will be invited to help plant flower bulbs in the communal gardens of a sheltered housing scheme and community allotment as well as presenting energy saving light bulbs to elderly clients of Age Concern after a solar boat trip. Yes, they will learn some sound science on the way (about climate change, biodiversity, organic burgers, food miles, and a lot more). And yes, though it will seem informal, even casual, it will be carefully and subtly choreographed. Even the beer.

Tensions and Opportunities at the Interface Between the Formal Curriculum and Voluntary Activities

Competing demands of coursework, part-time jobs to supplement loans and energetic social lives can mean that volunteering and sustainability are not usually high up the list of student priorities. Only a dedicated minority will make the time for a regular commitment to the local community or environment. Financial constraints and a packed syllabus means there is little time or money to organise activities not central to the curriculum, whilst past funding guidelines for student volunteering stipulated that projects should not be a compulsory part of the curriculum. However, by working with lecturers to identify volunteering activities of some relevance to their course or future employability, students may be inspired to participate actively, particularly if it becomes part of a group project with a social element. Formal recognition through optional modules or encouraging real-life case studies may get sustainability on to the university timetable but there is a danger that by becoming part of the curriculum, environmental education becomes a sterile exercise rather than a fun, hands-on, spontaneous event. So, although these off-site events as described here may not bring about immediate lifestyle changes, they may spark an interest or awareness amongst students that may be followed up later - the organic orchard might bear fruit in more ways than one.

References

Boyle, A., Maguire, S., Martin, A., Milsom, C., Nash, R., Rawlinson, S., Turner, A., Wurthmann, S. and Conchie, S. 2007 Fieldwork is good: the student perception and the affective domain. *Journal of Geography in Higher Education*, **31**, 299-317

Carbon Neutral Company 2007 *Carbon Offsets and the Process of Carbon Offsetting* [Internet]. <http://www.carbonneutral.com/pinfo/carbonoffsetting.asp>. [Accessed 20th August 2007].

Elliott, J.A. 2007 Acting sustainably: encouraging and crediting student engagement with sustainable development. *Planet*, **18**, 43-48

Reavey, D. 2007 Love it! Learn it! Live it! *Environmental Education*, **84**, 4

Sjerps-Jones, H. 2007 Engaging students with sustainability issues. *Planet*, **18**, 40-42

Acknowledgements

This initiative has benefited considerably from the enthusiasm and efficiency of Lucinda Healey and clients of Aldingbourne Country Centre.

It's Time We Changed the System

Bruce Nixon
Sustainability Consultant

Abstract

This workshop explores the issues underpinning our current unsustainable societies and explores how we can change these to achieve a more sustainable future. Today, collectively, we face the biggest crisis in recent human history. Every day there is more worrying news about global warming and the potentially devastating effects of climate change. People everywhere will be affected, especially the poor. But sustainability is much more complex than climate change. Sustainability embraces global economic and social justice, respect for different peoples and ending violence. A sustainable world protects Planet Earth and all its diverse life forms. We face degradation of the earth, increasing pollution, and growing shortages of fossil fuels, food, land and water, already leading to conflicts. If everyone consumed like Londoners, we would need three planets. Millions live in poverty and fear generated by out of control violence. The threat of nuclear proliferation and international terrorism grows. There can be no peace without justice. To a large extent the West has exported its problems. It is unaware of its violence and the hostility its foreign policies have generated. Why are people, governments and corporations so slow to understand and respond to this crisis?

At the root of the crisis is an unsustainable economic system and its underlying values, driven by consumerism; rich, powerful elites; large corporations; global institutions and governments too much influenced by big business; militarism and military economy; over use of 'science'; uncritical belief in global sourcing and globalisation as the way to end poverty; and GDP as the measure of progress. To change things, we need to see the whole system and make sense of it. We are part of a living system, an intricate, interacting relationship between the planet and all living things upon it. Living systems hit back hard if not respected. We need to transform our mindset and how we live and approach solving problems. It may seem a daunting prospect, but human beings created the situation and we can change it. People change the world. This paper will throw light on the situation, challenge, identify the key underlying issues, give positive models, offer ways forward, including how Gandhi's thinking may help us, and suggest key actions we need to take.

Keywords   Sharing expertise, capacity building for sustainability, changing behaviour, celebrating success, challenges for the future

Collectively, We Face the Biggest Crisis in Recent Human History

It is a wonderful world. For many of us in developed countries, things have never been better. However there always is an upside and a downside. The world faces what looks like the biggest crisis in recent history. Recent floods in England have brought it home to us. In an economy heavily dependent on fossil fuels, there are already signs of emerging fuel and food shortages and rising costs. Every day there is more news about the potentially devastating effects of climate change. People, especially poor people, and business will be affected everywhere.

The *Stern Review*, commissioned by the UK government, sets out devastating consequences and warns that the global economic cost of climate change to business and governments could eventually reach 20% of world GDP if nothing is done. The scientific consensus is that the environmental crisis is man-made, largely caused by CO_2 and methane. Even if, as some argue, it's mainly down to solar activity, we still face a crisis. However, it's much more complex than climate change. The two big issues are:

   (i)   the effects of continuing economic growth on the planet
   (ii)   poverty

Ecological harm and poverty are inseparably linked. A cynic might say that we, in the 'west', are only waking up as climate change starts to threaten us, no longer just other people! Climate change is a symptom of a malaise that is broader and deeper. We need a moral and spiritual re-awakening. As Meg Wheatley says 'It's our turn to help the world' (Nixon, 2006, Foreword).

We are consuming and destroying the planet's resources at a rapidly growing and unsustainable rate

Putting it bluntly, it's greed, taking more than our fair share. London's 'footprint' is huge: London requires 125 times its surface area to provide its needs. If everyone consumed like Londoners, we would need three planets, five at the Los Angeles rate of consumption! Yet most countries aspire to this unsustainable 'western' way of life.

We face degradation of the earth, increasing pollution, and growing shortages of fossil fuels, food, land and water, already leading to conflicts. We need to abandon the idea that we are the masters, everything is there for us to exploit and other peoples and species are relatively unimportant. The West has exported much of its manufacturing, with all the pollution problems, to poorer, developing countries less able to operate sustainably.

Human beings are part of an intricate, interconnected relationship between Planet Earth and all living things upon it. If we want a sustainable future, we need to treasure and protect this ecological diversity of which we are a part. Satish Kumar (Kumar, 2004), like Gandhi, says the whole of nature is holy; all life has intrinsic value. Everything is inter-connected and we are who we are in relationship to others. We need to respect different peoples, cultures and religions - and abandon violence in every form - thought, word and deed - including violence towards other animals and the planet of which we are a part.

Sustainability must include global economic and social justice

As we learn from the media and travel more, we become more aware of how fortunate we are and that it is very different for the majority of people in the world who are relatively or very poor. If we want a secure and peaceful world, in which people and business can flourish, it means tackling extreme poverty. We know the facts: millions live in poverty and face starvation; they are afflicted with disease much of which could easily be prevented or cured. Millions of children die. If they survive, their lives are stunted by lack of education and opportunity. Many live in fear and insecurity generated by violence.

There can be no peace or security without global economic justice and respect for difference. The big powers are largely unaware of their violence, militarism and the extent and effects of their huge military economies. They created nuclear weapons, leading to proliferation and the threat of nuclear annihilation. Unfair, colonialist foreign policies create hostility and contribute to growing international 'terrorism'. Other countries see clearly the contradictions between our postures and actions. State violence, imposing our way, looking for a quick dollar, and bullying are not the answers to these problems. We need greater awareness and a change of consciousness.

Problems cannot be solved at the same level of consciousness that created them. *(Albert Einstein)*

Growth isn't working well as a means of reducing poverty

Vandana Shiva (Shiva, 2005) calls it *mono-thinking* and *mono-culture* - the idea that one size fits all - an unproven approach that flies in the face of economic history (Ha-Joon Chang, 2007). It is rapidly fuelling climate change, global warming and degradation of the soil and ecological system. Rapid economic growth is inefficient and far too slow in reducing poverty. Between 1990 and 2001, for every $100 of growth in the World's per person income, only $0.60 contributed to reducing poverty below the $1-a-day level (New Economics Foundation Report, 2007). In the UK, growth benefits the richest 10 percent of the population, 10 times as much as the poorest 10 percent. In India, well over 100,000 farmers have committed suicide since 1993, largely as a result of debt and failed GM crops.

Instead of reducing poverty effectively, rapid economic development is making a growing elite of super rich people vastly richer, raising the incomes of middle classes and wealthier nations. We see this most graphically in Mumbai where, despite rapidly growing prosperity, 55% of the population live in slums. It is creating problems everywhere, most of all in poor countries and poor areas of rich countries, like northern England. Certainly some countries, such as Singapore have been lifted out of poverty, but in many cases, like our own, not through free trade. (Ha-Joon Chang, 2007). They enjoyed protection whilst developing their own economies. Adam Smith (1776) is misquoted by advocates of unrestrained free-market capitalism.

Although Britain is the 4th or 5th largest world economy, this success comes at a cost

This success is partly based on London's attractiveness as a place for billionaires to live and make money and the City's financial expertise including tax avoidance and evasion, off shore tax havens and money laundering. The already wealthy are best able to benefit from this expertise and ingenuity in getting richer. Taxes are 'perverse' in the sense that rich people pay least proportionately and can pay for the best advice on avoidance. Disproportionate wealth contributes to the problem of unaffordable housing in London and similar problems in the countryside.

Average total pay for a chief executive at £2,875,000, is more than 11 times the increase in average earnings and nearly 20 times the rate of inflation as measured by the consumer price index. The ratio between bosses' rewards and employees' pay has risen to 98:1, up from 93:1 a year ago - meaning that the pay of a chief executive is almost 100 times more than that of a typical employee. 10 years ago the pay differential was 39 times that of the average worker. Women bosses are left behind (The Guardian, 2007). There is a sharp contrast between the pension schemes of top directors and employees many of whom face uncertainty. 26 top directors will retire on annual incomes of between £500,000 and £1m plus; over 100 more can look forward to retiring on at least £200,000 a year and 80 FTSE firms retain final salary schemes for all or some of their directors whilst axing them for staff (Labour Research Department, 2007).

The happiest countries tend to have more equal income distribution

Like the USA, UK ranks low amongst countries with advanced economies on many measures of wellbeing and happiness: prison population, crime, child poverty, teenage pregnancy, alcohol and drug abuse, literacy, political alienation and upward social mobility. Social mobility in Britain is worse than in other advanced countries and declining - educational attainment is strongly related to family income (London School of Economics and Sutton Trust; *http://www.suttontrust.com/newsarchive.asp_a016*).

There is an escalating gap between rich and poor in UK and between North and South. The wealth gap is the widest in 40 years. There is a polarisation between the wealthy in Southern suburbs and the poor elsewhere (Joseph Rowntree Foundation, *http://www.jrf.org.uk/knowledge/findings/*). In the seventies, incomes were getting more equal; now the reverse is happening. There is growing poverty in the countryside: rural services are declining; and the rural population is ageing, as the young people cannot afford to stay there and migrate to towns. We now produce only 60% of our food (Commission for Rural Communities, *http://www.ruralcommunities.gov.uk/*). Fresh food production needs to be local and we are destroying its source. Sourcing for 'lowest cost' externalises and does not count social, health and environmental costs. It destroys communities and affects wellbeing. Low prices are an illusion when we, the taxpayers, pay for 'cleaning up' and our wellbeing suffers.

What We Need to do as Individuals, Organisations and Governments?

We are drifting. The disastrous Iraq war has diverted attention and vast resources from the biggest issues we face, namely the environment and poverty. We need to stop being in denial or behaving as if we are powerless to make any difference.

Reversing climate change

Rich countries bear the heaviest responsibility; we have the technological capability and the means. The 'west', seen by other nations to have created the problems, needs to show the way, set an example and help poorer nations develop their own ways out of poverty and into sustainability. We need to rapidly cut rising global CO_2 emissions, largely resulting from using fossil fuels, to a sustainable world average of 3 tonnes per person. Methane emissions, mainly coming from cattle and refuse dumps, and emissions from high-flying aircraft, especially damaging, are also rising. Wealthy people and countries pollute most; poor countries and people are worst affected. People in the UK and EU account for 12.5 tonnes (average) of greenhouse gases per capita per year and this is rising; the US and Canada some 20; China four; India two and sub Saharan Africa less than one ton (Goodall, 2007). The EU and UK, need to get down to three tonnes, perhaps aiming for two, an 80% reduction; some argue 90%. Individuals are directly responsible for 44% of CO_2 emissions - indirectly far more. Ultimately, the fairest solution may be a personal CO_2 or footprint limit for every person on the planet.

We all need to take action

The momentum is gathering. Large business is responding and new enterprises providing sustainable technology and housing are starting up. But people, business and government are doing too little, too slowly, to avoid catastrophe. UK government strategy is not joined up. Transport policy and strategy seems extraordinarily inconsistent with sustainability. Government schemes are too timid and its relatively cautious targets are unlikely to be met. International aviation and shipping emissions should be included in targets. Government has ample scope to make an impact and set a good example - the way it operates its buildings, its investments in infrastructure, sourcing decisions and the influence it can bring to bear on suppliers. The individual behaviour of ministers and civil servants such as how they travel is another opportunity. Enabling measures are needed to remove obstacles. Government needs to take bold measures to reward the sustainable, penalise the unsustainable, make sustainability affordable for everyone, nurture nascent green technology, help make 'going green' profitable and give local communities more responsibility and more say. Governments also need to bring about level playing fields internationally, global and regional frameworks, so that nations and corporations can act more responsibly without severely disadvantaging themselves (SIMPOL, *www.simpol.org.uk*).

Everyone has to take personal responsibility and use their purchasing and 'people' power. It is no good waiting for or blaming others - like government or business. Both will respond to a groundswell of opinion, consumer demand, purchasing power, lobbying and the political pressure of citizens. Governments and political parties want to gain or stay in power and not alienate powerful vested interests. Without understanding the full implications, political leaders sometimes jump at grand, easy solutions like bio-diesel or nuclear power. They want to avoid actions that may harm the economies or competitive advantage of their nations, alienate big business, deter investment or affect employment. Corporations face similar difficulties. These are complex problems, not easy to resolve. We also need to press for changes in the unsustainable economic system in order to remove the obstacles to change.

Why Are We, Our Governments and Corporations So Slow To Respond To This Crisis, When Effective Action is Urgently Needed?

Why do we continue to produce and drive heavily polluting cars, fly as usual when there is an emergency comparable to World War II? Why do years of successive summits and concerts, Live Aid and now Live Earth, produce so little action? Putting vested interests before global welfare, denial and resistance to change are part of being human. It is hard to admit that a mindset in which so much has been invested is not working.

It's the system!

The root of the crisis is an unsustainable economic system and its underlying values. Most people have good intentions and care about less fortunate people and the world our children and grandchildren will grow up in. But businesses cannot respond sufficiently and survive in the current system. We need whole system thinking. It is little use trying to change things by addressing symptoms. Problem solving rarely works except in the context of the whole system, as the history of

New Labour may be said to demonstrate. Instead, we need to try to see the 'whole system' and address the key underlying issues. We are part of a living system which cannot be controlled like a machine. Living systems are unpredictable and hit back hard if not respected, as climate change and 'the war on terror' show. We need to transform the way we live and how we try to solve our problems. We need more humility and a spiritual perspective (Gandhi, 1938; Kumar, 2004). We also need a better balance of male and female energies.

We are caught up in an unsustainable system driven by powerful elites, large corporations, militarism and a military economy and global institutions not sufficiently representative of all countries. The World Bank, World Trade Organisation and IMF are dominated by governments too much influenced by big business interests and uncritical belief in global sourcing and globalisation as the way to alleviate poverty and GDP as the measure of progress. The current global system was developed by politicians and economists committed to a free-market system (unlike their predecessors, such as John Maynard Keynes, Kenneth Galbraith and, today, Jeffery Sachs). Consumerism was created in the 40s alongside easy credit and built-in obsolescence, to keep US factories producing. It is a major obstacle to sustainable enterprise and sustainable living. Have we been duped? Are we 'slaves' to a system working largely for the benefit of corporations and wealthy elites?

A key part of the present system is debt, the debt money system, 'out of control financial markets', perverse taxation and massive tax avoidance that puts up the burden of personal taxation. Only 3% percent of money is issued by government or central banks. The rest is debt money created by banks, which thus make large profits. This, it is argued, fuels consumption, needlessly puts up the cost of public infrastructure, creates a large burden of debt and hardship - both for poor people and poor countries. Financial markets cause instability for businesses, create a focus on the short term, share values and short-term profitability and thus diverting attention away from the long term and stewardship. Taxes are 'perverse' in the sense that rich people pay least proportionately and they do not sufficiently encourage sustainability and enterprise. Taxes are also complicated and relatively inaccessible without expensive advice. Because almost all of us have a stake in this system, we need to look at it with an open mind. Also, to avoid damaging legitimate interests, changes need to be carefully considered, moderate and gradual, starting with the those that would make most difference and do least harm.

We keep talking about these issues but do not take action. James Robertson (Robertson, 1998; Robertson, 1998) puts forward comprehensive proposals for reform of the money system, taxation, including sustainable taxation and tax based on common resources - such as land whose value may increase enormously as a result of public investments and un-extracted fossil fuel energy - and a citizen's income that would replace current complicated, expensive and inefficient measures to alleviate poverty.

If we are to have sustainable lives and sustainable enterprises, we need to create a sustainable global economic system. We need a new economic system and reformed global institutions, focused on the key priorities: meeting human needs; protecting the planet; tackling poverty, disease and violence worldwide; giving everyone the chance to enjoy meaningful work; and healthy and fulfilling lives. These aspirations are expressed in the UN Millennium Goals. There is a growing consensus that to achieve them, *fair*, not *free*, trade is needed, giving each country, with support from richer ones, the freedom to develop its own unique way. It may seem a daunting but human beings created the system and we can change it. People change the world.

Gandhi's Thinking Can Help Us in the 21st Century

Arguably, he was the most successful and influential change agent of the 20th Century. He got the British out of India and has influenced some of the greatest leaders of our time! He called his campaign 'All rise' meaning everyone gains; everyone takes responsibility. He understood the need to find out what it was like for ordinary people and created a growing groundswell before embarking on change. His key principles are truth and non-violence. If only our politicians, journalists and business leaders would try them! It takes courage. *Truth* means diligently seeking and speaking the truth. He called his life an experiment with truth.

Non-violence applies to all life on the planet, non-violence in thought, word and deed. For him it meant resisting oppression non-violently through love. He understood that ends do not justify means: it is no use trying to end violence with violence. Today, especially 60 years after Hiroshima, we need non-violence as a worldview - non-violence in bringing about change; dealing with international conflicts; non-violence towards nature and women. The World Council of Elders is a step in this direction.

Gandhi would argue that the imposition of factory agriculture and inhuman conditions in factories is violence. He would regard nuclear energy as violence towards nature. He was also a strong advocate of modest consumption, local food and the primacy of localisation, especially devolving power to local communities to determine their futures. (Gandhi, 1938; Nixon, 2007).

What We Need To Do?

> The world has enough for everyone's need, but not enough for anyone's greed. (Mahatma Gandhi)

Principles for sustainability:

- reduce
- reuse
- recycle
- repair

Individuals need to transform the way we work and live. It means consuming less; minimising use of non-renewable and non-biodegradable resources; avoiding toxic substances and products that cannot be recycled. That rules out UPVC and nuclear power both of which use toxic processes and produce non-biodegradable waste. Obviously, we need to be flexible and make balanced decisions, as advised by Friends of the Earth and The Centre for Alternative Technology. For business, a prudent 'going green' strategy can make money, but you may want to do it anyway for ethical reasons. Businesses that respond to the challenge and growing customer awareness can enhance profitability and competitive position.

A model for sustainable businesses is Interface, a worldwide company producing floor coverings, fabrics for airliner seats, speciality chemicals and interior architectural products. Interface's principle is 'do well by doing good' says, septuagenarian, Ray Anderson, Chairman and founder of Interface. Companies like this are a minority but their number is growing, often from small beginnings. Sustainability is at the heart of Interface. Interface aims for a 'zero footprint' and is more than half way there. It has helped create a host of sustainable companies in its supply chain. Go to Interface's website to find out what they have done (www.interfaceinc.com). Another commercial example is Sherwood Energy Village, created on a former colliery site, providing a site for industry, housing, recreation and education. It exemplifies energy efficiency, promotion of renewable energy and biodiversity in all its developments. There are plenty more, large and small. A good national model is Sweden which aims to be nuclear free by 2010 and oil-free by 2020 (*Ecologist*, March 2007, pp.42-45).

How Does Radical Change Come About in Complex Systems?

We are part of a complex interacting system. How do complex systems change? Transformation comes about in a multitude of ways. To find our way in a complex, uncertain, world we need the collective creative intelligence of everyone in organisations and communities. If global institutions are to succeed, they need to adopt the same principle and be inclusive. The heroic leader, alone, or a small elite group of people, cannot possibly know what needs to be done. Transformation requires everyone to take leadership. Meg Wheatley defines leaders as 'anyone willing to help' (Berkana Institute, *http://www.berkana.org/resources/justourturn.html* and *www.berkana.org*; *http://www.congregationalresources.org/InterviewWheatley.asp*). To facilitate this process requires a different kind of leadership that both inspires and enables.

Change occurs through increased awareness, new understanding, realisation of a vital need. Ultimately, a change of consciousness leads to decision and action. Then the inherent creativity and inventiveness of human beings comes into play. There is a tipping point. Change comes about through evolution and revolution. Change happens, as we are beginning to see, through the small actions of millions of 'ordinary' people. It comes about through relationships and millions of conversations. Transformation *also* comes about through totally new ways of thinking (Albert Einstein), chance discoveries, (Charles Darwin, Sir Alexander Fleming), and inventions of geniuses, (Sir Timothy John Berners-Lee, inventor of the world-wide web). Extraordinary, visionary leaders like Mahatma Gandhi, Martin Luther King Jnr, Nelson Mandela and Winston Churchill give expression to the hopes of millions and change the course of history.

This may be seen as a somewhat optimistic view. Human behaviour is complicated. Lessons from changing organisations may be relevant but changing society is much more challenging. People say one thing and do another as polls reveal. Consumer behaviour is influenced by the desire to flaunt one's wealth and make a statement about who one is. So people may put photovoltaic panels or turbines on their roofs, sited where they can be seen, to display their affluence. Yet they may continue to live an unsustainable life style in most other respects - consuming, flying and driving as usual. On the whole, it is poorer people who actually live most sustainably! They simply consume less.

Then there is the 'cool factor'. According to some recent research, young women actually prefer young men who flout the green mantras. How can we make being green 'cool' or get people above that superficiality, is the big question? There is much debate about how to do this: *carrot* or *stick* or *communications* as they were used in World War II or maybe all three? But clearly governments will have to intervene by much more effective means if there is to be sufficient change in a world where affluence and aspirations are rising rapidly all over the world (BBC Radio 4, Analysis 19th July, 2007).

Can we really create a spiritual renewal? It would be a tragedy if things had to get very much worse before we acted sufficiently. In case you become discouraged by the seeming impossibility of radical changes, the key thing to remember is that *everyone* changes the world and that .....

> Whatever you do may seem insignificant, but it is most important that you do it. (Mahatma Gandhi)

I also find this quotation by Martin Luther King encouraging:

> Everything that is done in the world is done by hope.

How Can an Individual Help Bring About a Sustainable System?

The need for systemic change will be recognised as it becomes more apparent that efforts to solve the major problems are not working:

> The right way to do things is not to persuade people you're right but to challenge them to think it through for themselves. (Noam Chomsky)

There are five spheres in which we need to work: in *ourselves,* the source from which change begins; our *family and home*; our *community*; our *workplace*; the *world*.

> Be the change you want to see in the world. (Mahatma Gandhi)

- *First, be the change:* start by deciding who you are; what really matters to you, your values, purpose and beliefs. Why are you on this earth? Feel your embarrassment about being thought soft. Trust your instincts. Follow your energy and do what you feel passionate about. Be clear about what is most important to you and prioritise. Own up to your deficiencies and take responsibility for them. It all takes courage
- *Be a leader of transformation:* in your workplace, whatever it is. This means being an agent of change
- *Finally, we all need to be global citizens!* Lobby big business, national government, regional and global institutions. Play a constructive part in your community. Press for local, national and global change. It is our responsibility to be fully aware and informed, continuously

> Activism is my rent for living on the planet. (Alice Walker)

Getting sustainability into the heart of your workplace and society – an approach that works

Here is an approach that works. It applies to your workplace or community, however large, including changing the world. Base your approach on what you know about how complex systems change. Change comes about in emergent as well as structured, planned and designed ways. It comes about informally through relationships and conversations:

- *Prepare the ground for change:* change will come about when the time is right, when there is widespread recognition of the need and a groundswell has begun
- *Have a philosophy of seeing the opportunities in the big issues:* personal opportunity, business opportunity and opportunity to learn. Spread a philosophy of seeing the opportunities. The most successful people and enterprises are adept at seeing and grasping opportunities
- *Build trusting relationships:* see the best in everyone. Make friendships; get alongside the CEO; build partnership and alliances; have conversations; learn and inform yourself - be open hearted and open to contrary views. Be a trustworthy mentor. By listening to people, you will support and empower them
- *Network:* connect with people. This opens you up to synchronicity, the benign, unpredictable forces in the universe that will support you and give you what you most need. Start conversations. Connect people with one another. Be an enabler. This helps them to make things happen
- *Work with the energy for change:* with like-minded, 'crusading forces' in the organisation but also with resistance; respect and listen to the 'restraining forces'
- *Co-create:* adopt a whole system approach to change. Get the whole system into the room. Bring together key stakeholders, the full diversity of the system or your part of it. Help people articulate dreams and hopes. Help them identify and address the key issues that are getting in the way. Through engaging diversity, the most appropriate strategies for change will emerge and the successful implementation is more likely
- *Develop leaders of leaders who know how to enable:* help people articulate their dreams, and be clear about purpose and outcomes
- *Take inspiration from positive models:* every day there is exciting news about new initiatives. Study what works and enlarge it; find good models inside and outside your organisation. Interface, the international carpet company, and Sherwood Eco Village have already been mentioned example. Another example is the steps Eurostar is taking to go green (Railway Magazine, 2007).
- *Review progress regularly:* help people, evaluate and learn from what is working and not working, key issues in the system that need to be addressed and what needs to be done differently. Celebration, giving and receiving appreciation, fuels good energy and supports people in recovering and learning from setbacks and difficulties. Include yourself
- *Sustain yourself:* seek balance and prioritise your own wellbeing. Do things with mindfulness. (Thich Nhat Hanh, 1999) Give yourself time for renewal and reflection. Surround yourself with supportive friends *who will tell you the truth* - even if you may not like it

For articles on processes you can use to facilitate change, go to *Writings* at *www.brucenixon.com*.

Go radical. Here are some key campaigns that may help bring about system change. Google to get their websites:

- *Agriculture instead of agribusiness:* local food; food diversity; ending the degradation of planet earth and bio-piracy. (The Soil Association; Vandana Shiva; Garden Organic)
- *Company law reform:* enabling alternative forms of company ownership; widening the duties of directors to embrace the interests of all stakeholders, the environment, society as a whole (Centre for Tomorrow's Company; Rabbi Michael Lerner)
- *Ending poverty - Global trade - a radically new framework:* reforming unrepresentative global institutions like the World Bank, World Trade Organisation and International Monetary Fund and the unfair, unsustainable trading system they impose. (World Development Movement; NEF; Christian Aid; Oxfam; War on Want; Action Aid)
- *Ending violence as a way of resolving conflict:* personal, national and international. Strengthening nuclear non-proliferation, ending nuclear armament, abandoning nuclear power generation

and a Peace Council replacing the Security Council (CND; Friends of the Earth; Greenpeace; Oxfam; Oxford Research Group; Peace Pledge Union). Road Peace aims to end violence on roads

- *Localisation:* particularly giving power to localising communities and the production of local healthy food production and distribution; restoring high streets and village communities. (New *Economics Foundation*; Local Works; the Soil Association; Friends of the Earth; Garden Organic; Slow City; Slow Food; and Transition Towns)

- *Reforming democracy:* making it work better, decentralizing, unlocking local democracy, giving more power to local communities, making parliament more representative; giving greater power to parliament to scrutinize, inquire and prevent the executive withholding information and over-riding the wishes of citizens - e.g. going to war on a flawed premise, nuclear power and weapons. (One World Trust; Pressure Works; Charter 88; and New Politics Network's '*Power to the People*'; *WriteToThem.com*)

- *Sustainable buildings, cities, communities and transportation:* refer to Herbert Girardet's book *Cities People Planet - Liveable Cities for a Sustainable World* and website *www.underthesky.org.uk*; Transition Towns; and Transport 2000

- *New Economics and monetary reform:* reforming the debt money system; perverse and unsustainable taxation and the power of financial markets. (James Robertson - *working for a sane alternative* www.jamesrobertson.com; *new economics foundation*; Tax Justice Network; SP Worldwide International Simultaneous Policy Organisation; and Christian Council for Monetary Justice)

- *Wellbeing:* better measures of progress than GDP and continuing, unsustainable economic growth. (New Economics Foundation; UN Development Programme; and Millennium Development Goals)

Predictions

I don't like making predictions. I am sure to be wrong. Scaremongering is not constructive. Human beings are too creative to let total disaster happen. However, if we do not act decisively these consequences are likely, the first five predicted by Stern (*http://www.occ.gov.uk/activities/stern.htm*) who estimated:

- the global economic cost of climate change to business and governments could eventually reach 20% of world GDP if nothing is done
- a more than 75% chance of global temperatures rising by 2-3 % over the next 50 years and a 50% chance they will rise by 5%
- rising sea levels could leave 200 million people permanently displaced
- up to 40% wild life species could face extinction
- by 2080 sea levels round Britain are expected to rise 26 to 86 cm; flooding in coastal areas will be 10-20 times more likely; rainfall will decline by 50% leading to drought though wetter winters
- a world economy based on fossil fuel may be severely damaged leading to unemployment and possible collapse
- soon, everywhere, there may be mounting fuel, energy, water and food shortages and rising prices
- increasing social conflict, violence, war and terrorism
- rising numbers of refugees fleeing from countries where people are desperate, starving and sick
- diseases are likely to spread from other continents

If we take the necessary action now, we may become a little less affluent, but all of us, the poor majority on the planet, ourselves, our children and our children's children are likely to be a lot happier. Maybe, the universe is trying to teach us a lesson. Maybe too, we need to pay more attention to the lessons of history.

To Sum Up: What You Can Do

- be the change - get your own house in order
- see the crisis as an opportunity and grasp it
- make your own life sustainable - that includes YOU - save yourself as well as the planet!
- follow the mantra - reduce, reuse, recycle, repair
- aim to make your business and home carbon neutral
- reduce your 'footprint'
- buy sustainable goods; choose sustainable, ethical suppliers or help them so to become
- get well informed and fully aware: for example, read George Monbiot, look at the *New Economics Foundation* and use the *www*
- lobby political and business leaders and influence others

References

BBC Radio 4, 2007, Analysis, 19th July

Berkana Institute. [Internet].<http://www.berkana.org/resources/justourturn.html>. and [Internet]. <http://www.berkana.org>. [Accessed 3rd September 2007].

Commission for Rural Communities. [Internet].<http://www.ruralcommunities.gov.uk/>. [Accessed 3rd September 2007].

Council of Elders. [Internet].<http://www.theelders.org/elders/>.[Accessed 3rd September 2007].

El Diwany, T. 2003 *The Problem with interest.* Kreatoc Ltd.
[Internet]. <http://www.theproblemwithinterest.com/index.html.>. [Accessed 3rd September 2007].

Gandhi, M.K. 1938 *Hind Swaraj or Indian Home Rule.* Ahmehdabad: Jitenda T. Desai

Gandhi, M.K. 1969 *Eleven Vows.* New Delhi: National Gandhi Museum and Library

Goodall, C. 2007 *How to live a low-carbon life.* London: Earthscan

Guardian 29th August 2007 www.guardian.co.uk/executivepay/0,,543498,00.html

Ha-Joon Chang 2007 *Protecting the global poor, Prospect magazine,* **136,** July

Kumar, S. 2004 *No Destination - an autobiography.* Totnes: Green Books

Labour Research Department [Internet]. <http://www.lrd.org.uk>.[Accessed 5th July 2007].

Monbiot, G. 2006 *Heat, how to stop the planet burning.* London: Penguin Press

New Economic Foundation Report 2007 *Growth isn't working,* January 2006. [Internet]. <http://www.neweconomics.org/gen/uploads/hrfu5w555mzd3f55m2vqwty502022006112929.pdf>. [Accessed 3rd September 2007].

Nixon, B. 2007 *All Rise - how Gandhi's thinking can help us in the 21st Century.* Schumacher Institute Challenge Paper.

Nixon, B, 2006 *Living System - Making sense of sustainability.* Gloucestershire: Management Books 2000

Rail Magazine 2007. July 4-17, 35-37

Robertson, J. 1998 *Transforming Economic Life - a Millennial Challenge.* Totnes: Green Books

James Robertson J. *Working for a sane alternative.* [Internet]. <http://www.jamesrobertson.com.>. [Accessed 3rd September 2007].

Sherwood Energy Village. [Internet]. <http://www.sev.org.uk/about-us/energy-village-concept>. [Accessed 3rd September 2007].

Shiva, V. 2005 *Earth Democracy.* London: Zed Books

SIMPOL Simultaneous Policy Year *Globalising peace, justice, sustainability and prosperity.*[Internet]. <http://www.simpol.org.uk>. [Accessed 3rd September 2007].

Smith, A. 1776 *An Inquiry into the Nature and Causes of the Wealth of Nations.* London: Methuen and Co. Ltd

The Guardian 29th August 2007
[Internet]. <http://www.guardian.co.uk/executivepay/0,,543498,00.html>. [Accessed 3rd September 2007].

Thich Nhat Hanh 1999 *The Miracle of Mindfulness.* Uckfield: Beacon Press

Woodward, D. 2008 Of 'Misguided Notions' and Misguiding Nations: the Growth Report, Poverty and Climate Change. *Political Quarterly,* **79,** October-December

For more resources, go to Writings at <http://www.brucenixon.com>

In addition, useful sources of help include:

- Getting your house in order [Internet].
  <http://www.imc.co.uk/news/professional_consultancy_article.php?item_id=654&issue=18>.
- Envirowise - waste and water [Internet]. <http://www.envirowise.gov.uk/>.
- The Carbon Trust - energy and carbon [Internet]. < http://www.carbontrust.co.uk/>.
- Global Action Plan <http://www.globalactionplan.org.uk/>.
- ACORN <http://www.iema.net/acorn/>.
- Good Corporation {Internet]. http://www.goodcorporation.com/>.

GIS as a Basis for Sustainable Development in South African Municipalities

Elizabeth Hicken
Kingston University

Abstract

South Africa adheres to global sustainable development initiatives and acknowledges through its 2006 draft publication *A Strategic Framework for Sustainable Development in South Africa (NFSD)* (see the end of the paper for a list of acronyms) that the Government through various Acts has a legally binding obligation to take responsibility for the environment, the economy and society. In applying these principles as an emerging nation, South Africa is subject to the experiences inherent in Third World development and the multitude of obstacles that this may deliver. It is a large country with a varied and conflicted history, and the implementation of sustainable principles at ground level has placed substantial pressure on local governments to facilitate the globally originating commitments through their daily activities. The Constitution specifically places a duty on municipalities to fulfil their mandate of service provision to local communities in a sustainable manner. However, the *NFSD* acknowledged in 2005 that debilitating incapacities at local government level were the result of service delivery failures and, therefore, these objectives were not being met. This paper explores whether the Earth Observation technology Geographical Information Systems (GIS) could make a significant contribution to rectifying these inconsistencies, and facilitate sustainable development within the local governance sector in South Africa.

Keywords   GIS, sustainable development, South Africa, geomatics and GIS, African municipalities

Introduction

Sustainable development is a concept born from the need to address a number of global concerns related to the growth of human population and associated destructive development patterns. Global shocks, climate change and natural disasters as well as environmental degradation and poverty are the most relevant of these issues, and a succession of world-wide guiding documents have been produced since 1992 to address these concerns. South Africa adheres to global sustainable development initiatives like *Agenda 21* and the *2015 Millennium Development Goal* targets, and acknowledges through its 2007 publication *A Strategic Framework for Sustainable Development in South Africa (NFSD)* (see list of acronyms at the end of the paper) that the Government has a legally binding obligation to take responsibility for the environment, the economy and society.

In applying these principles, as an emerging economy, South Africa is subject to the experiences inherent in Third World development, and the multitude of obstacles that this may deliver. It is a large country with a varied and conflicted history, and the implementation of sustainable principles at ground level has placed substantial pressure on local governments to mediate sustainable practices through their daily activities. The country is in a transitional phase where significant macro challenges exist in the form of income inequalities, extensive poverty, and an unproductive settlement pattern which includes informal and slum areas. Furthermore, at a local level, South Africa exhibits development issues such as lack of adequate water, sanitation and electricity supply to settlements, poor land use management as well as a lack of basic housing, health, other services and infrastructure (DPLG,1998). This has created socio-economic and developmental issues as well as biological degradation.

The conclusions drawn in this report were compiled from a series of primary interviews conducted throughout the South African Provinces and collection of secondary information based mainly on primary research. The persons interviewed were selected to represent the full spectrum of stakeholders in the geomatics value chain in South African municipalities in all Provinces.

South Africa is run by three inter-connected tiers of Government whose jurisdictions range from national to local level. The Presidency, as leader of National Government, has been required to disseminate responsibility to a local government level to meet its strategic objectives. Although this has increased pressure on municipalities, it also means they are empowered to respond with resourceful solutions, which are providing opportunities for both the private and public sectors. The evident and growing investment in Information and Communications Technology (ICT) in the South African public sector signifies its contribution to growth and development during this phase. Information Systems, as a component of ICT, are a key element of the administrative foundation of municipal management, and specifically Geographical Information Systems (GIS), which provide information within a spatial context.

The *1998 White Paper on Local Government* (CC, 1996) identifies three systems of parallel municipal activity - institutional, political and administrative - within the context of transformation, cooperation and development. Since the primary objective of local government is the service of communities, a robust administrative foundation could produce not only the efficient daily delivery of municipal functions, but also provide support against political, natural, socio-economic and other unexpected shocks, thereby contributing significantly towards sustainable development.

Background

South Africa is home to an estimated 47 million people, about half of whom live in rural areas. It comprises nine Provinces which in turn are separated into District Councils or Metropolitan Areas (urban conglomerations). This study primarily focuses on the District Council (non-metro) regions whose administrative unit is the Local Municipality, and which together function as *Local Government*. The South African Constitution (Chapter 3, Section 40) stipulates that although all three spheres of Government (National, Provincial and Local) are connected and interdependent, they are also distinctively autonomous in their operations. Furthermore, within Local Government, the objectives of the District Council may or may not be those of the Local Municipalities whilst their resources may or may not be shared, depending on the particular Province and region. Overall, and within the South African legislative framework, local government is guided by the National *Department of Provincial and Local Government* and its strategic objectives.

There exists substantial evidence that the South African Government is committed to the mitigation of development issues at all levels, and the Constitution (Chapter 7, Section 152 1b,c,d) (CC,1996) specifically places a duty on Municipalities to fulfil their mandate of service provision to local communities by setting their objectives so as to:

(i)   provide democratic and accountable government for local communities
(ii)   ensure the provision of services to communities in a sustainable manner
(iii)   promote social and economic development
(iv)   promote a safe and healthy environment
(v)   encourage the involvement of communities and community organisations in the matters of local government

This is a constructive theory. However, in 2005 the *NFSD* acknowledged that the debilitating incapacities at local government level were the result of failure in service delivery which resulted in these objectives not being met (NFSD, 2006). The report further states that these incapacities were a result of the rapid delegation of responsibility to the local government tier, after South Africa's 1994 democratic elections, to integrate National strategies but without sufficient resources or knowledge. Although a number of bodies and initiatives have been established in the interim to assist local government in delivering its mandate and rectifying these incapacities, significant issues and challenges still remain.

The National Spatial and Sustainable Development Operating Frameworks Governing South African Municipalities

The *National Framework for Sustainable Development in South Africa* 2007 is a stakeholder discussion document and precursor to the *National Strategy for Sustainable Development* first conceptualised in 2005, but awaiting completion. As an interim measure, a raft of socio-economic, developmental and environmental Acts and Regulations guide local government in South Africa. The 2001 South African Census recorded 60 District Councils and 262 Municipalities (including all metropolitan areas) which are obliged to produce annual Integrated Development Plans (IDPs) (DLPG, 2000). These are short, medium and long term strategic plans for the successful management and development of the region, and link resources to objectives through comprehensive budgets (DLPG, 2005). The IDPs are the basis for municipal operations and are the main reporting mechanism to the public and higher levels of Government.

The South African *Municipal Systems Act (2000)* states that a Spatial Development Framework (SDF) based on land use management is an essential item of the Municipal Integrated Development Plans (DPLG, 2000). It further acknowledges the assimilation between the environment, development and poverty, placing emphasis on municipalities to deliver services in a sustainable manner (DEAT, 2002). The *Municipal Planning and Performance Management Regulations* (2001), derived from the *Municipal Systems Act*, state that the SDF must 'contain a strategic assessment of the environmental impact of the spatial development framework' (DEAT, 2002; RSA, 2001). Municipalities are concurrently guided by the *1998 National Environmental Management Act (NEMA)* which places responsibility for environmental management at all levels of Government and specifies the framework for Environmental Impact Assessments (EIAs) at project level (Swilling, 2006).

A notable concern, however, is that these strategic environmental assessments are produced as a direct response to developmental plans. In other words, environmental objectives mainly exist at a municipal level as a reactionary (or secondary) device to integrated planning, and environmental strategies are thus not truly integrated into municipal activities - there remains a trade-off (Swilling, 2006). However, the *1998 White Paper on Local Government* (DPLG, 1998) promulgates that: 'Planning for environmental sustainability is not a separate planning process, but is an integral part of the process of developing municipal integrated development plans' (Swilling, 2006).

Through the Presidency, National Government has linked economic development (particularly related to addressing imbalances) to spatial planning through *The National Spatial Development Perspective (NSDP)*(2003) to which all National Departments and Provinces are committed (Aboobaker, 2004). A number of projects have been initiated by Government to implement the NSDP, including the harmonisation of multi-level plans and monitoring techniques to evaluate *the space economy*. The NSDP acts as a guiding framework (Mohamed, 2004) and municipalities are expected to reflect this through their Integrated Development Plans (IDPs). At Provincial level, the equivalents are Growth and Development Strategies.

The Spatial Data Infrastructure Act (54) of 2003 defines the terms relating to the collection and sharing of public data. This is facilitated through the *National Spatial Information Framework (NSIF)* initiative of the Department of Land Affairs. It is acknowledged that spatial information and management is a key focus for local government leading to the creation of a National GIS Strategy (NSIF, 2007). Local Agenda 21 (LA21) is the global initiative which channels sustainable objectives to a Municipal level. LA21 shares parallel objectives with the Municipal IDPs by incorporating communities and environmental awareness more closely into projects and plans.

Notwithstanding environmentally conscious governance, fully established and integrated sustainable development principles and related spatial data management is still not fully evident in municipalities. The main areas of omission are identified as:

- a holistic environmental (biological) management approach decoupled from development (human and infrastructural) objectives
- detailed and standardised specifications for planning data, specifically statistics and geo-information for reporting
- a multilevel, standardised, interoperable and maintained spatial information environment for governance data
- the practical application, monitoring and reporting of legislation and guiding frameworks at local government level

Information and Information Systems as a Sustainable Commodity

The *Knowledge Economy*, based on information, is a modern tertiary economic sector embracing activities that demand highly-skilled labour, such as services, finance and technology (Opoku-Mensah, 2007). The global economy is in transition from an *industrial-based* society to *information* society where information and knowledge (the application of information) are fundamental to competitive economic advantage (Oshikoya and Hussain, 2007; Nyarko, 2007).

At this time of global flux, transparency is a prerequisite to changing realities, and therefore adaptation to environmental change. Transparency can be attained through a reliable and continual flow of information, which improves confidence and reduces uncertainty. Information is the foundation of policy development and therefore intrinsic to decision-making and governance. From a South African perspective, governing activities have been disseminated to a municipal level to enable the National Government to meet its policy commitments. Municipalities and their towns and settlements are required to become increasingly economically self-sustaining and to promote Local Economic Development (LED). Accessibility of Municipal data is critical, both to Government and the community at large. The *Municipal Property Rates Act (No.6, 2004)* specifies that each municipality is to maintain a landholdings database (Yirenkyi, 2006).

However, in many rural areas in South Africa the number of finite ratepayers is low, due to a large indigent population and informal settlement areas. Hence, information needs have to respond to this situation. Although the Municipal Integrated Development Plans provide a sound foundation for charting the course of municipal activities during a year, they are not prepared in a common format that will permit aggregation numerically or representation graphically to National level as the basis for comparison and trend determination. Maps and statistics may accompany, but are not a requirement of, the plans (RSA, 2001). Currently, there are no all-inclusive and integrated methods for feeding available municipal data into a central node from which information can be accessed to inform national policy decisions or to measure performance against targets such as the Millennium Development Goals (MDGs). Such potential can be illustrated by the United Nations Economic Commission for Africa's *MDG Mapper*, an online resource and clearing house for National African statistics relating to the achievement of the Millennium Development Goal targets, which has operated since 2007 (*http://geoinfo.uneca.org/mdg/*).

Dematerialisation (NFSD, 2006) is a concept linked with sustainable development; it is a process which aims to achieve proportionate, equal and maintainable improvements in the quantitative and qualitative lives and environs of communities by using fewer resources. This concept applies equally to information sub-structures where omissions, duplication, inaccuracies and general inefficiencies in the collection, transfer and use of data impede or delay sustainable governance and development. Within a national context, South African Municipalities currently rely on non-aligned information sources and channels ranging from National Census data to *ad hoc* local survey data. Dematerialisation of municipal information processes could improve the quality and timeliness of information transmission to improve decision-making. As the smallest unit of autonomous government, local authorities are ideally suited to act in collecting and transmitting in electronic format socio-economic, demographic and infrastructural data sets. The adoption and implementation of relevant information technologies would enable this process.

Geomatics and GIS: Application in South African Municipalities

Geomatics can be described as 'the integrated approach of measurement, analysis and management of the descriptions and locations of earth-based data' (School of Geomatic Engineering, University of New South Wales). Within this field, Geographical Information Systems (GIS) provides computer programmes that combine relational databases with spatial interpretation through a graphical interface, often output as a map. A GIS typically comprises five interrelating components: hardware, software, data, people and processes. GIS links data to spatial location and enables users to visualise an area in terms of its demographic, ecological, economic, infrastructural and environmental dimensions, and crystallises a person's ability to understand a scenario in the context of space. It translates information in the form of statistics and text into a picture and improves all round comprehension. Hence, it stimulates an ability to respond with faster and more informed decisions. From this picture, data can be added or removed as the situation changes, and so it provides a dynamic platform from which information can not only be visually simulated, but from which trends over time can be compared. Intrinsic to meeting global sustainable commitments like the *Millennium Development Goals* and *The Johannesburg Plan of Implementation* is the application of technologies like GIS.

Recognition of GIS as an *essential*, rather than a *nice-to-have*, tool in public sector administration in South Africa, coupled with the propagation of responsibility at the local level, has motivated National and Provincial Governments to create or increase budget allocations for geographical resources and skills. This trend is echoed on a continental level, particularly within the context of sustainable development in cities, as the United Nations acknowledged in *Agenda 21*. For instance, paragraphs 132 and 133 of the *Johannesburg Plan of Implementation* recommend countries to 'Promote the development and wider use of earth observation technologies, including satellite remote sensing, global mapping and geographic information systems...' and to 'Support countries, particularly developing countries, in their national efforts...' to achieve that objective (United Nations World Summit on Sustainable Development, 2002).

Since governments and municipalities are assigned specific geographic areas to govern, the relationship between the community and their spatial location and environment is critical (Mbense and Nkosi, 2006). Building on the concept of earth observation technology within the realm of local administration and service delivery, particularly in the developing world, there are a number of key features which emphasise the significance of electronic spatial data as a basis for sustainable decisions and actions:

- *Spatial Conceptualisation* of an area's status, issues and potentials is enabled and enhanced through GIS which provides a platform on which to make more informed decisions and create future scenarios. GIS can also incorporate live or regular updates thus producing data relevant to immediate planning and action
- *Land and property data* can be singled-out as the primary foundation on which decisions for government are made. The area, boundary, value, sensitivity, use, population characteristics and settlement patterns are what guides socio-economic activities and hence the state of environment, standards of living and economic prospects of a community. Most of a Municipality's Income results from land rates, sales and rentals and studies have shown that 80% of a local authority's business and 90% of its external inquiries are based upon spatial data (Compion, 2007). Municipalities are losing up to 15% of their income because of poor information base management and there exists a direct link between effective land use management and local wealth creation

- GIS, as one type of *Information System*, can be technologically integrated into full municipal administration systems and subsequently linked horizontally to other municipalities or vertically to District, Provincial and National level (or even continental and global). It is also a tool well suited to the internet, particularly in terms of data viewing and transfer
- The substructure of a GIS is a *database* and it facilitates the display of statistical data spatially for analysis. Demographic, infrastructural, socio-economic, environmental, image and other information can be overlaid, compared and trends determined, making it an ideal medium for communicating the MDGs
- GIS is ultimately a *cross-sectoral tool* which can be applied in any department to create process efficiency e.g. property land parcels can be related to rates (local taxation) data, with direct benefit to municipal planning and finance

Currently, the number and size of GIS departments and resources in South African Local Government varies from no skilled staff or no fully functioning systems, to small, but robust, units of up to about three skilled members who maximise GIS potential. Until now, municipal GIS infrastructure and continuity has been dependent upon particular persons committed to driving the process from within the municipality, and is usually limited to a function of specific projects and associated capacity building. Often, however, the turn around time for projects is too long, the projects are discontinued and the GIS infrastructure replaced. Along with a high rate of staff attrition in general and continual administrative re-structuring at all levels, this often creates unsustainable GIS working environments and poor delivery within municipalities.

In terms of local economic development, the most useful application of GIS is in a wide-usage format which is as user friendly as possible, like pension payout points, tourism and for local farmers to access information. Very technical and advanced GIS applications are not currently considered essential in all municipalities, but the rate of adaptation is expected to cascade as benefits are realised in local context.

GIS is only as useful as its weakest link and, in South Africa, this is normally a data issue. *Statistics South Africa* began a spatial data audit in 2006 to assess, collect and make available public data to all levels of government. This along with the *Spatial Data Infrastructure Act* is the main initiative currently governing public sector spatial data management, although neither speak of the urgent need for acceleration in data creation or alignment of data objectives between sectors. The South African Geospatial Analysis Platform (GAP) is one project that has emerged from a recognition of these limitations. This is a common mesoscale framework for sharing economic and development information and is applied as a method to update the *National Spatial Development Perspective* and create corresponding spatial profiles and maps. The basis of the framework is a standardised boundary layer of mesozones devised through spatial economic cluster referencing into areas of comparative size and was released directly to municipalities in 2006.

For the second phase of the project, the goal is a national alignment of economic and social data. The current functional specification is the creation of an integrated GIS platform populated with key human development and environmental interaction variables. The intention for the GIS platform of the GAP initiative is an open source, web-based, municipal exchange network to reduce duplication and software costs, and the supplementation of national and existing municipal data sources with local enterprise data. Although this project is not designed specifically to integrate sustainable development holistically into municipalities, it does aim to provide a basis for the combination of data from multiple levels and sources (CSIR, 2007b). Developments proposed include economic-ecosystem interactions, user feedback, web-enablement and international comparison (CSIR, 2007a).

Primary Obstacles to the Implementation of Integrated GIS in South African Municipalities

These include:

- GIS and Information objectives are not aligned horizontally or vertically (i.e. within Districts and Provinces and between Provinces)
- lack of communication of knowledge and objectives of GIS exists in all directions (i.e. intra and inter-Municipal, District and Provincial)
- GIS resources and budgets are not aligned with objectives
- general understaffing in government and therefore unrealistic workloads
- politics interferes with administrative efficiency and therefore impacts on successful and sustained planning and decisions
- poorly-managed, unstable and corrupt working environments exist in some municipalities
- lack of understanding, support and interest in GIS potential by municipal and other decision-makers
- South African municipalities in general are guided by numerous Acts and Regulations and report to various other levels of Government as well as the community; this can result in information and work overload within a high-change environment
- deficiency and/or inaccessibility in South African-base and other key data and datasets; generally a 'top down' data attitude is inefficient and many data sources are deemed unreliable or politically motivated

Secondary Obstacles to the Implementation of Integrated GIS in South African Municipalities

These obstacles are derivatives of the major obstacles:

- lack of resources (finances, equipment, time)
- incapacity (skills, management, plans)
- lack of a full understanding of Municipal processes and problems by GIS vendor
- lack of integration of GIS into daily activities as a decision-making tool (not only in isolation for map creation) (Mbense and Nkosi, 2006)
- isolation of GIS as an Information Technology function or other department-specific function
- no actual or conceptual definition of where GIS functions originate in a Municipality or who is responsible for driving them (lack of a cross-cutting integrated approach to GIS)
- lack of a broad understanding of GIS and technological uncertainty and resistance by general users
- the perception that GIS is expensive and difficult to use
- local data is not being sufficiently created or maintained

The general miscommunication between municipal needs and the potential of GIS applications often leads to squandered resources where solutions do not fit the problem and implemented systems are not fully utilised or maintained. Many municipalities are considered to have sufficient budgets for items like GIS sections, but the primary obstacles impede the success of utilising these funds efficiently.

Primary Drivers for Improved Municipalities Management Using GIS in South Africa

The principal drivers include:

- *awareness*: a growing recognition from local to global of the power of GIS in successful governance
- *environment*: a rapidly shifting technological society and increased technological transfer in the developing world
- *timing*: deficiencies in current municipal systems and the transitional phase of their development call for solutions (The South African Government issued a public call for participation in August 2007 for a review in the institutional arrangement of Provincial and Local Government which is to result in new and revised *White Papers* by end 2008)(DPLG, 2007b)
- *support*: collaboration from a district through to a continental and even global level is evident and growing; patterns in the similarity of obstacles and potential solutions in local governance is evident in the developing world
- *pressure*: the increase in natural disasters and growing restlessness in local communities due to poor service delivery is speeding up action to implement efficient and lasting systems
- *trends*: Government has acknowledged and continues to promote technology as a method to improve operations (NFSD, 2006)

Currently the main trend in the implementation of GIS in South African municipalities is as one element of a larger Information or Content Management System. Although this means that GIS can be fully integrated into daily municipal functions and made available to a wide range of users with varied skill levels, it also scales up the magnitude and costs of the installation, therefore reinforcing some of the negative perceptions listed above.

Recommendations for Integrating GIS into Local Government in South Africa

Although there are instances of GIS opportunities being implemented in municipalities in South Africa, there is no evidence of successful co-ordination, standardisation or experience sharing. Government intervention can be self-defeating unless there is careful consideration of these elements and a complete understanding of municipal and vendor issues. The South African Government has recently issued a tender for *Total Municipal ICT Solutions* and cabinet approved a policy in February 2007 to implement Free and Open-Source Software (FOSS) in government over the next five years. The current GIS software standard is proprietary IOL, 2007. The key concept for GIS-based systems is an environment which enables the cyclical nature of information feedback for development planning (Table 1).

Table 1 Summary of recommendations for the integration of GIS into local government

Opportunity description	Recommendation

Full information management systems for daily administration

GIS can be integrated as an element of a full Information or Content Management System for the daily running of municipalities. This means that multiple users in various departments with varying GIS skills can utilise the power of GIS on a common platform.	A number of vendors are implementing this in South African Municipalities. A variety of new and existing software can be used in conjunction with this, as well as being accessible over the internet. Existing systems need not be reinvented. Truly integrated systems processes are required, not just random linkages, with GIS as a cross cutting element or the foundation of the system. The Information Systems should create an enabling environment for the IDP process.

Systems before staff

The success in municipal GIS departments is currently a result of key staff members driving the process. While motivated staff are invaluable, systems cannot be dependent upon particular staff members to supply them with energy. Systems need to be in place regardless of the calibre of staff involved.	An agreement and adoption of a common Geo working paradigm including decision-making data flow and exchange amongst the tiers of Government can ensure stability. If GIS systems are results-driven and integrated into municipal operations then their full value can be gained despite a high staff attrition rate.

Systems independency

Municipalities do not generally like to be dependent upon private vendors to continually provide input since this can be disruptive, time-consuming and expensive. However, it has been recognised that a private sector contribution is essential.	By implementing the correct and lasting systems, and being specific about how these need to improve delivery, planning and reporting, Municipalities do not need to be continually referring to the implementing vendor.

Human resourcing and GIS training

The public sector typically offers lower salaries to GIS-skilled staff than the private sector, making it a less attractive work environment. The recruiting process and management of GIS staff can also be flawed if driven by non-GIS managers. If municipalities use proprietary GIS software packages, the associated training is generic and so the full ability of GIS, in terms of matching software to solutions, is lost.	A percentage of GIS staff resourcing and management should be handled or critically analysed by external or private sector persons familiar with GIS staffing. This requires the provision of supplementary GIS training to suit specific municipal needs.

Increase decision-maker awareness - empower technicians

Many GIS departments and personnel are run by managers who do not have a good grasp of GIS and its potential.	Information workshops and demonstrations between managers and technical staff can increase awareness and raise the profile of the GIS section. GIS technicians should be encouraged and incentivised to make suggestions and be proactive.

Increase general awareness through multi-level usage and campaigns

Some municipalities have a small or non-existent presence of GIS; others are limited to knowledge contained in the relevant departments.

Various levels of GIS can be made available to corresponding levels of user in terms of Geo-skills. A range of geo-enabled tools exist which suit very technical to non-technical Users. Many of the more basic tools are free or web-based. Non-technical users can be trained in basic map drawing and querying to free up technical users for more complex tasks. This is not only more efficient but increases general awareness of GIS within the municipality. GIS awareness campaigns by District and Provincial Government assist in raising GIS awareness in general.

Synergise experiences and access support networks – improve co-ordination

Many Municipalities and Provinces are not communicating shared experiences, including problems and successes.

Inter-Provincial and Inter-Municipal GIS workshops, forums and troubleshooting sessions would prove extremely beneficial. The DPLG (South African Department of Provincial and Local Government) has initiated an IT forum. Municipalities need to self-initiate horizontal as well as vertical working relationships across the Government tiers. Provinces need to be supportive in this role and follow suit.

Increase accountability and improve co-ordination

There is currently a lack of evidence of strategic and technical co-ordination between Government units (horizontally and vertically).

Designating and standardising responsibility at all levels will enforce accountability and hence results. The Provincial Department responsible for Development Planning is usually best suited for this role. A dedicated Municipal Strategic Manager guiding Information and Planning, including GIS, would be ideally suited at the Local level.

Efficient allocation of resources – understanding user needs

GIS is application driven; it can be customised and scaled to suit particular user needs and problems. Technology is also a tool to solve particular business problems, not an end in itself. South Africa's unique settlement pattern and institutional arrangement requires customisation of technology and systems. Some municipalities are more strategically placed to aid in the overall development of a Province, depending on their location, community and environmental conditions. Also, many outlying or small municipalities are not attractive places for skilled staff members to work in isolation, and cannot support GIS salaries. A more finite approach to resource allocation coupled with a detailed understanding of an area's particular needs should be approached. Needs across municipalities are similar although each region has its own unique set of issues and opportunities. Solutions need to be carefully designed to suit the particular municipality and the factors which influence its daily activities. Vendors need to pay particular attention to this.

Not all Municipalities require a fully-integrated GIS; but all require some degree of GIS functionality and access to more advanced GIS services at times. For smaller municipalities GIS is better provided as a more basic function of a full information system; in others, a fully functional advanced GIS is required. District, Provincial and Municipal offices should be available to field more advanced requests for guidance and support, especially from smaller municipalities. In certain regions, GIS staff can be shared and GIS projects outsourced or contracted. GIS budget resources could better be used by municipalities to collect new data or conduct local surveys to be fed back into a larger Information Management System, whilst still contributing to the Geo function. For example, online-based Information Systems are not a sensible option in some rural areas where telephone signal can be disconnected up to 50% of the time. Here, the concept of Shared Services is the key, representing more efficient use of a jurisdiction's resources. In certain Provinces this approach has been adopted in the form of Information Sharing and Management Centres.

Static and supporting maps

There exists a role for static maps and profiles like paper map publications and electronic PDF files. Another option is basic online mapping services.

Municipalities benefit from being provided with static map publications and area profiles created at higher levels. These act as a source of reference as well as powerful supporting documentation for motivation and decision-making. For example: District Profiles and Atlases. The best delivery method is CDs of dynamic map programmes for the unskilled user, from which maps can be printed. Current online Mapping Services need to be significantly improved both in terms of internet speed and data profiles.

Spatial and other data micro management

Much of existing municipal data is outdated and difficult to maintain, and has been acquired from a higher level or on an *ad hoc* basis. This top-down approach does not facilitate the efficient management of data at ground level, particularly in informal settlement areas. Statistics South Africa is currently the only legitimately recognised source of population information in the country for governance purposes. Various National parastatal bodies like energy suppliers and large private corporations are equally dependent on local information and are very willing to negotiate data exchange. The integration of socio-economic data is critical for establishing service backlog information. Various existing sources like Indigent Registers can be used as a basis from which to build a comprehensive information platform.

Municipalities should be empowered to collect and maintain their own datasets which, according to a set of standards, could be fed into an aggregated system. The South African census is conducted once every ten years with random and interim surveys to estimate changes in socio-economic and demographic information. Municipalities, as well as businesses, need more updated, relevant and accurate information. A potential revenue stream could be created by selling this information to private businesses. If Statistics South Africa worked even more closely with municipalities, this could help in resolving certain data collection problems. Similarly, cadastral and other local and community data should originate at Municipal level. This information, for example, could be fed online to the IDP nerve centre. A well maintained and referenced data hub linked to data sets for cities would have wide benefits.

Private sector participation

The South African public sector includes private sector procurement and consultation. However, more open, honest and ongoing two-way communication would be beneficial to highlight municipal users' needs and create a more common reference framework. The private sector currently has ambitions for the public sector which are not being met because their efforts do not receive a sufficient or ongoing response.

Capitalising on the expertise and mobility of private vendors and establishing links with the public sector through workshops and shared experience would highlight user needs and inform solutions.

Free and open-source software (FOSS)

The role of FOSS in GIS in South African municipalities is still in transition. There are advantages and disadvantages of both FOSS and Proprietary Software.

Ultimately a combination of FOSS and Proprietary software would be optimal. These systems can communicate with one another if standards like Open GIS are adopted. Unique municipal environments suggest unique solutions. Deliverables should be aligned and made amenable to aggregation to Provincial or National level.

Community involvement and behaviour change

Municipalities exist to serve communities. Lasting improvement in livelihood and environment can only be achieved through the holistic process of improving governance through management systems that accommodate changes in societal behaviour and that are aligned with local economic development. Many areas in South Africa are still party to tribal structures, and local people are therefore party to more than one system.

South Africa's challenges are too varied and complex for the Government, alone, to eliminate them, especially at the current rate of development. In many rural areas which experience extensive poverty, a sense of community and ancient tribal systems still exist. These can be leveraged to create joint goals through awareness-raising and community involvement.

Globalise

Link local objectives to National and Global Sustainable Development agendas and policies by aligning statistical targets.

Leveraging tools like online portals and mappers such as African Data Repositories and UNECA's (United Nations Economic Commission for Africa) *MDG Mapper*.

Linkage of Municipal Activities to Global Sustainability Agendas: Alignment and Measurement

National Sustainable Development principles are not sufficiently entrenched, aligned within South African municipalities or consistently evident amongst technical vendors. However, the *NFSD* includes municipalities (and other public sector entities) as responsible partners in the attainment of MDG Goal 7 to *Ensure Environmental Sustainability* including Targets 9 through 11. A set of global indicators has subsequently been developed to embody these targets. Indicators allow the quantification of otherwise unmeasurable concepts and such numerical feedback enables standardisation, comparison, indexing and trend determination of the status and progress of National development. Since indicators are dependent on the cultural environment in which they are measured, each country is tasked with their own particular compilation of indices. South Africa is making progress in this arena. For example, MDG Target 9 to 'Integrate the principles of sustainable development into country policies and programmes; reverse loss of environmental resources' could be measured through a set of indicators, one of which could be the 'change in protected area as a percentage of total country surface area'. Although the definition of key indicators is at an early stage, appropriate statistical information available by geographical area is ideally suited to graphical representation within GIS.

Conclusion

Technology alone cannot solve environmental, social and economic problems; rather, it is a medium through which to effect transparent reporting on the status and change in issues pertaining to the principles of sustainable development. Societal imbalances and environmental degradation require the direct application of their own particular solutions according to a complex set of causes embedded in cultural, infrastructural, legal and governance settings. Sustainability in the context of this study means self-reliance, and correct information management is critical to this concept. From the perspective of a Third World country, the provision of sound bottom-line planning data is key to sustainable development. GIS, a member of Geomatics or Earth Observation systems, can make a significant contribution to the handling and interpretation of the required information sub-structure. The argument that humanity needs to live a sustainable existence has been won; what now remains is how to achieve this objective.

Acronyms

DPLG: Department of Provincial and Local Government

EIA: Environmental Impact Assessment

EMP: Environmental Management Plan

FOSS: Free and Open Source Software

GAP: Geospatial Analysis Platform

GIS: Geographical Information Systems

ICT: Information and Communication Technologies

IDP: Integrated Development Plan

LA21: Local Agenda 21

LED: Local Economic Development

MDG: Millennium Development Goal

NFSD: National Strategic Framework for Sustainable Development (in South Africa)

NSDP: National Spatial Development Perspective

NSIF: National Spatial Information Framework

SDF: Spatial Development Framework or MSDF (Municipal Spatial Development Framework)

UNECA: United Nations Economic Commission for Africa

References

Aboobaker, G. 2004 *The Presidency produces the National Spatial Development Perspective (NSDP)*, South African Integrated Development Plan nerve Centre. [Internet].
< http://www.idp.org.za/content_CSIR/news/News_NSDP.html>. [Accessed 28th July 2007].

CC, 1996 Constitutional Court of South Africa, Constitution (Act 108 of 1996: Local Government. [Internet].
<http://www.info.gov.za/documents/constitution/index.htm.>. [Accessed 23rd July 2007].

Compion, J. 2007 An Integrated Spatial Information System for the City of Cape Town. *GIS for Environmental and Land Use Management Conference , 4 April,2007*

CSIR, 2007a. *Geospatial Analysis Platform (GAP)-Version 2, About GAP.*
[internet].<http://www.csir.co.za/websource/ptl0002/gap/Documents/About_GAP.pdf >.[Accessed 6th August 2007].

CSIR, 2007a *Geospatial Analysis Platform (GAP)-Version 2, Gap Development and Application Timeline.* [Internet]. <
http://www.csir.co.za/websource/ptl0002/gap/Documents/GAP%20timeline.pdf>. [Accessed 6th August 2007].

DEAT (Department of Environmental Affairs and Tourism), 2002 *National Framework Document: Strengthening Sustainability in the Integrated Development Planning Process (December 2002).* [Internet]
< http://www.environment.gov.za/soer/resource/IDP/0302%20draft%20IDP%20framework.pdf>. [Accessed 4th August 2007].

Ditsobotla, 2005 *The North West Provincial Government Ditsobotla Municipality: Spatial Development Framework, North West Environmental Management Series 6.* [Internet].
< www.nwpg.gov.za/sesdnw/Enviro.%20Publicat/Series%206.pdf>. [Accessed 5th August 2007].

DPLG (Department of Provincial and Local Government of South Africa) 1998 *The White Paper on Local Government (1998).*
[Internet]. < http://www.thedplg.gov.za/subwebsites/wpaper/wpindex.htm>. [Accessed 24th July 2007].

DPLG (Department of Provincial and Local Government of South Africa) 2000 *Local Government: Municipal Systems Act (32), 2000,* Chapter 5. [Internet].
< http://www.thedplg.gov.za/index.php?option=com_docman&task=doc_view&gid=50&Itemid=27>. [Accessed 28th July 2007].

DPLG (Department of Provincial and Local Government of South Africa) 2005 *Municipal Integrated Development Planning (IDP).*
[Internet].
< http://www.thedplg.gov.za/subwebsites/annualreport/IDP%20booklet.pdf> [Accessed 5th August 2007].

DPLG (Department of Provincial and Local Government of South Africa) 2007 *Strategic Plan 2007-2012.* [Internet].<
http://www.thedplg.gov.za/dmdocuments/Strategic%20plan%202007-2012%20Final%20cd.pdf>. [Accessed 24th July 2007].

DPLG (Department of Provincial and Local Government of South Africa) 2007 Newspaper supplement *Policy Talk: A Special Edition on the White Paper process on Provincial and Local Government. July/August 2007*

IOL, 2007 Independent Online article 22 February 2007 [Internet].
< http://www.ioltechnology.co.za/article_page.php?iSectionId=2888&iArticleId=3695987>. [Accessed 21st August 2007].

Michael, 1986. 'Tools for policy-making: Indicators and policy assessment', in Bulmer *et al.* (eds) *Social Science and Social Policy.* Cited in NFSD, 2006

Mbense, M and Nkosi, H. 2006 Obstacles in implementing GIS in government. *Position IT,* 31-34

Mohamed, H. 2004 *National Spatial Development Perspective to be updated*, South African Integrated Development Plan Nerve Centre [Internet].
< http://www.idp.org.za/content_CSIR/news/NSDP_updated_Article.html>. [Accessed 28th July 2007].

NFSD (The South African National Framework for Sustainable Development) 2006 *Draft Discussion Document for Public Comment.* Department of Environment and Tourism: *A Strategic Framework for Sustainable Development in South Africa,* **54** (9.1), **55** (9.2), **56** (9.3)

NSIF (The National Spatial Information Framework) 2007 Official Website. [Internet].
<http://www.nsif.org.za/>. [Accessed 25 August 2007].

Nyarko, Y. 2000 *Employment and the Knowledge Economy in Africa*, The United Nations Economic and Social Council, Economic Commission for Africa, Fifth Session of the Committee on Development Information [Internet].
<http://www.uneca.org/codi/codi5/content/E-ECA-CODI-5-2-EN.pdf>. [Accessed 23rd July 2007].

Opoku-Mensah, A. 2007 ' Information as an Economic Resource', in *African E-Markets: Information and Economic Development.* University of Copenhagen, Denmark and International Books: Centre of African Studies on behalf of the United Nations Economic Commission for Africa (ECA), Development Information Service Division (DISD)

Oshikoya, T.W. and Hussain, M.N. 2007 ' Information Technology and the Challenge of Economic Development in Africa', in *African E-Markets: Information and Economic Development.* University of Copenhagen, Denmark and International Books: Centre of African Studies on behalf of the United Nations Economic Commission for Africa (ECA), Development Information Service Division (DISD)

The Republic of South Africa 2001 Local Government: Municipal Planning and Performance Management Regulations, 2001. *Government Gazette No. 7146,* **434**, *24 August, No 22605, Chapter 2, s(4f), 5.* [Internet].
<http://www.info.gov.za/gazette/regulation/2001/22605.pdf>. [Accessed 4th August 2007].

Swilling, M. 2006 *Local Government and the Politics of Sustainability.* [Internet].
<http://www.dplg.gov.za/subwebsites/led/LEDConference14Aug2006/15Aug2006_Prof_Mark_Swilling.doc>. [Accessed 4th August 2007].

Yirenkyi, S. M. 2006 *A Study to determine the quality of GIS Support Service rendered to Municipalities in Kwazulu-Natal using Servqual Scale Approach.* South Africa: University Kwazulu-Natal

Reclaiming the Future – From Re-Using Construction Materials to one Planet Living® [1]

Jonathan Essex
BioRegional Development Group

Abstract

If everyone in the world lived as we do in the UK we would need three planets to support us. Therefore the UK should reduce its impact, our ecological footprint, by two-thirds to reach a sustainable and globally equitable level. The equivalent challenge for climate change is much greater. Based on a reduction of CO2e (carbon dioxide (CO_2), nitrous Oxide (N20), methane (CH4), perfluorocarbons (PFC), hydrofluorocarbons (HFC) and sulphur hexafluoride (SF6)) by 80% by 2050 globally, the UK is living at around a fifteen climate lifestyle.

Reclaiming and re-using construction materials is a response to this challenge. The business case for re-using construction materials highlights environmental benefits and potential cost savings. Reclamation saves embodied energy in materials: re-using 1 tonne of bricks as whole bricks saves around 880kg less CO_2 emissions, compared to crushing and re-using as aggregate. Sustainable construction must measure its impacts against resource use and carbon limits. To achieve *One Planet Living*[1], UK construction should aspire towards zero (fossil energy and waste), so waste is no longer viewed as a landfill problem but an embodied energy *resource*. This cultural change goes beyond comparing best practice and creating sustainable communities. An evaluation of whether construction is within environmental limits means 'closing the loop' on resource management and considering energy and waste over the whole life-cycle of the built environment.

Keywords   Reclamation, re-use, business-case, sustainability, construction

About the BioRegional Development Group

Jonathan Essex, the author of this paper, is Reclaimed Materials Manager for BioRegional Development Group. BioRegional is a visionary environmental organization dedicated to developing practical solutions for sustainable living.

BioRegional's construction materials reclamation team has over 10 years of industry experience in working with reclaimed, recycled, environmentally accredited and local materials. Projects include writing the materials strategy for the world renowned Beddington Zero Energy Development and playing a key role during the demolition process in the London Olympic Park, surveying around 60% (to date) of buildings, identifying materials that can be reclaimed and estimating CO_2 savings.

---

[1] *One Planet Living*® is a joint initiative of BioRegional Development Group and WWF based on 10 Guiding Principles of sustainability. The vision of One Planet Living is a world in which people everywhere can lead happy, healthy lives within their fair share of the Earth's resources. To find out more visit <u>www.oneplanetliving.org</u>.

Introduction

Policy framework: linking waste and energy

UK construction, through its responsibility for construction and maintenance of the built environment, currently accounts for around:

- 19% of the ecological footprint (James and Desai, 2003)
- 23% of the carbon footprint, including the embodied energy[2] contained within the materials and the process of construction (James and Desai, 2003)
- 32% of the total waste stream (DEFRA 2007, 26). Of the 90 million tonnes from construction and demolition, 69%[3] is recycled or re-used
- 30% of freight transport (Lazarus, 2003). Minerals and building materials account for 15% of total tonne-km transport by road and 13% by rail (Department for Transport, 2006)

As construction has a massive impact, it provides a major opportunity for reducing our ecological and carbon footprint, through material, waste and transport impacts. DEFRA's Waste Strategy for England (2007) states that:

> As a society, we are consuming natural resources at an unsustainable rate. If every country consumed natural resources at the rate the UK does, we would need three planets to live on. The most crucial threat is from dangerous climate change. Our goal is to make the transition towards what the WWF and BioRegional call One Planet Living.

The policy framework to drive improvements in construction's sustainability focuses on waste during the construction stage, and energy (climate change impact) once construction is finished (e.g. Zero Carbon Homes – the target for the Code for Sustainable Homes).

To consider its contribution to *One Planet Living*, the construction industry should join up the separate focii of construction waste and built environment energy use to set overall *resource efficiency* over the *whole life cycle* against environmental limits.

This paper examines the current energy and waste hierarchy, and construction practice, before investigating the re-use of materials as one opportunity for improvement.

Rethinking Energy and Waste – Towards Resource Management

Energy

To live within environmental limits we need to limit our total demand for the use of the earth's resources and the level of pollution, including greenhouse gas emissions, that our lifestyles produce. This is reflected in the Mayor of London's energy hierarchy (Mayor of London, 2004): be lean (reduce demand and energy efficiency), be green (on-site then off-site renewables) and be clean (prioritise low

---

[2] The embodied energy of a construction product is the energy required to abstract, process, manufacture and deliver it to site. It is commonly expressed in terms of CO_2 emissions.

[3] *http://www.defra.gov.uk/environment/statistics/waste/kf/wrkf09.htm*. In 2005, 90 million tonnes of C&D waste was produced, 28 million tonnes (i.e. 31%) went to landfill (including backfill at quarries, and landfill engineering).

carbon e.g. Combined Heat and Power). Various bodies have called for such an energy hierarchy to provide a policy framework within the UK's Energy Strategy (including Engineering Forum for Energy, 2006; Friends of the Earth, 2006; Department for Trade and Industry, 2007).

The demands on the construction industry to reduce carbon emissions are still limited. For example, the new Centre for Alternative Technology Report for a Zero Carbon Britain (2007) and Carbon Trust are both focused on reducing the carbon emissions from the supply chain to the construction industry. However, there are significant opportunities for the construction industry to measure and reduce the energy use not just in its companies and best practice, but in measuring its operations against environmental limits. Responding to this effectively requires sustainability to be embedded centrally into the construction process (Seymour and Essex, 2007).

Waste hierarchy

In contrast to DTI's energy strategy, DEFRA's waste strategy (2007) is centred upon the waste hierarchy. This contrasts with dominant practice within the construction industry which focuses on down-cycling (e.g. recycling of bricks into aggregate through crushing, scrap metal recovery) and the lower levels of this waste hierarchy. The predominance of cost constraints, often presented in terms of time and space to follow different approaches, has limited opportunities of reuse to architectural salvage and niche markets.

Figure 1: The waste hierarchy

Focusing on the top two levels as a priority requires reclamation to be prioritised. This could be done through providing sufficient time (rethinking contracts), space (reclamation yards), planning (audits) and management buy-in. Case studies showing the businesses and environmental benefits are included in the Appendix.

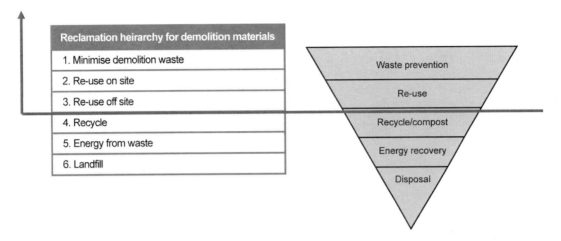

Figure 2: Reclamation hierarchy for demolition materials

This will save both physical waste and embodied energy:

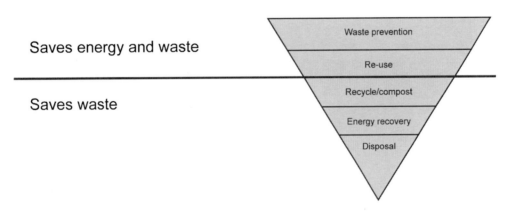

Figure 3: Saving in waste and energy

Reclamation – An Opportunity for Re-Thinking Construction

Definitions

In this paper the *Reclamation Industry* is assumed to comprise those involved in the salvage of materials for re-use; it includes those who physically carry out salvage and those who buy and sell materials for re-use.

The *Demolition Industry* is assumed to comprise contractors engaged with any project that involves deconstructing, dismantling or demolishing a building of any type.

Reclaimed materials are those that have been reclaimed from the waste stream and reused in their original form, with minimal reprocessing. They may be cut to size, adapted, cleaned up or refinished, but they are fundamentally retaining their original form.

Recycled materials are considered to be any materials taken from the waste stream and reprocessed and remanufactured to form part of a new product.

Re-using materials in their original form has the following benefits:

- replaces the need for new virgin materials
- reduces the energy demand for manufacturing new products
- retains the embodied energy of the material
- saves irreplaceable historic materials and craft skills from bygone eras

This cuts carbon emissions, offers significant environmental savings and saves money.

Reclamation and re-use of materials is not a new idea. Salvage has always formed an integral part of the demolition process. However, the construction and demolition industries have recently developed increasingly more innovative schemes to achieve high levels of *recycling* in their activities, rather than reclamation and material reuse.

Legislative drivers for reclamation in the UK – a brief overview (2007)

DEFRA - 2007 Waste Strategy

In 2007 DEFRA released a new waste strategy for England (DEFRA, 2007a). The strategy is framed in terms of *One Planet Living* (see above). This framework requires a shift from considering sustainability in terms of best practice to measuring impacts to achieve living within environmental limits. Annex C3 highlights the infrastructure and capacity needs for the sector. The key areas for investment are reprocessing capacity (e.g. gypsum wastes), materials exchanges and skills and knowledge sharing. In terms of materials exchanges the strategy highlights the future use of consolidation centres, smart logistics, material recovery facilities and exchanges for reclaimed products. Stakeholders have proposed large scale reclamation yards for steel and timber as a means of enabling reclaimed products to break into the mainstream supply chain (Lazarus, 2006). Site Waste Management Plans will be mandatory for larger sites as from October 2007. Segregation and on-site management of waste will make the relative costs of reclamation more favourable, especially when viewed alongside increasing cost of landfill (DEFRA, 2007b).

WRAP, BREEAM and Code for Sustainable Homes - Specifying Reclaimed Materials

BioRegional Consulting Ltd are currently undertaking two pieces of consultancy for WRAP which could support the strategy focusing on the whole waste hierarchy rather than prioritising funding for recycling. The WRAP Reclaimed Products Guide will sit alongside the existing Recycled Content Toolkit to aid the specification of reclaimed materials. This builds on earlier work by Salvo (Kay, 2001). WRAP are also undertaking a strategy to develop a recyclability indicator. This will provide an assessment as to whether buildings are being *'designed for deconstruction'* (Hurley, 2001; CIRIA, 2004; Falk, 2007). The 2007 update of the Green Guide to Specification (Building Research Establishment,

2007) includes a number of reclaimed products for the first time. These include reclaimed timber floorboards, roof tiles and bricks.

EU recommendations

The European Commission has been highlighting the disparity of waste recycling and re-use across Europe. In launching the Waste Management in Urban Regeneration report, BURA stated:

> The European Commission's working document on Construction and Demolition Waste suggests that member states should be recycling or reusing up to 85% of construction waste by 2010. At present the UK recycles 51%. To achieve the remaining percentage we need to shift perceptions and make significant changes. (European Commission, 2000)

Why Reclaim? - the environmental and economic benefits

Waste reduction, reclamation and local re-use can radically reduce the lifestyle environmental impact of individual construction products (DEFRA, 2007a, Annex C3, p.1). Figure 4 contrasts the environmental impact of reclaimed as opposed to new steel. Although new steel sections are made with 60% recycled content they still have 25 times the environmental impact of reclaimed and re-used steel sections. Re-use of reclaimed timber is estimated by BRE as having a 79% lower environmental impact compared to new.

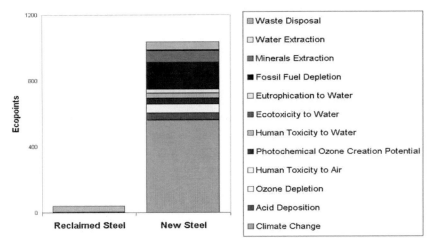

Figure 4 Components of the 96% environmental impact saving achieved by reclaiming and re-using steel sections [4]

Demolition in the UK provides an opportunity to reclaim and re-use vast amounts of construction materials. For example the 2012 Olympics in London has the potential to recover thousands of tonnes of old 'London Stock' bricks. The economic case stacks up because the cost of deconstruction is less than the resale value of the bricks. The main contractor can save money on disposal costs and recover costs from the salvage company. Typically, each tonne of bricks saves around 880kg of carbon dioxide emissions.

Reclamation can support local economic development. The number of jobs resulting from the re-use and recycling of construction materials is ten-times greater than those from landfill. New Economics

---

[4] Source: Building Research Establishment (BRE) lifecycle analysis, cited in Lazarus, 2006.

Foundation research (Sacks, 2002) shows there is a three-to-one benefit of local employment to the local economy. So, the choice to re-use or re-cycle has a positive local impact. This action is supported by Green-Works' experience in employment in re-use as compared to recycling (Crooks, 2007).

Reclamation yards: supporting a reclamation-led approach to demolition

To achieve these environmental and cost savings requires contracts and adaptation of the construction process to take a different, *reclamation-led* approach. Case studies where this has proved cost effective have been collated by BioRegional (2007).

One key aspect to achieving greater material re-use is to strengthen the supply chain, to match demand with supply. The construction sector in the UK is now looking to extend the use of web-based material exchanges (e.g. *www.salvo.co.uk*) to utilise industrial ecology (e.g. the national industrial symbiosis programme, *www.nisp.org.uk*).

However, in many cases the times when materials become available and can be used are not the same. Therefore, sufficient space to consolidate and store materials before resale is crucial. In the UK the space for *reclamation yards* has reduced in recent years while government funding has led to increased down-cycling.

Recent investment support by Transport for London for the London Consolidation Centre demonstrated significant savings from consolidating the supply of materials to construction sites. In a similar way, segregation and collection of construction and demolition materials for re-use could also be developed as a viable business.

This is certainly the experience in the US, where Habitat for Humanity ReStores operate as self-financing not-for-profit organisations in around 150 cities. These social enterprises provide jobs, support local communities and supply around 20% *of* DIY building materials, through reducing construction waste and re-use from taking a reclamation-led approach to demolition.

Other countries have demonstrated that when a number of demolition sites take a reclamation-led approach and a reclamation yard of sufficient scale exists locally then both this approach and business become viable. DEFRA (2007a, Annex C3, p.20) recognise that virtual material exchanges (e.g. Salvo, NISP) must be supported by investment in new consolidation and reclamation yards.

Conclusion

The choice to take a reclamation-led approach to demolition and specify reclaimed materials for new construction is aided by measuring the potential carbon, waste and cost savings. This information, together with increasing legislation and landfill tax, will help construction to view 'waste', increasingly, as an opportunity - both to reduce the climate impact of construction and as a business opportunity.

By measuring the 'embodied energy' of construction products and processes, the overall whole life cycle impact of construction can be managed and reduced. This will allow construction to shift from comparing 'sustainability best practice' within 'budget constraints' to consider how different approaches can 'maximise value' within 'environmental limits'.

References

Addis, B. 2006   *Building with Reclaimed Components and Materials*. London: Earthscan

BioRegional 2007 *A Reclamation Led Approach to Demolition*.[Internet].<http://www.bioregional-reclaimed.com/Case%20study%20files/BRJuly07.pdf>.[Accessed 3rd September 2007].

BRE 2007   *The Green Guide to Specification*. [Internet].
<http://www.bre.co.uk/greenguide/section.jsp?sid=435>. [Accessed 3rd September 2007].

CIB Publication 300 2005 *Deconstruction and Materials Reuse – an International Overview*. Rotterdam: CIB Secretariat

CIRIA C607 Report 2004 *Design for deconstruction: principles of design to facilitate reuse and recycling*. London: CIRIA

Crooks, C. 2007   The Three-Legged Stool: addressing the sustainability agenda in the real world. *Green-Works Conference. 6 June 2007*. [Internet]. <http://www.green-worksconference.com>. [Accessed 6th June 2007].

Department for Communities and Local Government 2006 *Code for Sustainable Homes (CSH)*. Yorkshire: DCLG

DEFRA 2007a *Waste Strategy for England 2007* - Annex C3 - Construction, demolition and excavation waste. [Internet]. <http://www.defra.gov.uk/environment/waste/index.htm>. [Accessed 3rd September 2007].

DEFRA, 2007b. Consultation on Site Waste Management Plans. [Internet].
<http://www.defra.gov.uk/corporate/consult/construction-sitewaste/index.htm>. **(Accessed 3rd September 2007].**

Department for Transport 2006 Transport Statistics, Great Britain. Yorkshire: Department for Transport

DTI 2007   *Meeting the Energy Challenge, A White Paper on Energy*. Yorkshire: DTI

Engineering Forum for Energy 2006 *Submission to the DTI consultation on 'Our Energy Challenge: Securing Clean, Affordable Energy for the Long Term.'*

European Commission 2000   *Management of Construction and Demolition Waste, Working Document No.1*, April 4th. [Internet]. <http://ec.europa.eu/enterprise/environment/index_home/waste_management/constr_dem_waste_000404.pdf>. [Accessed 3rd September 2007].

Falk, B. and Guy, B. 2007 *Unbuilding: Salvaging the Architectural Treasures of Unwanted Houses*. Newtown CT : Taunton Press:

Friends of the Earth 2006   *Energy Review 2006 Consultation Response*. Edinburgh: FoE

James, N. and Desai, P. 2003 *WWF's One Planet Living in the Thames Gateway report*. BioRegional Reclaimed

Helwegg-Larsen, T. and Bell, J. 2007   *Zero Carbon Britain: An Alternative Energy Strategy*. Centre for Alternative Technology. [Internet]. <http://www.zerocarbonbritain.com>. [Accessed 3rd September 2007].

Hurley, J., McGrath, C., Fletcher, S. and Bowes, H.M. 2001   *Deconstruction and re-use of construction materials*. London: BioRegional Development Group

Kay, T. 2001 *The Salvo Guide*. London: BioRegional Development Group Lazarus, N. 2003 *BedZED Construction Materials Report; Toolkit for Carbon Neutral Developments*. BioRegional Reclaimed. London: BioRegional Development Group

Lazarus, N. 2006 *Reclaimed Building Materials in the Development of the Thames Gateway*. BioRegional Reclaimed, 2006. London: BioRegional Development Group

Mayor of London 2004 *Green light to clean power: The Mayor's Energy Strategy*: London

Sacks, J, 2002 *The Money Trail: Measuring your impact on the local economy using LM3*. London: *new economics foundation*. [Internet]. <http://www.neweconomics.org/gen/z_sys_publicationdetail.aspx?pid=128>. [Accessed 3rd September 2007]

Salvo, 1997, 2007. BigREc Surveys 1997 and 2007.[Internet]. <http://www.salvo.co.uk>. [Accessed 3rd September 2007].

Seymour, L. and Essex, J. 2007 *Challenge to the UK Construction Industry; to live within environmental limits*. Published by www.ice.org.uk.

WRAP How to re-use, reclaim and recycle construction materials on site, WRAP. [Internet] <http://www.wrap.org.uk>. [Accessed 3rd September 2007].

Appendix 1: Example case studies of successful reclamation projects

Three UK case studies where a reclamation led approach has been taken are presented below. Further UK and international case studies are contained in the Reclamation Led Approach to Demolition guide[5].

Case Study 1: The Arkenside Hotel, Cirencester, UK

Contractor: *Minchinhampton Architectural Salvage Company*
Description: Complete building systematically dismantled, sold and reconstructed at a new site.
Items Reclaimed:
Complete building which had a Georgian-style façade constructed in fine Bath 'Ashlar' limestone and with wide early Victorian pine floorboards throughout.
Reclaimed and Reused: Over 800 tonnes of material
Time: 12 Weeks, 2006

Cost Comparison (£)			
Mechanical Demolition (approach not taken)		**Reclamation Led Demolition (approach taken)**	
5 week programme to crush and landfill 800 tonnes of material		12 week programme of careful deconstruction	34,000
TOTAL COST:	**£29,000**	**TOTAL COST:**	**£34,000**
		Income	
		3,600ft² pine flooring	4,480
		2,200 welsh slates	2,640
		880m² Cotswold flagstone	8,800
		Stone building	65,000
		TOTAL INCOME:	**80,920**
		NET INCOME:	**46,920**
		NET SAVING:	**£17,920**

The Arkenside Hotel in pictures

Arkenside Hotel, Cirencester, July 2006	Parapet wall, right wing, main facade

[5] Downloaded from *www.bioregional.com*.

| Clearing rubble to expose face stone | Numbering of stones before removal |

| Reclaimed materials: brick, joists, floorboards, precious metals (copper, lead), other metals, internal doors, door hardware, woodwork, general fittings | Left front door – scaffold poles used to support stone during dismantle |

| Careful dismantle of window cases to be used in the future | Cutting out the steel ties from the stone |

| Face stone measured, catalogued and inventoried onto pallets | Existing mortar is cut to release stone without causing damage to face edges |

| Arkenside Hotel, August 2006 | Arkenside Hotel, September 2006 |

Case Study 2: Deconstruction of Two large Victorian houses, Putney, UK (and re-use of building materials at Jubilee Wharf, Penryn)

www.zedfactory.com and www.zedstandards.com

Client: Robot Mother Ltd

Description: Two large Victorian houses in Putney were systematically deconstructed. The houses were typical construction of the era, i.e. brickwork constructed using lime mortar, timber joists and floorboards. These types of buildings have a high reclamation value in terms of both structural and non-structural elements. The non-structural reclaimable elements at Putney included timber doors, York stone paving, granite kerbs and bollards and terracotta copings.

Items Reclaimed:
All of the main building elements were reclaimed. The contractor extracted, processed and sold brickwork alongside the extraction of timber joists, floorboards and doors. BioRegional coordinated the haulage of this timber and the extraction and haulage of York stone paving, granite kerbs and bollards and terracotta copings.

Reclaimed: Over 237 tonnes of material

Comment: BioRegional Reclaimed were contacted early in the demolition process to identify materials with reclamation potential and advise on their successful extraction. A motivated client and the early involvement of BioRegional enabled significant rates of reclamation. Materials were often redistributed to the clients of other construction projects. For example, early stages of the building phase of Jubilee Wharf, in Penryn, coincided with the demolition of the Victorian houses in Putney.

A key factor in making high levels of reclamation possible was the allocation of a holding area to dry out timber and to store materials before they were required on-site. Another key factor was a dedicated architect and client.

Re-use:
Jubilee Wharf, is not only a highly efficient environmental building upgradable to a Zero (Carbon) Energy Development (ZED) but enhances re-used building materials that were reclaimed from other construction sites. This widens the consideration of environmental impact from energy at the use stage and waste during construction to measure and reduce the overall resource (energy and waste) impact over the whole lifetime of the development.

This £3.5 million ecological development comprises twelve community workshops, six residential units, a community nursery, a café, charity offices and a function hall. It was designed by ZED factory Ltd and BioRegional Reclaimed were contracted to source reclaimed materials. In addition to the granite sets, granite bollards and timberwork that were transported to Jubilee Wharf from Putney; BioRegional sourced additional reclaimed materials locally, including a maple dance floor and granite kerbs. The process of reclamation was carried out without significant additional cost, even after the timber planks had been treated for increased fire safety.

BioRegional's involvement in both projects resulted in significant quantities of various timber, brick and stonework being diverted from landfill for re-use. This reduced the financial cost to the demolition contractor of landfill taxes, reduced costs through re-use of materials elsewhere and environmental benefits through savings on virgin materials and embodied CO_2 that goes into producing the materials.

This process of reclamation was carried out without significant additional cost. For example, reclaimed timber planks remained cost neutral even after they were treated for increased fire safety. Additional time was required in the selection of materials on-site but this had been factored into the design phase and did not affect the critical path of the construction.

A key factor in making high levels of reclamation possible at Jubilee Wharf was the allocation of a holding area to dry out timber and to store materials before they were required on-site. This is a common challenge that BioRegional are working to resolve, for the London area at least, through the establishment of a large 'reclamation yard'. This would extend the opportunities for reclamation and reuse of construction materials, even at the scale of the London 2012 Olympic development in Stratford, East London.

The use of reclaimed materials here added to the environmental sustainability of the new development through landfill diversion, reducing pressures on virgin resources and avoiding the energy intensive processes associated with their manufacture. This sits well with other aspects of the sites' sustainability, such as its energy footprint and connections to the local community. This is about creating a cultural change as well as reducing resource and carbon impacts - sitting in the café you can admire the reclaimed floor, while being heated from a wood pellet boiler, sourcing fuel from Devon, and sampling locally grown produce.

Jubilee Wharf was completed in 2006.

Embodied Carbon Savings

Materials Reclaimed	Material Reclaimed	Embodied CO_2 saving
Timber	7 tonnes	15 tonnes
Brick	230 tonnes	200 tonnes
Various stonework	5 tonnes	1 tonne
TOTAL:	242 tonnes	216 tonnes

Putney and Jubilee Wharf in pictures

Putney house prior to demolition

Timber floorboards found throughout the property

York stone paving in the garden of the property, 5 tonnes of stonework reclaimed

230 tonnes of bricks reclaimed from the houses

7 tonnes of timber reclaimed from the houses in Putney including joists, floorboards and doors	Unwanted local authority granite kerbs stored at Jubilee Wharf prior to construction.

Jubilee Wharf	Reclaimed timber floorboards used for floor and ceiling finish at Jubilee Wharf

Case Study 3: Brick Reclamation at Diglis Basin, Worcester

Main Contractor: Tilbury Douglas
Reclamation Company: *Minchinhampton Architectural Salvage Company*
Items Reclaimed and Reused: Over 35 tonnes of bricks re-used offsite (75%) and Staffordshire Bricks re-used as a feature in new development on site.

Time: Six days, July 2007

Agreement*:* At the request of the conservation officer all of the bricks from the Finger Wharf were to be re-used or salvaged. There was little scope for on-site re-use of the bricks. The bricks were bound with lime mortar. The main contractor was paid 10p/brick by the reclaimer. Thus avoiding landfill or crushing costs.

Methodology*:* The buildings were dismantled panel-by-panel by rocking the wall with a 360 excavator and allowing it to gently fold so it falls in a controlled manner, with the machine bucket.

Panels were approximately 15' long by 12' high. Once on the ground the bricks were cleaned by hand and removed from the site. Gentle systematic collapsing of the wall, clearing as you go, greatly increases quantity of bricks reclaimed.

Around 12,000 red bricks (35 tonnes) were salvaged equivalent to 75% of the total bricks available. In addition, all of the Staffordshire Blue bricks which formed the archways were reused on site. It took six days using two pairs of brick cleaners working to reclaim around 500 bricks per person, per day.

The Impact of the Design *Charrette* Process in the Creation of Sustainable Community: The Case of Tornagrain

John Onyango
Mackintosh Environmental Architecture Research Unit, University of Glasgow
Karim Hadjri
School of Planning, Architecture and Civil Engineering, Queen's University, Belfast

Abstract

Sustainability is understood to be concerned with meeting the needs of the present without compromising the opportunities of future generations, implying an ability to maintain, and prolong, the *status quo* in spite of new developments in the built environment. Sustainable design processes thus take into account environmental, socio-economic and cultural issues through addressing the various indicators that tackle the design and management of built environments, building performances, and resource consumption.

Radical changes are planned in the Scottish planning system as evidenced by the Scottish Executive's publication of the Draft Planning Advice Note (PAN) in July 2006[1], with the aim of enabling Community Engagement that allows for openness and accountability in the decision making process.

This paper presents an independent and rigorous analysis of the *charrette* approach to future public engagement and its effectiveness within the Scottish Planning System with regard to the draft PAN 2005. It analyses how sustainable issues were addressed during the *charrette* at the proposed Tornagrain Settlement in the Highlands of Scotland. The analysis revealed that as a method of engagement the *charrette* could be effective in creating sustainable communities under certain conditions.

Keywords Inclusiveness, process, sustainability, community

Introduction

This paper introduces the location of the Tornagrain settlement and examines some basic definitions of sustainability, followed by setting the context in which the terms are used to critically assess the *charrette*. It defines the *charrette* approach as a method of community engagement followed by an analysis of how sustainable issues were addressed. Firstly, it is important to explore the meanings attached sustainability indicators.

The proposed Tornagrain settlement is located on the A96 corridor between the towns of Inverness and Nairn in the Highlands of Scotland. It features in the spatial development perspective for Scotland to the year 2025, as set out in the National Planning Framework for Scotland (2004). The framework identifies locations for new settlements at Whiteness, south of Nairn, Tornagrain and an increase in

---

[1] This document has since been issued as PAN 81. 2007. Community Engagement: Planning with People, Scottish Government, Edinburgh.

housing in the villages of Croy, Culloden, Culloden Moor and Crawder. In that period, it allocates a population of about 10,000 to the proposed Tornagrain settlement.

The Moray Estate Development Company (MEDC) owns over 2500 hectares of land within the A96 Inverness-Nairn corridor and has interest in the developments that are envisioned by the Highland Council (Figure 1). The MEDC took the initiative to engage the Highland Council in this vision for growth in the corridor but was not met with understanding. The MEDC, therefore, took the initiative and appointed Turnberry Consultants to analyse the best way to obtain optimum results from the development of its land holdings within the corridor. A report was sent to the Council in August 2004. In turn, Turnberry Consultants advised on the successes and failures of planned towns around the world and appointed consultants capable to tackling the problem at hand. They interviewed several international firms and recommended the appointment of Duany Platter-Zyberk[2] from the United

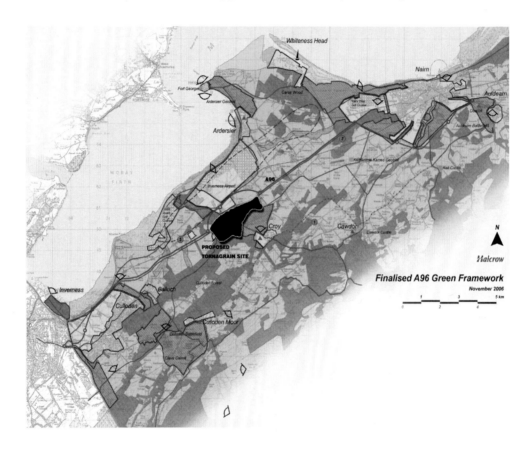

Figure 1   Location of Tornagrain Settlement
Source: Halcrow Group. (2006, p.3)

---

[2] The design team for the *charrette* was composed of several teams from USA, UK and Germany with over 20 professionals. These were:

        Duany Plater-Zyberk and Company-a leading US practitioners in New Urbanism
        Turnberry Consultants-a UK property and planning consultants
        DTZ- a consulting and research and property advice company
        Fulcrum- Consulting Engineers
        Applied Ecology Ltd- specialist in ecology and environmental management
        Savell, Bird & Axon- Transportation Planning
        Horner & MacLellan- Inverness based landscape architects

States as the lead consultant. The appointed team visited developments in: Denmark and Holland; the Scottish settlements of Nairn, Forres, Grantown-on-Spey, Cromarty, Argyll, Bute, Dunkeld and Edinburgh; Poundbury and Hampstead in England; and Kentlands near Washington, DC, Savannah in Georgia, and Seaside and Celebration in Florida in the United States. The objective was to understand issues of sustainability and not the replication of a particular model at Tornagrain.

The Scottish planning system on the other hand is undergoing radical changes as evidenced by the publication of Planning Advice Note 81 by the Scottish Government in July 2007. It aims at enabling community engagement that allows for openness and accountability in decision making. Two years previously, Moray Estates had taken steps to make a positive contribution to growth through a process named the *charrette*.

Methodology

The paper analyses the *charrette* as a method of community engagement. It deals with observations on attitudes, motivations and behaviour, and perceptions of people not as individuals, but as groups and clusters. The methodology used combines ethnographic and socio-scientific approaches and is based on a literature review of community engagement. It applies methods of qualitative analysis to unravel associative patterns through a combination of group interviews and questionnaires. It interrogates the participants' perception of the *charrette* as planning process to achieve a sustainable[3] new town development at Tornagrain. Questionnaires used to gather information on perceptions were triangulated with observations and notes taken during the process. The questionnaire had two parts: the first adapted from Nick Waites Associates[4] in the Enquiry by Design methodology; the second based on work by Drew Mackie Associates[5] focused on a structure map of organizations and persons participating in the process and networks of trust, respect and loyalty. Questionnaires were made available to the public immediately following the second public presentation. Structural mapping of organisations and persons involved in the process was built up while the meetings proceeded to unravel associative patterns. Several structured interviews were conducted with *charrette* participants and clients, and the meetings were video-taped for subsequent analysis.

Community Engagement

This section examines the nature of community and community engagement. The term community means different things to different people, reflecting different personal wants and needs balanced against the interests of the larger community. This paper starts with ideas from the report by Atherton *et al.* (2002, p.3) to the Community Development Foundation: to encompass all the inhabitants and users of a council area; all the inhabitants and users of a locality; and a network of people with a

---

[3] Sustainability is used here within the context of Satterthwaite (1997, p.1668) to include '...a diverse range of environmental, economic, social, political, demographic, institutional and cultural goals...' in relation to the issues of the desirability of the target population [stakeholder]. This requires referencing to long term political and social viability, thus providing starting points [process] rather than end points [products] of the development plans and agendas that match and fit the wants of the communities' future.

[4] Nick Wates can be contacted on Nick Wates Associates, 7 Tackleway, Hastings, East Sussex, TN34 1SP, United Kingdom. [http://www.nickwates.co.uk]

[5] Drew Mackie can be contacted on Drew Mackie Associates, 10 Winton Grove, Edinburgh EH10 7AS. drewmackie@m2ud.com

sustained common identity or interest. To fully comprehend the process of community engagement, a short literature review follows.

The traditional planning process in the UK is generally protracted, demanding on scarce resources and is sometimes unrelated to the realities and pace of life in the community (Hamdi and Goethert 1997, p.3). This method of planning has been widely criticised (Jacobs, 1961; Stretton, 1978; Gilbert and Gorgler, 1992; Devas and Rakodi, 1993). It places an implicit emphasis on: control; modelling; prediction and making certain; inhibition rather than promotion; and weakening and not supporting the pluralistic, spontaneous dynamics that shape communities. Its prime concern is to make plans rather than achieve real practical effects on the ground. Devas (1993, pp.72-73) argues that although comprehensive and broad, such plans often lack practical concern for social, economic and environmental issues. Furthermore, it is claimed that this approach segregates plan making from the decision making process with the consultants planning, the politicians deciding and the community receiving. It has its roots in the positivist (reductionism) or critical (post-positivist) models of enquiry that conceptualise planning as the control of land-use and urban development as a means of achieving a healthy and attractive urban environment (Mega, 1996, p.47).

The term community engagement was previously known as action planning, a term attributed to Otto Koenigsberger, and represents an alternative to the conventional planning process (Hamdi and Goethert, 1997, p.23). It aims to equip designers and planners, as enablers, with abilities to guide rather than control spatial, social and economic developments, and match the needs of the community with the goals of planning through a cyclic process of reflection, learning and revision. It developed over time due to the realisation that the planning process could not follow a tidy, linear sequence as initially envisioned because of limitations on the capacities of institutions involved and the nature of the political agendas and processes. The perception of the roles and responsibilities of the planners, and the practitioners' community, is transformed from provision to enabling and empowering the stake holders who form the community. Community engagement is driven by research into the physical, social and economic systems aimed at improving the process at the level of community through problem solving and strategic planning (Hamdi and Goethert, 1997, p.30). Thus, it can be argued to be a problem-based and community driven process to achieve goals through participation and reliance on a local knowledge base, drawing on the skills of experts from outside the community who act as catalysts. They introduce the necessary methods, techniques and ideas whilst at the same time disseminating principles that help remove legal barriers and provide legitimacy to the local community. Action plans are starting points [process] rather than end points [products] and are incremental rather than comprehensive. They provide clear visible outputs for the process of discovering common interests from within the community and subsequent convergence of interests from what initially appeared as sticking points.

Several underlying concerns have to be recognised in the community engagement process and transition from process to product, including an avoidance of excessive dependence on outsiders. The community needs to be assured that the plan will lead to visible developments within a set time frame and that learning from the process will be replicated in future projects. This is reflected in the level at which the community is engaged in one of the five different ways illustrated in Figure 2.

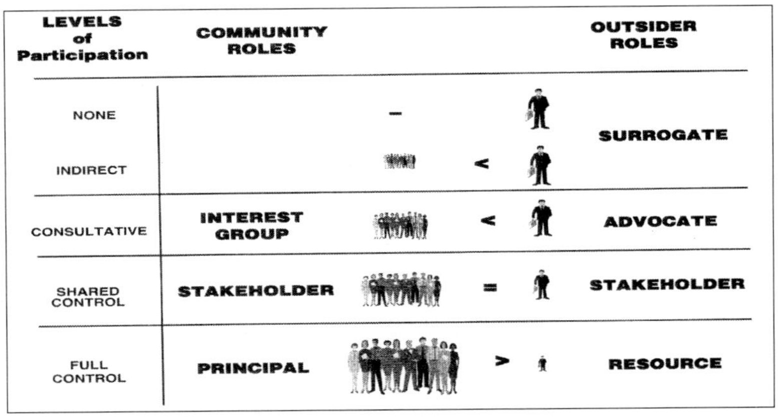

Figure 2   Levels of community engagement
Source: Hamdi and Goethert (1997, p.68)

From observation, the *charrette* at Tornagrain can be categorised at the 'consultative level' in most design issues and 'shared control' on policy issues. It has to be emphasised that the initiative to consult and engage the community was both client-driven and driven by government.

The Scottish Government has issued guidelines on good practice to achieve community engagement: these are summarized in Table 1.

Table 1   National Standards for Community Engagement

Involvement	Identifying and involving all interested parties
Support	Identifying and overcoming barriers
Planning	Gathering evidence of needs and resources
Method	Agreeing on method of engagement
Work together	Agree use clear procedures to empower
Information Sharing	Share necessary information with participants
Work with others	Multi-disciplinary process
Improvement	Actively develop skills and knowledge
Feedback	Cyclic feedback loops to improve
Monitor and evaluate	Constantly monitoring and evaluating of the process

Source: Communities Scotland

The paper will now consider how closely the *charrette* followed them and its contribution to sustainability.

Several methods are available to engage the community: two that are well-known are *Enquiry by Design* and the *Charrette*, used in the UK and US, respectively. *Charette* is the French word for cart and is often used to describe the final, intense work effort expended by art and architecture students to meet a project deadline. The use of the term is said to originate from the École des Beaux Arts in Paris during the 19th century, where proctors circulated a cart, or *charrette*, to collect final drawings whilst students frantically put the finishing touches to their work (Charrette Institute, 2006). The other definition of a *charrette* is the design/ planning process that takes place over one day (Hamdi and Goethert, 1997, p.95) and has been widely used in the UK since 1992 by various groups including the Prince of Wales' Institute of Architecture[6]. It assembles an interdisciplinary team, typically consisting

---

[6] The Prince of Wales' Institute of Architecture has since been reorganised to become The Prince of Wales Foundation. This is an educational charity which exists to improve the quality of people's lives by teaching and practising traditional methods of building. It can be contacted at 19-22 Charlotte Road, London, EC2A 3SG. [http://www.princes-foundation.org/index.html]

of the community, elected officials, planners, architects, engineers, developers, business owners and other stakeholders to create a plan that can be implemented within a specified time frame. The key element is the compression of the process to an average of between four to seven days. Participants work together through a series of feedback loops in brainstorming sessions, sketching workshops and other exercises. Meetings take place during the day and night, with participants coming together as a group at set times or breaking off into small working groups to consider issues in more detail whilst, at the same time behind the scenes, the core design team works continuously. The entire community participates whenever personal time schedules permit and without the need to take periods of leave from formal employment. Most stakeholders such as developers, architects, business owners, transportation authorities and local leaders participate throughout the scheduled meetings.

Typically, the *charrette* process is modified to fit different projects using the same basic strategy with the designers/ planners acting as catalysts and involving as many stakeholders as possible in a series of short, intensive design sessions. During the *charrette* there are times when collaborative hands-on sessions are used for participants to 'root-out' potential problems and identify and debate possible solutions. The forums are used for informing the community, building confidence and providing skills and knowledge.

Enquiry-by-Design, in contrast, is a method of public participation which relies on workshops to bring together major stakeholders at one time and in one location (place) to discuss, develop and draw possible urban design and planning solutions to specific, place-based problems. This process allows for options to be investigated interactively through design, and are debated, and illustrated in order to reach the community's preferred outcomes. The results of *Enquiry-by-Design* workshops are typically non-binding, and are aimed to encourage participants to think creatively, so enabling them to step outside their sometimes limiting and constraining roles. It provides the flexibility to consider and debate a wide range of possible options.

Sustainability and Indicators

This section outlines the parameters within which the term sustainability is used in this paper and how the indicators deemed to contribute to a sustainable community were addressed at the *charrette* under the four headings introduced in Table 2. Sustainability is understood to be concerned with meeting the needs of the present without compromising the ability of future generations to meet their own (Fookes, 2000, pp.29-30). This implies prolonging the *status quo,* a desire to leave a favourable heritage for future generations. It is thus concerned with the attributes of social, economic, cultural and even judicial aspects of life. The term is nebulous and difficult to define leaving opportunities for contestation (Mega, 1996, pp.133-4). Furthermore, Satterthwaite (1997, p.1668) claims that 'there is lack of a clear and agreed definition as to the meaning of 'sustainable cities'' and 'sustainable human settlements'.

This is one of the reasons why many projects under development are trumpeted as sustainable. Sustainability is thus a balancing act because a bad policy that is sustainable is not better than a bad policy that is un-sustainable (Marcuse, 1998, p.104). Reference to long-term political and social viability is, therefore, important and community engagement provides a useful starting point to examine ways for translating development plans into policy statements with regard to future states. Fresh governmental initiatives are currently exploring renewable sources of energy such as wind and solar power. The Scottish Government encourages sustainability and has published guidelines (PAN 81, 2007). Sustainable communities are places where people want to live and work, now and in the future. This is a community that meets the diverse needs of both the existing and the future communities, contributing to a high quality of life and using the environment in an appropriate manner. The PAN aims that such communities should be well planned, built to a high standard, safe and inclusive.

Sustainable indicators for development often address issues of the carrying capacity of natural resources; ecosystems; aesthetic qualities; human, built, and economic environments; social capital; diversity; and justice in renewable and non-renewable resources. It addresses needs of both the old and the young (inter-generational) and the relationship between human capital and the environment. A sustainable development will respect the local culture, uphold social justice and equity, and provide opportunities for meeting the skills, abilities, health and education of the communities. These embrace crime, provision of health care, shopping and recreational facilities, racial harmony, education and employment provision (Sustainable Measures, 2007).

Quality of life in cities is measured by various indicators. Grayson *et al.* (1994, p.10) adopt a model developed by the Quality of Life Group at the Universities of Glasgow and Strathclyde which measured quality of life dimensions based on a random sample of 1,200 people. The index addresses factors that affect community life, as indicated in Table 2.

Table 2   Indicators of quality of life

Social	Cultural	Economic	Environmental
Shopping	Shopping	Costs of living	Pollution
Racial Harmony	Racial Harmony	Shopping	Scenic ways
Crime	Education	Work/ Employment	Climatic changes
Education	Leisure	Crime	Energy uses
Leisure	Housing	Affordable Housing	Transportation
		Transportation	

Source: Adopted from *Environment and Planning A*, 1988, 21, 1659

Sustainable indicators for development address the carrying capacity of the environment, people and society through careful use of natural resources and ecosystems. They handle, sensitively, the aesthetic qualities of the human, built, economic and social environments and accept diversity and justice. They embrace renewable and non-renewable technologies, in local and non-local applications. In addition, they address inter-generational needs and the relationship between human capital and the environment. The next section shows how the *charrette* at Tornagrain used sustainablity indicators.

Inclusiveness and governance

The *charrette* was well advertised and interesting debates ensued in response to invitations for participation. This is evidenced by articles from the local and national press, some supporting the proposal, others opposed to it. At the start of the *charrette,* an opening session was held at Drummusie

Hotel. It was well attended with over 150 persons from the community. The representative from the Scottish Government gave the opening speech and welcomed the *charrette* as a new way of planning that may be used elsewhere. He emphasised that the issues were local and that the government, as observer, would not in any way interfere with the planning process.

Inclusion of the community in the decision making process facilitated both engagement and empowerment. As Harvey (1973, p.14) argues, inclusiveness is a reflection of social justice that operates on the principles of factual matters (process) and value (perception of the process). Inclusiveness was evaluated on two levels: firstly, using three sets of questions to establish the amount and kind of information that was available to the public living within the A96 corridor; the second level involved answers to a set of 15 questions to evaluate perception trust, fear of conflict, lack of commitment, avoidance of accountability and inattention to results. Analysis revealed that 72% of respondents held the opinion that the process was inclusive; only 17% disagreed and a further 3% strongly disagreed.

Well run

The *charrette* was effective and inclusive: community representatives were well represented and engaged positively in the deliberations. Participants included local elected leaders, associations of the various hamlets, and members – all of whom wished to debate the vision of the new proposal. The process enabled the community to build capacity and participate not only in the present but possibly future *charrettes*. It increased knowledge on issues of urbanism and sustainability. The process included selecting names for the neighbourhoods proposed in the *charrette,* thereby inspiring a sense of civic pride.

Active, inclusive and safe

Overall, 12 questionnaires were returned representing 8% from those who had attended large public meetings and 49% from smaller and more intense discussion meetings. The profile of respondents was as follows: 36% female; 64% male; 8% aged 20-35 years, 33% aged 36-49, 50% aged 50-64 and 9% aged at least 65; 92% were of British-White background and the remainder from other White backgrounds, conforming to the ethnic population profile of the Highlands revealed in the National Census 2001. Only 8% of respondents lived outside the A96 corridor.

Although, currently, there is a large population of Polish immigrants, they did not participate in discussions. Those who attended agreed the need for an integrated community, a cohesive neighbourhood and provision of amenities for people of all ages and income levels. Discussion favoured the intention to create opportunities for cultural, leisure, community and other activities. Child's safety was a particular parental concern given the alignment of the A96 highway.

Well-designed and built

The workshop on housing and economic issues was attended by 37 people of whom 12 were local residents in the A96 Corridor. The remainder were officers from various agencies and professional groups concerned with housing, social, health and economic issues. They included Balloch

Community Council, Ardesier Medical Practice, NHS Scotland, Inverness West Community Council, Scottish Executive, Inverness Chamber of Commerce, HIE, Highland Housing Alliance, NHS Highland, BRE Highland, Communities Scotland and Scotia Homes. The issues discussed included sustainable growth; housing types; housing costs; integration; amenities such as schools and health care. Issues affecting commercial and economic outlets, gated communities, and noise and type of economic activity were also raised.

There is a housing crisis in The Highlands with average prices starting at £100,000, well beyond the means of prospective purchasers with an annual income of £28,000. Agencies such as Community Scotland were therefore set up to assist those who could not climb the property ladder. The issue of noise from those repairing motor cycles or cars outside apartments was raised and, in response, the Housing Association representative stated that this was against Housing Association tenancy regulations. There was discussion and agreement that people should be enabled to work from home to supplement an income. A call emerged for the inclusion of self-build housing where the dwelling unit was completed with basic plumbing and electrical services. It was also suggested that the percentage of affordable housing should be increased from 25% to 35%, or more, given that land values rather than building costs raised problems. Traditional buildings such as those in smaller communities like Thin Horn are simple, yet appreciate quickly in value because of the quality of construction. Innovation and technology were thus seen as the way forward in housing provision, including: the use of recycled water; solar energy for passive heating; day lighting; and reduction in carbon dioxide emissions.

Thriving

The *charrette* also addressed issues of economics through the provision of mixed use developments that would provide mixed employment opportunities to communities to sustain family life. It was, therefore, important that any proposed community be located close to the nexus of transportation (airport and rail stop) and existing Business Park. It was emphasized that mixed use development is important including schools, a hospital, town centre, or library. Amenities such as schools, shops, and health clinics also needed long term investment and the developer proposed to subsidise such key services. Attention was drawn to the successful new town of Poundbury in Dorset, England. Andres Duany of DPZ outlined the difference between the development process proposed at Tornagrain and other types, pointing out that the client, Moray Estate, was a facilitator through provision of land and initial infrastructure. The key is working together in partnership with the architects, developers and others concerned with the proposal. Urbanism, it was clarified, was about human experience; one being able to have cappuccino at 11:00pm in the centre of the town.

Well connected

Sustainable communities need to be well connected with transport services and communications in support of regular trips for daily activities such as shopping, going to work or school, leisure pursuits, and visits to the doctor. Provision must be safe for various age groups, the young and the old as well as pedestrians, cyclists and vehicular users. There is need for well-designed car parking facilities that are not intrusive in the local environment.

The workshop on sustainable transportation was attended by 20 people, nine of whom were local residents in the A96 Corridor. The rest were officers from various agencies and professional groups concerned with transportation. It discussed the need to reduce long distance needs travel; innovative approach to traffic demands and management; the existing A96 highway; railway transportation and bus links, and the role of pedestrians in the planning process.

It was pointed out that the A96 is both a trunk road and arterial route. The proposal for Tornagrain was thus not just about roads, but opportunities, whilst the proposed railway station halt would create opportunities for linking bus routes and communities, and the airport and Business Park. The challenges of the busy road could be tackled by the bifurcation or even trifurcation of the A96. This allowed for possibilities of reducing speed yet maintaining capacity, whilst securing the safety of pedestrians. It was acknowledged that pedestrians' rights are essential for any sustainable and viable community.

It was proposed that settlement design would be based on 80m runs of street with three - four minutes walk (pedestrian sheds) to the centre. In a well-designed city the bus would stop only three times in a distance of three pedestrian sheds (400m x 3 x 3) and people could easily walk. An example, Poundbury, indicates that 25% of resdients walk to work or for daily needs. The sustainable solution does not exclude the car, but manages it, creating options for residence, shopping and by-pass construction. Some of the best shopping streets in the world comprise of six lanes and linked boulevards. Upton in Northampton illustrates this design where a walk-able community was created along a boulevard embodying the busy A45 road. Likewise, in London, Kensington High Street can be regarded as a tamed thoroughfare with enhanced commercial performance. Technology would play a role in promoting sustainability by ensuring the availability of real-time information on bus/ train location and associated investment in upgraded public transport.

Environmentally sensitive

Sustainable communities are environmentally sensitive in a holistic sense, designed and built to minimize the impact on climate change, carbon dioxide reduction and energy efficient technology. During the *charrette* process environmental issues were addressed in many ways. There were discussions on the merits of compact settlement form as opposed to urban sprawl with examples drawn from US cities. Impact assessment was conducted on archaeological sites to inform the master plan: five known sites of national importance and a further 31 sites elsewhere in the area were identified to minimize impacts through mitigation strategies. This included placing a 10m easement around each site and the adoption of such culturally-significant features in street name and neighbourhood designations.

The *charrette* process tackled affects on biodiversity recognizing the existence of four badgers on the site that would be protected. It was agreed that the ecological impacts of the by-pass, and water diversion and retention actions, should be studied further. Reduction of the impact of signage on the landscape was proposed through the use of tree planting before development. Slope analysis was undertaken prior to dealing with the impact of cut and infill programmes.

Sustainability issues are at the forefront of government policy and the public agenda determined by Planning Policy Statement 1,(1999, p.9). The questionnaire was used to check whether the four strands of sustainability were addressed during the *charrette* process:

- Social sustainability
- Economic sustainability
- Environmental sustainability
- Technical sustainability

Overall, only 50% of respondents felt that issues of social sustainability had been tackled during the *charrette* process; 27% expressed no opinion. Greater proportions, however, felt that economic (64%), technical (63%) and environmental (61%) dimensions of sustainability had been addressed.

Conclusion

The *charrette*, as an iterative process, results in strong team commitments and increases community participation. Local views and knowledge are linked to the wide professional experience of the design team enabling community and team consensus. However, there are a number of advantages and possible disadvantages associated with the process:

Advantages

- accelerated timescale
- wide publicity both negative and positive
- broad public access through different media and outlets
- concentration of technical skills and ease of communication within the technical team
- technical team commitment
- cost and interest of paymaster: it is estimated that the process cost £350,000, thereby demonstrating the level of commitment by Moray Estate

Disadvantages

- 'big-bang' consultation and high profile approach. If it goes wrong it could alienate the community and agencies. It could annoy potential agency allies in appearing to by-pass the normal planning procedures
- overwhelms and potentially sidelines legitimate alternatives in the momentum created dependence on personality of the facilitator: how does this get replicated without someone like Andres?
- seductive artistic imagery: could be seen as a sales pitch
- cost and interest of paymaster (estimated by some of the audience as £350,000) interpreted as buying the normal processes

It is our view that the process could not have been executed more professionally. Our experience of similar public consultation exercises across the UK shows this to be best-resourced and most smoothly conducted exercise. Its success is crucially focused on the skill, personality and style of the facilitator. Analysis of the *charrette* reveals that as a process of engagement, it was very successful, allaying fears of those who had misgivings to the proposed development and involving them *ab initio* in the decision making process. Throughout the process the facilitator, Andres Duany, constantly made assurances that everything was 'up-for-grabs' in the *charrette*, and that the team was in the hands of that process. The team echoed the wishes of the community on the broad scale but left the nitty-gritty details to the individual local architects, developers, marketing firms and the community who better understood the situation. Throughout, tact was used to redirect the attention of participants to the issue being discussed; this approach successfully accommodated negative comments within a broader context of positive achievement. Furthermore, debate was encouraged and time allowed further reflection on opportunities for change.

Andreas Duany, the facilitator, took the initiative in going to Nairn and engaging the business community on potential developments. His role as enabler in the engagement process and willingness to work with all parties was vital. It created the opportunities for smaller villages like Croy and oppositional communities like Nairn to engage in the process and seek assurances that their legitimate interests would not be dismissed. Creativity was used to illustrate and explore ideas and issues that were raised as potential problems. Indeed, one participant pointed to the range of choices available in the proposal which exceeded that normally available in current developments.

References

Atherton, G., Hashagen, S., Chanan, G., Garratt, C. and West, A. 2002 *Involving Local People in Community Planning in Scotland.* London and Glasgow: Community Development Foundation and Scottish Community Development Centre. [Internet]. <http://www.communityplanning.org.uk/documents/engcommunitiesincp.pdf>.[Accessed 18th October 2006].

Fookes, T. 2000 'Auckland's Urban Growth Management', in Memon, A. and Perkins, H. (eds) *Environmental Planning and Management in New Zealand.* Palmerston North: Dunmore Press

Gilchrist, J. 2006 *The Truman Show's architect dreams of a Highland Utopia.* Edinburgh: The Scotsman Newspaper. [Internet]. <http://living.scotsman.com/homes.cfm?id=951722006>. [Accessed 18th October 2006].

Halcrow Group 2006 *A96 Corridor Masterplan.* [Internet]. <http://www.highland.gov.uk/NR/rdonlyres/AD733ED1-EDB0-4BE7-91D8-9FFB194A9F37/0/a96interimreport.pdf on 18th October 2006>. [Accessed 18th October 2006].

Harvey, D. 1973 *Social justice and the city.* London: Edward Arnold

Leakey, C. 2006 *Informative and amusing but hardly impartial,* Inverness, Scotland: The Inverness Courier. [Internet]. <http://www.inverness-courier.co.uk/news/fullstory.php/aid/349>. [Accessed 18th October 2006].

Marcuse, P. 1998 Sustainability is not enough. *Environment and Urbanization,* **10,** 103-111

Mega, V. 1996 Our City, Our Future: Towards Sustainable Development in European Cities. *Environment and Urbanization,* **18,** 133-154

Office of the Deputy Prime Minister 1999 *Planning Policy Statement 1.* Norwich: HMSO

Rogol, M., Doi, S. and Wilkinson, A. 2004 *Solar Power: sector outlook.* CLSA Asia-Pacific Markets

Satterthwaite, D. 1997 Sustainable Cities or Cities that Contribute to Sustainable Development. *Urban Studies,* **34,** 1667-1691

Scottish Executive, 2004 *National Planning Framework for Scotland.* Edinburgh: Scottish Executive

Exploring the Changing Nature of Students' Attitudes and Awareness of the Principles of Sustainability

Eddie Cowling, Amanda Lewis and Sarah Sayce
Centre for Sustainable Communities Achieved through Integrated Professional Education (C-SCAIPE) Kingston University

Abstract

Education for Sustainable Development (ESD) has become increasingly significant within the built environment Higher Education curriculum. Kingston University's School of Surveying (KUSS) has long recognised the need for including sustainable development in the student learning experience. The HEFCE-funded Centre for Sustainable Communities Achieved through Integrated Professional Education (C-SCAIPE) has supported and assisted the School in incorporating sustainability, initially into the built environment curriculum, and subsequently aims to promote the underlying importance of sustainability across other professionally-accredited courses within the university.

This paper reports on how C-SCAIPE is exploring students' familiarity, understanding and interest in sustainable development and how these develop over their time at Kingston University. C-SCAIPE has investigated various aspects of sustainability in relation to the students' studies. Students' awareness and 'sustainability literacy' have been tracked, together with their interest in, and perceived importance of, sustainability issues to their courses and future careers, and how students' behaviour and lifestyle has been influenced by studying courses underpinned by the principles of sustainability.

Keywords C-SCAIPE, sustainability, higher education, built environment

Background

Achieving progress towards sustainability is critical to the future well-being of society; this has long been recognised by HEFCE (HEFCE, 2002) who have placed sustainable development as a major objective both organisationally and within their sphere of influence and activity. We are also currently within the United Nation's Decade of Education for Sustainable Development. It could be expected, therefore, that Higher Education institutions would be at the forefront of embedding sustainability both within their own institutional values and within the curricula that they deliver. However, with some notable exceptions, research commentary to date (Dawe *et al.*, 2005; Higher Education Academy, 2006; Roberts and Roberts, 2007) would suggest that ESD (Education for Sustainable Development) is still not widely developed. Within built environment education the need is large, given the acknowledged impact that buildings make to the economic well-being of the country; the social well-being of people and the impact on the environment.

It is within this context that C-SCAIPE (Centre for Sustainable Communities Achieved through Integrated Professional Education) has been established within Kingston University's School of Surveying aimed at 'producing graduates capable of working to create more sustainable communities.' At the core of C-SCAIPE's ambitions lies the intention that our students develop knowledge, skills and importantly the value sets to enter their professional lives with confidence and the ambition to make a difference. Whilst C-SCAIPE lies within Kingston University's School of Surveying (KUSS) its activities are scheduled to have impact beyond Surveying to embrace other built environment courses and, ultimately, other professional courses within the university.

C-SCAIPE's aims are ambitious; they could also be said to be difficult to judge in terms of success. The C-SCAIPE Team are aware of this and decided that one measure that could be used would be to monitor students' knowledge and personal commitments both at the point of entry to programmes and upon completion. As a frame of reference, the staff's changing knowledge and practices are being monitored in parallel; after all, if the staff do not lead the process of knowledge and value development, then it would be unrealistic to expect high levels of student engagement. This paper reports on the findings of the initial round of surveys of students entering Surveying programmes but it does not report on the related staff.

Background literature

The 'Education for Sustainability' agenda has emerged as a significant area of development within the Higher Education sector (Wals and Blaze-Corcoran, 2004). It is now widely recognised that it is important to consider how Higher Education institutions (HEIs) can embed sustainability into their teaching and learning programmes. Despite initiatives encouraging the implementation of sustainability into Higher Education such as the Higher Education Partnership for Sustainability programme (HEPS), and extensive academic discussion of appropriate pedagogic content for education for sustainable development (ESD), there has been little exploration into the effectiveness and changing student perceptions of sustainability on a micro, institutional level.

The Future Leaders Survey (Forum for the Future and UCAS, 2007) offers an insight into student attitudes to sustainability on a national level. Over 54,000 students responded to a questionnaire which was sent to all UK university applicants. Feedback suggests students consider sustainable development is an important factor when considering their university options. The survey reveals that architecture, and building and planning applicants placed the most importance on a university's reputation regarding sustainable development when choosing their university (74% regarding it as important or very important). Whilst this level of dis-aggregation is useful it may hide significant differences between the various built environment disciplines and there is a lack of understanding of how the level of interest may vary between, for example, a building surveyor and a planner. A cross-sectional study such as the Future Leaders Survey also fails to track how effective HEIs are in developing students' knowledge and attitudes as they progress through university in the way that a longitudinal study can. Another recent study (Pelly, 2007) indicates that 20% of building environment students said environmental considerations were 'very important' when choosing their career. So important in university; less so to a future career.

SQW Economic and Management consultants were commissioned to carry out an independent specialist review and evaluation of the HEPS Programme (SQW, 2006) in order to 'establish a pioneering partnership of higher education institutions seen to be achieving their strategic objectives through positive engagement with the sustainable development agenda and to generate transferable tools, guidance and inspiration to encourage the rest of the sector to do likewise' as envisaged by Forum for the Future (2004). Their evaluation examined the influence and impact of the HEPS programme on the 18 UK HE institutions enrolled. It explored the progress of the sustainable development agenda and investigated barriers faced by institutions and considered how such obstacles could be overcome.

The Council for Environmental Education's Guide (2004) is useful in providing advice how to implement and evaluate ESD learning programmes and to 'measure learning' in the area. However, it does not focus on the HE sector and does not provide case studies of where such evaluation has been applied. Furthermore, there are few studies at micro level that observe and map student awareness and perceptions at particular universities or across certain disciplines. Although studies such as those discussed above recognize the importance of measuring the effectiveness of ESD, little attention has been paid specifically to the most important stakeholders within Higher Education (HE), that of the students and educators. The study by Azapagic *et al.* (2005) is an exception. This study of engineering students world-wide attempted to identify and explore their level of knowledge and understanding of sustainability. It concluded that, although engineering students recognize sustainable development is important in the field of engineering, the level of knowledge is far from satisfactory and significant knowledge gaps exist.

The University of Plymouth is one of very few British HE institutions to have conducted an internal research programme assessing their own students' awareness and understanding of sustainability. A small-scale qualitative study was carried out during a Masters level Geography field trip. Additionally the university has conducted an online questionnaire aimed at students from a range of disciplines exploring students' current perceptions of sustainable development and sustainability (Kagawa *et al.*, 2006). The report is interesting as it highlights that student learning in this area is affected by the teaching delivery mode; inter-active teaching was found to be most effective. This is an approach adopted by C-SCAIPE.

From these studies, it is apparent that, despite a national drive to equip our future workforce with skills to promote sustainable development within their chosen field, and to increase students' understanding and interest in sustainability, the efficiency and success still remains largely under-researched. Further, although there is some evidence base of interest in sustainability when students enter higher education, their levels of knowledge and understanding at the point of entry remain unknown so there is no benchmark against which the 'value added' can be measured. This is what this research seeks to address.

Methodology

The baseline data for the research was collected via a self-completion questionnaire issued to all Kingston University School of Surveying (KUSS) first year students as they entered Level One. The questionnaire was also distributed to all postgraduate students in KUSS as they started their MA or MSc courses. The survey will then be repeated to the same sample as the students finish their courses;

the undergraduate students as they approach the end of their final year, and the postgraduate students as they advance towards the end of their MA or MSc courses. The process is to be repeated with each new intake of students, providing us with data from a variety of year groups. This longitudinal study will give us data that maps our students' awareness, enthusiasm and interest in sustainability at entry and exit points and gives us an empirical indication of how this develops over their time at Kingston University. It will provide evidence both on the level of rising knowledge and awareness in society generally and the effectiveness of the embedding of principles within the students' learning experience.

The self-completion questionnaire was the chosen method for the sake of efficiency and to minimise bias. It also allowed a large quantity of data to be collected with little effort required from students at a busy time of their year. For this reason, other methods such as interviews and focus groups were rejected. The survey consisted largely of Likert scale questions and closed rating scales. This kept questions short, clear and easy for the respondent to manage. Open-ended questions were used sparingly and only when appropriate. After collection, the data was analysed using the software package SPSS. Significance tests were carried out and open-ended question responses were categorized and coded for analysis in the statistical package.

The survey covered three broad themes:

(i) *Interest and perceived importance*

The goal of equipping students with the skills and knowledge to contribute to a sustainable future will be unfulfilled if the interest is absent, and if students do not realise the relevance of a grasp of the subject to their course and/or future careers. For this reason the students' *interest* and *perceived importance* of sustainability were researched, and constituted the prevailing theme of investigation in the study. It entailed questions regarding students' personal interest; whether the subject of sustainability influenced their political viewpoint; how relevant students felt sustainability will be (or 'was' in the case of the repeated survey) to their university courses; and if they felt an understanding of sustainability would better equip them for their chosen career path. A similar exploration was conducted through the staff questionnaire, the results of which will be reported elsewhere.

(ii) *Awareness and understanding*

Questions regarding *awareness and understanding* of sustainability were posed. This explored familiarity with the subject matter, investigating 'sustainability literacy' and investigated students' perceived relevance of the triple-bottom line.

(iii) *Behaviour and lifestyle*

Students' *behaviour and lifestyle* were explored. The respondents were probed as to how often they perform a range of activities such as recycling. The repeated survey will illustrate whether students' daily life changes over their time at Kingston University and if they become more or less 'environmentally conscious'.

Sample and Response Rate

A pilot study was initially conducted with 60 first year students. On the basis of the feedback from this survey the questionnaire was altered and modified to form the final version of the student questionnaire which was completed by 53% of Surveying undergraduates, and 55% of the postgraduates. Table 1 illustrates the response rate according to degree level. Table 2 shows the gender demographics of the survey (which are roughly representative of the School of Surveying demographic as a whole).

Table 1   Respondents according to degree level

Level	Frequency	Percent
Undergraduates	123	75
Postgraduates	41	25
Total	**164**	**100**

Table 2   Respondents according to gender

Gender	Frequency	Percent
Male	130	79
Female	34	21
Total	**164**	**100**

Results

(i) *Interest and perceived importance*

Students' enthusiasm and perceived relevance of sustainability were mapped via various questions. Respondents were asked to give a score out of 10 for how interested they are in sustainability (1 being not remotely interested, and 10 being very interested).

The overall mean score was fairly high at 6.8 and comparable to that in the UCAS study. However, Table 3 and Table 4 illustrate disparities of interest across the programmes and levels. Unsurprisingly, the MA Planning and Sustainability gave the highest overall average and the BSc Real Estate Management the lowest by some distance.

The perceived relevance of SD to the students' courses was investigated by asking if the students felt sustainability will be an important part of their course. As Table 5 indicates, 96% of students thought it would be very important or fairly important to their degree course. Whilst this could be seen as encouraging, it could be a function of their prior information on the Kingston courses including Open Day materials.

Disparities again emerged. For example 15% of the BSc Real Estate Management students thought sustainability would be of no importance to their course compared to the overall average of only 4%, whilst only 30% of this group thought it would be very important, in comparison to 43% overall.

Table 3   Mean score for undergraduates

Course Module				
BSc Real Estate Management	BSc Property, Planning and Development	BSc Quantity Surveying Consultancy	BSc Building Surveying	BSc Residential Property
5.89	6.85	7.22	7.07	7.22

Avg: 6.82

Table 4   Mean score for postgraduates

Course Modules		
MA European Real Estate	MA Planning and Sustainability	MSc Real Estate
6.38	9.14	5.93

Avg. 6.76

Table 5   How important will sustainability be to your course?

Overall response		
Response	**Frequency**	**Percent**
Not important to my course	6	3.7
Fairly important to my course	87	53.0
Very important to my course	71	43.3
Total	164	100.0

It was considered important to gauge 'entrenched interest' in sustainability when exploring students' interest in the subject. This meant investigating students' interest and perceived importance of sustainability away from the classroom and lecture theatres. Thus students were asked if they had an *active* interest in sustainability outside of their university course.

Figure 1 shows that a considerably higher proportion of postgraduates, than undergraduates, have an active interest in sustainability. Given that C-SCAIPE has an ambition of instilling value changes, the 'journey travelled' by the undergraduates will be important data for the staff team.

Following this closed question, students who do have an active interest in sustainability were asked to comment on what they did beyond their normal studies to develop their understanding of sustainability. Activities which emerged varied from watching particular television programmes or documentaries (highest response for both UGs and PGs) to being involved with a pressure group, attending external lectures, keeping newspaper cut-outs, and involvement in voluntary work or employment.

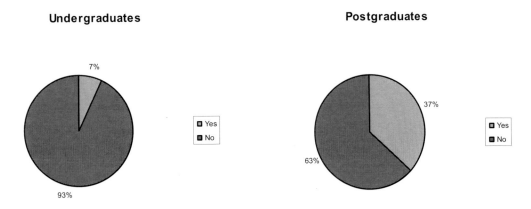

Figure 1   Undergraduate and postgraduate student responses to the question asking whether they have an active interest in sustainability outside of their university course

This line of enquiry continued with a probe as to whether students would support a particular political party if sustainable development was key to the party's political agenda. Figure 2 illustrates the results.

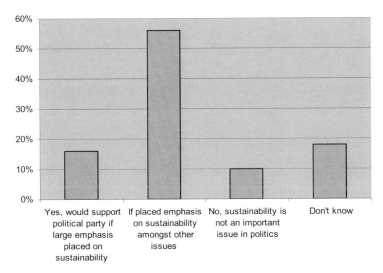

The fact that 18% of respondents replied 'did not know' may indicate that a good proportion of students are not engaged in politics and (despite its rising prominence) the place of sustainability on the political agenda.

Figure 2 Students' response when asked if they would support a political party that placed emphasis on sustainability

This question was cross-referenced with another exploring the extent to which respondents had studied sustainability prior to entering university. Of those who *had* covered sustainability before, 46% thought it would be important to their chosen career, whilst of those who had not been taught anything on sustainability, less than 30% thought it would be important, implying an exposure to the principles of sustainability before HE increases the perceived importance of a grasp of sustainability.

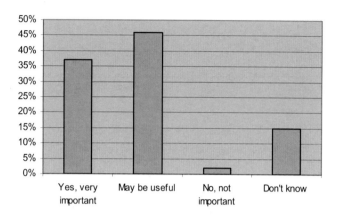

Students' perceived importance of sustainability knowledge to their future careers was investigated (Figure 3). 84% said an understanding will be important, or might be important, to their chosen career, suggesting widespread acknowledgement that an awareness of the principles of sustainability will contribute to the success of their careers and better equip them in the career path they choose.

Figure 3 Importance attached to an understanding of sustainability to students' chosen careers

There are also strong correlations with the question asking how important the students feel sustainability will be to their degree courses. Of those who said sustainability will be an important part of their course, 56% said it would be very important to their chosen career. 37% said it may be useful for their careers, and no respondents from this sample said it would not be important (7% said they 'did not know'). Of those who thought it would *not* be an important part of their degree course, 17% said it may be useful to their future career and a majority (83%) said they 'did not know'.

(ii) *Awareness and understanding*

Changing awareness, understanding, and 'sustainability literacy' were explored via a range of questions. Students were given a list of words, terms and topics, which they were asked to score, out of ten, for relevance to sustainability. Table 6 shows the terms used, and in descending order of perceived relevance.

(iii) *Behaviour and lifestyle*

It is one thing to teach or learn sustainability principles; it is quite another to adopt them as lifestyle choices. The questionnaire, therefore, sought to test respondents' actual behaviours: just how sustainable or 'green' are students outside university? The survey explored the frequency with which they perform a variety of activities. The question also attempted to give an indication of the carbon footprint of our students' and staff carbon footprint and any relationship between their views and their actions. Results of note include:

- over half of students routinely re-cycle their household waste
- only 2% of students routinely purchase fair trade produce (despite Kingston University being a fair trade university)
- of those with access to a car, a third of students use it for journeys of one mile or less on an 'often' or 'daily' basis

- when shopping, only 3% of students always use their own shopping bag (or old carrier bags) instead of using new ones from the shop
- only 3% of students routinely avoid choosing products on the basis of unnecessary packaging

Students' understanding of the 'Triple Bottom Line' was also briefly explored. A Likert scale of one to ten was again used as students scored how important social issues, economic issues, and environmental issues are to sustainability. 'Environmental' received the highest average across the board, scoring an average of 8.4 compared to 'economic' issues with 7.4 and 'social' scoring 7. Again this changed with level and course (postgraduates scoring all three far higher than undergraduates). Cross-referencing with the students' study of sustainability before entering university revealed that those with prior knowledge recognised the interrelation between the three areas far more than those who had not, scoring the topics of higher importance, and on a more even basis.

Table 6   Average scores of topic relevance to sustainability

Pollution	8.26
Energy	8.24
Climate Change	8.04
Conservation	7.71
Waste	7.44
Infrastructure	7.38
Town Planning	7.38
Transport	7.38
Regeneration	7.35
Carbon	7.29
Architecture	7.15
Self-Sufficiency	7.04
Health	6.96
Biodiversity	6.95
Kyoto Agreement	6.93
Housing Value	6.59
GDP	6.27
Enterprise	6.09
Gentrification	6.04
Crime	5.69
The Brundtland Report	5.60
Freedom of Info. Act	5.59
Pensions	5.46

Environmental or ecological words dominate the top places of perceived relevance. The Brundtland Report is perceived of lowest relevance and below the two 'ringers' which were included to detect how much consideration the students were taking over their choices, and to get an idea of how informed their choices were.

As expected, and promisingly, a closer look at the data informs us that this changes as the degree courses progress, all respondents from the MA in Planning and Sustainability gave The Brundtland Report 10 out of 10 for relevance. The three year mapping of the changing perceived relevance of these subjects to sustainable development will be an informative part of the study.

These results would demonstrate room for significant improvement in basic sustainability lifestyle habits. Given the price differential between many fair trade products and their non-fair-trade equivalents, the difference in habits could be explained by financial considerations but other behaviours point to students paying little regard in practice to their carbon footprint except with regard to re-cycling. The recycling example is interesting in that the university's Sustainability Team has run an active campaign for the last two years to promote awareness of the need to re-cycle and has set up mechanisms within halls of residence to support re-cycling activities. Given that the starting point of our students is a high level of interest in sustainability *in principle,* but that their personal choices lack evidence of sustainable living practice, it is imperative that the educators - and retailers - will need to work hard to make the sustainable choice that which students adopt. The repeated survey in three years time will hopefully suggest this has occurred, but much will depend on how far such choices are embedded in the value sets of staff.

Concluding Thoughts

There are encouraging indications that our students recognise the importance of an understanding of the principles of sustainable development. Indeed 37% of Kingston University Surveying students thought a good understanding of the principles of sustainability would be 'very important' to their chosen career, which contrasts, nationally, with only 20% of building environment students who had said environmental considerations were 'very important' when choosing their career (Pelly, 2007).

Despite the evident importance our students place on an understanding of sustainability regarding their future career in comparison to the national survey, it appears our students did not anticipate the significance sustainability would have on their degree courses in comparison to the Built Environment students nationwide; 74% of building and planning students said sustainable development was 'very important' when choosing their degree course, presumably with the assumption it would play a key role in their studies. This contrasts with only 44% of our students who believe sustainability will be an important part of their course.

These initial results suggest that when it comes to key life decisions such as voting, KUSS students place more importance on sustainability than Built Environment students at national level with 16% judging that sustainability was a very important issue to a political party's agenda, whereas nationally only 10% of Built Environment students think environmental considerations are very important when it comes to voting.

The disappointing result is that, in terms of personal lifestyle choices, even elementary actions towards sustainability have not been adopted.

Looking forwards, the overall results of the survey provide a useful benchmark from which to monitor change both in the views and knowledge of those entering our programmes. It also gives a base point from which the effectiveness of student learning about sustainability can be evaluated. The intention is that the survey will be integrated within the feedback from the current staff survey, and in time roll out to other departments and faculties in order that a full picture of Kingston's progress can be charted.

The survey data has illustrated that the School's emphasis on sustainable development has an opportunity to contribute greatly to the students' awareness of the subject given that they enter the courses with interest, but a low knowledge base. Given that it is increasingly important that they leave ready, able and committed to put understanding and knowledge of sustainable development into practice in the working world, the repeated survey on the eve of the same students' entrance into employment will hopefully provide a positively different dataset.

References

Azapagic, A., Perdan, S. and Shallcross, D. 2005 How much do engineering students know about sustainable development? The findings of an international survey and possible implications for the engineering curriculum. *European Journal of Engineering Education*, **30**, 1-19

Council for Environmental Education Evaluation Group 2004 *Measuring effectiveness: evaluation in education for sustainable development.* [Internet].
<http://www.cee.org.uk/documents/Measuring%20effectiveness%20evaluation%20in%20esd.pdf>. [Accessed 21st August 2007].

Dawe, G., Jucker, R. and Martin, S. 2005 *Sustainable Development in Higher Education: Current Practice and future developments*, A report for The Higher Education Academy. York: Higher Education Academy

Forum for the Future 2004 *On course for Sustainability: Report of the Higher Education Partnership 2000-2003*. London: Forum for the Future

Forum for the Future and University College Admission Service 2007 *The Future Leader Survey 2006/0 (11 June 2007)*. [Internet].
<http://www.forumforthefuture.org.uk/docs/page/165/495/Futureleaders0607.pdf>. [Accessed 21st August 2007].

HM Government 2005 *Securing the future: delivering UK sustainable development strategy*. [Internet]. <http://www.sustainable-development.gov.uk/index.asp>. [Accessed 12th August 2007].

Higher Education Partnership for Sustainability and Forum for the Future 2004 *On course for sustainability: Report of the Higher Education Partnership for Sustainability 2000-2003*. [Internet].
<http://www.forumforthefuture.org.uk/docs/publications/237/On%20course%20for%20sustainability.pdf. >.[Accessed 1st September 2007].

Higher Education Academy 2006 *Sustainable development in higher education. Current practice and future development: A progress report for employers, unions and the professions*. York: Higher Education Academy

HEFCE 2002 *Report 02/23 Evaluating the regional contribution of an HEI: A benchmarking approach*. United Kingdom: HEFCE

Kagawa, F. Selby, D. and Trier, C. 2006 Exploring students' perceptions of interactive pedagogies in education for sustainable development. *Planet-Centre for Sustainable Futures*. 17th December. Plymouth: University of Plymouth

Pelly, L. 2007 *Forum for the Future: Challenges to Engineering Education for Sustainable Development. Proceedings of the Engineering Professors' Council 2007 Annual Congress Meeting held at the University of Leeds*. Leeds: Leeds University

Roberts, C. and Roberts, J. 2007 *Greener by Degrees: Exploring Sustainability through Higher Education Curricula*. Plymouth: Geography Discipline Network

SQW Ltd Economic and Management Consultants 2006 Specialist Review and Evaluation of the Higher Education Partnership for Sustainability (HEPS). *Final report to the UK higher education funding bodies (HEFCE, SFC, HEFCW and DEL)*. 11th June. Bristol: HEFCE

Wals, A. and Blaze Corcoran, P. 2004 *Higher Education and the Challenge of Sustainability: Problematics, Promise and Practice*. London: Kluwer Academic Publishers

SME Engagement With Sustainability Issues: A Case Study From Surrey, UK

Ros Taylor, Simon Bray and Robert Gant
Kingston University
Kathy Morrissey
WSP Environmental, UK

Abstract

Environmental issues and the wider sustainability agenda are increasingly pertinent concerns for business and commerce. While major corporations have been relatively quick to realise the competitive advantages and reputational risk avoidance associated with adopting sound environmental and social policies, response from Small and Medium Enterprises (SMEs) has been slow, despite the availability of diverse training programmes and support. This is an important distinction given that in the UK SMEs engender half of all economic activity, employ more than half the work force, are significant producers of commercial waste and account for 80% of pollution incidents (Netregs, 2005). The social, economic and environmental impact of SMEs is thus very significant. This report discusses a survey of SMEs in Surrey, UK, undertaken to gain insight into SME understanding of sustainability issues from international legislation to immediate local concerns and to appreciate why the uptake of training and support opportunities remains poor. Associated seminars explored alternative and potentially more productive ways to enhance environmental and sustainability performance.

Results confirmed that transport, energy and waste were the primary concerns with issues such as climate change and biodiversity deemed to have little immediate relevance to SME practice. However, companies did appreciate and were keen to engage with social sustainability, for example donating unwanted but re-usable IT resources to schools and charitable organisations. Uptake of existing training provision was poor with 77% of companies surveyed unaware of the targeted provision available and others unwilling to allocate staff time for participation. In seminar discussion, government-, big business-, or local council-led sustainable procurement drivers supported by educational and practical guidance emerged as a key way forward to engage SMEs in the sustainability agenda and cascade good practice throughout the business community.

Keywords   SMEs, sustainability training, environmental awareness, sustainable procurement

Setting the Scene

In the last two decades, environmental quality has become an increasing concern for governments and individuals and has thereby driven the agenda for industry and commerce. However, SMEs have been reluctant to respond to this agenda and embed sustainability and improved environmental practices in business operations. Given that the 4.3 million UK SMEs account for 51% of national turnover and 59% of employment (DTI, 2006), the sustainable operation of these businesses is a national imperative. However, from a realistic perspective it has been argued that while 'there are undoubtedly many ways in which SMEs can improve their environmental performance …. It is questionable that within the present economic system environmental [and other aspects of] sustainability will ever be achieved' (Hutchinson and Chaston, 2007). Evidence supports this claim and confirms that SMEs produce significant environmental impacts (Williams and Lynch-Wood, 2001) accounting for an estimated 60% of commercial waste and 80% of pollution incidents in England and Wales (NetRegs, 2005). Reluctance on the part of management to acknowledge and respond effectively to this situation by adopting proven Environmental Standards has lead to a cumulative and significant impact on the environment (Hillary, 2000). It is recognised that such environmental disbenefits can be further aggravated by the concentration of SMEs in industrial estates and business parks which lack shared and responsive management services (Hillary, 2004). However, initiatives to remedy this situation and engage SMEs in environmental schemes have produced mixed results. Reasons for such disengagement are complex and range from perceived costs, an unwillingness to release staff for appropriate training to a perception of state over-regulation of the small business sector (Petts *et al.*, 1998; Hillary, 2004; Bradford and Fraser, 2008).

An approach to encourage the 'untapped potential' (Bradford and Fraser, 2008) of improved environmental management in SMEs is through sustainable procurement policies (Edler and Georghiou, 2007). Public procurement has been seen as a potential driver for SME engagement and has been demonstrated as a general tool to specify contract renewal (Dalen *et al.*, 2005). There are, however, apparent or perceived barriers to sustainable procurement (Thompson and Jackson, 2007) which may prevent the timely uptake of this ethos and inhibit public procurement officers from making informed choices. Amongst others, barriers in local government may be perceived as financial, legislation and insufficient priority from management (Borg *et al.*, 2006). When these factors are coupled with obstacles indicated by the SME sector, it is perhaps little wonder that SME voluntary uptake of environmental management training has, to date, seen limited success (Bradford and Fraser, 2008).

In Surrey there are approximately 50,000 SMEs (personal communication, Horton-Baker, 2007). These are situated within the jurisdictions of 11 local councils, the county council, government offices and various Further and Higher Education institutions. SME training and guidance has been offered already through several of these organisations including local councils, educational establishments and business support organisations e.g. Surrey Chambers of Commerce, BusinessLink Surrey. However, take up of a variety of well-organised schemes has been limited. This project, therefore, was designed to investigate reasons for the poor engagement with environmental management in Surrey SMEs. Supported by HEIF (Higher Education Innovation Fund), a team from Kingston University has consequently researched sustainability barriers and training awareness in Surrey-based SMEs. This investigation has included consideration of the validity and use of Sustainable Procurement in the public sector as a tool encouraging SMEs to engage with training opportunities.

SMEs in Surrey

Survey design

The research findings reported in this paper are derived from a survey of the environmental and sustainability issues faced by Small and Medium Enterprises in Surrey undertaken within the *Sustainable Business Practices for Small and Medium Enterprises* programme and co-ordinated by the Westfocus partnership based at Kingston University. The objectives set for that investigation were to:

(i)   determine awareness of sustainability principles in the business community
(ii)   define the impact of environmental factors and policy regulation on business operations and practice
(iii)   identify evidence of sustainable business practices in waste identification and management strategies in the Surrey economy
(iv)   probe sector attitudes to the further involvement of business in the community and engagement with Corporate Social Responsibility (CSR)
(v)   measure participation in existing training provision for sustainable business operations and the specification of future training needs
(vi)   establish how public and private organisation procurement policies can be used to influence SME attitudes towards the sustainability agenda

Evidence is drawn from a self-completion questionnaire designed to probe these key issues. The questionnaire was pilot-tested against a target of 50 companies drawn systematically from a database supplied by BusinessLink, Surrey. This proforma was mailed to company management in November 2005 and produced a response rate of 6%. Follow-up conversations by telephone with non-respondents confirmed that three main factors had accounted for the low rate of response: a lack of perceived and immediate interest in the topic as related to company policy and practices; the season of the year with the impending annual holiday break and imminent accounting deadlines; and non-contact (3 cases) due to an outdated sampling frame.

In response to this feedback, the self-completion questionnaire used for the main survey in January 2006 was re-framed and some questions re-worded. This was mailed, with a covering letter and reply-paid envelope, to the remaining 1550 registered members listed on the database. Notwithstanding these precautions, the final return produced only 94 usable questionnaires, accounting for 6% of members listed on the data base. The Post Office referred a further 95 envelopes as 'not known at this address'/'gone away'.

The findings analysed in this report are, *force majeure*, presented as being *indicative* rather than statistically *representative* of the behaviour and experience of business enterprises in the administrative county. The sample is geographically dispersed and, for a more sensitive interpretation, has been categorised initially into 13 sectors of business activity. Where appropriate, for tabulation, these categories have been re-grouped into six composite sectors to support further interpretation and commentary.

Profile of businesses

Figure 1 represents the numerical distribution of the 13 categories of business and organisation that responded to the survey and completed, satisfactorily, the standard proforma. The main clusters are found in the principal urban centres of the GU (48%), KT (20%) and RH (15%) postcode districts. Figure 2 provides further detail on the relative importance of the business sectors represented in these county-wide postcode districts.

Key structural features in business profile are represented as Figure 3. This confirms that finance and business (30%), professional services (20%); and computer/hi-tech (11%) businesses dominated the employment scene. Small business operations predominated. Overall, 38% of firms employed fewer than 5 people in full-time and/or part-time capacities and a further 30% between 5 and 9 personnel. Companies employing in excess of 30 people accounted for a further 14% of the total. Only 2 companies had workforces in excess of 100.

In excess of 80% of firms engaged in finance and business, computing/hi-tech and professional services employed fewer than 10 people. In contrast, those in manufacturing, construction and hotel and catering had more extended employment profiles. Furthermore, part-time employment characterised the smaller businesses: 49 employed females and 24 males in a part-time capacity.

Overall, 55% of companies occupied rented premises and 38% were owner-occupiers; these patterns of property tenure were similar across the postcode districts.

Sustainability and corporate social responsibility

Awareness of sustainability issues was weakly developed across all business sectors (Figure 3). This key finding justifies the thrust of the survey and sets the scene for targeted intervention.

Respondents were invited to react to a given definition for sustainability, *viz.* 'protection of the environment and prudent use of natural resources now and for future generations whilst promoting economic growth and social well-being'. Overall, 89% of respondents agreed with this statement. The few (mainly professional services, finance and business companies) who disagreed challenged the clarity and intention of the statement: amendments suggested included an extension of the wording to include ethical concerns and social sustainability, and a revised wording to reflect the competitive reality of the present-day business environment.

Findings confirm that, in general, companies have been tardy in addressing sustainability issues in a formal sense. Only 16 businesses claimed to have a formal environmental policy. In 15 cases the person completing the proforma had seen this company statement. It was claimed that this policy extended to suppliers (15 cases) and customers (6 cases). Furthermore, only three businesses held an accredited Environmental Standard (ISO14001(2) and unspecified(1)), whilst a further three claimed to be seeking accreditation (BS8555(1), ISO14001(1), and unspecified (1)).

Figure 1   Location of businesses surveyed

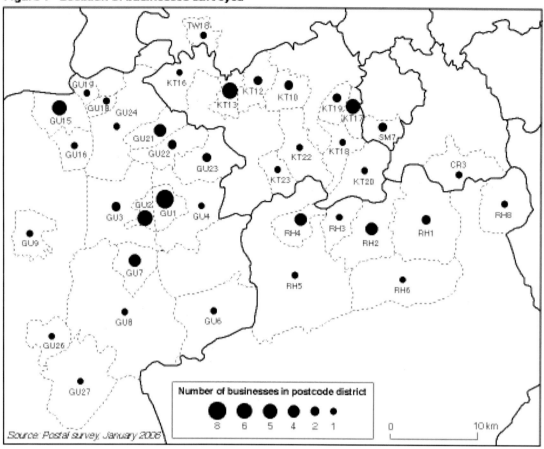

Figure 2   Principal business sectors

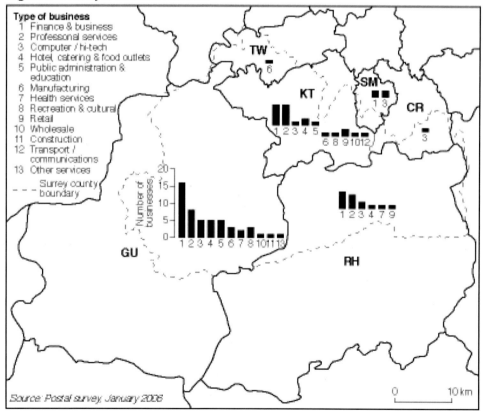

Figure 3 Profile of businesses

(a) Company structure

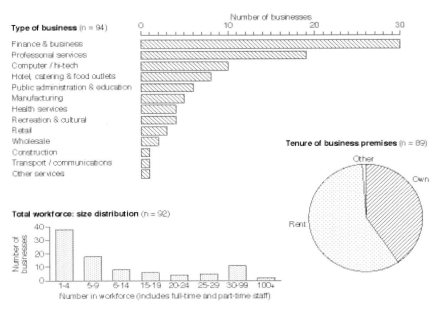

(b) Awareness of sustainability issues

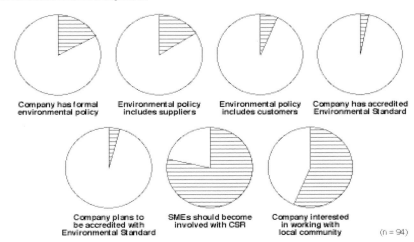

Source: Postal survey, January 2008

Engagement with CSR formed a further and important thrust of the survey. It was explained that such involvement would require recognition of the wider concerns of the communities in which they operated and the creation of effective linkages with, for example, local charities, schools and public groups. This challenge evoked a favourable and geographically-widespread response from 87 businesses, 85% of whom supported the position that SMEs should become actively involved in CSR activities. More specifically, a smaller subset of 62% representing proportionately all sizes of firm claimed to be interested in programmes devised by Surrey Community Foundation to help businesses work with their local communities.

Table 1 captures this spread of interest, and latent commitment, across all categories of business. It is significant that whilst respondents from typically smaller businesses in the finance and business and professional service sectors are largely prepared to become more involved in CSR, proportionately fewer members expressed an active interest in working with local communities.

Table 1   Attitudes towards Corporate Social Responsibility (CSR)

Business Sector	SMEs should become more involved with CSR?		Interested in working with local communities?	
	yes	no	yes	no
Finance and business	23	4	17	10
Professional services	14	3	10	17
Computing and hi-tech	8	2	5	5
Construction, manufacturing and transport	6	0	3	3
Wholesale, retail, hotel and catering	11	2	8	3
Public administration, recreation, leisure, health	12	2	10	5
Total	*74*	*13*	*53*	*43*

Source: Postal survey, January 2006

Environmental issues and business operations

Scaled questions were used to check the significance and impact on business operations of *international and national* agreements aimed at promoting environmental awareness and changing corporate and public attitudes towards the environment. These included the Kyoto Protocol, UK Climate Change Levy, UK Waste Electrical and Electronic Equipment Directive (DTI), UK Landfill Tax, UK Water Framework Directive, UK Envirowise Waste and Waste Water Initiative and UK Biodiversity Action Plan. Respondents confirmed that The UK Landfill Tax has had a significant, across-sector, effect on the operations of 19% of businesses. Then, in descending order of direct impact, and more evenly spread across business sectors, the effects of the UK Waste Electrical and Electronic Equipment Directive (DTI) (13% of businesses), UK Climate Change Levy (11%), Kyoto Protocol (9%) and UK Water Framework Directive (7%) featured as being less important. Finally, the impacts of the UK Envirowise Waste and Waste Water Reduction Initiative (3%) and UK Biodiversity Action Plan (2%) were confirmed as minimal.

Businesses were invited to scale the impact of seven important environmental issues on their operations. Table 2 identifies the proportions and sectors of companies that claimed environmental issues to exert at least a 'significant' impact on business operation and location. Overall, in excess of half the sample cited transport (75% of companies), energy consumption (62%) and waste disposal (62%). Pollution (46%) and water consumption (44%) followed closely. Climate change issues (37%) and protection of wildlife and habitats (31%), however, were judged to be less significant. Potential responses to these concerns varied by the size of firm. For instance, both the categories of firm employing fewer than five people and with a workforce exceeding 30 claimed that they could take a more proactive stand against energy consumption, water consumption, waste disposal and transport.

Firms of intermediate size, however, were less sure of their potential behaviour towards the stated range of environmental issues.

The pattern and strength of responses bear a general relationship to business type. For instance, transport issues had a special impact on: manufacturing industries; wholesale and retail distribution; hotel, catering and food outlets; and professional services. Energy consumption was likewise important for these sectors. Waste disposal, however, was understandably an issue of less significance for finance and business services, professional services and public administration and education than for companies in other sectors.

Table 2 **Companies claiming that environmental issues have either a 'significant' or 'highly significant' impact on business operation**

Business sector	Pollution	Climate change	Energy use	Water use	Wildlife and habitats	Waste disposal	Transport
Finance and business	12	10	16	11	8	18	24
Professional services	10	6	11	6	4	9	15
Computing and hi-tech	4	2	5	2	2	5	7
Construction, manufacturing and transport	4	2	6	3	4	6	7
Wholesale, retail, hotel and catering	7	8	11	12	5	11	9
Public administration, recreation, leisure, health	6	7	9	7	6	9	8
Total companies affected	**43**	**35**	**58**	**41**	**29**	**58**	**70**
As % of all companies	**46**	**37**	**62**	**44**	**31**	**62**	**75**
As % of companies claiming an ability to respond	**20**	**15**	**51**	**34**	**17**	**61**	**43**

Source: Postal survey, January 2006

A suite of questions challenged companies to reflect on their capacity to respond more fully to significant environmental issues that affected their operations. Findings confirm that whilst more than a third could take further action to deal with waste disposal (60%), energy consumption (51%), transport issues (46%) and water consumption (34%), relatively few felt able to deal with various pollution issues (20%), wildlife and habitats (17%) and climate change events (15%). Although there are no strongly-defined relationships between business sector and ability to respond to particular challenges, the declared ability of the public administration and education sector to reduce water consumption and deal more sustainably with waste disposal, and the computer-hi-tech sector, professional services and hotel, catering and food outlets to deal more effectively with waste disposal are noted.

Transport and the business environment

Traffic management schemes and parking regulations can effectively reduce and re-distribute traffic flows. In conjunction with car sharing and investment in public transport services these schemes can impact on the working environment and economic performance of businesses. They also impact on the life-style and journey patterns of the workforce. Findings from the survey highlight key issues on operating efficiency perceived by company management.

Overall, 66% of businesses surveyed claimed that vehicle parking and congestion charging had impacted on business operations. Such impacts were not differentiated by business sector.
Furthermore, 55% agreed that central government and local authority initiatives aimed at *reducing* vehicle parking and *relieving* congestion had affected the company. This opinion was voiced by over half the respondents in finance and business companies, hotel, catering and food outlets and professional services, and especially those in urban core locations. This pattern of concern was replicated for the impacts of traffic management on the travel-to-work patterns of company personnel. The dominance of small businesses in the employment profile distorts the proportionate analysis of journey-to-work flows and modal choice. Notwithstanding, the survey confirms a workforce dependence on private car travel. Employees at 84% firms used a car to travel to work; in 48% of cases this mode accounted for at least 75% of daily journeys. Characteristically, public transport, cycles and motor-bikes were each used by less than 25% of company employees. Walking, as a mode, was favoured mainly by full-time and part-time employees in small businesses situated close to home.

Waste identification and management strategy

It is recognised that waste materials from businesses can have a significant impact on the environment. In this context, several waste re-cycling and reduction initiatives have been developed and promoted in Surrey to minimise the consequences. Accordingly, businesses were invited to assess the 'significance' to their company of eight specified categories of waste, with an option to extend this selection.

Table 3 summarises the pattern of response and identifies those waste streams deemed to be 'significant' in the context of business practice. Paper and cardboard were deemed to be of foremost importance by 63% of businesses. Next in importance, at a reduced level, were electrical goods (29% of businesses), water (19%), plastic (19%) and chemicals (15%). Waste glass, metal and tyres were each 'significant' outputs from less than 10% of the businesses surveyed.

Waste paper and cardboard streams are 'significant' waste outputs from professional, finance and business services, computer/hi-tech enterprises and hotel, catering and food outlets. With the exception of the hotel and catering sector, these types of business are the principal sources of redundant computing hardware and electrical equipment. Chemicals, metal waste and plastic derive mainly from specific manufacturing, finance and business enterprises, and hotel, catering and food outlets.

Respondents were advised that Surrey County Council operated 'waste sharing' and 'waste swapping' schemes to allow firms to trade in waste products. Overall, 31% of companies claimed to be interested in such ventures. Two products were viewed as important in such trade: paper and cardboard (20%) and electrical goods, including redundant computer hardware (14%).

Businesses were asked to outline briefly the plans they had made to reduce consumption or to re-cycle types of waste they had earlier identified. This request produced a far-ranging and descriptive set of comments and actions. In total, 52 (55%) businesses responded to this invitation. Content analysis was applied to the free text and 70 response categories covering 104 responses were constructed. These categories were re-cast into 12 key themes which, in turn, have been re-grouped under the main headings of 'problems encountered', 'management policies and practices', and 're-cycling achieved'.

Eleven businesses claimed to have experienced *problems* in re-cycling waste. These included frustration with bureaucracy, the absence of appropriate local services facilities for specialised waste re-cycling and the financial costs involved.

Twenty-nine businesses cited *evidence of a positive company policy* and set of formalised actions to deal with waste recycling and to promote sustainable business practice. Several demonstrated a pro-active stance in negotiation with local authorities and the quest for specialist waste removal agencies. One larger organisation had invested in specialist equipment to compact waste cardboard before removal from site. Policies to reduce energy and water consumption and minimise the aggregate cost of public utilities and re-use waste materials were also evident across all sectors. A few firms had adopted policies to promote social sustainability. These included the introduction of a non-smoking work environment, provision of staff accommodation within walking distance of the workplace, insistence that cleaning agencies used water-based cleansing (not aerosol) materials and negotiation with clients to secure re-cycling objectives.

Fifty-nine businesses signalled evidence of *company achievements* in waste re-cycling. These actions displayed varying levels of commitment, but covered most business types. Re-cycling waste paper and cardboard and plastic packaging materials was of foremost importance. Six businesses had made provision for the sustainable removal and treatment of glass products. Others had negotiated the specialist collection for re-cycling of waste products such as chemicals, metal products and electrical components. Given the representation of IT-dependent professional and financial services in the survey, it is heartening to record policies for the donation of obsolete computing hardware to charitable organisations and successful schemes for recycling printer cartridges. In some small firms the (mainly part-time) staff removed the waste paper from the premises for recycling through a home-based service.

Table 3 **Types of waste identified by companies as being 'significant' or 'highly significant' to their business operation**

Business sector	Water	Electrical Goods	Chemical	Metal	Glass	Plastic	Paper/ cardboard	Tyres
Finance and business	5	8	2	2	3	3	19	2
Professional services	1	3	0	1	1	1	13	0
Computing and hi-tech	0	7	2	0	0	1	5	0
Construction, manufacturing and transport	2	2	4	2	0	3	3	2
Wholesale, retail, hotel and catering	4	2	4	4	1	5	9	1
Public administration, recreation, leisure, health	5	5	2	1	2	6	10	1
Total companies affected	17	27	14	10	7	19	59	6
As % of all companies	19	29	15	9	9	19	63	6
% expressing interest in waste share/swap schemes for specified waste product	4	14	2	3	3	7	20	2

Source: Postal survey, January 2006

Sustainable procurement

Government directives have targeted an increase in sustainable procurement practices for SMEs. Initiatives to achieve that objective have been trialled in Surrey. Responses given to the suite of questions focused on this issue confirm that 86% of businesses (across the employment range) supplied goods and services to other businesses; the remainder (especially financial services and hotel and catering and food outlets) dealt *directly* with private clients. In contrast, 34% of companies (including representatives from most sectors, and the smaller employers) supplied goods and services to the public sector.

Knowledge levels of locally-operating schemes tasked with promoting sustainable procurement initiatives were relatively low and poorly developed. For instance, only 12% of companies had knowledge of *public organisation* initiatives to target supplies from sustainable businesses, and only 11% (mainly larger employers) were aware of *private company* initiatives to achieve that objective. There were notable exceptions to this blanket designation amongst the 13% of companies that knew of initiatives raised by charities to target supplies from sustainable businesses, and particularly those in the finance and business sector.

However, a near-consensus (81% of all businesses, including similar proportions from all size categories) emerged that the public sector should use its influence on suppliers to encourage a reduction in trading impacts on the environment. The relatively lower subscription to this ideal from

businesses in the professional service and finance and business sectors is explained, in part, by the proportion of businesses that already maintained strong linkages with public sector clients.

Training programmes for sustainable business

For local businesses, Surrey County Council has promoted a series of *county-wide* initiatives to raise awareness of environmental impacts and sustainability issues. The main programmes are featured on Table 4 which indicates, by business type, those firms expressing either a 'strong interest' or 'high level of enthusiasm' for participation. In descending order of preference, Paper for Surrey (24% of businesses), Surrey Programme for Environmentally Responsible Business (18%), and Waste-wise Business Manual (17%) were, potentially, the most favoured. Few businesses expressed an interest in the activities of either Surrey Urban Diversity Plan (9%) or Surrey Car Share (8%). There is no marked clustering, by business sector, in potential affiliation to any of the schemes offered. However, further analysis by business size suggests that, with the exception of engagement with the Surrey Programme for Environmentally Responsible Business, the largest employers were the most interested in these working initiatives. Firms of intermediate size expressed relatively higher levels of interest in the Surrey Programme for Environmentally Responsible Business and the Surrey Urban Biodiversity Project.

Table 4   Companies registering either a 'strong interest' or 'high level of enthusiasm' for Surrey-wide initiatives to raise awareness of environmental impacts and sustainability

Business sector	Surrey programme for environmentally responsible business	Local paper for Surrey	Waste-wise business manual	Surrey car share	Surrey urban biodiversity project	Total companies in survey
Finance and business	6	9	5	4	4	30
Professional services	4	5	3	1	2	19
Computing and hi-tech	2	3	0	1	0	10
Construction, manufacturing and transport	0	1	2	0	0	7
Wholesale, retail, hotel and catering	2	3	3	0	1	13
Public administration, recreation, leisure, health	4	3	4	2	2	15
Total companies affected	**18**	**24**	**17**	**8**	**9**	**94**
As % of all companies	19	25	18	9	10	

Source: Postal survey, January 2006

Surrey County Council, in conjunction with BusinessLink Surrey, has also provided SUMS (Simple Utility Management Seminars), an environmental training programme for SMEs. The objective of SUMS is to raise environmental awareness and promote sustainable business operations. It is very significant that 77% of the businesses surveyed claimed to have no knowledge of the existence of such dedicated training provision. Larger businesses showed greater levels of awareness of training opportunities. Those employing fewer than 10 people expressed some interest but claimed that time constraints worked against participation.

So far, participation in formal training programmes has been minimal. Only 5% of the businesses (three from the business and finance sector, and one each from the computer/hi-tech and public administration and education sectors) had participated in the seminar programme. A further 16% (mainly small businesses, across all sectors) expressed an interest in training provision, but to date had been thwarted by pressure on time and a reluctance to release staff from key duties.

Two of the five businesses (one each from the computer/hi-tech and finance and business sectors) which had been represented at the environmental training seminars claimed to have subsequently changed business practice to conform more closely to sustainability precepts. For one, this has involved writing an environmental policy for the company, monitoring and reducing the consumption of water and energy, instituting more rigorous procedures for re-cycling of other waste products, and adopting more sustainable procurement practices. In conclusion, much remains to be done in targeting businesses and securing active participation in training programmes in a non-threatening environment.

The Way Forward

Evidence drawn from this *indicative* study of sustainability and business practice in Surrey shows that, overall, the business community agrees on the given definition and scope of 'sustainability,' notwithstanding the situation that only a few businesses have developed formal environmental policies or hold accredited Environmental Standards. It also indicates that although few SMEs have fully adopted the practices of corporate social responsibility, there exists a general willingness to become more fully involved with the local community, and belief that the public sector should use its influence on suppliers to encourage a reduction of trading impacts on the environment. Findings also show that businesses are prepared to take further action to deal with waste disposal, energy consumption and transport issues. Furthermore, SMEs in Surrey would be willing to deal more proactively through company policy with the administrative and technical problems connected to re-cycling and waste management, supported by Surrey training initiatives and central government intervention

Company participation in training programmes for enhancing environmental awareness and raising the profile of the sustainability agenda remains low across all sectors in the Surrey business community. This suggests that a more imaginative suite of actions and targeted dissemination of guidelines is required to overcome barriers to participation and assist in cascading good practice. To achieve this objective, and change environmental attitudes in Surrey SMEs, the benefits of customised training to company well-being, ethos and community engagement have to be demonstrated and realised. This should be facilitated through targeted information and dedicated training provision tailored closely to company needs, budget and expectations, and an active field programme of outreach activities.

References

Borg, N., Blume, Y., Thomas, S., Irrekb, W., Faninger-Lund, H., Lundd, P. and Pindare, A. 2006   Release the power of the public purse. *Energy Policy,* **34**, 238-250

Bradford, J. and Fraser, E.D.G. 2008 Local authorities, climate change and small and medium enterprises: Identifying effective policy instruments to reduce energy use and carbon emissions. *Corporate Social Responsibility and Environmental Management,* **15**,156-172

Dalen, D. M., Moen, E.R. and Riis, C. 2006 Contract renewal and incentives in public procurement. *International Journal of Industrial Organization,* **24**, 269-285

Department of Trade and Industry (DTI) 2006 *Small and Medium Enterprise Statistics for the United Kingdom, 2005.* SME Statistics Unit, Sheffield: Department of Trade and Industry. [Internet]. <http://www.sbs.gov.uk/smes>. [Accessed 8th August 2008].

Edler, J. and Georghiou. L. 2007 Public procurement and innovation-Resurrecting the demand side. *Research Policy,* **36**, 949-963

Hillary, R. (ed.) 2000 *Small and Medium-Sized Enterprises and the Environment.* Sheffield: Greenleaf Publishing

Hillary, R. 2004 Environmental Management systems and the smaller enterprise. *Journal of Cleaner Production,* **12**, 561-569

Horton-Baker, N. 2007 Personal communication. The number of SMEs in, and their financial contribution to, Surrey. Kingston upon Thames: Surrey Economic Partnership

Hutchinson, A. and Chaston, I. 2007 Environmental management in Devon and Cornwall's small and medium sized enterprise sector. *Business Strategy and the Environment,* **3**, 15-22

NetRegs 2005 SME-environment 2005 Surveys for England and for Wales. [Internet]. <http://www.netregs.gov.uk/netregs/1169119>. [Accessed 2nd January 2007].

Petts, J., Herd, A., Gerrard, S. and Horne, C. 1998 The climate and culture of environmental compliance within SMEs. *Business Strategy and the Environment,* **8,** 14-30

Thomson, J. and Jackson, T. 2007 Sustainable procurement in practice: lessons from local government. *Journal of Environmental Planning and Management,* **50**, 421-444

Williamson, D, and Lynch-Wood, G. 2001 A new paradigm for SME environmental practice. *The TQM Magazine,* **13**, 424-432

Lessons From the Frontline: Embedding Sustainability in the Higher Education Curriculum

David Turner, Kenny Lynch and Sue Swansborough
University of Gloucestershire

Abstract

Finding a way to give university students and staff a means of exploring the public, private and academic issues of sustainability is almost as complex as the issue of sustainability itself. The Department of Natural and Social Sciences at the University of Gloucestershire has taken the bull by the horns by introducing sustainability to all first year students studying environment-related subjects through the *Skills for Sustainability* module, a learning and personal development planning (PDP) module beginning in Induction Week.

The approach taken in the module is to use sustainability as a vehicle to introduce PDP and learning skills; raise awareness of disciplinary and interdisciplinary sustainability issues; engender an active learning approach in students; and involve a range of external agencies and internal resources to make the student experience more realistic and relevant. Engagement with sustainability issues came about in a variety of ways, including a 'Question Time'-style debate, sessions with specialists, research for group presentations and a visit to a sustainability project. Students built an e-portfolio through PebblePad which aimed to promote reflection on learning, develop skills for career paths and demonstrate how the module had affected behaviours related to sustainability issues.

Research into the development, delivery and reception of the module has highlighted both positives and negatives of 'selling/packaging' sustainability in this way to both students and staff. This paper explores these tensions and the possibility of applying this model to a wider university audience in the future.

Keywords   EBL, sustainability, curriculum, learning, skills

Introduction

This paper outlines the findings of an innovative approach to employ active learning through a skills-based module to introduce students to the widest experience of sustainability from day one in university life. The paper draws on the results of interviews and questionnaire feedback on the evaluation of the module as part of a wider PhD research study and explores the student and staff perceptions of participation in this learning experience. Interviews with seven staff members, eight students and an analysis of 60 questionnaire responses are presented as evidence for what did and did not work in this pilot module. The paper presents these findings in relation to the goals of embedding sustainability in an active learning approach which sought to deliver experiential learning through enquiry based learning methods employed by ten tutors delivering the module. The paper sets out a clear ethos for this approach in the literature and as interpreted locally and asks questions of the future of graduate learning that does not address the shifting labour market requirements of graduates. Finally, the paper sets out some clear lessons and recommendations for the future delivery of sustainability in the curriculum based on the findings and experiential learning from delivering this approach in 2006.

Approaches to Learning in Higher Education

Recent trends in Higher Education in Western societies have focused on achieving value for money in the level of public investment and student contribution through tuition fees. Western societies place considerable store on the performance of their HE sector, in particular the ability of this sector to contribute to national and regional economies (Morgan, 1997). Luke (2003) suggests that educational policy and pedagogy have been very strongly influenced by what he has described as 'corporate culture'. For example, corporate approaches to management and strategy have been introduced to educational management and education has been conceptualized as providing skills for employment and for employers. However, the fact that curricula are constantly changing and that, as a result of globalization, new technologies and increasing concerns about security and environment have been introduced, more and more 'basics' are being added to national curricula. Luke *et al.* (2005) caution that such a 'corporate rationalisation of post-secondary education' found throughout the Western societies has also been transferred systematically to Asian education systems with mixed results. This presents a real challenge for providers of higher education as universities are increasingly put under pressure to provide graduates with wider and more relevant skills needed by increasingly knowledge-based economies. For example, the Leitch Report (2006) proposes that the implementation of its main recommendations would ensure that the UK can be economically competitive as well as reducing poverty and inequality. In its foreword, the report argues that:

> In the 19th Century, the UK had the natural resources, the labour force and the inspiration to lead the world into the Industrial Revolution. Today, we are witnessing a different type of revolution. For developed countries who cannot compete on natural resources and low labour costs, success demands a more service-led economy and high value-added industry. (The Leitch Report, 2006, p.1)

One of the Leitch Report's main interim recommendations was about the projection of the skills make-up of the UK economy. The number of full-time entrants, aged 18 to 20, into Higher Education institutions in 2005/06 was 235,160, an increase from 198,970 in 1999/00 (DFES, 2007). In the last 25 years participation in HEIs has tripled (DFES, 2007). The big question now being asked is whether these entrants are being equipped with the necessary skills to enter the dramatically changing labour market of the 21st Century, a question asked by Stewart and Knowles (2000).

To meet this challenge, in June 2007 the UK Government created a Department for Innovation, Universities and Skills (DIUS) from sectors of the previous Department for Education and Employment relating to further and higher education, and parts of the Department for Trade and Industry relating to innovation and science. One of the first actions of DIUS has been to publish the government's response to the Leitch Report, *World Class Skills* (DIUS, 2007). This report argues:

As the Stern Review set out in compelling terms, we will not secure the future we all want for our nation, indeed for our planet, if we do not reflect our responsibility to the environment in all that we do. We need to ensure we have the skills necessary to protect and improve the environment we live and work in. (DIUS, 2007, p.3)

And later that:

Sustainable development - meeting the needs of the present without compromising the ability of future generations to meet their own needs - is a defining challenge of the twenty-first century. If the nation is to play its full part in challenging global poverty and combating environmental problems like climate change it is imperative that everyone in this country develops the skills of sustainable living and working. That means placing sustainable development at the heart of skills provision, ensuring that it is a fundamental goal of our economic and social progress. (DIUS 2007, p.20)

However, sustainability is not mentioned again and the key proposals are grouped according to those considered as 'for individuals' and those that are 'for employers'. This indicates the dominance of the corporate and individualist in UK government education and skills policy. Moreover, Luke and others have argued that there is a loss of values in education, as governments and curriculum developers have rushed headlong towards economically-demanded education at the expense of socially-relevant education. There is a focus on building content into curricula in order to create functioning employees at the expense of the development of thinking and the development of citizens to play a full part in society. However, Gallimore (undated) argues that there is evidence that 40% of recent graduate 'job-hunters' have at least once ruled out a potential employer because of the nature of the industry or because of publicity surrounding social or environmental practices. Employers are indicating that applicants for graduate jobs who can 'articulate their values clearly and assess how they fit in with the values of the organisation' can be very attractive. Where graduates are applying for jobs in the environmental or CSR sector, those who can express their values with clarity and commitment stand out as attractive.

The DIUS (2007) proposes that by 2020 more than 40% of the adult population in England will have a higher education qualification. This is an increase of 29% over 2005. Consequently, it is increasingly important that graduates have an ability to work with a wide range of professionals from different disciplines. Such collaboration will be increasingly important as emphasised in the Egan Review (2003). Hewitt (2004), the multinational human resource consultancy, argues that organisational structures are already changing. In the future more companies and institutions will organise their staff in a more project-focused way and this will reduce hierarchies. Organisations will be more focused on consumers than on producers and involve more independent consultants and outsourcing of activities. This means more of our graduates will change jobs more frequently, work in project teams, will be self-employed and will work with collaborators from a range of disciplines. Ensuring that they have the skills and attributes for such a career pattern requires changes to traditional undergraduate curricula (see also Roberts, 1995; Roberts and Powell, 1997).

Rationale for Skills for Sustainability

The Higher Education Academy (HEA) states that:

> Sustainability is a key area of development for the higher education sector and it is important to consider how best to embed it into learning and teaching strategies and curricula. We recognise the importance of increasing 'sustainability literacy' among students and the growing demand for sustainability skills among employers. Our programme aims to assist institutions and subject communities in their development of curricula and pedagogy to equip students with the skills and knowledge to live and work sustainably. (HEA, 2007)

Skills for Sustainability which is a compulsory module for all undergraduate students taking environment and related subjects, is an opportunity to introduce, as fundamental underpinning concepts, both active learning and sustainability. The module starts in Induction Week and then runs with weekly two-hour contact sessions for the whole of the first semester.

Linking module activities to the students' induction experience extends the process of support beyond the initial first week into their first semester as advocated by Lynch *et al.* (2006). This provides students with a connection from the induction experience into their course and access to interdisciplinary concepts and skills that will prove useful for their future within and outside the university.

The impetus for the module development arose from a desire to rationalise and redevelop two existing modules: *Environment and Society*, which aimed to provide an inter-disciplinary introduction to sustainable development; and *Learning Development*, which combined undergraduate study skills with introductory Personal Development Planning. This latter module was evaluated by students as lacking in subject content, whilst reinforcement of study skills in *Environment and Society*, for example in the sessions which supported the assessed group presentation, was perceived as repeating material already covered in *Learning Development*.

In addition, the design of the module was intended to make the skills and personal development planning element more 'active' and 'interactive' and to this end an enquiry-based learning approach was proposed (Justice *et al.*, in press (a); in press, (b)). Evidence from student feedback suggests that students' experience varied according to the tutor's approach.

Whilst some students clearly engaged with the expectation that the tutorial supported their learning, the main focus of learning was the tasks performed outside of the tutorial, such as reflection, investigation of issues in preparation for meetings, and team research and preparation for the presentation. These are elements recognised in the work of the Centre for Excellence in Enquiry at the University of Manchester (for example, Hutchings, 2006). However, some students assumed that most of the learning would take place in the classroom. The difference appears to be in the approach taken by tutors and the emphasis placed on enquiry-based learning as the main focus of student activity. This issue will be discussed further in a later section.

Research Questions

This section of the paper addresses the key questions raised in the previous discussion. This interpretation is a preliminary analysis of a case study-based educational research project based on student and staff experience in the development and delivery of a module designed with a two-fold agenda: delivering graduate skills through the medium of sustainability.

Data sets were prepared from in-depth interviews with selected staff engaged in the development and teaching of the module, and selected students. In addition, a questionnaire survey was administered to students towards the end of the module. The research programme addressed four themes; the focus for this paper rests on the final theme:

(i)   the extent to which the students appreciated the intention of the module in relation to the skills and content learning
(ii)   student experience of EBL
(iii)   level of engagement with the ePortfolio and PDP
(iv)   understanding of sustainability

Research Results

The questionnaire was distributed to all students in week 11 of the 13 week module, completed at the end of the learning session, and collected by Personal Tutors. The researcher analysed the results using SPSS and compiled a set of key tables.

Table 1   Self assessment of graduate skills (based on number of respondents)

Graduate skills measure	Strongly Agree	Agree	Neutral	Disagree	Strongly Disagree	Total	Mean
Importance of reflective learning	7	29	18	2	2	59	3.64
Personal Development Planning	13	35	8	2	0	58	3.84
Ability to plan and write essays	5	26	18	7	3	59	3.39
Benefits of interdisciplinary approaches	10	32	10	6	0	58	3.84
Work with others to deliver a presentation	25	31	3	1	0	60	4.32
Manage my time effectively	8	26	18	6	2	60	3.46
Become a more effective learner	8	27	19	5	1	60	3.54
How to source and reference	15	31	8	4	2	60	3.89
Understand issues of plagiarism	25	27	7	1	0	60	4.25

A key measure sought to identify the extent to which the module had achieved its primary aim of embedding graduate level skills to enable students to operate effectively at graduate and employability levels. To achieve this, a series of attitudinal scale questions were devised against the learning outcomes set for the module. These measures are listed in Table 1. With a median score for all measures of 4.0, it is clear that there is mostly a positive skew on self-perception of skills learned in the module to the upper end of the range.

On this basis, the module certainly succeeds in enabling students to develop the skills identified as important for undergraduates. What is of interest, however, is the absence of significant differences in performance on skills based on gender, age or personal tutor.

Student appreciation of the module

A key question in the research sought to establish how clearly the purpose of the module was presented at the outset of the learning process. For many (70%) the purpose was clearly presented as Table 2 outlines below.

However, for some the picture was less obvious. Almost all students who were 'not clear' or 'very unclear' were located in one of three tutor groups, emphasising the importance of the tutor in engaging with the core values of the module. In delivering a module that requires clarity and focus in selling the twin narratives of skills and sustainability, tutor engagement emerged as a leading predictor of student engagement with both the principles and goals of the module. As one student commented: '(The) Module aim could have been made clearer, as many of the lectures didn't seem to have an aim' (Student 36).

Table 2   The extent to which students had a clear understanding of the purpose of the module

Response	Number	%
Very Clear	4	7
Clear	38	63
Not clear	15	25
Very Unclear	3	5
Total	**60**	**100**

Sustainability in the curriculum

The Higher Education Funding Council for England identifies four areas of sustainability within its Sustainability Strategy that Higher Education Institutions (HEIs) should address:

(i)   role as educators
(ii)   generation and transfer of knowledge
(iii)   leadership of, and influence upon, local, national and international networks
(iv)   business strategy and operations (HEFCE, 2005)

Roberts and Roberts (2007) argue that for educators the generation and transfer of knowledge in their role as educators on sustainability are hampered by the looseness of the definitions around sustainability. So it is of little surprise that students encountered varying levels of engagement within *Sustainability for Skills*. What was achieved was a raising of awareness amongst students, not only of the importance of sustainability, but also its relevance to the curriculum. As Table 3 shows, only one student indicated that they were not aware at the end of the module of the importance of sustainable development in their field of study.

Table 3   Graduate Skills: Awareness of Sustainability

Graduate skills measure	Strongly Agree	Agree	Neutral	Disagree	Strongly Disagree	Total	Mean
Importance of sustainable development	20	34	5	1	0	60	4.23

This does not mean that the whole evaluation was positive: as discussed later, a theme emerged that some students felt that they formed part of a generation that was being asked to miss out, having to make sacrifices because of the of profligacy of previous generations. Strong feelings were voiced by some students who were unwilling to be deprived of consumption practices, such as foreign holidays, commuting by car and other aspects of hedonistic consumption enjoyed by their parents' generation. There were a number of key activities within the module designed to focus staff and students on learning about sustainability:

- Sustainability Question Time (Week 2)
- visit to Sustainable Thornbury (Week 7-9)
- utilising PebblePad to reflect on learning about sustainability (e-portfolio assessed)
- an (assessed) group presentation on sustainability

Two of these elements formed part of the assessment processes and were seen as an important way of ensuring engagement with sustainability as well as building up a wide range of graduate skills. In terms of the assessment processes students generally thought these were fair (79%).

Table 4   Student rating of the assessments

Response	Number	%
Very fair	5	9
Fair	40	70
Not fair	11	19
Very unfair	1	2
Total	**57**	**100**

This positive endorsement for the assessment process is somewhat surprising since one of the elements of the assessment, the use of PebblePad, received the largest share of criticism from the students on this module (Table 4). Two thirds of the students found PebblePad difficult or very difficult to use. Added to this difficulty, it was evident from student feedback that not all tutors delivered effective learning sessions that engaged the students around sustainability (the key aim of the module) whilst providing graduate skills learning opportunities. Student 36, for instance, commented that 'Many of the lectures didn't even touch on the theme of sustainability, especially the lectures with Tutors 3 and 4'.

Table 5 Student appreciation of the Sustainability Question Time

Response	Number	%
Very helpful	11	7
Helpful	34	63
Not helpful	5	25
Very unhelpful	3	5
Total	**53**	**100**

Such lack of a sustainability focus may well explain the negative feedback achieved for both the Question Time (Table 5) and Thornbury trips (organized across the module and provided for the tutors) (Table 6). This may have resulted from lack of briefing from the module tutor. It would appear that sustainability is not only new to students, but also for some tutorial staff.

Table 6 Attended the trip to see 'Sustainable Thornbury' a community in action

Response	Number	%
Yes	50	85
No	9	15
Total	**59**	**100**

Attempts to apply the theoretical elements of sustainability through a field visit to the Sustainable Thornbury project received a mixed student reaction. Some thought it 'boring' and 'pointless', 'not what was expected', 'too rushed', and 'nothing new'. Others thought it 'interesting', 'inspiring', 'showed what can be done and what needs to be done'.

Student expectations of what a sustainability project would look like were interesting. Some students expected 'windmills and solar panels', but found Thornbury a town with 'little practical evidence' of sustainability and were disappointed that young people were not greatly involved in the project. This, to them, was not their idea of an ideal sustainable community. Although 85% of respondents had attended the field trip to Thornbury, many found reason to doubt its relevance to the module. Typical responses include:

It was a waste of time. (Student 38)

I thought it was a good idea, but why travel all the way to Thornbury – SUSTAINABILITY. (Student 37)

It was what I expected, very sustainable in most ways but not in others (Student 31)

Findings

The research sought insights from all stakeholders involved in the delivery and participation on this module. A number of key points emerged from this feedback. In relation to the graduate skills learning, almost all the students agreed that:

- their skills in team working, citation, presentations and information gathering had been enhanced
- they had enjoyed the active learning approach and commented on enjoying independent learning and groupwork, the relaxed interactive style and discussions, and the opportunity to undertake their own research
- they were 'pleasantly surprised' that the method of learning was not traditional lectures

The most important learning outcomes apart from 'finding out about sustainability' were predominantly practical learning skills:

- how to reference
- learning about plagiarism
- group working
- developing a CV
- meeting other students and staff

This suggests that students perceive the module to be more effective at delivering skills enhancement over sustainability. Some students thought that the module lacked structure whilst others disliked specific sessions. There were widespread concerns over a number of issues relating to the software (PebblePad) designed to build the personal development plan and reflective learning portfolio. However, in terms of sustainability aspects of the module, students stated they better understood the context of sustainable development within their discipline, but also revealed confusion over the dual aims of the module. They were not sure whether the module was about sustainability *or* skills rather than a combination of these.

Discussion

The elements of the module that link most effectively to the theoretical debates about active learning in sustainability are compared with those of Dawe *et al.* (2005), demonstrating how successful has been the delivery of *Skills for Sustainability*. Dawe *et al.* (2005, pp.13-15) have proposed eleven elements within a framework of teaching approaches for education in sustainable development and these are grouped under three headings (the personal; re-connecting to reality; and holistic thinking). These interrelationships are expressed in Figure 1 as segments A-D; areas where there are doubts about the connections are depicted as segments E-G.

The module directly addresses four of these elements: lifelong learning, linking with local communities, real-life experiences and interdisciplinarity and critical thinking. As these are aspects of active learning they are represented by area C in Figure 1. The module also addresses three other elements: teachers as role models, teachers as learners/teachers; and systems thinking (Area A). For example, the learning opportunities provided space for students to develop systems thinking, such as getting students to link their learning into broader systems, such as ecosystems or social systems, particularly in relation to their own disciplines or the disciplines represented in the module cohort. An additional approach identified by Dawes *et al.* was that linking the learning with institutional environmental management systems (Area B). This was not explicitly addressed in the module, but feedback from some students had begun to do this as they challenged teaching staff to consider the way the module had been organised. The sustainability of 'bussing' a large group of students to Thornbury to meet a small number of people, when the latter could have come to the university at less expense and with reduced carbon emission, is a case in point.

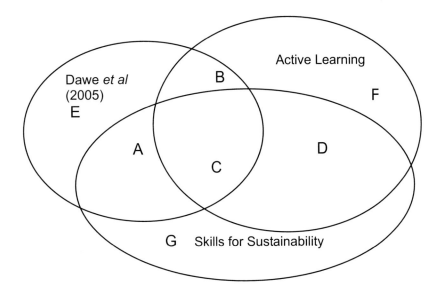

Figure 1   The inter- relationships between two learning styles and the module[1]

Perhaps most importantly, Dawe's seventh criterion aims to enact social change: students were challenged by tutors and other students to consider their beliefs and behaviour in relation to the theories they had encountered. For example, a number of students reported changes of personal behaviour with regard to management of household waste, adopting alternative transport modes for commuting and planting vegetables for home consumption. In addition:

> There's bits [of my behaviour] that I don't want to change, like I wouldn't want to have to get on a bus to come here….. and I wouldn't like to not be able to straighten my hair….and if I had the money, I'd want to buy an Aston Martin or a Ferrari and things like that. Everyone before us has been able to do what they want so why can't we?

> I've certainly begun to think about …how much carbon emission am I creating by buying those tomatoes in Tesco?…..I've certainly looked into buying English-based products more. It's….. led to a whole series of thoughts……next year I'm hoping to grow my own veg in the back garden.

Whilst others were frustrated by the apparent inability to achieve positive action:

> It's quite frustrating because all these good ideas that everyone has…. people have individual good ideas of how to make things more stable and better, but most of the time nothing actually gets done…. for anything to happen it's going to be years and years – why can't you just do it now?

---

[1] Source: Turner *et al.* 2007

This suggests that *Skills for Sustainability* did not specifically 'enact social change' as a result of active learning for all (area E) but did challenge students to consider current attitudes towards sustainability.

It is probable that some of the learning on the module was achieved through non-active or traditional didactic methods (Areas A and G). It is unreasonable to expect that a module covering so many disciplines and delivering wide skills and knowledge requirements could do anything but draw on the widest possible learning opportunities.

The module sought to link the theoretical elements of active learning to the practicalities of sustainability both within and across disciplines. This was achieved by enabling students to engage with, and learn, through the active application of the skills developed in the module to sustainability issues across a range of community projects and organisations, university student support departments, and other learning resources. For example, the students visited the 'Sustainable Thornbury' project (a small town twenty miles south of Cheltenham) to examine sustainability issues in a real-life situation. Subsequently, students were involved in the associated Higher Education Academy Sustainability Project, through access to the project's online learning resources.

Furthermore, student learning on the module was supported through a series of weekly podcasts made available using a blog interface in PebblePad. This initiative is supported by the Higher Education Academy sponsored Informal Mobile Podcasting and Learning Adaptation (IMPALA) project. The podcasts included extracts from the 'Question Time' debate and a debate on Fair Trade and Sustainable Development organised by the Gloucestershire Fair Trade Network, an independent interest group, which included participation from the Head of Corporate Affairs at Kraft and the Director of Public Relationships at the Fair Trade Foundation.

Conclusions

The first run of this new module appears to have been largely successful and has provided a forum for students to explore the issue of sustainability at the outset of their university lives. Students:

- engaged with a range of learning activities that ensured they are equipped with many of the skills required to learn in a higher education institution
- reported a change in their consumption practices as a result of discussing sustainable development issues as part of the module
- created reflective learning portfolios which provided evidence of deep thinking and considerable changes to their outlook and learning approaches

Student feedback highlighted that the tutors generally balanced the learning between encouraging students to think for themselves and supporting them in their learning. However different tutors 'bought into' the enquiry-based learning approach at differing levels (particularly using PebblePad) and adopted different activities according to their specialisms:

In conclusion, the module provides an innovative interdisciplinary introduction to sustainability, PDP and learning skills, and further redevelopment will ensure that a coherent and relevant enquiry-based learning experience is accessible to a wide cohort of students. This case study module has therefore set out to introduce students to active learning approaches which are important to their learning at the University of Gloucestershire. The module has also encouraged students to consider their values in relation to their behaviour and their careers, through personal development planning and their enquiries into sustainability issues thus addressing issues raised in the Leitch Review (2006), the DIUS (2007) response and the Egan Review (2006), the latter being explicitly addressed in the content of a podcast for the students, and finally in Roberts (1995) and Roberts & Powell (1997). In short this module has introduced students to basic 'sustainability literacy'. (HE Academy, 2007)

The feedback raises the need to ensure that the needs of learners and staff are met in an enquiry-based learning approach. Preparation for the next presentation of the module will need to address the tutors' 'buy-in' to enquiry-based learning and PebblePad, and their knowledge of how both work and why they are being used. The question of how the general presentation of the purpose and structure of the module is presented to students may require revision.

This model has the potential to transfer to other programmes where sustainability is seen as an issue of core relevance to the discipline. The module team would argue that the skills required in active learning correspond with those required to reflect and act upon a critical understanding of sustainability issues. Examples of this include developing the ability to think critically about behaviours and lifestyles, to link theories to practice and the experience of transformative learning.

Key recommendations for this module for next year have included a greater emphasis on EBL with all students completing the assessment through a problem-based learning approach based on making the university more sustainable. This will culminate in a Green Dragon's Den presentation for the most innovative ideas. Staff have been re-trained in the use of PebblePad and feedback from the students has been shared with Personal Tutors for the next academic year. Again, the research will seek to explore the learning achieved by students.

References

Dawe, G., Jucker, R. and Stephen, M. 2005 *Sustainable Development in Higher Education: Current Practice and Future Developments A report for The Higher Education Academy York*. York: Higher Education Academy

DfES 2007 *Higher Education* [Internet]. <http://www.dfes.gov.uk/inyourarea/natsumm.shtml>. [Accessed 21st August 2007].

Egan, J. 2003 *Skills for Sustainable Communities*. London: HMSO

Gallimore, J. no date *Values and Corporate Social Responsibility (CSR). Report of a combined project for the Philosophical and Religious Studies (PRS) and Geography*. Plymouth: Earth and Environmental Sciences (GEES) Subject Centre

Hewitt Associates 2004 *Preparing for the Workforce of Tomorrow*. Hewitt Associates, Houston [Internet]. <http://www.hewittassociates.com/Intl/NA/en-US/KnowledgeCenter/ArticlesReports/ArticleDetail.aspx?cid=1734&tid=48>. [Accessed 24th August 2007].

Higher Education Academy 2007 *Sustainability* [Internet]. <http://www.heacademy.ac.uk/ourwork/learning/sustainability>. [Accessed 21st August 2007].

HEFCE 2005 *Sustainable Development in Higher Education* [Internet]. <http://www.hefce.ac.uk/pubs/hefce/2005/05_28/>. [Accessed 21st August 2007].

Hutchings, W. 2006 *Designing an Enquiry Based Learning Course*. University of Manchester: Centre for Enquiry Based Learning

Justice, C., Rice, J., Warry, W. and Laurie, I. (*in press* a). Taking inquiry makes a difference – a comparative analysis of student learning. *Journal on Excellence in College Teaching*

Justice, C., Rice, J., Warry, W., Inglis, S., Miller, S. and Sammon, S. (*in press* b). Inquiry in Higher Education: reflections and directions on course design and teaching methods. *Innovative Higher Education*

Leitch Report 2006 *Skills in the UK: The Long Term Challenge. Leitch Review of Skills.* London: HMSO

Luke, A. 2003 After the Marketplace: Evidence, Social Science and Educational Research. *The Australian Educational Researcher,* **30**, 87-107

Luke, A., Freebody, P., Shun L. and Gopinathan, S. 2005 Towards Research-based Innovation and Reform: Singapore schooling in transition. *Asia Pacific Journal of Education,* **25**, 5–28

Lynch, K., Frame, P., Harwood, T., Hoult, E., Jenkins, M. and Volpe, G. 2006 'Transitions into higher education: processes, outcomes and collaborations', in Grigg, G. and Bound, C. (eds) *Supporting Learning in the 21st Century.* Peer reviewed proceedings. Auckland: Association of Tertiary Learning Advisors Aotearoa/New Zealand (ATLAANZ), 32-46

Morgan, K. 1997 The Learning Region: Institutions, Innovation and Regional Renewal. *Regional Studies,* **31**, 491–503

PebblePad Learning Ltd. 2007 [Internet].<http://www.pebblelearning.co.uk/>. [Accessed 3rd March 2007].

Roberts C. and Roberts J. (eds) 2007 *Greener by Degrees: Exploring Sustainability Through Higher Education.* Cheltenham: Curricula Geography Discipline Network

Roberts, C. 1995 Taking Responsibility: *Promoting Sustainable Practice through HE Curricula - Sport, Leisure, Hospitality and Tourism.* London: Pluto Press

Roberts, J. and Powell, J. 1997 Educating the Future - Engaging with Sustainability in Higher Education. *International Sustainable Development Research Conference.* Manchester. 7 - 8 April

Stewart, J. and Knowles, V. 2000 Graduate recruitment and selection: implications for HE. *Graduates and Small Business Recruiters,* **5**, 65-80

Swansborough, S., Turner, D. and Lynch, K. 2007 'Active learning approaches to develop skills for sustainability', in Roberts, C. and Roberts J. (eds) *Greener by Degrees: Exploring Sustainability Through Higher Education Curricula.* Cheltenham: Geography Discipline Network

University of New South Wales 2007 *Guidelines on Learning.* [Internet]. <http://www.guidelinesonlearning.unsw.edu.au/>. [Accessed 25th July 2007].

Sustainable Education Through Engagement

Michael Herrmann
Kingston University

Abstract

As the concept of sustainable development has become established as a priority underpinning future social and economic progress, so the call has gone out for the implementation of a curriculum for sustainability across all education sectors. However, little thought has been given to the pedagogical implications of such a goal. The author has had experience over the last ten years in the development of education for sustainability curricula in three UK Higher Education institutions and articulates an approach to sustainable education based around the principles of an experiential learning pedagogy.

Keywords   Experiential learning, citizenship, transformative, diversity, place

Introduction

According to Clark (1989), during the last 2,500 years there have only been two major periods of conscious social change, when societies deliberately 'critiqued' themselves and created new worldviews. She argues that with the rate of environmental change associated with science and technology, the prevailing worldview has grown in a maladaptive fashion, and we thus need to follow the example of the Athenian and Renaissance societies and (rapidly) enter a period of deep reflection and change.

As educators of the leaders of tomorrow's world, our higher education establishments play a crucial role in addressing any sense of helplessness and cynicism that may affect people, empowering them to realise their potential to deliver sustainable solutions for our common future. This paper aims to demonstrate the value of the adoption of a higher education pedagogy that is effective in this ambition, laying a particular emphasis on the notions and principles of 'citizenship' and 'experiential learning'.

Citizenship

The concept of citizenship is currently the subject of much debate within UK education and, since 2002, has been written into the National Curriculum as a statutory requirement for secondary schools. Citizenship is a very broad concept which applies notions of democracy, community, human rights and justice to the challenges and choices of living and acting in a modern society.

The Further Education Funding Council report (FEFC, 2000) for the UK Department for Education and Employment (DfEE) argued strongly for the inclusion of citizenship education within the FE curriculum, concluding that it should be recognised as a new key skill to sit alongside the six key skills already identified. It is reasonable to assume that the concept will have an increasing influence within HE in the coming years, although here, where curriculum planning remains relatively devolved, its impact will depend on the enthusiasm of individual departments and institutions. The citizenship education agenda clearly complements and supports the education for sustainability agenda and, indeed, the QCA's report specified concern for the environment as a key value and sustainable development as an essential component of knowledge and understanding:

> Pupils should acquire basic knowledge and understanding of particular aspects of society with which citizenship is concerned. One of five aspects listed is environmental and sustainable development. (QCA, 1998)

Speaking in support of an action plan for education for sustainable development (ESD) published by the UK Department for Education and Skills (DfES, 2003), the Secretary of State also emphasised the links between ESD and education for global citizenship.

Professor Sir Bernard Crick chaired the Advisory Group on Education for Citizenship and the Teaching of Democracy in Schools, publishing a report (QCA, 1998) that left no doubt about the radical nature of the concept when it stated that: 'We aim at no less than a change in the political culture of this country both nationally and locally'. It called for people to '...think of themselves as active citizens, willing, able and equipped to have an influence in public life'. This should include both an engagement with existing traditions of community involvement and public service, while helping young people to be '...individually confident in finding new forms of involvement and action among themselves'. Despite the prior publication of the Curriculum for Global Citizenship (Oxfam, 1997), the Crick Report (QCA, 1998) and those that followed it (DFEE, 2000a; DFEE, 2000b; QCA, 2000; Eurodyce, 2005) made little mention of global issues, restricting their focus to national, regional, and community concerns.

Given that we live in a globalised world where the activities and consumption of one part of the world create impacts to individuals and the environment in far off countries, any sophisticated consideration of sustainability needs to include awareness of global concerns. If institutions of higher education (HEIs) are to deliver a meaningful continuation of 'citizenship education' beyond that undertaken at primary and secondary school levels, it falls to the hands of educators in Higher Education to include such awareness-raising, establishing the notion of interdependence, and to attempt to accelerate the learning processes of their students towards a deeper understanding and commitment to ways in which they can contribute to the goals of sustainable development both during their higher education and into their professional careers (Richardson *et al.*, 2005).

Experiential Learning

> Tell me and I forget. Show me and I remember. Let me do and I understand. (Confucius)

Dewey (1938) and many later educational writers promoted the value to progressive education of learning by discovery. As if we need proof of this, educational psychologists claim that we retain eighty per cent of what we do, as opposed to just twenty per cent of what we hear and read (Cortese, 1997). Boud, Cohen and Walker (1993) went on to say that 'learning can only occur if the experience of the learner is engaged, at least at some level'. Empirical research (Gigliotti, 1990) has demonstrated that the incorporation of research and action skill training activities into curricula can lead to overt positive environmental behaviours. However, is an experience alone sufficient for learning to occur, or is it also necessary for some kind of mental processing to take place? As Mason (2000) points out, 'If experience in itself was so valuable, then humans who are enmeshed in experience ought to be more knowledgeable than they are. Sadly the conclusion that can be reached is that we do not learn from experience'. It seems that in order to gain knowledge from an experience it is important to first process the information and issues raised.

Experiential learning goes beyond traditional (didactic) teaching by shifting the focus from the transfer of knowledge and skills to the process of learning, and thus includes opportunities for an enriched and accelerated learning experience (Dennison and Kirk, 1990). Costas Criticos describes how 'Experience has to be arrested, examined, analysed, considered and negated to shift it to knowledge (Boud *et al.*, 1993). The Development Training Advisors Group defined a learning cycle that summarises this: do, review, learn, apply (Kirk, 1987). One of the main roles of the teacher in an experiential learning context is thus to facilitate the students in their critical analysis and reflection of the material and phenomena witnessed.

This critical thinking allows a learner to assimilate the lessons that can be learnt from an experience, and thus adjust their response when next faced with a comparable situation (Schön, 1983). Experiential, or experience-based learning, has been defined as the learning that occurs when changes in judgments, feedings or skills result for a particular person from living through an event or events (Chickering, 1977). Others have described it as 'the insight gained through the conscious or unconscious internalisation of our own or observed experiences which builds upon our past experiences or knowledge' (Beard and Wilson, 2002). Each definition takes account of the whole person, including their emotional responses (Boud *et al.*, 1985; Boud and Walker, 2000). The synthesis of these emotional responses is via one's own personal experience (including memories, training, knowledge, preconceptions and prejudices); as well as via one's imagination (for example, anticipation and visualisation).

It has been claimed that 'emotions and feelings are the key pointers both to possibilities for, and barriers to, learning' (Miller and Boud, 1996), and it follows that the emotive 'lessons' that connect with our personal psyche are likely to be the ones that maintain currency for us. We are more likely to remember what we feel, than what we are merely told. Nobel (2002) has articulated this when arguing that experiential learning is more personal or individualized, may be acquired unconsciously, and is thus usually more permanent (than traditional forms of teaching and learning). This 'deep learning' allows students to extract personal meaning and more profound understanding from course materials and experiences. (Warburton, 2003) Although experiential learning can be regarded as the earliest approach to learning for the human race, until relatively recently its significance and potential has not been fully recognized. Since the work of Dewey there has been a recognition that learning occurs as an iterative process of planning, action and reflection.

Whilst echoing Dewey's earlier awareness that all learning is, in effect, learning from experience, Boud (1989) considered the learning process in a broader perspective (Boud *et al.*, 1993). Usher and Soloman (1999) went on to point out that this learning from experience invariably takes place in 'the lifeworld of everyday contexts'. Experiential learning may thus remain largely unstructured, taking as a starting point direct life experiences rather than beginning with theoretical principles or concepts (Nobel, 2002). Sometimes referred to as 'learning by doing' or 'personal learning', it can be seen as an active rather than passive process (Burnard, 1991); whereby we learn by taking part and discovering 'something that is personal to us, whereas in the lecture approach, we are more passive; we adopt knowledge (from the public domain)' (Nobel, 2002).

It is also worth noting that 'unlearning' can represent as important a gain from experiential learning as 'learning'; 'flexibility and openness to the possibility of mistake or error can be important in learning' (Moon, 2004). Experiential learning shares many similarities with 'problem-based learning' as described by Jucker (2002), Steinemann (2003), and Warburton (2003). This is an approach that is said to allow students to move beyond passive reception of information towards learning that remains relevant and inspiring, as learners develop solutions to potentially complex, 'real world' contexts (Schmidt, 1993; Brown *et al.*, 1989). Problem based learning typically involves the refinement of solutions through collaborative, iterative processes akin to the rational, deductive, problem solving approach of scientific method (Walton and Mathews, 1989).

According to Moon (2004), one of the connotations of experiential learning is that there is usually a formal intention to learn (from experience), and it is this active process that distinguishes experiential learning from 'everyday' learning. Rather than being concerned with the mere accumulation of material of learning, the focus thus shifts to the process of changing, or 'transforming' conceptions (Bowden and Marton, 1998). As Beard and Wilson (2002) have pointed out, by contrast with traditional pedagogical approaches, an experiential learning methodology emphasises the learning 'activities' themselves, with greater consideration being given to the holistic nature of the experience. Under the supervision of a tutor, students are thus more likely to be 'setting their own agenda'; identifying suitable subject matter, identifying an appropriate approach, and reflecting on their own, and peers' progress.

Reflective practice journals and self and peer review are typical of the experiential learning pedagogy (Anderson *et al.*, 2000). The exercise of this degree of influence on the direction and nature of the learning process can empower individual learners in ways that more traditional approaches rarely manage. This sense of control over the learning experience may in turn engender a sense of care and responsibility in students; for themselves, for their actions, and for the actions of others (Griffin,1992). The learning that takes place through active engagement, whether through a 'live' project, or by direct contact with the actual environment can give rise to 'a heightened relational sensibility and sense of ethical responsibility' (Sterling, 2003). This realisation can occur whether the teaching occurs in a natural habitat or on a concrete campus devoid of rich ecology.

Following such a teaching methodology, the subject matter may not necessarily be familiar to the teacher or to the students. As a result, the learning experience can become more interactive, fresh and vital, and it could be said that there occurs a 'democratisation of the learning process', with a teacher assuming the role of facilitator (indeed, co-learner) rather than pedagogue. With the educator assisting the learning, rather than necessarily providing the actual material of learning (Anderson *et al.*, 2000), we come closer to what Peter Senge (1990) describes as an effective learning organisation;

one where people are continually learning to see the whole together. This encourages cooperation between learners (Coppola, 1996; Cockrell *et al.*, 2000), and can allow a progressive expansion of the capacity of the learners to nurture fresh and expansive patterns of thinking. As well as enabling collective aspiration to bloom, the shared focus on 'real' problems can also result in greater levels of competency and more effective learning (Peterson 1997; Friedman and Deek, 2002; Gabbert *et al.*, 1986).

A considerable additional benefit is that motivation levels are likely to be increased as students (and staff) realise the benefits of synergy whilst working together or contributing to one another's projects, as well as by virtue of gaining a sense of ownership over the learning experience. This is central to the notion of an effective 'learning organisation', where 'people continually expand their capacity to create the results they truly desire, where new and expansive patterns of thinking are nurtured, where collective aspiration is set free, and where people are continually learning how to learn together' (Senge, 1990). Cleary the ability to deliver an effective and fulfilling learning experience is likely to define 'the organisations that will truly excel in the future will be the organisations that discover how to tap people's commitment and capacity to learn at all levels' (Senge, 1990).

A key benefit of an experiential learning pedagogy is the development of a concept of 'meaningfulness' in the minds of the students - a student motivated to learn, almost on a 'need-to-know' basis, is more likely to value and enjoy the experience than a student who sees little purpose in the activities (Moon, 2004). Perhaps it is this intention to learn that distinguishes experiential learning from traditional learning.

It has been observed that environmental education programmes that tend to limit their activities to the promotion of environmental knowledge and understanding 'do not tend to lead to the development of a citizenry that is capable of resolving environmental problems' (Einstein, 1993), and that increasing awareness of environmental problems without providing a positive outlet into which students can channel emotional energy 'may increase apathy and despair among students' (Einstein, 1993). David Orr concurs when he states that the study of environmental problems is 'nothing short of a lesson in despair if the teaching goes no further' (Orr, 1992). Of course the study of environmental problems is vital in order to contextualise matters, and as an awareness-raising exercise may preface an exploration of viable alternatives and solutions. Acknowledging the relationship between the activities of design, manufacture and consumption, and the manifest environmental problems of the planet is a first step. Once this mental connection is made, the concerned student can make plans to adjust their practice, and plan to influence the actions and intentions of clients and colleagues.

Learning through diversity

The author has found that mixed ability, age, culture, background and discipline groups can be accommodated, and can enrich the study experience for all. If properly organised, students can work at different speeds, focusing on different aspects of a project, then coming together to share views, knowledge, and prior learning experiences. As Dennison and Kirk point out, differences can contribute to the learning experience of students, not least because students are often more receptive to the comments and observations of their peers than those of their tutors (Dennison and Kirk, 1990).

It is important to consider that experiences can be stored in our memories for a great many years before being recalled and analysed as evidence to explain a new situation. Thus experiential learning is enriched through access to a greater repository of collective experience.

Learning from place

The physical environment within which an institution of higher education (HEI) is placed represents a convenient and appropriate starting place for students to begin to assess the positive and negative impacts of human activity on natural and human systems. Ultimately it is the landscape that connects all human activities and is where evidence of problems (and opportunities) can be discovered. As Robert Thayer points out 'landscape is where the current conflict between technology and nature is most easily sensed; it is also the place where any attempt at resolution of the conflict must be tested and proven' (Thayer, 1994). The experience of landscape is felt at all levels too, from the performance of practical functions through to deep psychological and spiritual meaning. This consideration brings with it several implications - that students might benefit from involvement with their immediate physical (preferably natural) environment, that this may well involve establishment of some sort of relationship with local community (stakeholders), and lastly, that the very learning environment itself may play an important part in the efficacy of the learning process. A substantial university research programme on learning environments in the US noted that:

> there are three avenues an institution can promote to foster active student learning. First, certain teaching methodologies, such as problem based learning, promote active student involvement. Second, the classroom furnishings can either enhance or hinder active student learning. Thus, tables and moveable chairs enhance while fixed-row seating hinders active learning. (Source:*http://www.-lib.iupui.edu/itt/planlearn/execsumm.html*) [Accessed: 2/2/2002].

These observations open up the possibility of moving teaching and learning outside the traditional classroom, into outdoor learning environments. Removed from the rigid formality of an indoor classroom, studio or lecture theatre, with its lectern, raked and immovable seating, hemmed in by walls, an outdoor setting may have much to offer. It is postulated here that in such a setting, the learning process is more likely to be transactive, with learners interacting with other learners, with facilitators, and with place and space. Merely 'being' in nature as the learning environment is a powerful experiential intervention in itself.

Walking the talk

If our HEIs themselves cannot demonstrate good environmental practice, the integrity of the taught programme may be undermined; also staff and student perceptions, attitudes, and morale regarding their institution are likely to suffer negative consequences. In the UK we have much to learn from the experience overseas. During the 1990s, several US colleges developed programmes that included the active engagement of students with environmental issues. The widely acclaimed and emulated ULSF courses in Environmental Literacy Institutes (ELIs) depend upon participatory learning using the environment as a basis for integrated, interdisciplinary education. They aim to draw participants into current environmental problems by requiring active involvement to find realistic solutions. Specific case studies are chosen as the subject for experiential teaching and learning, emphasising the use of local environment as a laboratory. By bringing learners from a wide variety of cultural and professional backgrounds together to share thoughts and experiences, a rich, contextual educational experience is created.

A leading proponent, Dr. Bruce Grant, Widener University (USA), implores that a 'Campus Ecology' curriculum constitutes 'an essential and largely untapped resource to teach principles of urban ecological design for sustainability'. This can lead to a sense of personal empowerment through problem solving and by enabling students to become agents of change for urban environmental sustainability (Grant, 1999). Tom Kelly concurs with this sentiment, adding that through this sense of empowerment, students can be emboldened to take on issues of institutional change. Clearly, this will represent a challenge to more conservative, less progressive institutions. If handled skilfully, however, the mobilisation of the student body can represent a powerful engine to help deliver environmental improvements. Institutional efforts to involve students must be wholehearted and serious; learning focused on sustainable practice will be undermined and even negated by apparent environmentally insensitive behaviour (Ali Khan, 1995).

David Orr and colleagues at Oberlin College, Widener, Tufts, and Brown Universities have been exploring the huge potential that is offered to students, staff and institutional practice by adopting a thoughtfully developed curriculum for environmental education. Their work demonstrates that the mutual benefits are not only desirable, but are also eminently achievable, even within the existing academic framework. Jay Hair, President of the US National Wildlife Federation, concurs when she comments that:

> Institutions of higher learning, where visionary thinking often rubs against the daily demands of institutional life, are uniquely positioned to help invent the greener communities needed for the next century. (Hair, cited in Grant 1999)

> Colleges and universities are thus leverage institutions. They can help create a humane and liveable future, rather than remaining passively on the sidelines, poised to study the outcome. (Orr, 1992)

Other colleges, world-wide, have also been exploring these ideas, motivated by a growing public awareness of impending environmental crisis which is driving statutory commitment to improvements in environmental performance and provision. In UK HEIs, experience is accumulating. Noteworthy examples of activity that has sought to 'make tangible' the experience of sustainability include a pioneering cross-disciplinary 'Environmental Studies' module at the Surrey Institute of Art and Design (now University of the Creative Arts); the community design activities of the Leeds Metropolitan University, Landscape Architecture BA, 'Design and Community' unit; the Ecodesign BA Course at Goldsmiths College, London; and 'live projects' undertaken by students on the Loughborough Product Design and Technology BSc and Leeds Metropolitan University Design BA courses. In terms of campus developments, Bradford's 'Ecoversity' initiative and the Genesis Centre for Sustainable Construction at Somerset College rate as outstanding examples that demonstrate the untapped potential of HE campuses to provide 'living laboratories' where staff and students can witness sustainable interventions first-hand.

Conclusion

An authority on sustainable education, Stephen Sterling, describes the distinction between 'first order' learning and 'second order' learning. The former is adaptive, and tends to leave assumptions unchallenged, whilst the latter involves critical reflection that examines these basic assumptions. At a deeper level still, third-order thinking (and learning) encourages core values to be challenged and assumptions about the world to be reconceived. Thus it represents a truly transformative level of learning. Peter Senge summarises this by saying that learning is, at a simple level, the process through which new knowledge, values and skills are acquired. At a deeper level, it involves 'a movement of mind' (Senge, 1990). In order to build upon the citzenship agenda that is now being actively promoted in primary and secondary education, UK HEIs need to identify and adopt an effective pedagogy for sustainable education. This is likely to involve moving beyond the dry and passive study of sustainability theory through the active engagement of learners that is possible with experiential learning and which can allow students to 'take ownership' of their learning, and better enable the synthesis of lessons learned. It is perhaps only at this point that the shift of consciousness may occur in individuals and in society that Einstein called for when he said that we can't solve problems by using the same kind of thinking that led to the problems arising in the first instance.

References

Ali Khan, Shirley 1995 *Taking Responsibility, Promoting Sustainable Practice through Higher Education Curricula*. London: Pluto Press

Anderson, D, Johnson, R and Milligan, B. 2000 *Quality Assurance and Accreditation in Australian Higher Education: An Assessment of Australian and International Practice. Canberra: Evaluations and Investigations Programme*. London: Higher Education Division, Department of Education, Training and Youth Affairs

Beard, C. and Wilson, J. P. 2002 *The power of experiential learning: A handbook for trainers and educators*. London: Kogan Page

Beard, C and Wilson, J 2006 *Experiential Learning: A Best Practice Handbook for Trainers and Educators*. London: Kogan Page

Burnard, P. 1991 *Experiential Learning in Action*. Aldershot: Avebury

Boud, D. 1989 The role of self assessment in student grading. *Assessment and Evaluation in Higher Education*, **14**, 20-30

Boud, D., Keogh, M., and Walker, D. 1985 *Reflection: Turning Experience into Learning*. London: Kogan Page

Boud, D., Cohen, R. and Walker, D. 1993 'Understanding learning from experience', in Boud, D., Cohen, R. and Walker, D. (eds) *Using Experience for Learning*. Buckingham: SRHE and Open University Press

Bowden, J. and Marton, F. 1998 *The University of Learning*. London: Kogan Page

Brown, J. S., Collins, A., and Duguid, P. 1989 Situated cognition and the culture of learning. *Educational Researcher*, **18**, 32-42. [Internet]. <http://www.exploratorium.edu/IFI/resources/museumeducation/situated.html>. [Accessed 2nd February 2007].

Chickering, A. W. 1977 *Experience and learning: An introduction to experiential learning*. New York: Change Magazine Press

Clark, M. 1989 *Ariadne's Thread – The Search for New Ways of Thinking*. Basingstoke: Macmillan

Cockrell, K.S., Caplow, J.A. and Donaldson, J.F. 2000 A context for learning: collaborative groups in the problem-based learning environment. *The Review of Higher Education*, **23**, 347-63

Coppola, B.P. 1996 Progress in practice: teaching and learning with case studies. *The Chemical Educator*, **1**, 1-13

Cortese, A. 1997 *Engineering Education for a Sustainable Future* [online]. Second Nature. [Internet]. <http://www.secondnature.org/programs/starfish/biblio.nsf >. [Accessed 21st August 2000].

Dawe, G., Jucker, R. and Martin, S. 2005 Sustainable Development in Higher Education: Current Practice and Future Developments. York: Higher Education Academy   <http://www.heacademy.ac.uk/4074.htm>. [Accessed: 20th June 2007].

Dewey, J. 1938 *Experience and Education*. London: Collier Macmillan

DFEE 2000a Advisory group on education for citizenship. *Citizenship for 16-19 Year Olds in Education and Training: Report of the Advisory Group to the Secretary of State for Education and Employment.* London: Further Education Funding Council

DFEE 2000b *Developing a global dimension in the school curriculum* 0015/2000. London: DFEE

DFES 2003 *Sustainable Development Action Plan for and Skills.* London: DFES

DFES 2004 *Putting the world into world-class education – An international strategy for education, skills and children's services.* London: DFES

DFES 2005 *Developing a Global Dimension in the School Curriculum.* London: DFES

DFID 2003 *Enabling Effective Support: Responding to the challenges of the global society: A strategy of support for the global dimension in education.* London: Department for International Development

Einstein, D. 1993. The Campus Ecology Research Project: An Environmental Education Case Study. [Internet]. <http://www.fpm.wisc.edu/campusecology/cerp/thesis/3_cerp.htm>. [Accessed 11th September 2001].

Eurodyce 2005 *Citizenship Education at School in Europe.* Brussels: Eurodyce European Unit

Friedman, R.S. and Deek, F.P. 2002. Problem-based learning and problem-solving tools: synthesis and direction for distributed education environments. *Journal of Interactive Learning and Research,* **13,** 239-57

FEFC 2000 Citizenship for 16-19 year olds in education and training: report of the independent advisory committee. [Internet]. <http://www.post16citizenship.org/files/citizenship_report.pdf >.[Accessed: 20th June 2008].

Gabbert, B., Johnson, D.W. and Johnson, R. 1986 Cooperative learning, group-to-individual transfer, process gain, and the acquisition of cognitive reasoning strategies. *Journal of Psychology,* **120,** 265-78

Griffin, C. 1992 'Absorbing experiential learning', in Mulligan, J. and Griffen, C. (eds) *Empowerment through Experiential Learning: Explorations of Good Practice.* London: Kogan Page

Jucker, R. 2002 Sustainability? Never heard of it! Some basics we shouldn't ignore when engaging in education for sustainability. *International Journal of Sustainability in Higher Education,* **3,** 8-18

Levett, R. and White 2006 Sustainability carrots and sticks: the benefits and risks of sustainable development in HEIs - Report to HEFCE. Levett-Therivel Sustainability Consultants.   [Internet]. <http://www.hefce.ac.uk/pubs/rdreports/2006/>. [Accessed 2nd February 2007].

Mason, J. 2000 Learning from experience in mathematics, in Boud, D., Cohen, R. and Walker, D. (eds) *Using Experience for Learning.* Milton Keynes: SRHE and Open University Press

Moon, J. 2004   *A Handbook of Reflective and Experiential Learning.* London: Routledge Falmer

Noble, M. 2002 *Accrediting Experience.* Workshop paper given at NUCCAT Annual Conference. November. Manchester

Orr, D. 1992 *Ecological Literacy: Education and the Transition to a Postmodern World.* Albany: State University of New York Press

Oxfam 1997, reprinted 2004 *A Curriculum for Global Citizenship.* Oxford: Oxfam

QCA 1998 *Education for Citizenship and the Teaching of Democracy* (The Crick Report). London: DfEE / QCA

QCA 2000 *Citizenship at Key Stages 3 and 4 Initial Guidance for Schools.* London: QCA

Peterson, M. 1997 Skills to enhance problem-based learning. *Medical Education Online.* [Internet]. <http://www.med-ed-online.org/f0000009.htm#f0000009>. [Accessed 2nd February 2001].

Richardson, J., Irwin, T. and Sherwin, C. 2005 *Design and Sustainability: A Scoping Report for the Sustainable Design Forum*. London: Design Council

Schmidt, H.G. 1993 Foundation of problem-based learning: some explanatory notes. *Medical Education*, **27**, 422-32

Schön, Donald A. 1983 *The reflective practitioner. How professionals think in action*. U.S.A.: Basic Book

Senge, P. 1990 The Fifth Discipline. New York: Doubleday Currency

SQW 2006 Scoping study for a strategic review of sustainable development in higher education: A report to the HEFCE, SQW. [Internet]. <http://195.194.167.100/pubs/rdreports/2006/?o=1>. [Accessed 20th June 2008].

Steinemann, A. 2003 Implementing Sustainable Development Through Problem-Based Learning:Pedagogy and Practice. *Journal of Professional Issues in Engineering Education and Practice*. October

Sterling, S. 2001 *Sustainable Education: Re-visioning Learning and Change*. Totnes: Green Books

Sterling, S. 2002 A Baker's Dozen-towards changing our 'loaf' in *The Trumpeter*. <http://trumpeter.athabascau.ca/content/v18.1/sterling.html>. [Accessed 20th January 2006].

Sterling, S. 2003 *Whole Systems Thinking as a Basis for Paradigm Change in Education: Explorations in the Context of Sustainability*. PhD Thesis. Bath: University of Bath

Usher, R. and Solomon, N. 1999 *Experiential learning and the shaping of subjectivity in the workplace. Studies in the Education of Adults*. **31**, 155-163

Thayer, R. 1994 *Gray world, green heart: technology, nature, and the sustainable landscape*. New York: John Wiley and Sons

Walton, H.J. and Mathews, M.B. 1989 Essentials of Problem-Based Learning. *Medical Education*, **23**, 542-558

Warburton, K. 2003 Deep learning and education for sustainability. *International Journal of Sustainability in Higher Education*. **4**, 44-56

Working with Experience: Animating Learning. London: Routledge

Towards a Definition of Sustainability Literacy for the Built Environment Professions

Paul E. Murray
University of Plymouth

Abstract

Although sustainability has been adopted as a core theme by professional bodies across the world, little work has been published on how individual professionals can be supported in making the changes needed to transform their industry. This research links the concept of sustainability literacy, and the knowledge and skill attributes that individuals need to live and work in a sustainable manner with the construction industry which accounts for over 40% of all resources extracted from the Earth's crust, 50% of CO_2 emissions and employs, globally, more than 111 million people. Sustainability-relevant knowledge and skill themes that apply to the design, construction and management of the built environment are identified through a two-stage international literature review. These are used to develop prototype sustainability literacy profiles for individuals to self-assess the sustainability knowledge and skill levels they require inside the workplace. However, as sustainability literacy refers to life inside and outside work, the profiles also consider the generic knowledge and skill sets needed for background, 'big picture' understanding. This paper documents the development and piloting of the profiles which proved a useful starting point for professional and personal development and for the embedding of sustainability within construction education programmes.

Keywords   Sustainability literacy, built environment, construction industry, knowledge, skills

Introduction

Sustainability is increasingly being recognised as the emerging paradigm for twenty-first century living. Individuals, communities and local, national and international institutions are all adopting sustainability as an aspirational ideal essential for achieving the long term goal of sustainable development, as articulated in Gro Harlem Brundtland's report *Our Common Future* (WCED, 2007). The construction industry is particularly important to sustainable development because of its significance to humanity, and because of its impacts on the natural environment. We use the fruits of construction to support our civilisation and to express the human condition. We project our vision of ourselves, our religious beliefs, cultural prestige and personal egos through buildings, national monuments and the built infrastructure. We also reflect wealth through the property we own or control; Professor David Pearce of the research body CRISP points out that in the UK built assets account for 70% of our man-made wealth (Pearce, 2003, p.xi). Construction has always been important economically and today in many countries construction accounts for over half of capital investment; in the case of the UK and US, between 8% and 10% of GDP (DTI, 2006, p.9; Pearce, 2003, p.x; *Contructioneducation.com*, 2007). Construction output is used as an economic indicator, for example the USA Census Bureau cites the number of housing starts, building permits and new home sales as key economic indicators (USCB, 2007). Furthermore, according to the Confederation of International Contractors Associations (CICA, 2002, p.7) the industry employs directly 111 million people worldwide, including 2.1 million in the UK (DTI, 2006, p.9), demonstrating its social importance. Nevertheless, and notwithstanding its socio-economic relevance, the construction industry's strongest link to sustainable development lies with the scale of its negative environmental impacts. The design, construction, management, use and disposal of construction assets accounts for between 40% and 50% of all materials extracted from the earth's crust (Edwards, 1999) and in developed countries between 40% and 50% of all energy used (CICA, 2002, p.7). The industry is therefore heavily implicated in many of the global problems humanity now faces, including global warming, the loss of biodiversity, pollution and the loss of resources to future generations.

The link between construction and sustainability is being increasingly recognised by the industry's professional bodies, as evidenced by recent changes in their educational criteria (Table 1). While the increased focus on sustainability and construction is self-evident, little has yet been published on how individual professionals need to change and equip themselves to operate within the emerging sustainability paradigm. This is where the concept of Sustainability Literacy is helpful.

Table 1   Professional bodies and sustainability-related accreditation criteria (Derived from Murray and Cotgrave, 2007)

Professional body	Sustainability-related accreditation criteria
Royal Institute of British Architects (RIBA)	2002 Criteria includes design-specific social, cultural and environmental learning outcomes, and specific skills requirements
National Council for Architectural Registration Boards	Inclusion of some elements of environmental design and social responses to environment within Education Standards 2007
Chartered Institute of Building (CIOB)	2005 Educational Framework refers to environmental aspects and broad social, ethical and cultural issues. Some specific skills requirements relate to sustainability.
Institution of Civil Engineers (ICE)	
Institution of Structural Engineers (IStructE)	Need for sustainable development delivery in degree programmes with detailed guidance on sustainability-relevant knowledge, skills and attitude development published July 2005 by the Joint Board of Moderators
Chartered Institution of Services Engineers (CIBSE)	
Royal Institution of Chartered Surveyors; (RICS)	2005 RICS announcement about the need to address education for sustainability
Royal Town Planning Institute (RTPI)	2004 educational guidelines include sustainability, social, economic and environmental contexts and development of appropriate knowledge

Sustainability Literacy is the term coined by Forum for the Future to describe the attributes a person needs to live and work in a sustainable manner (Dyer and Selby, 2004). Forum's working definition for a sustainability literate person is someone who:

> understands the need for change to a sustainable way of doing things, individually and collectively, has sufficient knowledge and skills to decide to act in a way that favours sustainable development, is able to recognise and reward other people's decisions and actions that favour sustainable development. (Parkin *et al.*, 2004, p.9)

The United Nations, business organisations and aid charities emphasise the role of values in promoting sustainable lifestyles. Psychologists argue that although values, attitudes and beliefs are significant in motivating human actions and equipping professionals with appropriate knowledge and skills, these alone may not put the construction industry on a truly 'sustainability footing'; work is also needed to develop the values of the people working within construction to motivate and support their pro-sustainability behaviour. So, it can be inferred that there are three core components of sustainability literacy:

(i)   sustainability knowledge
(ii)   sustainability skills
(iii) sustainability values

Defining Sustainability Literacy Elements

Whilst delivering values-based education is a complex endeavour (Murray and Murray, 2007, pp.288-89), most construction educators are familiar with the idea of equipping learners with profession-related knowledge and skills. The emerging 'sustainability paradigm' referred to in Murray and Cotgrave (2007), however, requires shifts in the type and nature of the knowledge and skills delivered to construction students to ensure that future graduates have enhanced levels of sustainability literacy. In this context, identifying the sustainability-related knowledge and skills relevant to construction professionals is a useful starting point.

Forum for the Future defines knowledge as information leading to understanding and skills as abilities that are acquired through education or experience (Forum for the Future, 2002; 2004). Parkin *et al.* (2004) proceed to describe the knowledge and skills-base needed to support sustainable development as the:

> Intellectual and practical tools that enable them to take decisions and act in a way that is likely to contribute positively to sustainable development. They will be able to take decisions on specific matters ...... applying the 'at the same time' rule, that is taking environmental, social and economic considerations into account simultaneously, not separately. (Parkin *et al.*, 2004, p.9)

Parkin's vision implies that learners need to have a good grasp and deep understanding of the sustainability agenda generally, as well as detailed discipline-specific knowledge and skills. Advice on how to practically elicit the sustainability-related knowledge and skills relevant to a particular discipline has been offered by Forum for the Future and the University of Tennessee (Forum for the Future, 2004; McKeown, 2002). Helpfully, Forum for the Future has defined a list of specific sustainability knowledge and skill themes that can, theoretically, apply to anyone regardless of their discipline (Table 2; Table 3).

Table 2 Examples of generic sustainability knowledge themes (Derived from Forum for the Future, 2004, p.13)

Examples of sustainability knowledge sets
• Basic ecology, energy generation and supply, low carbon futures
• How to maintain health/wellbeing
• Understanding of equality and diversity, ethics, human rights
• Citizenship, government, local and regional strategies, risk, regulation, personal rights and responsibilities, effective organisations
• Best practice in industry, environmental management, business case for SD, material and energy use
• Basic economics, value concepts, cost/benefit analysis, whole-life costing, funding streams

Construction professionals, however, operate within a highly technical field and will therefore require discipline-specific *and* generic knowledge and skills if they are to provide a meaningful contribution to sustainability through their work. Forum for the Future recommends deducing discipline-based sustainability knowledge and skills using what they call the 'Antofagasta Model' (Forum for the Future 2002, p.5). This learner-centred model illustrates the world in which we operate as concentric circles with 'self' at the centre to deduce the relationships between sustainability, the person, other people and organisations around them, and the environment they work within.

This approach was considered in 2005 by the University of Plymouth when a comprehensive sustainability audit of undergraduate construction programmes was proposed (Murray, Goodhew and Turpin-Brooks, 2007). However, the extensive research undertaken by a range of authoritative bodies on the environmental impact of the built environment could make the use of the Antogafasta model inappropriate for the competency-focused construction discipline. In considering this, an international literature review was carried out with the aim of identifying this body of knowledge and classifying the main discipline-related sustainability knowledge and skill sets appropriate to a sustainability literate construction professional.

The sources consulted included among others, the Building Research Establishment (Howard *et al.*,1998); Constructing Excellence, the independent body working to enhance construction industry efficiency in UK (Constructing Excellence, 2004); professional bodies (the Chartered Institute of Building (CIOB, 2004; CIOB, 2005); the Engineering Council (2000); the Construction Industry Council (2002); UK government agencies (DTI, 2004); the Quality Assurance Agency (2002); and the US Green Building Council. The review findings were merged with Forum for the Future's generic sustainability knowledge and skills profiles to create a coherent schedule of 65 knowledge and 31 skill sets that included 55 discipline-specific and 41 generic elements. These were then used to underpin the 2005 audit of Plymouth's construction curricula, resulting in the identification of a small number of additional knowledge sets (Murray, Goodhew and Turpin-Brooks, 2007).

Table 3   Sustainability skills (Derived from Forum for the Future, 2004, p.14)

Understanding need for change	Knowledge and skills to act	Recognising and rewarding
Long term thinking	Leadership (by example)	Empathising
Futures planning	Parenting	Communicating
Solutions oriented approach	Teaching skills	Appreciating others' views
Articulating barriers/opportunities	Creating ownership	Developing/sustaining relationships
Critical thinking	Managing information	Team working
Assimilation/organisation	Change management	Working with diversity
Confidence to challenge	Patience, negotiation, diplomacy	Managing stakeholder relationships
Confidence to go above minimum standards	Strategic visioning	Advocacy
Inclusivity skills	Case-making	Specifying
Listening/reflection	Taking responsibility/leading	Consensus building
Absorbing/giving information	Decision-making	Capacity building
	Linking legislation	

Following the development of the auditing profiles, further work was carried out to make them more suitable to use as vehicles for individuals to self-assess their personal level of sustainability literacy. Further research was undertaken to take advantage of more recent developments in Education for Sustainable Development (ESD) and to enhance the accuracy and currency of the profiles.   On reflection, it was found that the skills categories were ambiguous. For example: are identifying barriers and solutions and problem solving generic or discipline-related skills?

Table 4   Sustainability skill themes
• Leadership Skills
• Management Skills
• Communication Skills
• Learning and Teaching Skills
• Personal Skills
• Sustainability-specific Professional Skills

Table 5   Sustainability knowledge themes
• Generic sustainability knowledge
• Background on Construction Links to Sustainability
• Energy In Design & Management
• Sustainability / Environmental Assessment Tools
• Waste Issues
• Construction Materials Issues
• Health, Safety, Welfare
• Pollution, Contamination Water Resource Issues
• Law/Regulation
• Construction Business Practices

As a result, a single sustainability skills category was created, combining the two previous categories and supplementing them with the findings of the updated research on sustainability skills published by the ODPM (Egan, 2004; ODPM, 2004), Construction Skills (CITB, 2005), the Construction Industry Council (CIC, 2004), the Higher Education Academy (HEA, 2006) and Oxfam (Oxfam, 1997). Additional research on discipline-based knowledge was also undertaken consulting sources that included the DTI (2006), the JBM (2005), the BRE (2005), the Royal Academy of Engineering (RAE, 2005), the USGBC (2005), the University of Cambridge (2006) and the American Institute of Architects (AIA, 2006). Following this work, the original 96 elements were expanded to 217 knowledge and skill sets organised within ten knowledge themes and six skill themes (Table 4 and Table 5).

Notwithstanding the fruits of this work, it was recognised that anyone trying to self-assess sustainability literacy by using an exhaustive checklist of knowledge and skills would quickly lose heart and deeper questions needed to be asked about the attributes individuals already possess, to what level, and which knowledge and skills they need to cultivate further to suit their aspirations. Furthermore, the literature reveals a significant level of confusion amongst academics themselves in relation to what the baseline terms 'sustainability' and 'sustainable development' actually mean in different contexts (Murray and Murray, 2007, p.285); an important factor to bear in mind in the development of any practical sustainability literacy self-assessment method.

In defining the qualities of the proposed sustainability literacy profiles, it was recognised that they should preferably be:

- capable of being self-administered
- formative, and informative
- user-friendly
- learner-centred, thus flexible for adaptation to different audiences (lecturers, students, professionals)
- sufficiently challenging and motivating to move an individual forward (transformative)

Five broad approaches were examined.

Questionnaire approach: Questionnaires are commonly used to measure perceptions, views, awareness levels and attitudes using open/closed questions, ranking systems, Likert scales, etc. A successful questionnaire will need to include the following attributes: a benchmark or standard against which to measure the minimum acceptable level of knowledge or skill required; use of accessible language; inclusion of a number of open-ended questions (to ensure depth); and a major commitment in development time. A sustainability literacy questionnaire would necessarily be long and time-consuming (if not tedious) to respond to. The format would have to be flexible enough to take into account different people's knowledge/skill starting points and it might prove difficult to avoid bias in question-setting. Furthermore, the issue of 'questionnaire fatigue' could not be ignored. Nevertheless, an element of questioning could be of value.

Health Impact Assessment Approach: Health Impact Assessments work by considering the possible positive and negative impacts of (for example) a new building or a new service on health. This approach is of interest because it is holistic and crosses boundaries (for example linking an individual's age and sex with lifestyle, social and community networks, physical living and working environment, infrastructure and schooling). Also Health Impact Assessments are potentially formative and developmental in nature and have great potential to inform any future Sustainability Literacy competency self-assessment model.

NVQ Competency Assessment Approach: NVQ competency assessments involve a detailed definition of the benchmarks needed to perform particular vocational functions as well as requiring inhibitive levels of individual subject expertise and time to develop and undertake.

Sustainability Toolkit/workbook approach: Flexible learning toolkits and learning packs for construction students have proved both popular and successful (Murray, 2005). The University of Plymouth developed sustainability-specific flexible learning materials for lecturers and students through the recently completed SLICE Project (Goodhew, 2003). Goodhew's materials, of all the subject-specific publications produced through SLICE (Murray, 2005), proved to be the most popular with lecturers; the use of such resources is undoubtedly helpful and could include scope for longitudinal progress-mapping. However, the SLICE experience was that developing high quality transferable materials is expensive and time consuming; SLICE developed nine sets of subject specific materials over a three year period at a project cost of over £300,000.

Scenario-based approach: Scenario-based approaches can potentially link with or integrate the best of other approaches. A scenario that enables someone to compare their own analysis of the requirements for 'wise action' to pre-defined 'model' would be formative, informative, and potentially motivational. Take the simple generic scenario of a decision to reduce consumption of water (either personally, professionally, or both). In analysing what is needed to reach this decision various bodies of knowledge and skills are required:

- knowledge of current consumption and methods of reducing that consumption
- knowledge of the direct benefits of reducing consumption, to individuals, communities, society and to the environment
- knowledge of the less obvious indirect, potentially unforeseen, real and perceived benefits (like improved self-esteem, perhaps, because the decision is in line with deeply held values)
- negotiation skills (with colleagues or family), parenting skills, leadership skills, teaching skills and goal-setting skills
- appropriate values to motivate the decision

Although this scenario approach has merit, it is difficult to see it as stand-alone; it is probably most suitable for use in face-to-face workshop and training settings (Murray and Murray, 2007, p.295) and is probably best considered as a supplement to the use of self-assessment sustainability literacy profiles. In addition, 'sustainability training' workshops were developed to help individuals engage with sustainability at a personal level. The workshops aim to link the three components - knowledge, skills and values - to the notion of living and working in a sustainable manner. They were used both as a clearing ground for piloting the sustainability literacy profiles and as an important supplement. In terms of the profiles, initially, basic knowledge and skills questionnaires were piloted with workshop groups providing open feedback on their use. The feedback from workshops indicated that the questionnaires, as expected, were unwieldy and uninviting and further development followed. Learners were then invited to identify the knowledge and skills relevant to their work under the categories identified in Table 4 and Table 5, and to self-assess personal competency levels for each detailed element. The basis of the self-assessment was a visual traffic light system utilising bronze, silver and gold award levels (Table 6).

Table 6   Sustainability competency award levels for construction professionals

BRONZE AWARD LEVEL			SILVER AWARD LEVEL			GOLD AWARD LEVEL		
◊	◊	◊	◊	◊	◊	◊	◊	◊
Basic awareness Understand awareness only the basics			Becoming familiar with some aspects		Good general knowledge	Detailed knowledge in some areas		Detailed knowledge in most areas

Each individual involved was asked to mark up sample profile sheets to identify, graphically, their self-perceived level of attainment for each knowledge/skill set and target level, the latter being based on future career aspirations and interests. For example, if knowledge of the BREEAM environmental assessment method was being assessed and the individual aimed to become a BREEAM assessor, then an attainment level at the high silver or low gold levels would be an appropriate target. If their current level features as a low bronze, it would suggest the need for a clear plan of action for self-development.

The completed profiles (available from the author), comprise thirty pages of profiles containing:

- 39 generic knowledge sets
- 129 discipline-specific knowledge sets
- 49 skills sets

In addition, the profiles include spaces for emerging issues, knowledge and skill sets to be added/included by the user.

The second wave of profile pilots involved twenty-five undergraduate and postgraduate students. Feedback suggested that the profiles are easy to use and their graphical quality was helpful. However, concern was expressed over the accuracy of using self-perception techniques, and if the entire thirty page profile were to be completed, the task would almost certainly prove off-putting. Overall, however, the feedback was encouraging as participants recognised the value of the profiles in considering their current position and future plans in relation to their personal and professional development.

Conclusions

What has become clear from the work to date is that the definition of what constitutes sustainability knowledge and skills will change and expand over time as new understanding and new solutions to the sustainability 'crisis' arise. The current 217 elements which constitute a helpful starting point in defining sustainability competencies for construction professionals have already proved helpful in the design and delivery of education programmes. However, if the profiles are to be used to help individuals self-assess their sustainability literacy, further work will be required to enhance their usability. The likely direction to proceed will be to translate the paper-based format of the profiles into an online editable hyperlinked digital format, which if well executed, could provide an accessible, inviting and efficient support for personal and professional development.

References

AIA 2006 *Ecology and Design: Ecoliteracy in Architecture Education.* Washington: AIA

BRE 2005 *Ecohomes 2005 Specification.* Watford: Building Research Establishment

CICA 2002 *Industry as a Partner in Sustainable Development: Construction.* CICA Paris: Confederation of International Contractors Associations for UNEP

CIOB 2004 *Sustainability and Construction.* Ascot: Chartered Institute of Building

CIOB 2005 *CIOB Educational Framework 2006.* Ascot: Chartered Institute of Building

CITB 2005 *Sustainability Skills Matrix for Built Environment Professionals; CITB Construction Skills.* [Internet]. <http://www.constructionskills.net/strategicinitiatives/sustainabledevelopment>. [Accessed 1st July 2007].

CIC 2004 *Built Environment Professional Skills Survey 2003/2004 – Survey results.* London: Construction Industry Council

Constructing Excellence 2004 *Demonstrations of Sustainability. The Rethinking Construction demonstrations and how they have addressed sustainable construction issues.* London: Rethinking Construction Ltd. [Internet]. <http://www.constructioneducation.com>. [Accessed 1st July 2007].

DTI 2004 *Sustainable Construction Brief 2.* London: Department of Trade and Industry. [Internet]. <http://www.dti.gov.uk/files/file 13939.pdf>. [Accessed 2nd July 2007].

DTI 2006 *Review of Sustainable Construction 2006.* London: Department of Trade and Industry. [Internet]. <http://www.dti.gov.uk/files/file34979.pdf>. [Accessed 14th July 2007].

Du Plessis C. 2001 *AGENDA 21 for Sustainable Construction in Developing Countries.* A discussion document. Report for CIB and UNEP-IETC. Pretoria: CSIR Building and Construction

Dyer, A. and Selby, D. 2004 *Education for Sustainable Development. Stage 2 bid to HEFCE.* University of Plymouth: Centre of Excellence for Teaching and Learning

Edwards, B. 1999 *Sustainable Architecture: European Directives and Building Design; 2nd edition.* Oxford: Architectural Press

Forum for the Future 2002 *Learning for Sustainable Development. A curriculum toolkit.* London: Forum for the Future

Forum for the Future 2004 *Sustainability Literacy: knowledge and skills for the future. Taking it on.* London: Forum for the Future

Goodhew, S. 2003 *Sustainability and Construction. SLICE Learning Pack 1.* University of Plymouth: Student-centred Learning in Construction Education

HEA 2006 *Sustainable Development and Higher Education: Current practice and future developments. A progress report for senior managers in Higher Education.* York: Higher Education Academy

Howard N., Shiers, D. and Sinclair M. 1998 *Green Guide to Specification. An environmental profiling system for materials and components.* Watford: Building Research Establishment

JBM 2005 *The Design and Content of Engineering Programmes. Annex D – Sustainability.* London: Joint Board of Moderators

McKeown, R. 2002 *Education for Sustainable Development Toolkit: Version 2.* University of Tennessee

Murray, P. 2005 *FDTL Project /03 Student-centred Learning in Construction education, Final Report.* Plymouth: University of Plymouth

Murray,P. and Cotgrave, A. 2007 Sustainability Literacy: the future paradigm for construction education? *Structural Survey,* **25,** 7-23

Murray, P., Goodhew, S. and Turpin-Brooks, S. 2007 Environmental Sustainability: Sustainable Construction Education; a UK case study. *International Journal of Environmental, Cultural, Economic and Social Sustainability,* **2,** 9-22

Murray, P. and Murray, S. 2007 Promoting Values in Career-based Programmes. A case study analysis. *International Journal of Sustainability in Higher Education*, **8,** 285-300

Oxfam 1997 *Oxfam's Curriculum for Global Citizenship.* Oxford: Oxfam

ODPM 2004 *The Egan Review: Skills for Sustainable Communities.* London: ODPM

ODPM 2004 *Summary of Responses to Egan Review of Skills - Public Consultation 2004.* London: ODPM

Parkin, S., Johnson, A., Buckland H. and White E. 2004 *Learning and Skills for sustainable Development: Developing a sustainability literate society.* London: HEP

Pearce, D. 2003 *The Social and Economic Value of Construction. The construction industry's contribution to sustainable development.* London: CRISP Support Unit (www.nCRISP.org.uk)

QAA 2002 *Building and Surveying Subject Benchmark Statement.* Gloucester: Quality Assurance Agency for Higher Education

RAE 2005 Engineering for Sustainable Development: guiding principles. London: Royal Academy of Engineering

University of Cambridge 2006 *The IMPEE Project: What do Engineers need to learn about sustainable development?* Cambridge: Cambridge University

US Census Bureau 2007 *Manufacturing, Mining and Construction Statistics.* [Internet]. <http://www.census.gov/const/www>. [Accessed 2nd August 2007].

USGBC 2005 *Green Building Rating System for New Construction and Major Renovations.* Washington: US Green Building Council. [Internet]. <http://www.usgbc/LEED>. [Accessed 4th June 2007].

WCED 1987 *Our Common Future, World Commission on Environment and Development.* Oxford: Oxford University Press

Delivering on the Promise: Success and Failure in Academic Knowledge Transfer

Paul Micklethwaite
Kingston University

Abstract

British Universities are increasingly engaging in 'knowledge transfer' activities. Significant government funding is available to allow academics to formally engage with business, public sector and community partners.

Knowledge transfer is a recent phenomenon on this scale. It may be a new kind of activity for the academics involved, so there is a need to share best practice on 'how to do it'. Successful examples are available, and promotional material ensures that all knowledge transfer projects are presented as being successful. However, we may learn more from cases which are less successful, or even unsuccessful. Such examples are more difficult to find in the promotion, dissemination and reporting of knowledge transfer.

This paper considers some of the less successful, more problematic aspects of knowledge transfer project design and delivery, based on personal experience as an academic engaged in several projects in the area of Designing for Sustainability. The paper addresses notions of success and failure in knowledge transfer, highlighting a potential mismatch between real and reported success, and potential tension between useful outcomes and assessed project outputs. It also identifies some potential pitfalls in project design and delivery.

Keywords Knowledge transfer projects, success, failure

What is Knowledge Transfer?

> Knowledge transfer is about exchanging good ideas, research results, experiences and skills between universities, other research organisations, business, government, the public sector and the wider community to enable innovative new products, services and policies to be developed. (ESRC, 2007)

Knowledge transfer is often discussed via the metaphor of a dialogue or conversation between the research community and potential 'users' of research. The ultimate purpose of this dialogue is to get research applied in policy and practice. This goal is often related to national economic competitiveness; if the UK is to compete in the global marketplace it needs to exploit, commercially, its research base by successfully converting research into innovation. The academic research community is seen as particularly ripe for this kind of strategic exploitation. However, the gains need not be solely economic:

> Successful innovation is about the creation and implementation of new processes, products, services and methods of delivery which result in significant improvements in outcomes, efficiency, effectiveness or quality across public, private and voluntary sectors. (ESRC, 2007)

Support for this kind of activity may come from UK Government or European Union sources. In 2004 the UK Government announced a ten-year Science and Innovation investment framework in which knowledge transfer is prominent (HMSO, 2004). Recent political emphasis on knowledge transfer is, therefore, due to continue, and it will presumably persist as a source of funding for universities, via such mechanisms as the Higher Education Innovation Fund (HEIF).

Academic knowledge transfer is a collaboration between academic researchers and non-academic partners. HEIF began in 2001 to '[support] institutions to engage in a broad range of knowledge transfer activities with business, public sector and community partners, for direct or indirect economic benefit.' (HEFCE, 2007) Government-funded research councils such as the Economic and Social Research Council (ESRC), the Engineering and Physical Sciences Research Council (EPSRC), and the Arts and Humanities Research Council (AHRC) offer similar schemes. Through these schemes, academic researchers have increasing opportunities to apply their research in a more concerted way. As a result, 'knowledge transfer' may be a new kind of activity for many academics, who may not be used to engaging with wider non-academic audiences in the cause of innovation, however broadly defined. There is, therefore, a need to share best practice in 'how to do' knowledge transfer.

Knowledge Transfer Reporting

Successful examples of knowledge transfer projects are widely available via the marketing and dissemination activities of knowledge transfer schemes such as those funded by the HEIF. Promotional material ensures that all knowledge transfer projects are *apparently* successful i.e. they are presented as being, and so are seen to be, successful. This observation probably applies equally to any case in which continued or further funding depends to some extent on a demonstration of success in the reporting of previously completed projects. While success stories can be inspiring and instructive, we may, however, learn more from cases which are less successful, or even unsuccessful. Such examples are more difficult to find in the promotion, dissemination and reporting of knowledge transfer activities. This paper was prompted in part by a perception of a mismatch between knowledge transfer as it is typically reported, and personal experience in the delivery of several such projects which are now outlined.

Examples from Designing for Sustainability

This paper is based on personal delivery of knowledge transfer projects in the areas of Designing for Sustainability. These projects include collaboration on many individual design development projects seeking to accelerate the introduction of more 'sustainable' products to market. None of these projects were Knowledge Transfer Partnerships (KTPs). Projects included various modes of knowledge transfer, including public lectures, professional training, one-to-one business support, and large-scale multiple-partner industrial collaboration. While some of these activities might be seen as 'delivery' oriented (one-way), the dialogical spirit of knowledge transfer was to some extent present in each.

Delivering on the Promise

The title of this paper has several potential dimensions in our discussion of academic knowledge transfer:

(i)   the promise to collaborating partners (living up to what you say in your promotional material)

(ii)   the promise to funders (living up to what you say in the funding bid)

(iii)   the promise of knowledge transfer as a mechanism (realising the potential to contribute to economic and social well-being, both in general and in specific cases)

In the knowledge transfer projects discussed here, often a form of provider-client relationship took hold between the academic researcher (myself) and an individual collaborating non-academic partner (for example, a sole trading designer) or between the university and a collaborating company or external organisation. A relationship initiated as knowledge transfer from the academic side was often perceived as a form of consultancy from the non-academic side. There is a need to manage the expectations of the non-academic collaborating partner, and establish the intended nature of knowledge transfer as a dialogue. There is a danger that promises are made up-front, for example, in seeking to recruit partners which may be difficult to deliver on, compromising the potential of knowledge transfer as a mechanism for collaborative innovation, and the academics involved.

Success and Failure

It is worth considering notions of success and failure in knowledge transfer projects. The ESRC lists separately the potential benefits to 'those carrying out the research' and 'those using research'. (ESRC, 2007) Academics are likely to be the former. According to the ESRC, the benefits of engaging with the audiences of your research are to:

- gain better understanding of the needs of potential users
- inform and improve the quality of your research
- gain valuable skills and experience
- develop networks and improve your influencing skills
- increase the prospects of your research being applied
- enhance your reputation
- increase your opportunities for further research funding and career opportunities
- open up the opportunity of joint funding

From the same ESRC source 'some of the benefits of working collaboratively' are to:

- increase the scope of your research and attract extra funding for the project
- apply evidence-based knowledge and expertise to important business problems or research agendas
- gain experience of current business or policy development and assist strategic change and learn complementary project management skills
- generate research ideas and teaching material relevant to business/policy makers
- enhance your reputation as well as your research and teaching skills
- develop and strengthen your networks
- increase your chances for future funding
- improve your career opportunities

These two lists of success factors are fairly identical. In my own experience, from which this paper is written, networking with wider academic and non-academic communities engaged in sustainable design and sustainable business was a clear personal benefit. Moreover, not only did I become better-connected with relevant audiences and communities, to some extent those communities also became strengthened via workshops and other events. The needs of potential users of my research and knowledge certainly came to the fore, with the result that I quickly learned the limits of my expertise in the attempt to make the transition from academic researcher to real-world facilitator of change. The sudden need to apply knowledge which had hitherto been more abstract presented challenges, and addressing these challenges certainly forced me to consider the relevance of my expertise to design and business practitioners, even if my interventions were not always successful.

The immediate measure of success or failure for knowledge transfer activity is via the metrics imposed to measure project outputs. The relevance and meaningfulness of these project outcome targets is not always clear. The metrics used to assess whether these targets have been met may, equally, not always be easily intelligible. In such cases some creativity and imagination can be required to translate what you are actually doing on a project into the assessment categories provided. Where imagination fails, activities may simply not appear on the report sheet. This can create tension if what you might consider to be useful outcomes are not assessable as valid project outputs. The official success of a project, in terms of the targets met, can become divorced from what you may consider to be actual meaningful achievement. In this sense real and reported success may be quite different. This can engender a feeling of 'trying to succeed in spite of the system', of playing a game in which the final result does not reflect what actually took place on the field.

Evaluating the success of a project on these terms also requires the involvement of specialist independent auditors to carry out an assessment of the officially recorded version of the project. On large funding programmes this supports a dedicated administration and auditing sector, a layer of professional activity which exists solely to implement the evaluative instruments of the funding programmes. These assessments typically require a significant paper trail for each collaborative contact and relationship. Much effort is devoted by the academic to satisfying these impressive administrative and recording requirements, perhaps to the detriment of the collaboration itself as partners are repeatedly chased for statements and signatures. Anecdotal estimates vary as to how much of a project's budget and resource is typically spent directly benefiting successful collaboration, for example working with a collaborating partner. The most pessimistic estimates can be as low as 10%.

Within this kind of context, it may be tempting to inflate the success of a project to the funder and other actual and prospective audiences. This is important if the reputation and credibility of funders, partners and individuals involved suffer as a result of the level of reported success being different from that of perceived or actual success. This may engender distrust of future activity by those involved, on the part of audiences who remain unconvinced of the spin given to a completed project. For the individual academic, there are also risks in terms of maintaining personal integrity and gaining satisfaction from involvement in a particular project.

'Top 5' Knowledge Transfer Pitfalls

Some problematic aspects of the design and delivery knowledge of transfer projects are now presented. These derive from personal experience. They are not presented in any particular order. Both operational and strategic issues are addressed, perhaps prompting discussion of which are inevitable and which avoidable.

Driven by funding, not by need

Academic research project proposals are submitted in response to funding calls by, for example, the research councils. Money is made available for particular types of project, with some perhaps being ring-fenced for proposals in a specific subject area. The process is similar for projects categorised as knowledge transfer rather than research. A successful application will meet the criteria of the funding call; it may be based on reflecting back to the funder their own statements as to what they are seeking to support. Understandably, applications may be designed primarily to satisfy funding criteria, or at least take those criteria as their starting point. In some cases, bids may be made simply to secure jobs, irrespective of the value of the project being submitted. For knowledge transfer funding criteria to successfully reflect prevailing cultural and policy priorities, it is vital that communities of research users are included in their formulation, hopefully ensuring the relevance of approved bids.

Unrealistic output targets: 'chasing the numbers'

Any funding application is required to give output targets: how many training events will be held; how many businesses will be 'advised' or 'assisted'; how many of those businesses will be from minority groups. High and challenging targets will clearly mark out a project as being ambitious, and therefore perhaps more eligible for funding. Yet as these targets accumulate, the burden on delivery can quickly become onerous. It may be tempting to inflate the figures to win the bid, but this may become problematic to deliver. In some cases it may be simple naivety that dictates how many minority-owned new businesses in a certain sector and geographical area are to be supported. This may particularly apply when the bid is written by someone who will not be involved in project delivery. Whatever the cause, the result can be a prolonged exercise in 'chasing the numbers', however unrealistic these may prove to be. This can lead to some interesting machinations in prioritising who to work with, in what way, and for how long. If the metrics for working with a business are, for example, a one-off consultation or five full days of assistance, with no intermediate measure, there is no incentive to pursue cases which may progress but are unlikely to be converted from the lower to the higher metric. Tactical decisions might then be made within the project delivery team to pursue further targets at the expense of other perhaps worthwhile outcomes which would be invisible to the project's auditors. A more sensible approach would be to seek to redefine the targets, and thus the scope of the project, but this may not be possible.

Ephemerality

The timeline of a two-year knowledge transfer project working with a number of small business partners might look something like Figure 1.

This example project includes ongoing recruitment of collaborators. A phase of initial 'brand building' is needed to raise awareness of the project among its target audiences in order to recruit participants. This effort must first be planned. It should also be preceded by the design of transparent procedures and protocols by which to conduct multiple collaborations. As a result, there may be little recruitment in the first six months. This launch phase might be speedier if those involved have relevant prior experience, or are building on existing activity (clearly preferable to a 'cold start'). A final closure phase is also likely, in which efforts are focused on completion of final project reporting. The delivery phase of the project, in which active collaboration takes place, may thus effectively be limited to the middle section of the timeline shown in Figure 1. Project legacy is also relevant. Much effort may be devoted to establishing a project, as suggested, but this may not always include a consideration of continuation beyond the project's end. In such cases opportunities to consolidate and build-on the success of a project may be quickly lost.

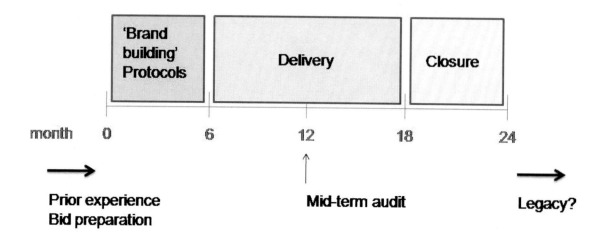

Figure 1   Timeline of an example two-year knowledge transfer project

The reporting burden

What if usable and acceptable procedures and protocols to handle collaborations are not set up in advance of recruitment? These may not be provided by the funders, in which case much effort will be devoted to *post-hoc* attempts to impose consistency on the paper trail generated by those live and messy real-world collaborations. If clear reporting procedures are not in place from the start, or those used are found to be unacceptable to the funders, then problems will arise. This problem increases in line with the level of reporting required. In some cases it can seem that the reporting procedure becomes more important than the actual outcomes achieved by a project, resulting in a culture of 'ticking boxes' rather than doing more, perhaps, meaningful work.

Managing expectations

Delivering on the promises made to collaborating partners in knowledge transfer is basically a case of living up to what you say in your promotional material. Pressure to recruit partners may lead to exaggerated early promises which delivery may not live up to. An obvious key requirement is that you are qualified to deliver on any promises made; a failure to manage expectations can only result in dissatisfaction. This boils down to conveying an accurate and consistent message across all modes of communication; otherwise your promises can quickly begin to overstretch your capacity to deliver. A tendency to promise too much may lead to academics 'bending over backwards' to satisfy expectations. A related issue is the level of coordination that exists in the academic provision on a knowledge transfer project. This is especially pertinent where academic engagement is spread across several individuals or institutions. Internal mechanisms must be in place to ensure consistent and coordinated academic involvement in collaborations with external partners.

Conclusions

This paper considers some of the less successful, more problematic aspects of knowledge transfer project design and delivery. It derives from personal experience as an academic engaged in several projects in the area of *Designing for Sustainability*. The paper attempts to identify some of the pitfalls in project design and delivery. It evaluates notions of success and failure in knowledge transfer, highlighting potential mismatch between real and reported success, and potential tension between useful outcomes and assessed project outputs. This discussion is particularly relevant to the field of sustainability from which the examples cited in this paper are drawn. The challenge of moving towards more sustainable development is primarily that of putting theory into practice, hence the theme of this conference. This is an area in which knowledge transfer can have a significant impact in effecting positive change by generating productive collaboration between academics and the 'real world' beyond academia.

By examining the 'negative case' of less successful aspects of knowledge transfer, the author hopes to make a constructive contribution to worthwhile future activities, particularly in the area of sustainability. The issues raised here may apply more broadly, in which case it is hoped that this discussion alerts others to some of the pitfalls in project design and delivery. This paper responds to a perceived lack of best-practice guidance in this kind of academic work. Knowledge transfer is a potentially powerful mechanism to facilitate collaborations between academics and new partners. The views expressed here are intended to help us deliver on that promise.

References

ESRC 2007 *Knowledge Transfer* [Internet]. <http://www.esrc.ac.uk/ESRCInfoCentre/Support/knowledge_transfer>. [Accessed 9th August 2007].

HEFCE 2007 *Higher Education Innovation Fund* [Internet]. <http://www.hefce.ac.uk/reachout/heif>. [Accessed 9th August 2007].

HMSO 2004 *Innovation Investment Framework 2004 - 2014*. <http://www.hm-treasury.gov.uk>. [Accessed 9th August 2007].

Framing the 'Subject': Developing Dimensions of Sustainability Literacy

Janet Davies
Massey University, New Zealand

Abstract

This paper explores the shape of post-school education for sustainability, where the educational aim is to develop the sustainability literacy of learners. Selected definitions of sustainability literacy are examined in respect of their underlying conceptualisations of 'literacy'. James Gee's (1996; 2004) ideological model of literacy as social group Discourse is used to inform understanding of sustainability literacy. How the development of such literacy may be supported in tertiary education is investigated and a framework for the development of sustainability literacy is suggested.

Keywords   New Zealand, sustainability literacy, Discourse, social practice, learning and teaching

Introduction

The scale, urgency and range of the task to slow down, arrest and hopefully remediate damage to the earth's systems requires an educational response that inverts the usual hierarchies for action. While education from birth and during pre-school and school clearly remains important, of greater urgency is education for those who are adult today. Adults are in a position to make significant change to individual behaviours and to influence family, community and wider societal systems and processes.

Despite media reports of adults' desire to act more sustainably, individual action is selective and public understandings of sustainability are limited, at best, to environmental sustainability and rarely include issues of social justice. Recycling, energy efficiency and organic gardening are now part of public consciousness, however, action depends not only on individual awareness, but on the development of local and national government policy that supports sustainability.

Education for sustainability is needed at every level of post-school education. It will be argued that this includes: higher education through mainstreaming in undergraduate programmes; vocational education and training through mainstreaming education in sub-degree programmes; professional development across the workforce, including special provision for policymakers and politicians; and community education in respect of everyday practice.

Although there is considerable agreement among post-school (tertiary) sustainability education practitioners and researchers that the goal of education for sustainability is sustainability literacy, there is little consensus about the nature of such literacy or the way in which such literacy should be developed. Discussion centres on sustainability 'content' as derived from a range of conceptions of sustainability, while 'literacy' is not overtly examined and remains an unarticulated and underpinning assumption.

Constructions of 'sustainability literacy'

Sustainability literacy in higher education is defined by Dale and Newman (2005) as the acquisition of a set of critical skills, facts-based and process-based. The Higher Education Academy Subject Centre for Geography, Earth and Environmental Sciences (2005) takes a broader perspective identifying skills and understanding, including understanding of the views and values of others. Forum for the Future (2004) go further, identifying sustainability literacy as understanding, knowledge and skills and, in particular, understanding to appreciate the need for change and the ability to appreciate good practice in others.

Taking a lesson from ecology, Fritjof Capra (1996) defines ecoliteracy as understanding the principles of ecology and being able to embody them in the daily life of human communities. While he points out differences between ecosystems and human communities, in particular self-awareness, he notes the commonalities and suggests that much can be learned from the fundamental principles by which ecosystems operate, including interdependence.

These conceptions of sustainability literacy range from skills to increasingly broad understandings that include attitudes and actions. The grounds on which one should accept or reject them as theoretically sound formulations of 'literacy', regardless of the concern with sustainability, are not articulated.

What is 'literacy'?

As Rockhill (1993, p.166) has argued, 'literacy is much more than a set of reading and writing skills - literacy is always about something'. In recognition of context, multiple literacies have been conceptualised, for example, scientific literacy and music literacy, where area-specific concepts and skills have been identified. Acquisition of these concepts and skills is deemed to constitute literacy. This 'cognitive deficit' model of literacy (Gross, 1994) relies on the identification of defining concepts and skills by subject experts. Although this approach has broadened, in particular, to include practice in the area and the nature of the discipline, it fails to recognize individual interests or social and political issues.

Street (1984) and others (for example, Gee, 1996) reject such approaches in place of literacy as social practice. Whereas traditional 'autonomous' models of literacy present literacy as neutral and universal, literacy as social practice provides an 'ideological' model which recognises the 'embeddedness' of literacy in culture and ideology (Street, 2003). Street argues that literacy cannot be 'given' neutrally and then have 'social' effects.

James Gee (1996; 2004) identifies literacy as fluency in a 'Discourse' (with a capital 'D') - a social group's 'way of being in the world', which entails communication via language, illustrations and icons and includes appropriate behaviours, shared knowledge and beliefs, and attitudes and values consistent with those of the group. Members of a group engaged in permaculture, for example, will participate in a permaculture Discourse through a common language, artefacts, practices and values.

Features of social group Discourse are evident in the science cultures investigated by Karin Knorr Cetina (1999) and others (Labinger and Collins, 2001). Knorr Cetina identifies fundamental differences in social practice between science disciplines, and between individual topics within disciplines, where different types of questions are pursued, and different theories, language, methods and equipment are used. These epistemic cultures have contrasting aims, forms of inquiry, practices and organization.

In this paper I use James Gee's (1996; 2004) understanding of literacy as fluency in social group 'Discourse' to explore possibilities for the development of sustainability literacy.

Developing Literacy

According to Gee (1996) all individuals acquire a primary Discourse, that of the home, through acculturation. This Discourse provides a taken-for-granted way of being - how to behave, what to wear - and includes language, and its vocabulary and syntax, that only has meaning within this frame. Gee identifies all other Discourses in which individuals participate as secondary and acquired through acculturation and learning.

The closeness between the primary Discourse and a particular secondary Discourse influences the ease with which the secondary Discourse may be acquired. Thus an individual who has been brought up in a family that behaves sustainably is likely to have a primary Discourse that is closer to a secondary Discourse of sustainability than an individual who has not, and will have less difficulty adopting the values and beliefs of the Discourse.

Gee's (1996) theory of social group Discourse recognizes an individual's apprenticeship to a Discourse until they have been accepted into the institutions of the social group and achieved fluency in the Discourse. Apprenticeship, however, may persist where this does not occur. In later work Gee (2004) points out that an individual does not have to support everything in a Discourse in order to participate, rather they are involved in an 'affinity space' associated with the Discourse. Similarly, Knorr Cetina's (1999) work on the cultures of knowledge settings identified 'loose collections' of individuals working in each of the areas she investigated, high energy physics and molecular biology.

While membership of, or apprenticeship to, a Discourse suggests Discourses are fixed Gee (1996) explains how 'liberating literacy' brings about change to a Discourse. All individuals are members of a number of Discourses and some of the Discourses in which an individual participates may be conflicting, for example, a Discourse of deep ecology will be in conflict with a Discourse of triple bottom line economics. Where conflict occurs, critical examination of aspects of one Discourse in the light of the other, for example the independence of economic, social and biospheres in the light of the interdependence of systems, may bring about change to underpinning ideology and to social practices. A disposition to challenge aspects of a Discourse facilitates development of meta-knowledge of the Discourse and liberating literacy.

A similar argument is made by Anthony Giddens (1984) in his theory of structuration which recognizes the role of individuals in maintaining or changing social systems (essentially patterns of behaviour) through individuals' interpretation of the systems. It is notoriously difficult to change entrenched behaviours as individuals rationalise and maintain the social systems created by their interpretations. This Giddens calls 'practical consciousness'. To change the social systems individuals need to develop 'discursive consciousness' through critical self-reflection and through critical examination of the systems in discussion with each other.

The issue remains: how these processes can be facilitated through tertiary education, including higher education, vocational education and training, professional development and community education.

Effective Tertiary Education for Sustainability

I have argued that the aim of education for sustainability is the development of sustainability literacy, that literacy is acquired through the acquisition of fluency in social group Discourse which may lead to the development of liberating literacy, and that there are many sustainability literacies which differ according to the social group Discourse. These literacies include sustainability literacies relating to everyday societal practices, for example permaculture as discussed above, to academic disciplines, for example, economics or biology, and to vocational training and work. The Discourse of sustainability specialists in academia provides a sustainability literacy that reflects the interests of this emerging social group.

Sustainability literacies relate to secondary Discourses and acquisition of these Discourses occurs by acculturation and learning. Tertiary education may assist with acculturation by providing an appropriate environment and period of time for acculturation to occur, but is directly responsible through teaching for facilitation of the learning that takes place.

Ideally, teachers and students together create curriculum (understood in this discussion to be all the learning and teaching activities undertaken) through democratic processes (Beane, 1997; 2002). In education for sustainability, democratic curriculum development would be grounded in current student and teacher Discourses of sustainability as a starting point for discussion, critical examination and the development of liberating literacy.

Such curriculum development is entirely possible in community education and professional development where education is oriented directly to the needs of the learner. Everyday sustainability literacies relating, for example, to Discourses of recycling, energy efficiency or organic gardening, could be supported and developed through informal and non-formal community-based education. In New Zealand and elsewhere increasing government legislation is putting pressure on employers to act sustainably and to support the development of sustainability literacy amongst employees. While professional development needs to occur across the workforce, programmes are especially important for policy-makers who both advise politicians and administrators in respect of possible policies and provide detailed articulation of policies that have been determined. Politicians, with their responsibility to determine policies, are the most urgent group for development of sustainability literacy. Critical examination of the practices and values of current Discourses and the development of discursive consciousness provides the conditions for liberating literacy and change to these Discourses.

In higher education and vocational education and training, however, courses are highly constrained, in particular by qualification requirements. Curriculum decisions are usually made well in advance of any teacher-student engagement. The onus thus falls on administrators and teachers to engage in professional development for education for sustainability and to develop programmes and courses and construct curricula that make provision for the development of student sustainability literacy.

As discussed, the development of liberating literacy requires a disposition to challenge aspects of a Discourse and thereby develop meta-knowledge of the Discourse. This high quality learning outcome requires a deep approach to learning, where 'approach' is defined as both the learner's intention in respect of learning and their process of learning (Marton and Saljo, 1976; Marton and Booth, 1997). The work of Ference Marton and his co-workers underpins a field of research into learning and teaching in tertiary education which has been highly influential over thirty years and continues to be so. This research informs the current discussion. A deep approach, as opposed to a surface approach, entails the intention to understand ideas for oneself and to relate ideas to previous knowledge and experience, look for underlying principles, check evidence and examine logic and argument. Such an approach is consistent with the highest conceptions of learning, namely learning as 'seeing something in a different way' and learning as 'changing as a person' (Marton, Dall'Alba and Beaty, 1993).

Teaching that fosters a deep approach to learning adopts a student-focused strategy aimed at changing students' conceptions, rather than a traditional teacher-focused strategy for transmitting information (Prosser, Trigwell and Taylor, 1994). Students are more likely to adopt a deep approach when they perceive that they have good teaching, freedom of choice in curriculum decision-making and an absence of overloading with subject content (Entwistle, 1997). Ramsden (2003) identifies, in particular, teaching and assessment that fosters long-term engagement with the learning task and teaching which demonstrates the lecturer's personal commitment to the subject matter and stresses its meaning and relevance to students.

Emerging research is showing that the learning outcomes valued by teachers and learners in tertiary education are holistic and at odds with the often fragmented outcomes specified in tertiary curricula or professional standards. In a study of higher education in five different disciplines (biological science, economics, electrical engineering, media studies and music), Entwistle (2005) identified distinctive epistemological and academic cultures. He found the fundamental objective of teachers in the study was to inculcate their students into the 'ways of thinking and practicing' of the discipline. In complementary work, learners in vocational education (Hodkinson and James, 2003) and in the early development (apprenticeship phase) of their working lives (Rainbird, Fuller and Munro, 2004) were found to perceive learning as 'becoming', for example, a teacher, careworker or IT engineer. These studies suggest that learning is the development of self-identity, whether as disciplinary or vocational practitioner or professional.

The message for education for sustainability is clear, learning needs to be oriented to holistic outcomes, for example, sustainable horticulture (rather than individual horticultural skills that may contribute to sustainability). And teaching needs to support the individual's personal search for identity, in this example to becoming a sustainable horticulturalist. Education for sustainability through developing sustainability literacy as fluency in social group Discourse reflects this concern with holism.

Further, the institutional context in which learning takes place has been found to mediate the process of 'becoming'. Brennan and Osborne (2005) have shown the process is influenced by the diversity of student cultures developed in learning institutions, and the diversity of ways in which students with different social and educational backgrounds contribute to, and interact with, these cultures. They stress the complexity of interaction, across social and organizational variables. These cultures have great significance for student engagement in education for sustainability in a system which Brennan and Osborne point out associates status with different types of organizations and with different subject areas.

The following listing summarises key features of effective tertiary learning and teaching:

- a deep approach is related to high quality learning outcomes
- learning outcomes are academic, professional and personal
- holistic learning outcomes are valued by learners and teachers
- learners see learning as a process of 'becoming', e.g. a nurse
- holistic approaches recognise the learner as a whole person
- learning outcomes are related to learner personal biographies
- effective teaching is highly contextualized
- learning is related to learner interaction with student, professional or workplace cultures

Framing the 'Subject'

Literacy as fluency in social group Discourse provides a holistic framework for sustainability literacy and a goal for education for sustainability that is consistent with the holistic outcomes shown to inspire student learning. A Discourse embodies a social group's 'way of being in the world' - its communication via language, illustrations and icons, patterns of behaviours, knowledge, attitudes and values – dimensions which provide a theoretical frame for curriculum.

This perspective on literacy accounts for the development of multiple sustainability literacies through Discourses relevant to everyday sustainable social practice, specific industry-related sustainability practices and sustainability in further and higher education that may be discipline based or relevant cross-institutionally. It recognises the significance of an individual's primary Discourse in engaging with secondary Discourses, again consistent with the significance of personal biographies and dispositions in learning.

The 'subject' of education for sustainability includes both what is learned and how it is learned. In framing the subject in terms of sustainability literacy, acquiring fluency in social group Discourse or changing the Discourse through liberating literacy includes:

- acculturation and learning through examining values, beliefs and perspectives; and constructing understandings
- developing discursive consciousness through critical examination of routinised social practices
- challenging sustainability Discourses through membership of other Discourses
- the learner 'changing as a person'
- recognising many sustainability literacies, including everyday, work-related and disciplinary literacies

Conclusion

Sustainability literacy in terms of social group Discourse - a group's 'way of being in the world' - provides an holistic framework for curriculum development and a holistic outcome for learning that is valued by learners and teachers. This theoretical perspective recognizes the ideological nature of literacy and accommodates the variety of everyday, industry-related and disciplinary sustainability literacies.

The development of sustainability literacy within this perspective involves both acculturation and learning. This is likely to involve fundamental change to learners' perspectives and high levels of learning, including 'changing as a person'. Such learning requires a deep approach to learning and learner-centred teaching. Where education for sustainability is undertaken in formal tertiary education, prior development of teacher sustainability through professional development is a key component. Such professional development is ideally founded in participants' critical examination of existing Discourses, leading to change in the Discourse and liberating literacy, and is equally relevant across the workforce.

References

Beane, J. A. 2002 Beyond Self-Interest: A Democratic Core Curriculum. *Educational Leadership*, **59**, 25-28

Beane, J. A. 1997 *Curriculum integration: Designing the core of democratic education.* New York: Teachers' College Press

Brennan, J. and Osborne, M. 2005 *The organizational mediation of university student learning*. Working Paper 2. The Social and Organisational Mediation of University Student Learning (SOMUL) Project. Milton Keynes: The Open University

Capra, F. 1997 *The Web of Life: A New Synthesis of Mind and Matter*. London: Flamingo

Dale, A. and Newman, L. 2000 Sustainable development, education and literacy. *International Journal of Sustainability in Higher Education*, **6**, 351-362

Entwistle, N. J. 2005 Learning outcomes and ways of thinking across contrasting disciplines and settings in higher education. *The Curriculum Journal*, **16**, 67-82

Entwistle, N. J. 1997 'Contrasting perspectives on learning', in Marton, F., Hounsell, D.J. and Entwistle, N.J. (eds) *The Experience of Learning*. 2nd Ed. Edinburgh: Scottish Academic Press

Forum for the Future 2004 *Sustainability Literacy: Knowledge and Skills for the Future*. Report from Forum for the Future's consultation workshop [Internet].<http://www.forumforthefuture.org/>. [Accessed 8th May 2007].

Gee, J. P. 1996 *Social Linguistics and Literacies: Ideology in Discourse.* 2nd ed. London: Taylor and Francis

Gee, J. P. 2004 *Situated Language and Learning: A Critique of Traditional Schooling.* London: Routledge

Giddens, A. 1984. *The Constitution of Society: Outline of the Theory of Structuration.* Cambridge: Polity Press

Gross, A. G.1994 The roles of rhetoric in the public understanding of science. *Public Understanding of Science,* **3**, 3-23

Higher Education Academy Subject Centre for Geography, Earth and Environmental Sciences. 2005. Education for Sustainable Development for GEES students in UK Higher Education. [Internet]. <http://www.gees.ac.uk/>. [Accessed 19th September 2005].

Hodkinson, P. and James, D. 2003 Transforming learning cultures in Further Education. *Journal of Vocational Education and Training,* **55**, 389-406

Knorr-Cetina, K. 1999. *Epistemic Cultures: How the Sciences Make Knowledge.* Cambridge Massachusetts: Harvard University Press

Labinger, J. A. and Collins, H. (eds) 2001 *The One Culture? : A Conversation about Science.* Chicago: University of Chicago Press

Marton, F.M. and Booth, S. 1997 *Learning and Awareness.* Mahwah. New Jersey: Lawrence Erlbaum

Marton, F.M. and Saljo, R. 1976 On qualitative differences in learning. II – Outcome as a function of the learner's conception of the task. *British Journal of Educational Psychology,* **46**, 115-127

Marton, F., Dall' Alba, G. and Beaty, E. 1993 Conceptions of learning. *International Journal of Educational Research,* **19,** 277-300

Prosser, M., Trigwell, K. and Taylor, P. 1994 A phenomenographic study of academics' conceptions of science learning and teaching. *Learning and Instruction,* **4**, 217-231

Rainbird, H., Fuller, A. and Munro, A. (eds) 2004 *Workplace Learning in Context.* London: Routledge

Ramsden, P. 2003 *Learning to teach in higher education. 2nd Ed.* London: Routledge

Rockhill, K. 1993 'Gender, language and the politics of literacy', in B. V. Street (ed) *Cross-cultural Approaches to Literacy.* Cambridge: Cambridge University Press

Street, B.V. 1984 *Literacy in Theory and Practice.* Cambridge: Cambridge University Press

Street, B.V. 2004 *Understanding and Defining Literacy: Scoping Paper for EFA Global Monitoring Report 2006.* Paris: UNESCO

Communicating Sustainability in a Higher Education Environment

Alan Strong and Lesley Hemphill
University of Ulster

Abstract

International drivers such as the UN Decade of 'Education for Sustainable Development' and national sustainability strategies and programmes have transformed sustainable development thinking. It is, therefore, paramount that higher education graduates bring conceptual thinking and an awareness of the breadth and depth of sustainability to their future professional careers, and capture these changes. An appraisal of sustainability-related drivers and challenges, across international and national perspectives, has brought focus to the need for curriculum development and changes.

This challenge to integrate sustainable development (SD) into under-graduate teaching in order to provide a platform for further and informed experiential learning is addressed through an appraisal of pedagogical material. This has led to a fresh approach to 'communicating sustainability' across several built environment professions in a multi-discipline environment for university entrants, whilst providing both SD-driven mindsets and a basis for further in-depth studies. Evaluation of innovative teaching techniques and interactive learning environments has informed this study and acted as a catalyst for further creative inter-disciplinary activities and programmes.

The University of Ulster Sustainable Development Group (SDG) (see list of acronyms at end of paper) has pursued this transformation as it has diligently sought to design for, and initiate, curricula changes. SDG has benefited from being part of the Royal Academy of Engineering 'Engineering Design for Sustainable Development' network.

Keywords Sustainability, pedagogy, inter-disciplinary, built environment, communications, online testing

Transforming Sustainability

International perspective

In the latter half of the twentieth century, sustainable development (SD) has evolved as a reaction to environmental degradation which is associated with the depletion of non-renewable resources such as fossil fuels, minerals and aggregates, as well as erosion of the ozone layer, pollution and the warming of the Earth's atmosphere owing to the production of carbon dioxide (Ratcliffe and Stubbs, 1996). The evolution of the concept of SD has its origins in early environmentalist thinking, through to the notion of 'limits' and crisis thinking as identified by the publications of the Club of Rome in its 'Limits to Growth' report and the Ecologist's 'Blueprint for Survival' which shook the Western World out of its complacency over affluence and resource availability (O'Riordan, 1976). They focused attention on an environmental catastrophe in which humanity would be thrown out of the 'balance of nature' unless the character and direction of industrial civilisation were fundamentally altered (Torgerson, 1995).

The term sustainable development became fashionable during the 1980s in the World Conservation Strategy and the Brundtland Report (Moffatt, 1995) by stressing the need for the simultaneous achievement of development and environmental goals (Mitlin and Satterthwaite, 1996). This international importance and value of sustainability was firmly established by the United Nations General Assembly as it charged its World Commission on Environment and Development Chairman, Gro Harlem Brundtland, to develop 'Our Common Future', following on from earlier UN work on 'common crisis' and 'common security' (WCED, 1987), and producing the classical definition of Sustainable Development as being 'development that meets the needs of the present without compromising the ability of future generations to meet their own needs'. The Brundtland message was directed towards people whose well-being was the ultimate goal of all environmental and development policies: in particular, the Commission addressed the young, recognising that the world's teachers have a crucial role to play in bringing the final report to them, an equivalence for education.

The UN Conference on Environment and Development met in Rio de Janeiro in 1992, under the informal name of Earth Summit. A total of 108 governments, represented by Heads of State, adopted three major agreements aimed at changing the traditional approach to development:

(i)   Agenda 21 - an action plan for achieving SD in the 21st century, integrating the goals of environmental protection and economic development, and ensuring SD became a permanent principle of the UN

(ii)   The Rio Declaration on Environment and Development - a series of principles defining the rights and responsibilities of States

(iii)   The Statement of Forest Principles - a set of principles to underlie the sustainable management of forests worldwide

This document consisted of forty chapters setting out policy areas dealing with *social* and *economic* issues, and the conservation and management of resources to allow for future development (Ratcliffe and Stubbs, 1996). In addition, two legally binding Conventions aimed at preventing global climate change and the eradication of the diversity of biological species were opened for signature at the Summit, according a high profile to two initiatives: The United Nations Framework Convention on Climate Change; and The Convention on Biological Diversity (UNCED, 1992).

The Johannesburg Earth Summit 2 in 2002 re-affirmed the commitment to the Rio principles, the full implementation of Agenda 21 and the Programme for the Further Implementation of Agenda 21. It also committed to achieving the internationally agreed development goals, including those contained in the United Nations Millennium Declaration and in the outcomes of the major United Nations conferences and international agreements since 1992. The plan of implementation would build on the achievements made since Earth Summit 1 and expedite the realisation of the remaining goals. Hence Earth Summit 2 sought to enhance international cooperation. These efforts promoted the integration of the three components of sustainable development - economic, social and environmental protection - as interdependent and mutually reinforcing pillars. Poverty eradication, changing unsustainable patterns of production and consumption, and protecting and managing the natural resource base of economic and social development became overarching objectives of, and essential requirements for, sustainable development (UN, 2002).

Earth Summit 2 emphasised that education was critical for promoting SD. It requires the mobilisation of necessary resources and highlights the need to integrate SD into education systems, at all levels, to promote education as a key agent for change including development, and the implementation, monitoring and review of education action plans (UN, 2002). It also sought to meet the specific Millennium Development Goal of 'achieving universal primary education, ensuring that, by 2015, children everywhere, boys and girls alike, will be able to complete a full course of primary schooling' (UN MDG, 2000).

National perspective

In 1999, the United Kingdom set out a strategy to deliver a better 'quality of life' through sustainable development. Six years later, it reviewed that strategy to take account of changes within the UK, such as devolution of governmental powers to Scotland, Wales and Northern Ireland, and to regional bodies and local government, and of international issues arising from the World Summit on Sustainable Development (UN, 2002). This resulted in the UK Government *Securing the Future Sustainable Development Strategy* 2005 which had a new purpose and principles for SD, and newly-shared priorities agreed across the UK. The strategy contained:

(i)   a new integrated vision building on the 1999 strategy, and stronger international dimensions
(ii)   five principles - with a more explicit focus on environmental limits
(iii)   four agreed priorities - sustainable consumption and production, climate change and natural resources
(iv)   protection and sustainable communities
(v)   a new and more outcome-focused set of indicators with commitments to look at new indicators such as well-being (DEFRA, 2005)

In contrast, the Northern Ireland Sustainable Development Strategy included two additional 'agreed priorities': firstly, Learning and Communication for Sustainable Development; and, secondly, Governance and Sustainable Development. As the most recently devolved government to establish a SD strategy, it attempted to focus sharply on communications, education and departmental ownership as more central roles (DOE, 2006).

Educational Changes

International perspective

The United Nations continued its contribution to the SD journey and its transformation, designating 2005 - 2014 as the Decade of Education for Sustainable Development (DESD) and appointing the United Nations Educational, Scientific and Cultural Organization (UNESCO) as the lead agency for its promotion. The basic vision of the DESD is a world where everyone has the opportunity to benefit from quality *education* and learn the values, behaviour and lifestyles required for a sustainable future, and for positive societal transformation. This translates into four objectives:

(i)   facilitating networking, linkages, exchange and interaction among stakeholders in ESD

(ii)   fostering an increased quality of teaching and learning in education for sustainable development

(iii)   helping countries make progress towards and attain Millennium Development Goals through ESD efforts

(iv)   providing countries with new opportunities to incorporate ESD into education reform efforts (DESD, 2005)

National perspective

The Higher Education Funding Council for England grasped this nettle in its *Sustainable Development in Higher Education* report which agreed on the potential contribution by the HE sector to SD in the:

- role as educators
- generation and transfer of knowledge
- leadership of, and influence on, local, national and international networks
- business strategy and operations (HEFCE, 2005)

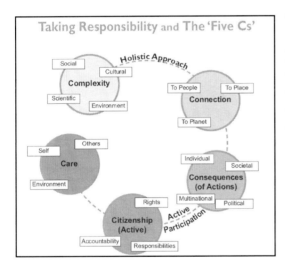

The commitment by the UK Government to SD in Education is also demonstrated by its Schools Action Plan. 'SD will not just be a subject in the classroom: it will be in its bricks and mortar and the way the school uses and even generates its own power. Our students won't just be told about SD, they will see and work within it: a living, learning, place in which to explore what a sustainable lifestyle means' stated the UK Prime Minister in promoting this UK Schools Sustainable Development Action Plan 2005/06 (DfES, 2005). Education can provide the integrating glue in promoting and demonstrating sustainable living, through a continuum of building on a strong foundation of environmental sustainability which supports teaching on the complexity of holistic systems, leading to behavioural change and thereby facilitating informed choices and concern for quality of life for those in both a local and global context.

Figure 1   Sustainable living by responsibility

A sense of responsibility and active participation can lead to lasting sustainable living, as shown in Figure 1 (ESD NI, 2005).

Behavioural change perspective

Individual behaviours are deeply embedded in social and institutional contexts, as we are guided as much by what others around us say and do and by the 'rules of the game' as we are by personal choice.

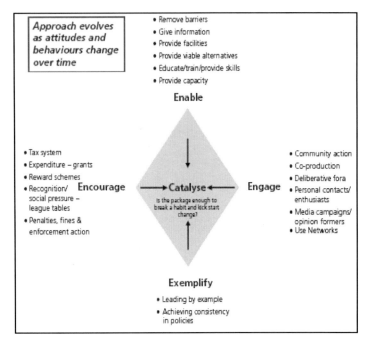

It is evident that the aspiration to deliver sustainability has been translated into a link to the education and training of society at all levels, with education and communications playing key roles. Everyday experiences play an important role in society's informal learning from media advertising to specific programmes on television, radio, magazine or news articles. This complex mixture of personal, psychological, social and governmental decisions provides an environment in which SD behaviour can be realised (DEFRA, 2005). Experience can be drawn from the 'motivating, sustainable consumption' aspect of sustainability as it addresses consumer behavioural change. It draws on the evidence base for different models of change (Fig. 2).

Figure 2   Behavioural change paradigm

A concerted strategy is needed to make it easier to behave more sustainably by: ensuring that incentive structures and institutional rules exist to *encourage* sustainable behaviour; *enabling* access to pro-environmental choice; *engaging* people in initiatives to help themselves; and *exemplifying* the desired changes within Government's own policies and practices (Jackson, 2005).

Industrial perspective

This paper is written in the context of the built environment as it represents the product of urban planning and architectural processes, and of various construction activities that take place in a defined spatial organisation. These processes aim to meet the needs of communities, industries and governments, and require a knowledge and understanding of scientific and engineering principles. Buildings dominate the built environment and are supported by an infrastructure and utilities framework. The adequacy of the built environment can be judged by its suitability in meeting people's basic needs such as shelter, food and employment. However, as nations develop, the provision is more readily assessed against a higher regime of criteria such as comfort, access, wealth and communications. In this regard the built environment impinges upon the natural environment to meet these needs of society, and is therefore at the boundary between environmental effects and human requirements (Strong and Hemphill, 2006). In terms of scale and impact, it is assessed that the UK Construction Industry has an annual expenditure of at least £80 billion and employs over 2.7 million professionals and tradesmen, whilst it is anticipated that these indicative figures will grow by 2.5% annually in the next 5 years due to London 2012 Olympic Games developments (CIC, 2007).

Built environment disciplines

The traditional professions of civil engineering, architecture, construction/building and quantity surveying remain central to the delivery of phases in built environment design and construction, and have been well served by a comprehensive supply of educational programmes at technician, undergraduate and post-graduate levels. The further development of built environment disciplines, as shown in Figure 3, reflects the need for skills in other equally important themes, whilst representing the breadth of the built environment processes across strategic and land planning, holistic and detailed design, procurement and construction, and facilities operation, maintenance and replacement.

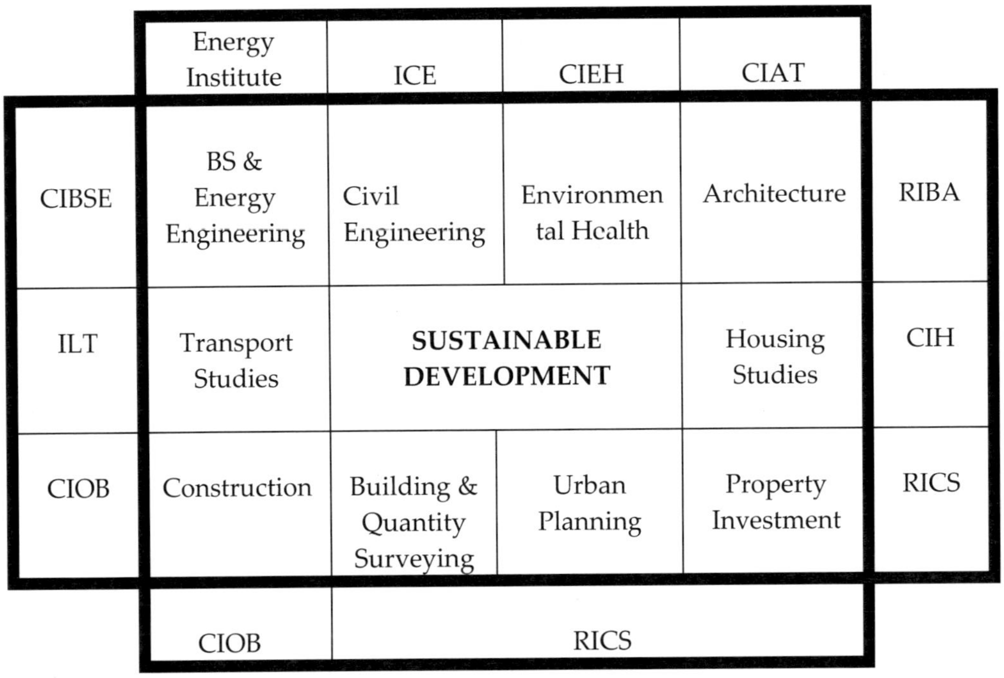

	Energy Institute	ICE	CIEH	CIAT	
CIBSE	BS & Energy Engineering	Civil Engineering	Environmental Health	Architecture	RIBA
ILT	Transport Studies	**SUSTAINABLE DEVELOPMENT**		Housing Studies	CIH
CIOB	Construction	Building & Quantity Surveying	Urban Planning	Property Investment	RICS
	CIOB	RICS			

Figure 3   Built environment disciplines and professional bodies

Figure 3 shows the wide-ranging built environment under- and post-graduate education provision at the University of Ulster, allowing opportunity for creative and inter-disciplinary learning and teaching as well as unified research and development (UU, 2007).

The vocational and professional nature of built environment professions demands regulation for both academic standards and the provision of under-pinning education towards professional status such as chartered engineer, builder, surveyor, architect, planner, environmentalist or environmental health officer. These professional bodies identified in Figure 3 play traditional roles, primarily as member organisations, in accrediting or approving educational programmes and representing the body in advocacy and learned society functions. They also have 'royal charter' responsibility functions in statutory roles for health and safety and ethics. Leadership and responsibility for SD falls within this latter category. The Institution of Civil Engineers, as one of the oldest professions, in conjunction with other leading construction bodies, has developed significant corporate SD strategies (ICE, 2007). This new professional response to the sustainability agenda is reflected mainly in the objectives and education accreditation requirements of the professional bodies, with some progressing to more deeply-embedded sustainability through operations and implementation. This accreditation focus has both driven and challenged higher education to include sustainability in academic courses (Strong and Tierney, 2007).

Graduates from the built environment courses have immense opportunity to develop fulfilling careers, to gain long-term employment, obtain rewarding salaries and be agents for change in SD and ethics, at home and abroad, and in the public and private sectors. These employability and influencer roles have been cited as key marketing tools to attract undergraduates, whilst the deeper role of professional leaders has been studied, confirmed and recorded by the Royal Academy of Engineering (Royal Academy, 2006).

Sustainable Development in the Built Environment Curricula

Drivers for change at University of Ulster (UU)

The University of Ulster School of the Built Environment set out to address the challenge of integrating sustainable development into its curricula. However, it encountered the traditional 'single discipline' approach in which each course, and its advising professional body, operated in isolation from allied disciplines. The formation of the UU Sustainable Development Group (SDG) in 2001, supported by funding from the Royal Academy of Engineering in its 'Engineering Design for Sustainable Development' programme, sought to address this deficiency and separation across teaching and learning activities, mindful of the key DESD driver which provided a reference network for UU activity. Subsequently, The Royal Academy of Engineering developed 12 Guiding Principles to support the UK-wide network, embracing creativity and innovation in providing balanced solutions across economic, social and environmental sectors (Royal Academy, 2005). In tandem, the Funding and Research Councils raised the teaching and research imperative to deliver material on SD (EPSRC, 2006). This quest for SD transformation focused on embedding SD principles and practice into engineering courses primarily through pedagogy and case studies.

UU SDG Strategy for SD Integration

The UU SDG commenced its task of SD integration from a low base. It initiated its work by conducting a *module audit* to determine explicit and implicit references to SD in all built environment module objectives. Whilst a new Environmental Engineering course rated satisfactory with 45% of modules including SD, more traditional Quantity Surveying and Civil Engineering courses, accredited by RICS and ICE, respectively, scored under 5%. From this audit, which confirmed a weak position, was produced a *Position Paper* on SD integration and application within a new ROAMEF framework that applied to all SD proposals:

- Rationale – the purpose(s) that the teaching or case study is intended to fulfil
- Objectives – the project objectives that will ensure delivery of the pedagogy material
- Appraisal – the justification that the project will meet the purpose(s) described in the Rationale
- Monitoring – the arrangements for ensuring that the project proceeds to the plan
- Evaluation – the arrangements for *ex-post* examination of the utility in meeting its purpose(s)
- Feedback - the application to subsequent projects of lessons learned in the execution

The appointment of a Sustainability Visiting Panel (SVP), drawn from external experts representing the economic, environmental and social pillars of SD, gave further momentum to this difficult challenge. The twice-yearly SVP meetings allowed the SDG work to be tested and brought vital advice and support. This provided momentum and clarity to the development of a continuum approach to the SD integration.

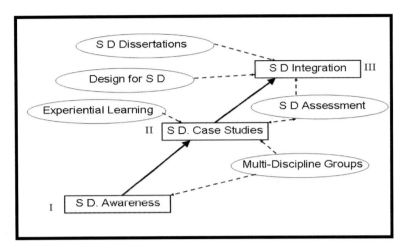

Figure 4 The UU continuum for sustainability in curricula

Evaluation and interaction with the Royal Academy Network led to a deeper appreciation that the holistic and cross-disciplinary nature of SD curricula required a range of understanding and skills. It confirmed that SD embraced academic depth of certain themes such as structural engineering analysis and an integrating breadth of information so as to ensure balanced thinking and sustainable solutions. This broad approach also extended to decision making, risk taking, design selection, materials choices and many more issues as each sustainability-driven consideration sought sufficient response and balance to the competing demands of environmental, social, economic and resource management zones.   A continuum for sustainability education designed to provide a foundation of SD *Awareness* [Phase I] and support more detailed studies in lectures was informed by *Case Studies* [Phase II] to facilitate and underpin a range of SD *Integrative Projects* [Phase III], design teamwork and individual studies (Fig. 4).

This continuum facilitated an appreciation of how SD can influence the built environment processes of concept, design, construction and maintenance as related to typical themes such as planning, biodiversity, design, facilities management, construction, environment, social impact, waste management, water resources, transport systems and urban development.

Education pedagogy

Whilst this paper is not primarily concerned with teaching and learning systems, nor about the plethora of pedagogy outputs which are currently being developed in higher education, it is important that the integration of SD into the built environment curricula employs relevant and effective methods to cover teaching, learning, assessment and evaluation. The accreditation of higher education teaching has clearly become more professional, and a new raft of higher education academies have supported this drive (Fry *et al*. 1999; HEA, 2003). Table 1 identifies a range of issues which arise in the effective delivery of teaching and assessment systems.

Table 1   Issues in delivering teaching, learning and assessment

Practice Development	Student Learning	Outcomes-based Planning	Principles of Assessment
• Learning from Lectures	• Student Motivation	• Interactive Learning Environments	• IT for Teaching & Learning
• Employability	• Student Supervision	• Experiential Learning	• Reflective Practice
• Quality & Standards	• Student Guidance	• C P D	• Small Group Activity

Communicating Sustainability Module

The platform for the UU approach is the SD awareness phase of the continuum delivered to a range of built environment disciplines through a 'Communicating Sustainability' (Year 1) undergraduate module, as shown in Fig. 3.

Communicating sustainability module

The objective to provide a Year 1 experience in SD for a range of built environment disciplines in a higher education academic school was driven by the following sustainability-motivated matters:

- existence of vocational courses meeting professional body accreditation requirements
- requirement for simultaneous multi-discipline delivery to several professional groups
- growing sustainability awareness experience to underpin future studies
- responsiveness to international and national trends in sustainability
- challenge and ignite students' social conscience
- mobilisation of motivated staff
- design of rigorous assessment for sustainability information

The initial module design was set at Level B (Year 1) with a CAT weighting of 10 credit points. It was developed as a 'forced marriage' between standard teaching in Information Technology (IT) and SD [Model A]. It later evolved into a partnership with SD material taking a leading role [Model B]. Further developments caused the IT material to be reduced, primarily as students already had basic IT skills, and allowed the structuring of a 20 credit point module in which SD was integrated with new teaching on Geographical Information Systems (GIS) [Model C]. Fig. 5 shows this evolution.

Module profile

Model B demonstrates the structure, content, learning outcomes and assessment of the Communicating Sustainability module. Its objectives cover knowledge of SD contexts, student appreciation and rudimentary measurement of SD in the built environment, basic knowledge of proprietary software applications and ability to demonstrate adequate oral and written skills. The module delivered and blended wider SD international contexts, local initiatives and measurement with communication and IT skills through an educational focus on key sustainability themes of water, transport, energy, construction, planning, regeneration, sustainable communities and social issues.

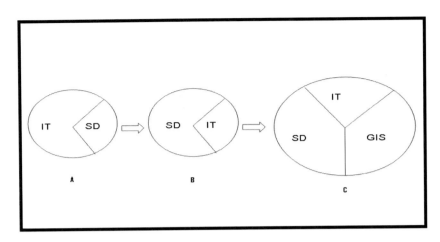

Figure 5   Evolution of sustainability awareness module structure

Although learning outcomes could be tracked across the headers of Knowledge and Understanding, Intellectual Qualities, Professional/Practical Skills and Transferable Skills, the 'mode of delivery' was identified as critical to students' acceptance and engagement.   A series of short challenging and stimulating SD interactive lectures by motivated staff and visitors included primary SD themes, and an emphasis was placed upon student-centred learning, supported by seminars and practical workshop sessions in the computer laboratory.   The UU interactive learning environment ensured that material was accessible from a WebCT portal and this was reinforced by access to reading resources via the highly acclaimed UU Learning Resource Virtual Built Environment Library (VIBEL, 2007), and display material on external SD events and information through WebCT announcements.

Module assessment has sustainable development as its core. It covers generic Personal Development Planning, Excel spreadsheet tests, Oral and PowerPoint presentation and a written SD-topic report. Innovation in assessment practice includes a purpose-built online test in a closed-book environment in which students are presented with a series of questions in multiple choice, true/false and 'matching statement' formats, drawn in random from a bank of 120 questions.

Module review

This module, delivered to eight built environment disciplines, is subject to annual scrutiny by Student Staff Consultative Committees (SSC), Course Examination Boards (CEB), Student Module Evaluations (SME) and Annual Subject Monitoring (ASM), in addition to periodic Professional Body (PB) accreditation and University Subject Review (USR) procedures.   Furthermore, the Sustainable Development Group (SDG) subjected the sustainability awareness concept and material to assessment and review through:

(i)   documented Student Feedback (SF) on both the SD awareness lecture series and SD online testing
(ii)   availability to the Royal Academy of Engineering (RAEng) 'Engineering Design for Sustainable Development' Annual Workshops
(iii)   the Annual Meeting of the UU Sustainability Visiting Panel (SVP)

Feedback set out in Table 2 has supported module development.

Table 2   Feedback and actions

Source	Comment	Module Team Response
CEB	Module Marks – high average	SD Assignment element more rigorous
SME	Inter-disciplinary sessions appreciated	SDG reinforce SD links in subsequent years
SSC	SD Lectures – complex material	Lectures accessible on WebCT portal
SF	Online test – not difficult	Test changed from open-book to closed-book
ASM	Generic nature recognised	Module promoted to further courses
USR	SD module fulfilled several LO's	Staff Training in module concept and material
RAEng	Online SD Test welcomed	Exchange with Sheffield University for SPeAR
SVP	Online questions piloted	Test modified & corrected
SVP	Desire to assist with delivery	Visiting lectures received voluntarily
SF	Lectures style and quality not consistent	Lecture team reviewed and enhanced

Conclusions

This paper has presented a structured approach to the challenge of communicating sustainability in a higher education environment. The compelling drivers in international and national jurisdictions are set at both generic governmental level and in the context of education, highlighted by the UN Decade of Education for Sustainable Development 2005 - 2014, to provide a vital backdrop to the transformation of sustainability education. Within the wide range of activities associated with the provision of the built environment, several professional bodies play key roles in protecting the well-being of members and society, across issues including ethics and education, whilst bringing sharper focus to, and appreciation of, the sustainability agenda. They are enthusiastic in addressing SD at strategic and operational levels, within their governance and at accreditation phases in higher education programmes. This has supported the imperative to introduce SD at an early stage in undergraduate degree courses, to establish a foundation for further studies and ensure that SD is seen as a holistic and integrative study area.

The UU vision for, and journey towards, the evolution and development of sustainability education in eight built environment disciplines has been conceptualised as a continuum with a customised 'Communicating Sustainability' module delivered to Year 1 students. Key conclusions derived from a five year delivery period indicate that:

- SD awareness has a prolific international context and cuts across government and society
- stimulating introductory lectures are important to gain early multi-disciplinary engagement
- access to a comprehensive range of quality support material gives wide opportunity for reading
- use of e-learning and online SD testing is both a student learning experience and a motivation to understand SD
- SD material sits adequately alongside the teaching of Geographical Information Systems
- student teamwork is enhanced through SD multi-disciplinary teaching groups and mini case studies
- a balance between academic staff engagement and external expertise ensures SD currency
- sustainability awareness must be used as a pointer to deeper SD studies across several topics
- change in student behaviour and conscience can be an indirect outcome
- professional bodies can contribute to, and learn from, this innovative academic model

Furthermore, the Sustainability Awareness module provides a sound basis for informing further developments and a deeper understanding of the *place* and *purpose* of SD in curricula and the *practice* of corporate and individual professional life. This evaluation has led to:

- development of an array of mini and major case studies for multi-discipline application
- application of the ROAMEF framework to all aspects of the SD teaching and research activity
- multi-discipline activities such as an 'Emotive Evening' event in which four built environment final year student cohorts address contemporary issues such as 'making poverty history', 'social inclusion' and 'climate change' in an integrating manner and social venue
- increased industrial liaison, through research and consultancy, with social enterprise organisations
- greater collaboration with SD Research communities and as a catalyst for change with single theme research studies
- concerted efforts to link and integrate design with SD thinking, holistic and balanced solutions and SD evaluation frameworks
- interaction with, and contributions to, Higher Education Academy programmes *vis-à-vis* Geography Earth and Environmental Sciences (GEES), Centre for Education in the Built Environment (CEBE), Council for Higher Education in Art & Design (CHEAD), Centre for Sustainable Communities Achieved through Integrated Professional Education (C-SCAIPE), and the Engineering Subject Centre at Loughborough

It is anticipated that the journey towards fulfilling and transforming sustainability education can be translated into other (less technical) higher education themes and discipline groups as the concepts, methodology and application of SD have resonance with human, social, natural, manufactured and financial capitals.

Acronyms

ICE: Institution of Civil Engineers

CIAT: Chartered Institute of Architectural Technologists

CIEH: Chartered Institute of Environmental Health

CIH: Chartered Institute of Housing

CIOB: Chartered Institute of Building

ILT: The Chartered Institute of Logistics & Transport

RIBA: Royal Institute of British Architects

RICS: Royal Institution of Chartered Surveyors

SD: Sustainable Development

SDG: Sustainable Development Group

SVP: Sustainability Visiting Panel

UU: University of Ulster

References

CIC 2007 *Labour Market Intelligence Report 2006-07*. London: Construction Industry Council

DEFRA 2005 *The UK Government Sustainable Development Strategy. Securing the Future*. London: Department for Environment Food and Rural Affairs

DESD 2005 *UN Decade of Education for Sustainable Development*. New York: UN

DfES 2005 *Learning for the Future - the Department for Education and Skills (DfES) Sustainable Development Action plan 2005/06*. London: DfES

DOE 2006 *First Steps toward Sustainability - A Sustainable Development Strategy for Northern Ireland 2006*. Northern Ireland: Department of the Environment

EPSRC 2006 *Sustainable Urban Environment Cluster*. [Internet].
<http://www.epsrc.ac.uk/ResearchFunding/Programmes/InfrastructureAndEnvironment/Initiatives/SUE/default.htm>.
[Accessed 2nd August 2007].

ESD NI 2005 *Education for sustainable Development - Good Practice Guide for Primary, Secondary and Special Schools*. Interboard ESD
Group – Northern Ireland. [Internet].
<http://www.welbcass.org/site/cass/mfc/downloads/ESD%202005%2001%20Dec%2005.pdf>. [Accessed 2nd August 2007].

Fry, H., Ketteridge, S. and Marshall, S. 1999   *A Handbook for Teaching and Learning in Higher Education*. London: Kogan Page

HEFCE 2005 *Sustainable Development in Higher Education. Statement of Policy 2005/08*. [Internet].
<http://www.hefce.ac.uk/pubs/hefce/2005/05_28/>. [Accessed 2nd August 2007].

ICE 2007 *Sustainable Development Strategy and Action plan for Civil Engineering July 2007 Statement from ICE, ACE, CECA, CIRIA
and Construction Products Association*. London: ICE

Jackson T. 2005 *Motivating Sustainable Consumption- a review of evidence on consumer behaviour and behavioural change*. Report to the
Sustainable Development Research Network. London: SDRN

Mitlin, D. and Satterthwaite, D. 1996 'Sustainable development and cities', in Pugh, C. (ed) *Sustainability, the Environment and
Urbanization*. London: Earthscan

Moffatt, I. 1995 *Sustainable Development: Principles, Analysis and Policies*. Lancashire: Parthenon Publishing Group

O'Riordan, T. 1976 *Environmentalism*. London: Pion

Ratcliffe, J. and Stubbs, M. 1996 *Urban Planning and Real Estate Development*. London: UCL Press

Royal Academy of Engineering 2000 *Educating Engineers for the 21st Century*. London: The Royal Academy of Engineering

Royal Academy of Engineering 2005 *Engineering for Sustainable Development: Guiding Principles*. London: The Royal Academy of
Engineering

Strong W.A. and Hemphill L.A. 2006 *Sustainable Development Policy Directory*. Oxford: Blackwell Publishers

Strong W.A and Tierney C.A. 2007 Review of Sustainability profile of Built Environment Professional Bodies. Unpublished
report. University of Ulster

Torgerson, D. 1995 'Policy analysis and public life: The restoration of "phronesis"', in Farr, J., Dryzek, J. and Leonard, S. (eds)
Political science in history: Research programs and political traditions. Cambridge: Cambridge University Press

UN 2002 *World Summit on Sustainable Development. Plan of Implementation*. [Internet]. <http://www.un-
documents.net/jburgpln.htm >. [Accessed 12th August 2007].

UN MDG 2000 *UN Millennium Development Goals*. New York: United Nations Department of Public Information

UNCED 1992 *Report of the United Nations Conference on the Environment & Development – Annex 1: The Rio Declaration, June 1992*.
Rio de Janeiro: United Nations

UU 2007 *Built Environment Courses at University of Ulster*. [Internet]. <http://www.engj.ulst.ac.uk/be/teaching.php>. [Accessed
4th July 2007].

WCED 1997 *World Commission on Environment and Development. Our Common Future*. Oxford: Oxford University Press

C-SCAIPE and the Decade: From Local to Global

Manuel Gomes
Lisbon University
Amanda Lewis
Kingston University

Abstract

This paper represents the outcome from an informal research secondment to C-SCAIPE (The Centre for Sustainable Communities Achieved through Integrated Professional Education) at Kingston University within the framework of the United Nations Decade of Education for Sustainable Development (UNDESD). Collaboration between C-SCAIPE at Kingston University's School of Surveying and the Centre of Geographic Studies at Lisbon University supported Manuel Gomes' PhD Project *Education for Sustainable Development within formal curriculum in the context of UNDESD*. This compared the aims and activities of C-SCAIPE with those of the UNDESD and forms the basis of this report.

The presentation highlights the importance of 'focus' within the delivery of Education for Sustainable Development (ESD) as a means of engaging with the UNDESD. It examines how C-SCAIPE which has a very specific focus contributes to ESD, and emphasises the importance of partnerships flowing from the Strategy for Education for Sustainable Development (SESD), and the need to maintain the links formed between ESD stakeholders and projects.

Keywords   C-SCAIPE, Education for Sustainable Development (ESD), educational partnerships, sustainability, UNDESD

Introduction

The paper is supported by the outcomes of an informal secondment which took place on the C-SCAIPE premises within the framework of the UNDESD, 2005-14. The relationship involving C-SCAIPE in Kingston University's School of Surveying and the Centre of Geographic Studies, University of Lisbon in the form of Manuel Gomes' PhD Project *Education for Sustainable Development within formal curriculum in the context of UNDESD* was initially an informal arrangement. It resulted in a substantial report comparing the aims and activities of C-SCAIPE with those of the UNDESD. Overall, the paper highlights four themes:

(i)   The importance of Education for Sustainable Development (ESD) within the UNDESD
(ii)   How C-SCAIPE contributes to the UNDESD
(iii)   The importance of educational partnerships
(iv)   The need to maintain links formed between stakeholders and projects

A brief examination of C-SCAIPE's overarching objectives, the goals of UNDESD and aims of SESD demonstrate synchronicity and adequate evidence of C-SCAIPE's contribution to the Decade and the UNECE (United Nations Economic Commission for Europe) Strategy, and its role as an important partner in the promotion of ESD. In addition, C-SCAIPE not only contributes to educational practice and embeds sustainability within the curriculum and its value sets for Sustainable Development, but also enhances curriculum strategies for the implementation of the teaching and learning process.

One significant aspect in implementing the Decade's objectives is that C-SCAIPE crosses the border between policy levels (UNDESD, SESD, SDAPES) and local action close to communities (from global to local). In this manner C-SCAIPE contributes towards sustainable communities improving sustainability indicators for places, spaces and objects to combine meaning and beauty with utility. Settlements are 'human' in scale and form. Diversity and local distinctiveness are valued and protected. C-SCAIPE recognises that cultural diversity is a rich asset for individuals and societies. The protection, promotion and maintenance of cultural diversity are essential requirements for sustainable development for the benefit of present and future generations.

In support of each C-SCAIPE objective, this paper presents a case study to establish how important staff feel its contribution is to the ESD. Another exercise is based on a proposal of Quality Criteria for ESD-Schools from the European Network for School Development through Environmental Education (SEED).

The outcomes of these two exercises show that C-SCAIPE and its associated staff believe that it is very important for C-SCAIPE to contribute to ESD and generally approved the majority of the quality criteria for recognising how one School, at university level, contributes to ESD. In the end it can be confirmed that the School of Surveying is rapidly moving towards becoming an ESD-School.

From Global to Local: the importance of ESD within the UNESD

In December 2002, under resolution 57/254, the United Nations General Assembly proclaimed the United Nations Decade of Education for Sustainable Development (UNDESD). This was recommended by the Johannesburg Summit to cover the period 2005-2014. In December 2003 Resolution 58/219 reinforced the importance of Education for Sustainable Development (ESD) and the need to promote public awareness and wider participation in the UNDESD.

UNESCO has been tasked to lead UNDESD and develop a participative International Implementation Scheme (IIS). This scheme is not prescriptive but does provide a useful tool and overall guidance for all partners, as to how, when, why, and where they can contribute to UNDESD. The IIS addresses five objectives for the Decade (Table 1):

Table 1 Five objectives for the decade

(i)	To give an enhanced profile to the central role of education and learning in the common pursuit of sustainable development
(ii)	To facilitate links, networking, exchange and interaction among stakeholders in ESD
(iii)	To provide a space and opportunity for refining and promoting the vision of, and transition to, sustainable development – through all forms of learning and public awareness
(iv)	To foster increased quality of teaching and learning in ESD
(v)	To develop strategies at every level to strengthen capacity in ESD

The IIS also proposed seven inter-linked strategies to increase the promotion and implementation of ESD (Table 2):

Table 2   Seven strategies for the decade

(i)	Advocacy and vision-building
(ii)	Consultation and ownership
(iii)	Partnership and networks
(iv)	Capacity-building and training
(v)	Research and innovation
(vi)	Information and communication technologies
(vii)	Monitoring and evaluation

Meanwhile, in Vilnius, on the 17th and 18th March 2005 the Economic Commission for Europe (ECE) adopted the United Nations ECE (UNECE) Strategy for Education for Sustainable Development (SESD). This strategy identifies Sustainable Development features of UNECE regions, including economic vitality, justice, social cohesion, environmental protection and sustainable management of natural resources. In the context of UNDESD, both the UNECE strategy and the IIS should facilitate the introduction and promotion of ESD. This strategy proposed six objectives (Table 3).

Table 3   Six objectives of the UNECE SESD

(i)	Ensure that policy, regulatory and operational frameworks support ESD
(ii)	Promote SD through formal, non-formal and informal learning
(iii)	Equip educators with the competence to include SD in their teaching
(iv)	Ensure that adequate tools and materials for ESD are accessible
(v)	Promote research on and development of ESD
(vi)	Strengthen cooperation on ESD at all levels within the UNECE region

From Table 3 it can be appreciated that the SESD has a long way to go in delivering the objectives of DESD across Europe. However, at a national level, ESD in the United Kingdom has progressed.

- The Sustainable Development Commission (2004) recommends that sustainability be embedded in higher and further education, and that appropriate interdisciplinary studies and research are promoted (Sustainable Development Commission, 2004)
- The Sustainable Development Action Plan for Education and Skills (SDAPES) England, launched by the Government in September 2003, recognises the need for change. The action plan reviews how we teach and learn about sustainable development throughout our lives; how we generate skills, knowledge, and understanding to fulfil our duty as global citizens; and how we manage our operations to support future generations

SDAPES encourages wider participation in sustainable development in education and skills in both formal and informal education through four key objectives (Table 4).

Table 4   Four Objectives of SDAPES

(i)	*Education for Sustainable Development* – to inspire and stimulate knowledge and awareness of sustainable development among children, young people and adults
(ii)	*Environmental Impact of the Department for Education and Skills and its partner bodies* – working closely with key partners across the education sector to identify current levels of sustainable development activity, and identifying what more needs to be done
(iii)	*Environmental Impact of the Education Estate* - how schools, colleges and universities learn about, and manage, their operations to support the environment, society, and economic growth
(iv)	*Local Partnership Activity* – how schools, colleges and universities engage children, young people and adults in sustainable development, in their local communities

Through the National Curriculum, the Department for Education and Skills (DfES) intends to build capacity within subjects such as citizenship, geography and science. These are already used to explore different aspects of sustainable development in various contexts and thus enhance the opportunities for pupils to think innovatively and prepare them to grow into responsible decision-makers and informed problem solvers.

Further Education (FE) and Higher Education (HE) institutions are developing into sustainable organisations, promoting themselves as beacons and sharing examples of best practice with institutions.

From National to Local: the C-SCAIPE CETL

In 2004 Universities in England had the opportunity to bid for the status of Centre for Excellence in Teaching and Learning (CETL) through a scheme designed to promote pedagogic activities funded by the Higher Education Funding Council for England (HEFCE) for an initial period of five years. Kingston University's School of Surveying seized this opportunity and created C-SCAIPE - Centre for Sustainable Communities Achieved through Integrated Professional Education - one of 74 CETL initiatives across the country.

Kingston University is situated in Kingston upon Thames, Surrey, in south-west London. It was founded in 1899 as Kingston Technical Institute offering courses ranging from Chemistry, Electrical Wiring and Building Construction to Nursing, Dressmaking and Clay Modelling. It became a university in 1992. Currently, it has structured in seven Faculties and C-SCAIPE sits within the School of Surveying (KUSS) in the Faculty of Art, Design and Architecture (FADA).

C-SCAIPE was inaugurated in September 2005 in recognition of the School's history of delivering high quality education for aspiring professionals and track record of innovative research into sustainability issues in the property sector. It moved into its new premises in August 2006 and was formally launched in October 2006. C-SCAIPE's overarching aim is to: 'promote a deeper understanding of the requirements of professional education in order to produce graduates capable of working to create more sustainable communities'. An holistic view of sustainable principles will be embedded within curricula and teaching delivery initially within the built environment based on live projects embracing a multi-disciplinary, inter-professional perspective. To achieve this aim, eight objectives were set to satisfy and action the remits of HEFCE and C-SCAIPE (Table 5).

Table 5   Eight objectives of C-SCAIPE

(i)	To reward existing staff excellence, enthuse and motivate colleagues, and to also achieve excellence, thereby enriching their own career opportunities and fulfilment, and the experience of those they teach
(ii)	To ensure that curriculum and assessment design incorporate sustainability issues as they relate to each subject area, thus enhancing KU graduates' understanding of sustainability from perspectives beyond their own discipline
(iii)	To enhance and increase the existing project-based learning and assessment experience for students and thereby build on what has proved to be a successful means of implementing Action Learning and engaging with elements of the KU Teaching and Learning Strategy within KUSS
(iv)	To develop new cross-faculty and interdisciplinary initiatives, generate debate about sustainability and its relevance to different stakeholders
(v)	To formalise and extend connections with practitioners and the local community and to provide students with the opportunity to address sustainability issues within a live, practice-based context
(vi)	To deepen and increase the educational interface between academics and practitioners, develop practitioner understanding of sustainability and to better inform their own decision-making
(vii)	To disseminate best practice in delivering sustainability across curricula, both throughout KU and external organisations
(viii)	To assist the university in moving forward in its own path towards embedding sustainability principles by working with others in the university in the field of research-informed curriculum development and student engagement

There exists a clear synchronisation between the overarching aims of C-SCAIPE, UNDESD and SESD (Table 6). Furthermore, there is evidence that C-SCAIPE can make a significant contribution to the Decade and UNECE strategy through its emphasis on relationships between the global and local.

It is recognised that whilst the underlying goals, objectives and strategies of the Decade should be common, each major region Africa, Latin America, Europe, etc. will have its particular strategy to deliver sustainability. The SESD is a way to promote the objectives of the Decade in the European Region.

Therefore, C-SCAIPE works with various stakeholders to promote ESD practices and live projects in Kingston University (teachers, students and other staff) and the metropolitan region.

Table 6   Links between DESD, SESD and C-SCAIPE

The overall goal of the UNDESD is:	To integrate the values inherent in sustainable development into all aspects of learning, and to encourage changes in behaviour that allow for a more sustainable and just society for all.
The aim of UNECE Strategy for ESD is:	To encourage UNECE member states to develop and incorporate ESD into all relevant subjects within their formal and informal education systems.
The overarching aim of C-SCAIPE is:	To promote a deeper understanding of the requirements of professional education in order to produce graduates capable of working and therefore creating more sustainable communities. An holistic view of sustainable principles will be embedded within curricula and teaching; delivery initially within the built environment based on live projects embracing a multi-disciplinary, inter-professional perspective.

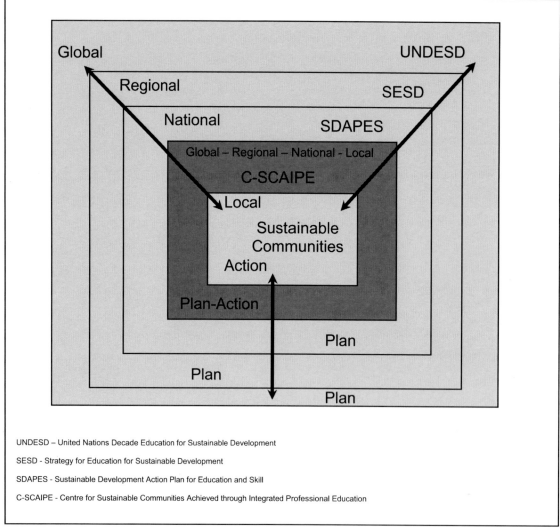

Figure 1   From Local to Global. From Decade to C-SCAIPE Communities

Figure 1 highlights the local dimension of C-SCAIPE's vision, activities and practices such as: digital platforms, reports, papers, internet sites, and projects with others universities (in Europe and Latin America) and various stakeholders. Through curriculum content, C-SCAIPE contributes to, and promotes, the goal of the Decade and UNECE strategy (Table 7). Examples of national-scale projects include the:

(i)   HEA-ESD collaborative network of universities involved with a variety of ESD projects, co-ordinated by the Higher Education Academy. The purpose of the project is to help institutions and subject communities develop curricula and pedagogy that will give students the skills and knowledge to live and work sustainably. The aims are to research and support the development of ESD in HE; to build capacity amongst individuals; and to assist the co-ordination and dissemination of policy. These are to be achieved through funding projects, an e-newsletter, working with the subject centres and running workshops and other events

(ii)   Ecoversity Student scheme where C-SCAIPE works with Bradford University. This three year project has six activity strands which aim to embed sustainability into the curriculum and educational experience of students

Table 7   C-SCAIPE levels contribution to ESD, from local to global

Level	Partners	Examples
Local	Kingston University and projects with various stakeholders in the community	Workshop Speak UP. Organized by C-SCAIPE with the Partner.
National	Development of projects with other universities and stakeholders in the UK	HEA-ESD is a collaborative network of Universities involved with a variety of diverse ESD projects co-ordinated by the Higher Education Academy
Regional	Development of projects with other universities and stakeholders in Europe	Collaboration in research field of ESD as an example, the informal protocol involving C-SCAIPE, Kingston University and the Centre of Geographic Studies at Lisbon University
International	Development of projects with other universities and stakeholders outside Europe	*Sustainability in Practice from Local to Global: Making a Difference* (Conference at Kingston University, 2007)

At the regional level is a dialogue between C-SCAIPE and CEG within the framework of the 41 principles of the UNECE. The need exists for increased cooperation and partnerships between stakeholders in research and development activities, ranging from identifying issues to working with new knowledge, its dissemination and application. The results of research and development activities should be shared with actors locally, regionally and globally, and be incorporated into different parts of the education system, experience and practice. The outcomes of UNDESD will impact on the lives of thousands of communities and millions of people as new attitudes and values inspire decisions and actions, making sustainable development a more attainable ideal, as affirmed in the IIS. This approach recognises that in the midst of a magnificent diversity of cultures and life forms we are one human family and one Earth community with a common destiny (Earth Charter, Preamble). Cultural diversity in the present is recognized as a heritage of the world community. The introduction to the Universal Declaration on Cultural Diversity 'The cultural wealth of the world is its diversity in dialogue' raises cultural diversity to the level of 'the common heritage of humanity as necessary for humankind as biodiversity is for nature' and makes its defence an ethical imperative out of respect for the dignity of the individual (UNESCO, 2001).

Traditional knowledge should be valued and conserved as an integral part of ESD. The International Implementation Scheme (IIS) for UNDESD reminds us that indigenous peoples have a particular role through having an intimate knowledge of the sustained use of their environments, and being particularly vulnerable to unsustainable development. Also the UNECE strategy recognizes the importance of the traditional knowledge for ESD as explained in Principle 17; the ESD principle should foster respect for, and understanding of, different cultures and embrace contributions from them. The role of indigenous peoples should be recognized and they should be a partner in the process of developing educational programmes. In conclusion, Table 8 illustrates that C-SCAIPE is a significant player in the implementation of UNDSED objectives. This Centre is a link between the various policy levels (UNDESD, SESD, SDAPES) and community action (from global to local) through live projects involving a variety of stakeholders and contributing in various measures towards sustainable communities and improving sustainability.

Table 8   General indicators of a sustainable community

(i)	Resources are used efficiently and waste is minimized by closing cycles
(ii)	Pollution is limited to levels which natural ecosystems can cope with and without damage
(iii)	The diversity of nature is valued and protected
(iv)	Where possible local needs are met locally
(v)	Everyone has access to food, water, shelter and fuel at reasonable cost
(vi)	Everyone has the opportunity to undertake satisfying work in a diverse economy: the value of unpaid work is recognized, while payments for work are just and fairly distributed
(vii)	People's good health is protected by creating safe, clean, pleasant environments and health services which emphasize prevention of illness as well as proper care for the sick
(viii)	Access to facilities, services, goods and other people is not achieved at the expense of the environment or limited to those with cars
(ix)	People live without fear of personal violence from crime or persecution because of their personal beliefs, race, gender or sexuality
(x)	Everyone has access to the skills, knowledge and information needed to enable them to play a full part in society
(xi)	All sections of the community are empowered to participate in decision-making
(xii)	Opportunities for culture, leisure and recreation are readily available to all
(xiii)	Places, spaces and objects combine meaning and beauty with utility. Settlements are 'human' in scale and form. Diversity and local distinctiveness are valued and protected

Source: LGMB – Local Government Management Board, 1995, in Huckle, J. and Martin, A, 2001

C-SCAIPE and Education for Sustainable Development

C-SCAIPE uses a rich vocabulary of sustainability terms in its literature which has a bearing on ESD. C-SCAIPE addresses the concept of sustainability in terms of the 'triple bottom line': economy, environment and society, reaffirmed at the Johannesburg Summit, as being the three pillars of sustainable development (Table 9).

Table 9   C-SCAIPE: embedding sustainable and sustainability words

• Sustainable communities • Sustainable principles • Sustainable issues • Education for sustainable society • Development of a sustainable society • Integrating sustainable research • Sustainable economic development	• Holistic view of sustainability • Delivering sustainability across curricula • Establishing sustainability as an area of our professional expertise

The International Implementation Scheme (IIS) accepts these three areas as key to sustainable development (society, environment and economy), adding culture as an underlying dimension. It highlights the focus of ESD as embracing the concept of respect at the centre: respect for others, including those of present and future generations; respect for difference and diversity; respect for the environment; and respect for the resources of the planet which we inhabit.

C-SCAIPE, in unison with the Higher Education Funding Council for England (HEFCE, 2002), confirms the view that 'achieving sustainable economic development is critical to the future of society' (Objective 1). This is in harmony with the three key areas of Sustainable Development illustrated in Table 10.

236

Table 10   Key areas of Sustainable Development

(i) *Society:* an understanding of social institutions and their role in change and development, as well as the democratic and participatory systems which give opportunity for expression of opinion, the selection of governments, the forging of consensus and the resolution of differences

(ii) *Environment:* an awareness of the resources and fragility of the physical environment and the effects on it by human activity and decisions, with a commitment to factoring environment concerns into social and economic policy development

(iii)*Economy:* as a sensitivity to the limits and the potential of economic growth and their impact on society and on the environment, with a commitment to assess personal and societal levels of consumption out of concern for the environment and for social justice

Source: International Implementation Scheme (2005)

Furthermore, C-SCAIPE recognises that sustainability has yet to be fully embedded within educational practices where 'A holistic view of sustainable principles will be embedded within curricula and teaching…' It is recognised that one of the key barriers to the development of sustainable society is the limited understanding of the concept of 'sustainability', other than from a single environment-focused perspective. Within the built environment, this is exacerbated by limited communication across the professions and between professionals and the wider community of stakeholders who use the buildings that we create and manage. This can be changed by encouraging communication between the different cultural and professional fields in Higher Education (C-SCAIPE Bid 2, p.1).

However, the way to face the concept of sustainability lies in the UNDESD vision of strongly linked pillars (environment, economy and society) as seen within SESD. ESD is still developing as a broad and comprehensive concept, encompassing interrelated environmental, economic and social issues. It broadens the concept of environmental education (EE), which has increasingly addressed a wide range of development subjects. ESD also encompasses various elements of development and other targeted forms of education. Therefore, environmental education should be elaborated and complemented with other fields of education in an integrative approach towards education for sustainable development (UNECE Strategy for EDS, 2005, p.4).

However, the environment-focused perspective can, on the one hand, have limited understanding of the concept of sustainability and, on the other, limited understanding of environmental impacts associated with economic factors. In relation to this idea, Bell (1998, p.239) claims: 'As environmental impacts cannot be accurately quantified or measured precisely, and are influenced by political priorities and economic factors, Sustainable Development and social responsibility became complex issues'. Brown (1998, p.91) argues economic growth is a major component of development - indeed it has until recently been seen by some as both the means and the goal of development. However, it is within the environment that human action takes place and we have to understand the environment as a complex organization. Gomes (2002) states that '… the environment … constituted with biophysical components in interaction with people and their activities, ……..is a global system of dynamics, open and complex relations, and just one modification in a variable of the system can develop an effect far away'.

237

ESD extends the conceptualisation of sustainability beyond the environment. It shares the philosophy of the Decade made evident by the IIS:

- the Decade is a far-reaching and complex undertaking. Its conceptual basis, socio-economic implications, and environmental and cultural connections make it an enterprise, which potentially touches on every aspect of life
- this plan presents three key areas of sustainable development - society, environment and economy, with culture as an underlying dimension
- ESD is fundamentally about values, with respect at the centre
- the values, diversity, knowledge, languages and worldviews associated with culture strongly influence the way issues of education for sustainable development are dealt with in specific national contexts

C-SCAIPE, as demonstrated on its web site (*http://www.c-scaipe.ac.uk/suss_definitions.html*), accepts a number of different definitions of sustainability with relevance to its activities and stakeholders. One of the key objectives is to engender greater understanding of the different definitions of sustainability with relevance to its activities and stakeholders. These include: broad and popular definitions (Encarta Dictionary), The Brundtland Definition, UK Government's Definition of Sustainable Development, The Precautionary Principle, Inter-generational Equity and The Triple Bottom Line and the well known definition derived from Brundtland: 'Meeting the needs of today without compromising the ability of future generations to meet their own needs' (Our Common Future, 1987).

Although the concept of SD is clear, three issues demand consideration:

- the concepts of understanding held by various stakeholders or institutions
- the divergence between theory and practice
- relationships of scale between the local and global

In this context, and with respect to these definitions, C-SCAIPE undertakes Education for Sustainable Development.

C-SCAIPE in Action: Local to Global (Contributions to ESD)

The C-SCAIPE Project (Bid 2) proposes a strategy to assess the work in progress. The monitoring and evaluation strategy links each objective to a specific process of review and a target. The First Annual Operating Statement (August, 2006) specifies a level of achievement for each objective. In this section attention is focused on Objectives 2, 3 and 4 which are linked to the teaching and learning process.

Embedding sustainability within the curriculum (Objective 2)

Key Objective 2 was realised by a curriculum review (KUSS) in June 2006. The programme of module review is an integral part of the implementation plan and is expected to be successfully rolled out to the whole of KUSS course delivery (75 modules) by the end of year two. The revalidation (2006-2007) of 45% of the School's modules was a boost to confidence against an original target of 30% (Table 11) In addition, several more modules incorporated sustainability issues in their assessment without revalidation.

Cross-Faculty curriculum reviews are scheduled by August 2007 (Table 11). The time-consuming task of auditing and reviewing has been re-prioritised in favour of projects on the ground which in the short term are more influential and effective in disseminating key lessons.

This activity will be expanded to include modules and courses in other professional fields both within and beyond the home Faculty.

Changes in delivery methods (Objective 3)

C-SCAIPE considers it important for ESD to break away from the traditional lecture mode. Through action-learning it advocates a move towards embedding social, environmental and economic sustainability principles in a range of inter-professional disciplines where students become more aware of set values, more inclined to be self-confident and take ownership of their learning.

A 'live' project at master's level to integrate Social Work and Planning has been devised, though not yet executed. Social Work students need to be able to understand the urban environment from the prospective clients' point of view: for example, a single mother pushing a pram with another child toddling beside her while she walks into town to do some grocery shopping and visiting various locations. Professional planners need to appraise Town Centre Management issues or an integrated public transport system. It is intended that both sets of students should walk through Kingston together, one may be seated in a wheelchair, another have an arm bandaged and, yet, another be blind-folded. The route for their journey has been documented visually and other material will be made available to help them complete the assessment. Students will make a personal record of the journey and encounters, writing up reflections and debating the issues raised in an open forum.

Table 11 Objective 2- Consolidation

Objectives	Participants	Initial Achievements	Timescale	Completed
To ensure that curriculum and assessment design incorporate sustainability issue	KUSS staff initially Other KU staff subsequently	Review KUUS u/g curriculum	Sept 05 – June 06	YES
		Review home Faculty curriculum	Feb 06 – Aug 06	No (see below)
		Initial KUUS and home Faculty module case studies undertaken 30% of KUSS u/g modules to incorporate sustainability in course documentation leading to validation event	Oct 05 – June 07 Jan 06 – Nov 06	YES YES
		Cross-faculty review of curriculum	Feb 07 – Aug 07	ON SCHEDULE

Evidence of a substantial shift away from traditional lecture-based delivery towards a more dynamic, interactive mode, encouraging discussion and debate within the professional courses has been substantiated and will form a critical measure of success. Sources of evidence derive from a variety of site visits supported by C-SCAIPE in the academic year (2006-07) and which ranged from a half-day visit to an ecologically-designed housing development in Bedzed, a whole day visit to the Ecobuild and Cityscape conferences and exhibitions to a five-day residential field trip to Dublin. These visits formed part of the delivery and assessment for the students which involved issues of sustainability.

Student feedback *via* the Student Staff Consultative Committee, practitioner support and staff experiences constitute important elements within the monitoring process. During 2007, C-SCAIPE is undertaking a two-year interim evaluation of its work. Part of this process involves gaining the views of students, staff and practitioners on the impact (or otherwise) of C-SCAIPE. An External Evaluator has been engaged to interview a dozen stakeholders to complement this evaluation. The report will be posted on the C-SCAIPE website following submission to HEFCE.

The evaluation process for learners is robust and includes:

- Qualitative data: module evaluation forms are given to all students at the end of each module.
- Quantitative data: end-of-module forms; and the end-of-year results will be compared to those of preceding years to determine the impact of C-SCAIPE and its effects on the School's retention rate

Attrition rate (Objective 3)

The attrition rate is a major issue facing professional courses. In this context the creation of C-SCAIPE will help to address this obstacle by enabling the School to embrace a teaching and learning strategy driven by the needs and requirements of the student and in supporting workshops, tutorials, visiting speakers, site visits, presentations and debates. This is exemplified by two events at C-SCAIPE: the Institute of Social Science seminar *Education, Hope and Action. An Exploration of the Meaning and Pactice of 'Pedagogy of Hope'*, led by Dr Sarah Amsler; and the Workshop *Speak UP*, led by Dr Amanda Lewis. In addition, the First Annual Operating Statement 2006 shows that the objective to enhance and increase the existing project-based learning and assessment experience for students had been realised.

Cross-disciplinary engagement (Objective 4)

Table 7 highlights linkages between C-SCAIPE, DESD and SESD aimed at integrating the values inherent in sustainable development into all aspects of learning, thereby encouraging changes in behaviour. This is consistent with the aims of the UNECE Strategy for ESD to encourage UNECE member states to develop and incorporate ESD into their formal and informal education systems. Cross-disciplinary engagement is fundamental and C-SCAIPE believes it should be extended to other Faculties in Kingston University during the next five years. Tentative discussions have already taken place with three of the six Faculties.

One further example of cross-disciplinary engagement is that with the Faculty of Science (School of Geography, Geology and the Environment) through the conference *Sustainability in Practice: From Local to Global: Making a Difference* in September 2007. Members of the School of Geography, Geology and the Environment have also used the C-SCAIPE Debating Chamber and Reading Room for events relating to sustainability.

School of Surveying Towards ESD-School

This paper outlines C-SCAIPE's contribution towards ESD in respect of rewarding existing staff, ensuring that curriculum and assessment design incorporate sustainability issues and the development of new cross-Faculty and interdisciplinary initiatives to generate debate about sustainability and its relevance to stakeholders. C-SCAIPE contributes not only to ESD but also to UNDESD.

What is the vision of C-SCAIPE staff regarding this involvement? To understand that vision C-SCAIPE staff completed two questionnaires: one focused on Quality Criteria for ESD-Schools at university level; the second related to staff perception of C-SCAIPE objectives in promoting ESD. The first is based on a proposal of quality criteria from the European network: School Development through Environmental Education (SEED). This network is linked with ENSI (Environmental Schools Initiatives), a decentralized network of national authorities and research institutions of the OECD (Organisation for Economic Co-operation and Development). ENSI is a UNESCO partner in the implementation of UNDESD.

The publication *Guidelines to Enhance the Quality of Education for Sustainable Development* lists 53 quality criteria within three fields: quality criteria regarding the quality of teaching and learning processes (1 to 33); quality criteria regarding the school's external relations (34 to 47); and quality criteria regarding the school's external relations (48 to 53). These criteria have been used as a starting point for reflections, debates and further development regarding future work on ESD among educational officials, teachers, headmasters, parents, and students (Quality Criteria for ESD-Schools, 2005, pp.4-5). Manuel Gomes' PhD Project was used for C-SCAIPE staff to probe and evaluate these quality value criteria and recognise how one school at university level contributes towards Education for Sustainable Development.

By using the expression ESD-Schools the authors of Quality Criteria (SEED) aim to stress that there are new challenges for schools that wish to engage in ESD-oriented development. ESD is not only dealing with aspects of people's dependence on the quality of the environment and access to natural resources now and in the future, but also with aspects of participation, self efficacy, equality and social justice as essential perspectives in preparing pupils for their engagement in sustainable development (Quality Criteria for ESD-Schools, 2005, pp.4-5).

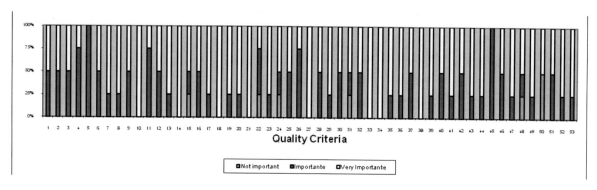

Figure 2   C-SCAIPE staff perception of Quality Criteria for ESD-Schools

Figure 2 shows that the majority of staff responses clustered at 'very important'. Eight of the criteria were chosen by 100% of respondents; and 17 by 75%. Only six quality criteria were accorded ratings of 'not important'. These results confirm that, in general, C-SCAIPE staff agreed with the effectiveness of these measures in indicating how one university School contributes towards Education for Sustainable Development.

The second questionnaire shows that the C-SCAIPE staff feel that the objectives of the Centre contribute in an important way to Education for Sustainable Development. Figure 3 captures the distribution of scores against criteria which range from '1 not important' to '10 very important'. Most answers scored between 7 and 10; only one criterion was rated at 2 (Objective 1), one at 5 (Objective 3) and one at 6 (Objective 8). Levels 9 and 10 are favoured by staff and underline Objective 2 *viz*. to ensure that curriculum and assessment design incorporate sustainability issues; Objective 7 *viz*. to disseminate best practice in delivering sustainability across curricula; and Objective 8 *viz*. to assist the university in moving forward in its own path towards embedding sustainability principles..

Score Awarded	1	2	3	4	5	6	7	8	9	10
1. To reward existing excellent staff										
2. To ensure that curriculum and assessment design incorporate sustainability issues										
3. To enhance and increase the existing project-based learning and assessment experience for students										
4. To develop new cross-faculty and interdisciplinary initiatives										
5. To formalise and extend connections with practitioners and the local community										
6. To deepen and increase the educational interface between academics and practitioners										
7. To disseminate best practice in delivering sustainability across curricula										
8. To assist the university in moving forward in its own path towards embedding sustainability principles.										

Answer	25%	50%	75%	100%

Figure 3   C-SCAIPE staff perception of the contribution of the Centre objectives for ESD

These questionnaire results confirm that the School of Surveying is developing towards an ESD-School based on Quality Criteria at university level. Future developments to consolidate progress and enhance recognition would include seeking permission for the use of the Decade logo and promoting further protocols for collaboration in ESD with overseas institutions.

References

Bell, M. 1998 *An Invitation to Environmental Sociology*. London: Pine Forge Press

Breiting, S., Mayer, M., Mayor, M. and Finn, M. c2005 'Guidelines to Enhance the Quality of Education for Sustainable Development'. in Austrian Federal Ministry of Education, Science and Culture (ed) *Quality Criteria for ESD-Schools*. [Internet]. <http://seed.schule.at/uploads/QC_eng_2web.pdf>. [Accessed 13th May 2007].

Centro de Estudos Geográficos n.d. [Internet]. <http://www.ceg.ul.pt/>. [Accessed 13th May 2007].

Convention on Protection and Promotion of the Diversity of Cultural Expressions. Paris, 20 October 2005. [Internet]. <http://unesdoc.unesco.org/images/0014/001429/142919e.pdf>. [Accessed 13th May 2007].

C-SCAIPE 2004 *Bid for a Centre for Excellence in Teaching and Learning (CETL) for Sustainable Communities Achieved through Integrated Professional Education*. Kingston University

C-SCAIPE 2006 *First annual operating statement 2006*. Kingston University

Earth Charter [Internet]. <http://www.earthcharter.org/>. [Accessed 13th May 2007].

Gomes, M. 2002 Itinerários Ambientais. Percursos e Formação. Lisboa: Ministério da Educação.
Guidelines for the use of the UN Decade of Education for Sustainable Development logo. [Internet]. <http://portal.unesco.org/education/admin/file_download.php/guidelineslogo.pdf?URL_ID=38235&filename=11086463293guide lineslogo.pdf&filetype=application%2Fpdf&filesize=134000&name=guidelineslogo.pdf&location=user-S/>. [Accessed 13th May 2007].

HEFCE, 2002 *Report 02/23 Evaluating the regional contribution of an HEI: A benchmarking approach*, UK: HEFCE. [Internet]. <http://www.hefce.ac.uk/pubs/HEFCE/2002/02_23.htm>. [Accessed 13th May 2007].

Huckle, J. and Martin, A. 2001 *Environments in a Changing World*. London: Pearson Education

Sustainable Development Commission (2004) *Shows promise but must try harder*. [Internet].<http://www.sd-commission.gov.uk>. [Accessed 13th May 2007].

Sustainable Development Action Plan for Education and Skills (SDAPES). [Internet]. <http://www.dfes.gov.uk/publications/5yearstrategy>. [Accessed 13th May 2007].

UNDESD 2005 *International Implementation Scheme for the United Nations Decade of Education for Sustainable Development*.[Internet]. <http://www.senternovem.nl/mmfiles/Implementation%20Scheme%20DESD_tcm24-121648.pdf>. [Accessed 13th May 2007].

UNECE 2005 *UNECE Strategy 2005*. [Internet] <http://www.bneportal.de/coremedia/generator/unesco/de/Downloads/Hintergrundmaterial_int/UNECE_3A_20Strategy_20for _20ESD_20_28engl._29.pdf>. [Accessed 13th May 2007].

UNESCO Universal declaration on Cultural Diversity. Adopted by the 31st Session of the General Conference of UNESCO. Paris, 2 November 2001. [Internet]. <http://unesdoc.unesco.org/images/0012/001271/127160m.pdf>. [Accessed 13th May 2007].

Workgroup of UNDESD coordinated by the Portuguese National Commission UNESCO. [Internet]. <http://www.unesco.pt/pdfs/docs/LivroDEDS.doc>. [Accessed 13th May 2007].